Women and Islam

Women and Islam

ZAYN R. KASSAM, EDITOR

Women and Religion in the World
Cheryl A. Kirk-Duggan, Lillian Ashcraft-Eason,
and Karen Jo Torjesen, Series Editors

 PRAEGER

AN IMPRINT OF ABC-CLIO, LLC
Santa Barbara, California • Denver, Colorado • Oxford, England

Library of Congress Cataloging-in-Publication Data
  Women and Islam / Zayn R. Kassam, editor.
    p. cm. — (Women and religion in the world)
  Includes bibliographical references and index.
  ISBN 978-0-275-99158-6 (hard copy : alk. paper) — ISBN 978-0-313-
08274-0 (ebook) 1. Women in Islam. 2. Feminism—Religious aspects—
Islam. 3. Muslim women—Islamic countries—Social
conditions. I. Kassam, Zayn R.
  BP173.4.W694   2010
  297.082—dc22   2010031249

ISBN: 978-0-275-99158-6
EISBN: 978-0-313-08274-0

14 13 12 11 10   1 2 3 4 5

This book is also available on the World Wide Web as an eBook.
Visit www.abc-clio.com for details.

Praeger
An Imprint of ABC-CLIO, LLC

ABC-CLIO, LLC
130 Cremona Drive, P.O. Box 1911
Santa Barbara, California 93116-1911

This book is printed on acid-free paper ∞

Manufactured in the United States of America

305.4869
W

To all who work for gender justice

Now, among those whom We have created there are people who guide [others] in the way of the truth and act justly in its light.

—Qur'an 7:181

And thus does their Sustainer answer their prayer: "I shall not lose sight of the labor of any of you who labors, be it man or woman: each of you is an issue of the other."

—Qur'an 3:195

One who partakes of good deeds and is a believer shall enter paradise, and shall not be wronged by as much as [would fill] the groove of a date-stone.

—Qur'an 4:124

It is [the divine being] who has created you [all] out of a single soul, and out of it brought into being its mate, so that one might find rest in the other.

—Qur'an 7:189

Once social change begins, it cannot be reversed. You cannot uneducate the person who has learned to read. You cannot humiliate the person who feels pride. And you cannot oppress the people who are not afraid anymore.

—César E. Chávez

Contents

Acknowledgments

This volume would not have been possible without the vision of Cheryl Kirk-Duggan, Lillian Ashcraft-Eason, and Karen Jo Torjesen, who envisaged a series of works that would bring together the way in which women were addressing contemporary and local issues through a globalized, and often religious, consciousness. I would like to thank each of the contributors to this volume for generously responding to my request to share their thinking and research with a broader readership. With great regret and sadness, I note that Louise Halper, whose chapter on Iranian women is included in this volume, passed away before its publication. Audrey Bilger's thoughtful suggestions were extremely helpful. Working with the editors at Greenwood Press, Praeger Publishers, and ABC-CLIO, the publisher of Greenwood Press titles, has been a pleasure and I thank each one for attending to the myriad details involved in bringing a project such as this to light. My profound gratitude for Kathleen Mirante, who so kindly offered a place in which to read, reflect, and write. Her generosity is boundless, and for that I am deeply grateful. My thanks to my sister, Tazim R. Kassam, for her wise counsel, support, and encouragement. And finally, as with all such work, any blemishes are mine alone.

Claremont, California, 2010

Introduction

Zayn R. Kassam

The subject of Muslim women or women in Islam continues to provoke horror, fascination, pity, anger, sadness, and at times, vitriolic
reactions against both Muslim men and Islam. The chapters in this
volume, on the other hand, will, it is hoped, invoke a different kind of
response, perhaps of admiration for the work of many of these women. More
realistically, this volume hopes to stimulate further discussion over more so-
ber understandings of challenges faced and strategies employed by Muslim
women around the world in attending to the realities of daily life. Each chapter takes us to a different part of the globe and affords us a glimpse into the
many diverse ways in which Muslim women are actively involved in addressing the conditions imbedded in their discrete environments, taking up the
opportunities afforded to them, and, in some instances, creating spaces for
an energetic engagement with what it means to be a Muslim woman in a globalized world.

This volume was conceived as the volume on Islam in a series titled
Women and Religion in the World. Its intent is to focus on contemporary
selected experiences of women and how their lives interface with religion.
Each volume is organized according to five themes: (1) Women, Family,
and Environment; (2) Socioeconomics, Politics, and Authority; (3) Body,
Mind, and Spirit; (4) Sexuality, Power, and Vulnerability; and (5) Women,
Worldview, and Religious Practice. Although the boundaries between each
of the themes are permeable, the chapters under each theme illumine different lenses through which the theme may be engaged.

As the chapters reveal, the challenges Muslim women face arise both
from within and outside, whether in relation to Islam or their national

contexts, and have as much to do with cultural and religious codes as they do with politics, economics, education, and the law. Thus, the various chapters take on many important challenges. The overarching question might be, How do women draw upon their faith to address their local issues? For instance, under the first theme, Women, Family, and Environment, we may ask, how do familial connections help women ameliorate their environment in such war-torn areas as those in Indonesia in their attempts to facilitate peacemaking and peace building? How do women in Iran enact democratic change to family law under a seemingly authoritarian regime? How do women better respond to the needs of their families in light of the social dislocations brought about by structural adjustment policies enacted in Morocco in ways that run counter to accepted social roles for women? Thus each chapter under each theme brings out various facets of how the overarching theme, when examined in specific locales, reveals some interesting specificities but also points the way to some commonalities that might facilitate transnational linkages.

For the second theme, Socioeconomics, Politics, and Authority, the two chapters included here ask the following questions: How do British Muslim women enter the political realm, given that such activities have largely been consigned to Muslim men as spokespersons for their communities? How do Malaysian Muslim women reconfigure the place of women in society, given the patriarchal slant in Islamic family law? Both chapters point to ways in which women in two highly different contexts, one non-Muslim and one majority Muslim, attempt to carve spaces of authority, one political, and one legal and social.

The chapters for the third theme, Body, Mind, and Spirit, engage the relationship between frameworks of reality and praxis by focusing on the following questions: How do Muslim women academics living in non-Muslim-majority countries engage with sacred and authoritative texts in order to propose ways in which both the understanding and the praxis of Islam could reflect the gender equity they see at the core of Islam? On the other hand, how do those who subscribe to gender complementarity rather than gender equity use the pathways of education to inculcate their understanding and praxis of Islam? How do Western academics produce knowledge about African women, and how do Ethiopian women in particular draw upon their faith tradition to address issues of marginalization and poverty?

The chapters discussing the fourth theme, Sexuality, Power, and Vulnerability, have as their unifying thread the issue of violence against women and the vulnerability of women as they engage such questions as the following: How do North African women playwrights grapple with violence against women and violence against nations as cultures come into contact with each other? How do Muslim women in Indonesia invoke politically charged religious justifications as they campaign in support of or against the issue of plural wives, polygyny? How do expatriate Iranian women's memoirs relate to the war on terrorism?

Finally, chapters placed under the fifth theme, Women, Worldview, and Religious Practice, examine the following questions: How do European Muslim women create a Muslim life in an increasingly Islamophobic context? How do Southern Californian Shi'ite Muslim women draw upon female role models to construct their spiritual and social identities? How do young Canadian Muslim women construct an identity that is empowering rather than oppressive?

Posing such questions enables an examination and understanding of the real issues with which Muslim women grapple, in each of these highly disparate contexts, rather than dwelling on the privations that being Muslim is supposed to inflict on Muslim women. From the many studies that are now available on gender in Islam and Muslim women, perhaps among the most significant are those that problematize easy assumptions about the role and place of women in Muslim societies and religion. For instance, Leila Ahmed, in her magisterial work titled *Women and Gender in Islam*, traces how the Qur'an, the sacred scripture for Muslims, while clearly viewing women as ontologically equal in stature to men, assumes a social role for them in keeping with the Arabian context of the day without essentializing women as inferior. Moreover, she shows how the Qur'an came increasingly to be interpreted in ever-narrower ways for Muslim women as Muslims entered societies in which patriarchal norms were well established. Barbara Stowasser reinforces this view in her study *Women in the Qur'an, Traditions, and Interpretation*, in which she examines interpretations of the Qur'an and the *hadith* literature in the Muslim medieval period (circa 9th through 13th centuries). She additionally makes the case that Muslims were bringing their interpretations in line with the Byzantine and Persian contexts in which these discourses were generated. Asma Barlas in her work titled *"Believing Women" in Islam: Unreading Patriarchal Interpretations of the Qur'an* examines such interpretative strategies further through asking the theological question, What is the nature of God? Is the divine being misogynist? She finds not only that the divine being is far from being misogynist but also that there is no evidence for essentializing men or women in the Qur'an; rather, differences between humans are predicated on their degree of righteousness or piety. Valentine Moghadam, in her study of women in Muslim societies titled *Modernizing Women: Gender and Social Change in the Middle East*, finds along with Leila Ahmed that colonization has played its own role in generating contemporary discourses on women both from within the Islamic discursive tradition as well as from outside it, that is, from the Western discursive tradition. In this respect, the Other was formulated—and women played a large role in such a formulation—in such a way that the West could be seen as feminist and liberal and democratic, whereas the East—into which Muslim societies were placed—was seen as a place for privation and oppression of women, very much a place to be redeemed. In addition, Moghadam's work points out the state's interests in facilitating a state-sponsored feminism that has had as much to do with opening up spaces for women to advance socially as it does with holding back legal reforms to pacify political interests, especially those such as Islamism, which pose a viable threat to the secular state. Such observations notwithstanding, she finds in her study titled *Globalizing Women: Transnational Feminist Networks* that the rate of literacy and economic capacity growth among Muslim women has been robust; however, the larger forces of globalization have, in their wake, brought both opportunities as well as a downward spiral in women's economic opportunities and increased Islamist surveillance of women. The contributions of others are noted in Roxanne Marcotte's chapter included in this volume, most notably those of Amina Wadud and Rifaat Hasan, alongside those of such younger scholars as Etin Anwar and Kecia Ali.

Thus, to come to a fuller understanding of how Muslim women's lives interface with religion, the evidence provided in this volume is that while the Islamic cultural and legal legacy may provide some impediments to the full realization of women's potential or to gender equity, Muslim women themselves are in fact turning to their religious tradition to argue, on its own terms, that gender inequity is by no means Islamic. Rather, the issues they face are very much connected to larger socioeconomic processes such as globalization and the war on terrorism, as well as to more regional processes such as conflict over limited resources, and more specifically to legal and political and social processes within their respective societies.

The remainder of this introduction details highlights of each of the chapters included in this volume.

PART 1: WOMEN, FAMILY, AND ENVIRONMENT

Louise A. Halper (in memoriam) engages a discussion of Islamic law in the context of Iranian women's activism in examining whether democratic change is possible within Islamic law. Interrogating the widely held view that Muslim women "benefit from a regime of secular law and suffer under religious law," Halper points out that the situation of women under Islamic law in Iran is quite comparable to that of Turkish women under secular Turkish law and not at all like that of women under Taliban-inflected Islamic law in Afghanistan. Rather, she argues, a more compelling determinant of women's status may, in fact, be "the salience of women to the political process and their active involvement in it," a hypothesis that is tested in conjunction with laws on marriage and divorce in Iran. Noting the strides that have been made in Iranian women's literacy rates, school and university enrollments, and fertility decreases and employment increases in the two decades between 1980 and 2000 since the inception of the Islamic regime, Halper asks how such data are compatible with the reinstitution of Islamic law and how such improvements in women's status have been effectuated and what role they themselves have played.

Since the law of marriage and divorce exercises a huge impact on the lives of women, Halper focuses on two legislative innovations occurring in 1993 and 1996 to the Divorce Reform Law of 1989, between Ayatollah Khomeini's death in 1989 and Mohammad Khatami's inception as president of the Republic of Iran in 1997. A rich historical summary of the law of marriage and divorce pre- and post-Revolution illustrates the strategies women began to utilize once Khomeini reinstituted Islamic family law. Often they used the *mahr*, a predetermined sum to be paid to the wife in the eventuality of the husband's death or divorce, to negotiate a more favorable situation than they were entitled to under the law. The indigence into which newly divorced women were placed in cases where the *mahr* was practically worthless also motivated attempts by the women's press and women's organizations to draw attention to the issue. Halper traces the new interpretive moves made by clerics attempting to reconcile feminism with Islam, whose work was published in such women's magazines as *Zanan*, and by women members of the Majles, the Iranian parliament, who sought to find religiously legal ways to address inequities experienced by women under the Iranian Islamic marital regime.

An examination of the political education and participation of women before, during, and and after the Iranian Revolution reveals that Islamist women, although they subscribed to the notion that "women's primary roles were in the family, also supported women who wanted or needed to work outside the home" and "became advocates for interpretations of the *shari'a* more open to the concerns of modernist women." The participation of women in the war effort during the Iran-Iraq War as well as in the labor force during and after the war led to the call for overt government support for the promotion of women's social participation and to the subsequent formation of institutions establishing a direct connection between the government and women's issues. The successes achieved by women after the Iranian Revolution demonstrate that democratic change is indeed possible under Islamic law.

Etin Anwar's chapter looks at the impact of conflict on human security, especially for women, and national security. She examines how social

and cultural gender constructs correlate with gender activism in the peace
and reconciliation process in such Indonesian conflict zones as Sambas,
Aceh, and Maluku. The religious education system, the *pesantren*, dissemi-
nates the naturalized view of women as weak and men as strong, leading
to social convention in which males are seen as pillars providing sustenance and authority for the household. The state further appropriated
women's sexuality as "mothers of the nation" within the national plan for
development in gendered ways, underscoring the role of women as supporters of men, considered the true champions of the state, and inscribing
the roles of women within the marital regime as responsible for the private
sphere while the public sphere was relegated to men. Despite the entrance
of some women into the highest corridors of power, the majority of women
find themselves in jobs associated with their sex.

Anwar interrogates the causes of conflict in Indonesia, examining first
the political conditions followed by a questioning of the assumed correlation between levels of testosterone and male-engendered violence. Noting
that violence is culturally constructed, Etin argues that the power of
destruction held by men gives them the power of domination over women
and generates gendered prestige and power systems embodied through the
performativities of masculinity and femininity. The social and cultural specificities within which conflicts are located suggest that national security
outweighs human security, including the well-being of women and children. In investigating accounts of violence against women in conflict
zones, Anwar notes that women's sexualities became the site regularly
transgressed and tortured for political deployment, while women also suffered mental and physical deprivation, all horrors into which children were
socialized as they observed what was done to adults. The ostensibly Christian-Muslim conflict in Maluku led to at least a half million displace-
ments, increasing poverty for women and children especially.

Anwar examines three models to investigate the role of women in
peace and conflict resolution activism: the essentialist, constructivist, and
exclusivist. Grassroots organizations working on the essentialist model,
which views the rightful place of women as mothers, as wives, and in the
private sphere, reveals that solidarity is built in bringing women together,
say, for example, as mothers or as women who have lost their husbands to
war or religious or ethnic conflict, enabling the issues they face collectively
to be addressed. The constructivist model of activism draws upon such
female psychological traits as nurturing and caring to advance peacemaking and peace building. Bringing together women from parts of the community that are in conflict with each other enables commonalities of
experience under war conditions to emerge, building solidarity and allowing the women to approach their menfolk to lobby for the end of hostilities

and to give up violence, its tactics, politics, and mediums. In this regard, forgiveness plays a key role in generating a sense of the common need for human security and togetherness. The third model, exclusivist activism, utilizes the restrictive gendered access to public space by enlarging the traditional role of women as homemakers. By engaging in social activism and humanitarian endeavors, they work to meet the needs of displaced persons, providing food, health facilities, microcredit loans, and education for the children. In addition, they organize prayers and demonstrations and meetings in order to bring about a "peace zone." Thus, despite the fact that peacemaking and conflict resolution are often part of a gendered process in traditional societies, women have utilized the avenues of agency open to them to transform them into tools to achieve the goal of security shared by both genders.

Rachel Newcomb turns to a discussion of nongovernmental organizations (NGOs) and Moroccan women's activism. While such an NGO as the Najia Belghazi Center founded by middle-upper-class women and located in a lower-middle-class neighborhood in Fes, Morocco, might report a remarkable amount of success in helping women with legal advice in cases of domestic conflict and divorce, as well as providing job training, at the same time it faces several challenges that consume valuable resources of time and effort. For instance, it encounters the social expectation that it has unlimited resources; on the other, it is viewed with suspicion as a tool of Western imperialism or an embezzler of grant funds, or both. In addition, the widespread view that the family should be the source of assistance in most matters works against the NGO's aim to build solidarity among women across class lines. Newcomb questions whether such challenges can be attributed to entrenched class differences or the oft-leveled criticism of insufficient religiosity and argues, rather, "that religion, local custom, and larger structural inequalities must be considered together in instances where the activists' efforts to foster social change failed."

For instance, such processes accompanying globalization as structural adjustment policies (SAPs), deregulation, and privatization have reduced government spending, seen declines in school enrollments for girls, and increased unemployment. Consequently, the government has encouraged the formation of NGOs to step into the social services breach while incurring criticism for failing to deliver on its responsibilities as a nation-state. Nongovernmental organizations dealing with women's issues touch a particularly sensitive nerve, given the country's attempt in 2000 to reform the *mudawana*, the legal regime governing personal status law. The move sparked debates on whether proposed reforms were anti-Islamic or not and revealed the state's uneasy alliance with conservative Islamists while also attempting to be progressive. Reforming the *mudawana* would also undermine entrenched male familial authority; however, no longer in place were the protections for women that were built into the patriarchal system, protections such as the community support that ensured an abused or divorced woman had some recourse and financial support. As the country moved into line with global neoliberal economic patterns, the traditional tribal structure was unseated by a cash economy and capitalist structures that counted among its casualties the disintegration of local networks and familial resources.

What purpose do NGOs serve? Newcomb points to two viewpoints: first, that NGOs work in tandem with states to contribute more efficiently to "development" than governments do within the framework of neoliberal capitalism, providing for social needs where governments fail; and second, that NGOs work outside the state in order to demand radical societal change. The NGO examined by Newcomb fits into neither of these categories; rather, she argues, they strategized to gain acceptance among conservative elements while at the same time attempting to address the very real issues their clients brought to them. Avoiding joining the fray of political debate over the *mudawana*, they sought instead to make a focus on violence against women their key mission, bringing programs and skill-building approaches to bear on helping women build the capacity to address the situations in which they found themselves.

However, despite some successful outcomes, for various reasons, such strategies did not attain the solidarity among women and the capacity building hoped for by the NGO. Newcomb deftly analyzes the various social, economic, and cultural factors that impede their ability to address the inequities women brought to their attention. The demands of the global economy coupled with the state's inability to work for gender justice within the constraints placed on it by IMF-led programs of structural adjustment give rise to social issues that are far greater than any NGO, even under the best of circumstances, can be expected to handle. As Newcomb notes, the problem is further compounded by class, religious, and cultural factors, but to name these as the sole reasons for NGO failure without recognizing the state's role in signing on to structural adjustment programs or failing to address the feminization of poverty must also be acknowledged.

PART 2: SOCIOECONOMICS, POLITICS, AND AUTHORITY

Narzanin Massoumi's chapter turns to the role of British Muslim women in the formation of an alternative leftist political party, Respect, formed by peace activists in the aftermath of protests against the wars in Iraq and Afghanistan. How do these women negotiate between their religious and political identities? Do they draw upon religious precepts or secular values to justify their political engagement? In order to address such questions, Massoumi invokes Peter Mandaville's notions of translocalities, that is, spaces in global cities where Muslims live as minorities and which afford "Muslim intellectuals the opportunity to express and encounter alternative readings of Islam" (Mandeville 2004, 135). In facilitating the development of a critical vision on Islam, including the questioning of its own parameters, Islam has emerged as a mode of contesting authority in that Muslim intellectuals are able to assert the capacity of each Muslim to engage in *ijtihad*, or independent intellectual effort. An ethnographic study conducted in 2007 also revealed that such Muslims invoke the notion of pluralism to open dialogue with others.

Engaging in *ijtihad* has enabled such Muslims both to reconsider their relationship to non-Muslims and to open up spaces for political participation for women. Events such as the Rushdie affair, the riots in the *banlieus* of Paris and in Britain, and the attacks on American soil on 9/11 have led to a focus on Muslim men that has overlooked the political participation and agency of Muslim women, seeing the latter rather as victims in a climate of increasing Islamophobia. Suggesting that feminist rejections of religion and multiculturalism as tools for reinforcing gender inequality replicate essentialist binaries reminiscent of Orientalism, Massoumi argues that it is not necessary to espouse essentialism in order to construct a coherent social identity. Feminist Orientalism, most readily apparent in Western feminist desires to "save brown women," as Gayatri Chakravorty Spivak famously quips, represents Muslim women as the oppressed Other in order to affirm its own identity as liberated and free. Further, such Western feminists as Susan Moller Okin argue against multicultural policies, suggesting that these serve to prevent minority Muslim women from being rescued from their patriarchal cultures. Such ideas have grown increasingly popular in Britain over the issue of the veil and complement militant foreign policies in the Middle East as well as anti-Muslim racist attitudes found in both Europe and North America. Massoumi carefully critiques both essentialist and antiessentialist positions with respect to multiculturalism, including at the more conciliatory end of the spectrum Rogers Brubaker's argument that even when social groups invoke such essentialism in order to invoke ethnic, religious, and racial identities, social scientists must not perpetuate such self-reification in their analysis. Rather, Massoumi argues, following Tariq Modood's prompt, that "groups can be seen to have what he calls family resemblances without assuming some kind of inherent essence." Massoumi also finds useful Pnina Werbner's distinction between different types of essentialism, namely, reification and objectification, freighted negatively and positively, respectively.

It is within the context of these larger discussions of groupings, essentialism, and multiculturalism that Massoumi takes on her examination of

politically involved Muslim women Respect activists, querying what they
see as the source of their identity and whence they draw the values that
drive their political participation. She found that participants identify two
triggers that spurred their activism and further clarified their sense of identity. First, the events of September 11 translated into a wake-up call for
many of these women, who saw the importance of their religion and simultaneously concluded that how they understood their religion was inherently a political act. In this connection, the concept of social justice in
Islam enabled them to develop "a coherent identity 'that made sense'" and
also allowed them to acknowledge that they were Muslims first. A few minority voices, however, demur from this view, suggesting that adopting the
identity of being Muslim reflexively in response to post-9/11 Islamophobia
allows someone else to set the terms of one's identity. Second, they sought
to change the predominant view that donning a headscarf signifies an
oppressive patriarchal relationship. By becoming involved in politics, all
but one respondent sought to act as ambassadors for their faith to show
that they, as Muslim women, were able to make their own decisions.
Espousing the views that Islam does specify rights for women and that
examples from the Prophet's life and from those of his wives inculcate
playing an active role in society, some of the women suggest that it is important to trace patriarchal understandings of the role of men and women
in Muslim society to culture, and not to religion. Drawing such distinctions between a pure Islam and a cultural Islam allows them to negotiate a
gendered public space within their own communities as well and to contest the solely male ownership of the political sphere.

In concert with other studies that have reached similar conclusions,
Massoumi finds that "the gendered divisions between the Muslim community are distinct from that which is imagined in popular discourse."
Dubbed the "uncles' club," Muslim men who already hold positions of
power in the state or government-funded bureaucracy were seen as holding women back from political participation, as well as being corrupt and
as not fairly representing the Muslim communities that had elected them.
Thus, these women find it necessary to articulate an alternative conception
of community, one that does not appeal to an abstract global community
but, rather, responds to concrete issues that need to be addressed. They
link their on-the-ground antiwar activism and service to their local populations as a political act that is necessitated by their religious values. In so
doing, they also challenge the liberal and secular prejudices concerning
gender equity in such religious communities as their own.

Massoumi then engages secular liberal feminists who consider religious feminism, or in this case, Islamic feminism, to be an oxymoron.
Rather, argues Massoumi, the secularist stance is itself exclusionary; and

as the women in the study have shown, it is possible to invoke Islamic feminism to refuse "particular boundaries that are drawn out for women" as new political communities develop in non-majority-Muslim contexts.

Azza Basarudin examines Malaysian Sunni Muslim women's praxis to determine how women balance their religion with the demands of a rapidly changing world. Taking as her case study the Malaysian Muslim professional women's organization named Sisters in Islam (SIS), Basarudin argues that "their intellectual activism is a contested site of alternative knowledge production in (re)claiming their faith to (re)imagine a transformative Muslim *umma* (community) inclusive of women's concerns, experiences and realities." Suggesting that the strategy employed by Sisters in Islam constitutes a faith-centered intellectual activism, which draws upon the sources of the Islamic tradition as well as the larger human rights discourse to effect a "reform from within," the author invokes and builds upon Abdullahi Ahmed An-Nai'm's concept of cultural mediation to show how Sisters in Islam brings the local into conversation with the transnational in order to campaign for women's rights within a specifically postcolonial Malaysian Muslim public sphere.

The politicization of Islam in the public sphere in response to the British colonial legacy of "economic divide, ethnic distrust, and political discontent" led to an Islamic revivalism that brought in its wake the Arabization of Malaysian Islam, including gender relations. Women have steadily been incorporated into the economy commencing with Prime Minister Mahathir bin Mohamad's development agenda that brought educational and economic opportunities to women. However, increasing Islamization in the form of "the rising trend of the totalizing discourse of conventional Islam" has increased surveillance of women's comportment and dress, as well as calling for a return to family values that promote veiling, gender segregation, the erosion of women's rights under Islamic family law, and subsuming women's rights under family and national development. Caught in the larger political struggle for hegemonic rule, Malay Muslim women have become emblematic of the purity of Malay culture and Malaysian Islam and are thus subject to intense scrutiny, policing, and legislation with a larger context of "racial, ethnic, and religious tension, factionalist politics, and state repression."

It is in this context that Sisters in Islam was formed to address biases toward women in Islamic family law. Under the guidance of Amina Wadud, a group of professional women went back to the text of the Qur'an to understand how this foundational Islamic scripture understood gender and, moreover, what tools were available from within the Islamic tradition for the realization of gender justice. Basarudin traces the process whereby Sisters in Islam developed various strategies to address gender inequality in the specifically Malaysian context, albeit with a transnational consciousness of gender. A key strategy has been to develop and draw upon hermeneutical recovery projects aimed at reexamining patriarchal monopolies on religious knowledge and gender constructions. The revival and reform of Islamic knowledge is brought to the public sphere through conferences, workshops, legal clinics, and the like, in order to facilitate discussions of religious beliefs and practices. Doing so creates a more informed and hence responsible and responsive citizenry able to bring faith to bear on the challenges of globalization, especially insofar as these relate to and impact gender and gendered practices. Such efforts are further undergirded by publications ranging from press releases to letters to newspaper editors, legal memoranda, working papers, and scholarly books. In addition, Sisters in Islam has developed an international profile, thereby encouraging a sharing and enriching of resources and strategies beyond the local to the global.

The connection of praxis to theory is nowhere more readily seen than in the legal and sociocultural regimes that govern the lives of women, which in Malaysia, as in most Muslim majority countries, are informed and legitimated by religious interpretations. Thus, Basarudin pays special attention to polygamy-monogamy campaigns and moral policing initiatives and to the role that Sisters in Islam has played and continues to play in bringing gender justice to bear on these issues within the context of Islamic family law. Challenges to Sisters in Islam's legitimacy and authority are to be expected; however, its work must be seen, Basarudin argues, as "fracturing" conventional Islamic hegemony; that is, "SIS's intellectual activism is seeping through the cracks to rupture the delicate relations of power." Indeed, Sisters in Islam's intellectual activism may be squarely placed within the stream of recovery projects that are grounded in a belief in Islam's inherent gender egalitarianism, given its moral and ethical vision.

PART 3: BODY, MIND, AND SPIRIT

Roxanne D. Marcotte turns her attention to scholarly activism on the part of diasporic Muslim women academics, some of whom have sought to propose what we would call feminist, and which are yet nonetheless Islamic, ways to understand the religious tradition insofar as it pertains to women. Turning to Mandaville's idea of translocality, in which one analyzes not how "people and cultures exist *in* places but rather how they move *through* them," Marcotte suggests that such Muslim scholar activists "criticize both cultural and traditional understandings of Islam that reiterate the hegemonic discourses of patriarchal and even misogynist interpretations of Islam." Their scholarly activities have opened up "new discursive spaces for thinking new possibilities for change." Focusing on the nexus of spirituality, scholarship, and activism, Marcotte argues that examining the context in which scholar activism takes place is essential in shedding light on the new discursive spaces that are opened up as a result. June O'Connor's identification of Muslim feminist activity as comprising "rereading, reconceiving, and reconstructing" and Anne Roald's alternate model of reselection (of source material) and reinterpretation of such source material provide frames through which to consider the works of such Muslim scholar-activists as Fatima Mernissi, Amina Wadud, Asma Barlas, Etin Anwar, Kecia Ali, and Riffat Hassan, who choose to remain Muslim while at the same time engaging the Islamic tradition to critique gender injustices and to propose a more gender equitable understanding of Islam and its institutions and practices. While the Moroccan scholar Fatima Mernissi was successful in mounting an incisive feminist critique of the semisacred status accorded to the *hadith* literature (narratives recording the doings and sayings of the Prophet Muhammad as conveyed by a chain of transmitters ending with his close companions), other indigenous scholars have suffered an ignoble fate, even death as in the case of Mahmoud Mohamad Taha, the Sudanese thinker, for attempting to address gender inequities. Thus, Marcotte argues, new diasporic discursive spaces allow Muslims in non-Muslim contexts "to explore, through their scholarship and their activism, new understandings of gender equality in Islam."

Noting that religion often remains undervalued in maintaining community and individual cohesiveness for immigrant minorities in host countries, Marcotte advances the view that Martin Baumann's tripolar model linking the historically and culturally religious community, the country of origin, and the country of residence can provide an additional lens through which to identify the discursive space occupied by a Muslim gender scholar-activist through the imposition of a fourth element, Islam, with such interrelationships represented in a Venn diagram (see Figure 6.1). Thus, a Muslim academic who has studied Islam in the academy is able to inhabit and also critique her historically and culturally specific Islamic tradition while negotiating her host country's culture. The writings of Leila Ahmed, Riffat Hassan, and Asma Barlas, all of whom find in their studies of Islam a more equitable treatment of women than is often practiced or inscribed in social institutions, are given as examples to illustrate the point that the struggle for gender justice undertaken by these scholar-activists was rooted as much in their scholarly work as it was in the positive evaluation of their faith with regard to the gender justice affirmed therein. For Leila Ahmed, the experience of a "women's Islam" serves to point to the increasingly misogynist interpretations overlaid onto the fundamentally ontological and moral equity with which women are treated in the Qur'an. For Hassan, the biblical view of Eve (which entered Islamic discourse very early on) informs the manner in which women are treated in the discursive and interpretive literature produced by Muslims in the early centuries, thereby laying the foundations for an unequal treatment codified in social and legal institutions. Barlas takes both these viewpoints further, arguing that neither the central principle of *tawhid* or singularity of God espoused by the Qur'an nor the principle of God's justice allow for father-right, the basis of patriarchy, to be supportable within a Muslim context; nor do they allow for misogyny, since that would go against God's fairness in deploying justice.

While the work of each of the foregoing three scholar-activists points to a "rereading" of the Qur'an, the next two scholar-activists brought into view, Etin Anwar and Kecia Ali, argue in their work for a reconsideration of the *shari'a*, the Islamic legal corpus, often faulted for its perceived inequitable treatment of women. Anwar suggests that when from within their cultural location women together "voice concerns of social, cultural, psychological, and political realities that oppress them," they are more able to find appropriate ways of addressing long-standing patriarchal inscriptions and practices. Ali addresses such inscription in the legal corpus, arguing that rather than discarding it in favor of placing reliance for authoritative injunctions only on the Qur'an, *shari'a* injunctions must be engaged seriously, especially in Western contexts where these have moral or ethical force rather than legislative power, as they do in Muslim-majority contexts, in order to "address new issues that are particular to diasporic environments." Thus, with respect to developing a more just sexual ethics, for which classical Muslim formulations are structurally inadequate in the contemporary climate, she suggests that Muslim women's contemporary experiences form the starting point for mining classical texts using a gyno-centric *ijtihad*—in this case, understood as a gender-sensitive hermeneutical struggle or effort—to determine their relevance in addressing contemporary sexual justice issues. The challenge remains how to "think about sexual intimacy within the constraints of God's revelation to humanity without becoming limited by patriarchal notions that deny women's lived experience and potential as fully human, fully moral, and fully sexual beings." She envisions a future in which women will serve as legal resources and practitioners in the manner that male imams do currently within their religious communities.

Marcotte then turns to examining the scholarly activism of such converts as Amina Wadud to Islam. It may be falsely assumed that converts are those least likely to interrogate "canonical" interpretations of their new faiths. Amina Wadud, however, takes on precisely such a challenge, that is, "the arrogance of those men who require a level of human dignity and respect for themselves while denying that level to another human being," as she takes seriously the notion that one "cannot stand on the sidelines in the face of injustice and be recognized as fully Muslim." She, too, calls for a new hermeneutic in understanding the Qur'an's injunctions dealing with gender, and for making women's experience part of the ongoing discourse on gender justice.

Khanum Shaikh examines the spaces that have opened up in recent decades for women's religious education. In particular, she investigates the workings of an organization called Al-Huda International, which has succeeded in reaching out to urban upper-class women, in an attempt to understand how and why this organization has attained such a high degree of success in delivering Islamic education. What kinds of subjectivities are found to emerge through participation in their activities, and how are the politics of gender played out? A study published in 1994 notes a move toward *madrassa*, or religious seminary, training for girls aged 11–15 in order to combat what was perceived as a threat emerging from Westernization, which was ostensibly projecting liberation but was seen as in reality promoting "obscenity and immorality." In the same year, Al-Huda International appeared on the scene as a space for women to study the Qur'an and its exegesis (*tafsir*) in a self-proclaimed attempt to promote Islamic values free of sectarianism and to strive for the upliftment of deprived classes. Dr. Farhat Hashmi, a graduate of Glasgow University in Scotland, began her efforts in Islamic education through private classes held at her home in an upper-class neighborhood in Islamabad, Pakistan, which soon led to the establishment of Al-Huda Academy, which offered one- to two-year-long diploma courses of instruction for women and girls in many urban cities in and beyond Pakistan. Over time, Al-Huda has extended its reach to Europe, the United States, and Canada and as part of its outreach goes into rural areas, slums, and prisons.

Shaikh points out that particularly for the Pakistani context, it is salient to note that a woman has broken into the male preserve of the dissemination of religious education. In doing so, Hashmi has mobilized the upper and middle classes of women, earning her credentials not from a traditional *madrassa*-based institution but, rather, from a European institution. The reasons for her success, observes Shaikh, include "technological sophistication, pedagogical philosophy, accessibility, *dawah* as a strategy for outreach, and a funding base," each of which is explored in further detail.

What kind of subjectivity has arisen as a result of increasing women's access to religious education pertaining to the Qur'an and its exegesis? Shaikh argues that she notes a conscious distancing from feminism; there is, rather, a "gendered form of moral agency" whose goal is "not to challenge normative prescriptions of gender and sexuality but, in fact, to inhabit these roles." Unlike the women featured in Marcotte's essay who struggle for gender equality, these women argue for a gender complementarity that further reinforces hetero-normative social roles. Accompanying such normative roles as wife, mother, and homemaker is a renewed emphasis on religious observance as well as Arabized religious dress, a move that often generates resistance from both family members and people from similar class backgrounds. Perhaps the strongest critique among several that have been advanced of Hashmi's approach and tutelage has come from Riffat Hassan, also an academic and theologian, who suggests in no uncertain terms that Hashmi is simply further reinforcing centuries-old male patriarchal interpretive norms without paying attention to Islam's overarching principles of social justice, including gender justice. Shaikh herself finds it problematic that her interviewees acknowledge neither the historically long-standing plurality of approaches to the Qur'an nor their role in the politics of the production of (Islamist) Islamic discourses.

Patricia H. Karimi-Taleghani offers a scholarly platform for dialogue on epistemological questions on how knowledge about African women and societies is produced, with specific reference to Ethiopia. She observes that apart from the continued imperialist gaze, both Western and African, which colors much writing on Africa and gender issues, current epistemologies often neglect "the role of African women's spirituality in their activism, particularly because that activism pertains to daily existence within urban African contexts." The chapter examines the features that influence women's economic situation and considers the indigenous values and organizations employed by Ethiopian women social activists.

In examining gender ideology in Africa, Karimi-Taleghani poses the question, "Just how much does ecological deprivation affect ideological control of scarce resources, especially in times of war, food crises, fuel shortages, and urban overpopulation?" She suggests that the ecological environment determines women's access to land, labor, and the products of that labor and is sanctioned through ritual. Historically, "prestige" crops that employed plow culture and more specialized skills, as well as cash crops produced under colonial rule, in dominated by men, whereas women were relegated less fertile lands and produced crops essential for feeding the family and employed hoe culture. The development of gender ideologies and ritual practices as well as legal systems to undergird male control of and access to more fertile lands also played a role, under colonial rule, in dominating and controlling women's productive work, restricting the access of women to land and technology, and often pushing women into greater poverty as they worked with fewer resources to feed their families.

In being self-reflexive about her own epistemologies in producing knowledge about gender in such African societies as Ethiopia, Karimi-Taleghani notes her own historically African roots and the oral knowledge that was passed down to her from other women in her family. She reflects on the spiritual retentions that are exhibited in the principles of a respect for nature, the symbiotic relationship between the physical and the metaphysical environments, the tangible nature of the spirit world, and the enduring connection to Africa, as well as her own academic training and fieldwork in Ethiopia. All of this, she notes, "enable me to enter Africa in different ways, to hear differently and report differently because I have experienced differently."

Having outlined her position with respect to her study of gender activism in Ethiopia, Karimi-Taleghani notes that the parallel and symbiotic gender systems of old are now viewed in fragments because of the intrusion into Africa of colonialism, intellectual chauvinism, and capitalism and as a result of the concomitant patriarchal ideologies that accompanied these. Consequently, African women's lives are now subjected to a "double patriarchy" in which African women are subordinated twice—by indigenous patriarchies and by Western white and male-focused lenses and theories. The oversimplification of African women as a monolith ignores the specific and localized identities within the many nations in Africa. Further, both state and international policies and economic regimes exercise an impact on preexisting indigenous gender relations. Parallels in indigenous gender systems were evident in metaphysical and political spheres and in gendered role expectations, while allowing for female subordination to be redressed through female institutions and metaphysical tools. Such systems have been undermined with the advent of Christianity, Islam, and colonization, as well as state-sponsored institutions. Nonetheless, spirituality is central to the traditional female world, and studies have shown that the sacred and the secular are of a piece in addressing colonial and contemporary challenges.

Karimi-Taleghani then asks, "To what degree have Ethiopian women been included or excluded from leadership roles and political participation within state and local structures?" Further, she asks, how do female institutions and organizations serve as avenues for change, and to what extent does women's spirituality aid in transforming their environments in order to meet family needs? She finds that much (but not all) "of the spiritual world of most women in Ethiopia revolves specifically around the feminine body and its reproductive functions." In addition, women's organizations in Ethiopia draw upon the teachings of their respective faiths, as well as indigenous spirituality and education, in order to organize women and provide training and other services that address the poverty in which many communities live. The efforts of state and international agencies are also noted with regard to gender development, environment, and biodiversity, all of which affect the lives of women. Data gleaned from both the organizers and the recipients of a transnational aid organization named Tesfa Ba Los Angeles, founded in the United States by expatriate Ethiopians, reveal that spirituality informs the desire of American Ethiopians to help the communities and women of Ethiopia, while eco-spiritual considerations inform the programming undertaken to ameliorate living conditions and poverty in Ethiopia itself.

PART 4: SEXUALITY, POWER, AND VULNERABILITY

Taking us to dramatic literature produced by North African Muslim women, **Laura Chakravarty Box** suggests that such literature provides "a bridge between the sphere of the personal or domestic and that of the national or international." Observing a shift since the inception of the war on terrorism from the sociological toward the political, Box traces the rewriting, by the Algerian French author Fatima Gallaire herself, of the play *Princesses*, first written in 1988 and revised in 2004 with a new ending. Rarely performed with its original ending, in which the protagonist is beaten to death by older village women, the play was revised by the author, who expressed her wish to change the ending, which she did in 2004, indelibly changing the character of the protagonist from one of victim to one who exercises a chilling agency not unlike that of her oppressors. Box sees in this shift a new note of pessimism regarding the ability of generations to work together for social change.

The chapter's attention then turns to the Tunisian playwright Jalila Baccar, whose play *Khamsoun*, initially banned in Tunisia, was performed in Tunis in 2008. Another play, *Araberlin*, takes up the subject of hybridized Arabs in Berlin in a post-9/11 era while reflecting perhaps metaphorically on politics at home, where it has not yet been performed. Engaging the question of for whom such women playwrights produce their works, the author observes that their recent work shows a greater preoccupation with world politics, subsuming the individual to the context in which the individual operates. The theme of resistance against occupation and oppression is increasingly brought into greater prominence even as the theme of violence against women ostensibly occupies center stage.

Nelly van Doorn-Harder turns to how spirituality factors into Indonesian women's struggles with respect to gender roles. Observing that the quest for developing a spirituality is on the rise and finds expression in a myriad number of activities, including Qur'an readings, meditation, and chanting, van Doorn-Harder considers various understandings of spirituality to draw out the power of spirituality to transform society. Accordingly, her chapter considers women "whose faith moves them to become advocates for women and transform society according to their specific vision of Islam," women who are both liberal and Islamist. What binds these divergent visions of Islam is their common appeal to the Qur'an as providing the blueprint for gender roles in society. Specifically, van Doorn-Harder takes up the struggles of women around the issue of polygamy, or more accurately, polygyny, in order to examine the role of spirituality in activism both for and against the practice. Complicating the issue further is that those who wish to see the implementation of *shari'a* law in Indonesia support polygyny on that basis, as a religious right.

The decade of upheaval since the fall of the Suharto regime in 1998 has resulted in heightened religiosity, whether in Islamist radicalism or what has been termed "overmoralization," as Indonesians sought to restore what they felt was the loss of morality that accompanied the political and natural upheavals of the decade, or in liberal activism that found itself increasingly preoccupied with campaigning for women's rights as the calls from Islamists for legalizing *shari'a* grew louder. The decade also saw a shift toward the much-needed relief work in such locales as war-torn Aceh as an expression of spiritual life. The issues encountered in such relief work include addressing the Islamist call to restrict the role of women in public life, limiting their choice of occupation, and restricting their mobility without male supervision. Islamist women have sought to socialize such ideas, including such practices as wearing the veil and promoting polygamous marriages, whereas others have fought to retain and promote women's religious and civil rights in the face of an increasing drive to Arabize Indonesian Islam and make its legal systems more consistent with *shari'a* law. While the latter did not succeed at the national level, it has made some headway in the form of by-laws or state laws, as in the state of Aceh, which declared *shari'a* law to be the law of the state in 2002. Such considerations have led to debates about polygamous marriages, the role of the woman as spouse, her call to *ikhlas* (sincerity of faith), and the parameters of violence in all its forms. Regardless of where they are on the ideological spectrum, what unites activist women is the practice of their faith, however conducted, and a struggle between literalist and liberal understandings of the Qur'an, mirroring the larger societal move from a communal sensibility to a more individualistic orientation.

Turning to the issue of polygamy, van Doorn-Harder explores the notion of *ikhlas* and how it has been reconceptualized by both Islamists and liberal Muslims alike in order to support or argue against the practice, respectively. The case of Ninih, the wife of a well-known preacher, is taken up to show how Ninih invoked the notion of *ikhlas* upon hearing news of the secret second marriage of her husband. This notion of *ikhlas* is one that involves an active sense of acceptance and resignation in the hopes that by being a virtuous wife and accepting polygamy—thought to be prescribed in the Qur'an—she would go to heaven. Islamists here promote polygamy because they view it as insurance against such Western vices as single parenthood and broken families.

Such views are also directed at girls, for whom literature is produced to show, on the one hand, the "friendly" face of Islam while, on the other, simultaneously undermining individualism and encouraging conformance to *sharia*, including polygamy. Girls are implicitly taught that a high sense of *ikhlas* should result in accepting one's fate as something God has sent one's way.

Despite such a reductionist view of the virtue of *ikhlas*, antipolygamy activists come from a position that it is important to draw upon the lived experiences of women. In their view, polygamy is a form of psychological abuse. The notion of *ikhlas* is reinterpreted to show that it may in fact be understood in a positive manner to argue for monogamy, with marriage understood as a partnership between equals rather than as an institution promoting a master-slave relationship between the husband and wife. In such a view, marriage may be construed as an act of devotion entailing *ikhlas* "practiced from the principles of voluntary choice, equality, justice, well-being, pluralism and democracy." Another antipolygamy activist appeals to the Qur'anic notion of *tawhid*, ascribing unity to God, to suggest that there can be no subordination between humans, since God alone is above humans, regardless of their sex. This view further argues that in spirit, the Qur'an was moving toward monogamy as the preferred form of marriage.

The stakes of how Indonesian women confront polygamy are high, for this issue is emblematic of a larger move toward a *sharia* mindset that would also yield immense political power to Islamists.

Khani Begum explores the recent proliferation in literary memoirs by Iranian women. She suggests that rather "than expressing a genuine desire to understand the experiences of Islamic women and their culture on their own terms," there are "underlying sociopolitical and psychological reasons for *this* particular trend at *this* particular time in the West." She believes that "they implicate U.S. political and economic interests ... by drawing attention to the relevance of these personal memoirs for U.S. and Western policies regarding the West's relations with Islamic societies in general and Iran in particular." Drawing upon Edward Said's observations regarding the relationship between the construction of knowledge about Islam and "the political, economic, and intellectual situation in which it arises," Begum notes that a new kind of Orientalist discourse is being generated in the writings of "insiders," who "occupy varying positions of power, especially during critical global political crises." Thus, her chapter examines recent Iranian women's literary memoirs in order to examine their own vested interests in power and authority. Such a discourse gives women a voice and informs Western readers while simultaneously reifying Western stereotypes of Islamic culture and Muslim women.

For instance, in adopting the form of the literary memoir, a form that is new to the preferred Iranian literary forms of poetry and drama, Iranian women are engaging in a transgressive act that goes counter to traditional prescriptions of self-effacement. Similarly, the parameters and regulations instituted under the fundamentalist regime in Iran around filmic depictions of male-female relationships has sparked innovative film-making styles and techniques in Iran and the Iranian diaspora, making Iranian cinema one of the most dynamic film mediums globally. At the same time, Begum suggests, there is a continuum in the Western fixation on the veil and the harem, whether exercised in the past through travelers' accounts or in the present through interest in the "unveiling" Muslim women offer in biographical narratives and films in that both are a way to know the Other, interpreted through categories familiar to the viewer's experience, with the Other being determined as exotic and mysterious when failing to accord with such experience. Michel Foucault, Edward Said, and others have noted the reflexivity of the scopic eye in defining its own sense of self when examining the Other.

The process of selection with respect to which works and filmic productions are brought to critical and scholarly attention and acclaim likewise reveals an interesting feature, with films exhibiting humanistic values shared with the West receiving more attention than films that challenge preconceptions of the Other. The shift from viewing the Orient as object to be desired, as during the time of colonization, to object to be feared, during the present era of globalization, has also sparked an even greater interest in the Other woman. Thus, the heightened interest in women's literary memoirs serves both to affirm Western humanistic values in battling patriarchal structures around the globe and to investigate possible answers to the perplexing question of "why do they hate us?" invoked in Iranian rejection of Western culture.

In this respect, Iranian women, as with other subaltern women, become the "native informant" brought into public view by publishers in response to current events "that have generated the fear and paranoia evidenced in the rhetoric of the war on terrorism." Their narratives, in the form of films and literary memoirs, are thus made to do the work of the earlier Orientalist writings, which emphasize Western humanistic values while simultaneously identifying its enemies. Turning to Hamid Dabashi's observations on Azar Nafisi's much-acclaimed memoir, *Reading Lolita in Tehran*, Begum reinforces her claim that such works work in tandem with current geopolitical agendas in justifying belligerence toward the Other. Works that might run counter to popular presuppositions of Iranian women's plight, such as the filmmaker Tahmineh Milani's *The Hidden Half*, for which she was arrested and then released (although charges are still pending), rarely get the kind of coverage accorded such a film as Marjane Satrapi's *Persepolis*. While the first examines a *hijab*-wearing woman's portrayal of her participation in the Iranian Revolution (1978), the latter portrays an Iranian woman's experience of the Revolution that finds much more resonance with Western conceptions of the same, despite the fact that both narratives are individual and highly specific tellings of the same story, pointing to the plurality of ways in which the Iranian Revolution was experienced. An exception must be made in the case of Shirin Neshat, whose art installations are much more widely known and acclaimed. Although her works fall more in line with the complex portrayals found in Milani's films, rather than being relegated to the margins since it does not work as well as works like Nafisy's and Satrapi's do in service of imperial designs, Neshat's art has taken on a life of its own and has crossed several boundaries to encompass photography, performance, literature, and art.

PART 5: WOMEN, WORLDVIEW, AND RELIGIOUS PRACTICE

Kari Vogt turns to an examination of Muslim women's religious practices in Western Europe. Noting that the presence of Islam in Europe dates largely from immigration flows in the 1950s, Vogt observes that the "broader political and social context of decolonization and specific economic and political choices made by European countries during times of economic growth or decline" must be taken into account in any discussion of European Muslim women's practices and worldviews. Numbering between 15 million and 20 million, many second- or third-generation European Muslims have taken full citizenship in their countries and are to be distinguished from more recent arrivals fleeing their countries of origin because of political unrest or from the migrants that came under family reunification programs as a result of changes in immigration laws. Such differences account, in part, for the diversity of attitudes to religion, social, and moral questions found in European Muslim communities. In addition, the already diverse ethnic and cultural backgrounds of the women in such communities contribute to the diversity of viewpoints and practices. Muslim familial practices pertaining to marriage and divorce have led to public debates resulting in the formation of Muslim women's associations aimed at representing and supporting their communities. The public debate over the headscarf and its subsequent banning in France in 2003 and then parts of Germany continues to be an issue of concern in Europe, both within and outside Muslim communities.

While the home has traditionally been the locus for Muslim women's religious practice, increasingly the mosque is becoming "an important arena for women's activities." Thus, rituals that previously used to be performed only at home—the *aqiqa* ceremony (head-shaving) performed after the birth of a child, for example, or the *Qur'an-khwani* (the recitation of the entire Qur'an), at the time of a person's death—are now often also being performed at the mosque as well. Increasingly, women are organizing such communal events as the provision of *iftar* (fast-breaking snack or meal) during the fasting month of Ramadan. Shi'ite women meet in homes or in the women's section of the *hosainiyeh* to conduct mourning ceremonies during the month of Muharram.

Some younger-generation Muslim women seek ways of learning about and understanding "authentic" Islam and may search out another mosque community, mentor, or Sufi *shaykh* (one sufficiently advanced in the spiritual life so as to be able to instruct others), as many of the latter take female disciples. A mosque in Oslo, Norway, for example, organizes special programs, including lectures and social events. Women also form such non-mosque-related organizations as the An-Nisa Society in London that provide a range of services and programs.

Women associated with more traditional Islamic movements gather at homes or reserve sections of the mosque for their devotional practices. Vogt examines a number of such movements among Moroccan, Pakistani, and Turkish Muslims in order to provide a better understanding of how women create spaces within which to sustain their faith despite and in response to the gender segregation encouraged by such movements. In addition, women have organized autonomous associations that cross ethnic and cultural boundaries, communicating with each other in European languages and addressing women's concerns while also bridging their communities with non-Muslim European authorities without giving up their commitment to their faith. Although traditional communities do not allow women to preach to mixed audiences, women nonetheless are legitimately permitted to preach to women-only audiences, leading to the development of female religious specialists. Since Al-Azhar University in Cairo began admitting women in the 1970s, several women have trained as Islamic scholars and have begun nonritual preaching. Although many such preaching activities take place in the languages of the country of origin, as women's networks arise, the language of such instruction has increasingly begun to be a European language.

Studies indicate that many European Muslims prefer the "Islam of the heart" rather than a strict legalistic Islam and view as the crux of Islam the five pillars rather than the interpretations of Islam that led to the creation of the *shari'a*. While attempting to educate themselves on Islam, religious Muslim women do not appear to be antagonistic toward European culture, which they also appreciate and engage both personally and professionally. It is important for them to claim their right to live as Muslims in European societies. Although they fight prejudice from both within and outside their Muslim communities, Muslim women in Europe are consciously creating networks and organizations and pursuing knowledge of Islam in order to sustain their religious lives within a diasporic context to create spaces of authority and engagement both within and outside their communities.

Bridget Blomfield looks at the female role models drawn upon by Shi'a Muslim women to construct their spiritual and social identity, also considering the intercessory and redemptive roles served by such models. These models are invoked during the days of ritual commemoration of the slaughter of the Prophet's grandson Husayn and his loyal band of family members and followers during the ill-fated battle near Karbala (present-day Iraq) between Husayn's forces and those of the Ummayad caliph Yazid led by Shimr. Among these role models are such women as Fatima, the daughter of the Prophet who was also the wife of Ali, whom the Shi'a consider the legitimate successor to the Prophet. Fatima's daughter Zaynab is also revered, as is Fatima, for her struggle on behalf of justice and her resistance to oppression. Blomfield traces the many ways in which Fatima is a role model as a person who is pure, the ideal wife and mother, one who stands up for justice and against oppression, and also examines her spiritual role as the progenitor of the Imams, the mother of compassion, and the bearer of divine wisdom. Zaynab is sent as an outraged sister and mother who defends her family after the massacre of her brother and family members and friends at the court of the Ummayad caliph Yazid. She has thus become a symbol of courage for Shi'a women.

Believing that emulation of Fatima's and Zaynab's laudable characteristics is necessary, Shi'a women retell stories of the two women at various occasions throughout the year, especially during the 10 days of mourning in the month of Muharram. Blomfield illustrates how these two women associated with the events at Karbala serve to model, as suggested by Kamran Scott-Agahie, the "new woman" who stands up to Western oppression, even as she may have been co-opted by the Islamists. In other words, Fatima and Zaynab together "make a modern, pious woman who is politically and religiously involved," that is, a woman who deals with her grief and loss by becoming a public activist. Such activism calls for freeing themselves from patriarchal constraints in order to practice a moral, pious lifestyle of their choosing. For example, as Lara Deeb's work suggests, Shi'a women in Lebanon view their faith as activism through which they can address injustice by offering education and support in their centers.

Blomfield notes that participation in the Muharram rituals commemorating the death of Husayn and members of his entourage serve to configure Shi'a women's worldviews and their hope for redemption. Further, these rituals structure time and place in a manner that enables the entering into sacred space while establishing continuity with formative events of the past, thereby allowing the past both to inform and to address the sufferings of the present. Blomfield adds her observations of Muharram rituals performed by women in Shi'a communities in Southern California. Here, she observes how women's bodies, too, as with their homes and centers, become sites of ritual enactment, allowing the "women a different perspective of human suffering by putting their personal sufferings in the context of the larger issues that the Prophet's family faced." In addition, the Muharram rituals are grounded in a theology that merits reverence and mourning for the Prophet and the Imams and their family with justice and redemption in the afterlife and with the courage to withstand suffering in the present.

Katherine Bullock's examination of the autobiographical narratives of three young Muslim women in Canada reflects on the relationship between religion and women's activism. Nadira, Mona, and Samana are three *hijab*-wearing young Muslim women who self-consciously publicly identify themselves as Muslims "by wearing a headscarf and long wrist- and ankle-length clothes out of a conviction that this is a religiously mandated dress." Although such points of view are part of the diversity of Muslim perspectives and are not always considered liberatory from a feminist point of view, the author argues that the reformist and anticolonial activist-inflected interpretation of Islam espoused by these women "can contribute to women's empowerment, rather than necessarily being a source of oppression."

Two of the women were raised in activist environments; the third was propelled into activism in response to the hostile stares she encountered one day during the first Gulf War. All three were active in Muslim organizations first either as children or as students at school or university. All three are activists. Bullock examines the role of religion in their activism and finds that religious teachings play a central role in the women's desire to be activists working toward social upliftment in a multilayered consciousness that extends from the individual to the family to society.

In terms of how religious upbringing and the decision to don *hijab* relate to growing up Muslim and female in Canada, one young woman, Nadira, reports her surprise at learning that men and women are treated differentially in some Muslim communities (including within Canada), for that was not her experience. Moreover, her decision to wear *hijab* is inflected by her growing spirituality and attention to religious praxis influenced by the writings and teachings of the medieval theologian and mystic al-Ghazali (d. 1111). For her, the *hijab* is a symbol of "educational advancement and moral liberation." Gender inequities among Muslims, in her view, must be addressed through *shari'a* because these are, in her view, the result of the wanton desires of some Muslims and not illustrative of the faith's teachings. Another woman, Mona, reflects on the moral accountability of both men and women to suggest that both genders are equally responsible for activism. In this respect, the role models of such older Muslim women as Sheema Khan, director of the Council on American-Islamic Relations (CAIR), provided for such women as Samana, the third woman whose narrative is included in this analysis, have also been critical in their own formation as Muslims and activists.

Bullock's research shows how these young women understand concepts of gender equity in ways that allow them to continue practices that seem, from a feminist point of view, to be reinforcing gender hierarchies and inequities. Drawing upon Yasmeen Abu-Laban's suggestion that Muslim women's political behavior—in this case, activism—be understood based on their own understandings, Bullock finds that young Muslim women such as the ones whose narratives have been examined here have opened up spaces through which they can balance their commitments to their faith with their commitments to, and indeed expectations for, women's equality.

PART I

Women, Family, and Environment

CHAPTER 1

Law and Iranian Women's Activism[*]

Louise A. Halper

A widely accepted view, both in scholarly and more general writing, is that Muslim women benefit from a regime of secular law and suffer under religious law. Thus, we are accustomed to conflating the situation of women in countries as diverse as Iran and Afghanistan and thinking both dreadful. But in fact, indicators of women's advancement in Iran[1] are quite comparable to those of women in Turkey, which has a secular tradition that is now 85 years old. On the other hand, in Afghanistan, the situation of women continues to be abysmal. At a glance, then, it appears that the presence or absence of *shari'a* as the law of the state is at the least nondeterminative, whatever influence it may have. It is in fact my hypothesis that the situation of women is impacted less by the nature of the legal regime than by their political status, that is to say, by the salience of women to the political process and their active involvement in it. Iran is my key example, and modifications in the law of marriage and divorce there constitute my data, so to speak.

Let me first set out some actual data. With respect to literacy, illiterates as a percentage of Iranian women 15 to 24 declined from over a third in 1980 to less than 10 percent in 2000.[2] Over the same period, the illiteracy rate for the entire population of adult women was cut in half, from about 60 percent to about 30 percent.[3] As for education, the number of

[*]This chapter adapted from Louise Halper, "Law and Women's Agency in Post-Revolutionary Iran," *Harvard Journal of Law and Gender* 28 (2005): 85, 113. Used by permission.

women in secondary school as a percentage of the eligible age group more than doubled from about 30 percent to almost 80 percent.[4] As of 1999, for every 100 boys in primary school, 96 girls were enrolled, indicating that boys and girls were almost equally likely to be learning basic literacy and numeracy skills.[5] In 2000, half of all Iranian university students were women,[6] as were 60 percent of entering students,[7] who were selected on the basis of a difficult nationwide exam. Twenty-seven percent of working-age women were in the labor force as of 2000, up from 20 percent in 1980.[8] In terms of health, life expectancy went up by 11 years between 1980 and 2000 for both Iranian men and women.[9] With respect to family planning, "levels of childbearing have declined faster than in any other country," going from 5.6 births per woman in 1985 to 2.0 in 2000,[10] a drop accomplished by a voluntary, but government-sponsored, birth-control program.[11]

As these figures reveal, since the Islamic Revolution, women in Iran are more literate and have more years of education than women under the monarchy. They are also longer lived and more likely to be in the workforce after schooling. They are likely to marry later and have greater control of their reproductive lives than women under the monarchy.

Some of these changes, for example, longevity and education, are certainly at least in part reflective of the redistributive character of the Islamic Republic, which, while it has not had a great deal of success in growing the economy, has readjusted the share of national wealth going to lower-income quintiles. Both men and women in this group have benefited from expanded availability of schools and health care within the popular classes. But beyond redistribution of wealth, these data bespeak a residue of attention to and focus on the situation of women hardly predictable if we turn our focus to the Islamic Republic's initial commitment to *shari'a* law interpreted in the patriarchal terms familiar to Islamic jurisprudence in Iran under the monarchy.

How are these data compatible with the reinstantiation of *shari'a* as the law of the state under the Islamic Republic? To what extent does that law continue to govern? By what mechanisms have the improvements reflected in these data been effectuated? What role have women themselves played in this improvement? These are important questions, particularly today, for they strongly implicate the issues of religion, law, gender, and activism.

I would like to examine these questions through the lens of the law of marriage and divorce. It is probably the case that the law of marriage and divorce is the central locus of gendered contact with the law in the courts and on the books. Most women will not have to testify in a criminal or commercial case, will not be victims of criminal acts, will not commit acts denominated sexual crimes; but most will be married, and many will be divorced. They will be a party to a marriage contract whose terms will shape their lives, and many will find that contract governing the terms under which the marriage is dissolved and their futures arranged. Thus, the law of marriage and divorce is of importance to women and is, in fact, the site at which their active intervention to shape the law is most likely to be seen. This is indeed the case in Iran, where the law of marriage and divorce has, since the Islamic Revolution, been a topic of interest to many women and an issue for women's organizations, as well as the women's press.[12] Women's involvement in this issue has had consequences for the law of marriage and divorce, demonstrating both the extent to which women's activism impacts the concerns of the state and the extent to which the state must respond to women as a constituency.

This discussion focuses particularly on two legislative innovations in the law of marriage and divorce from the mid-1990s, in the period after the death of Ayatollah Khomeini in 1989 and the election of Mohammad Khatami as president of the Islamic Republic in 1997.

The starting point should be the status of the law of marriage and divorce before the Islamic Republic constitutionally denominated *shari'a* as the law of the state. Prior to that, the law of marriage and divorce was supposed to be compatible with *shari'a*, as interpreted by leading clerics. Under Shah Mohammad Reza, a new law, the Family Protection Law (FPL), was adopted in 1967 and amended in 1975. That law, which compliant clerics had held as being *shari'a* compatible, constrained the unilateral power over divorce that was the husband's prerogative under classical Islamic law. Instead, the FPL said no divorce was final until ratified by the judge, who had to be satisfied with arrangements for custody and for the family's post-divorce maintenance. Moreover, the new law added maltreatment to the very limited circumstances (long desertion, insanity, impotence) under which the wife could initiate an action for divorce. Further, the husband could not register a second marriage without the first wife's consent, thus limiting his rights to polygamous marriage. These changes were procedural, but they had an impact on the substantive law.

After the overthrow of the Shah at the end of 1978 and almost immediately after Ayatollah Khomeini's return to Iran in February 1979 from 13 years of exile, Khomeini declared the FPL "un-Islamic" and declared that any person who remarried after being divorced under the FPL was an adulterer. But although Khomeini abrogated the FPL and replaced its lay judges with clerics who would administer *shari'a*, no particular legislation was put in its place. Instead, judges were left to decide for themselves how the broad outlines of *shari'a* were to be applied to particular cases. Nor were procedural rules amended, leading judges to try to fit the new legal structure into the old procedure and vice versa. This state of affairs continued, with bits of mending and amending for more than a decade. Not until the Divorce Reform Law of 1989 were the sources of law applying to marriage and divorce in the Islamic Republic of Iran (IRI) agreed upon and legislation passed to rationalize them with existing rules and opinions. In 1992, that law was further amended, resulting in the creation of a new family code that while similar to the FPL went further in protecting women in respect to divorce and custody.[13] That law was further amended in 1993 and 1996, on both occasions to the wife's advantage. By the time Mohammad Khatami was elected president of Iran, with a stunning 80 percent of the women's vote, the law of marriage and divorce was not only the equivalent of the FPL in terms of its provision for women, but in some cases the law exceeded its protections.[14] I want to focus in particular on the amendments of 1993 and 1996, as they indicate a new approach to the ways in which the Islamic law of marriage and divorce can be applied in a state context through new or reclaimed interpretive strategies. To do so requires some brief examination of classical marriage law.[15]

As indicated, in *shari'a*, marriage is considered a contract entered into by the two parties, each having different rights and responsibilities, which are themselves gendered. Thus, the husband is required to maintain the wife for both their lifetimes and for hers, if she survives him or if he divorces her by *talaq* (a mode of divorce in which a male verbally divorces his wife in front of witnesses by pronouncing the word *talaq* three times). In order to provide for her support, he is required, upon marriage, to endow her with a capital sum, known as the *mahr*, capable of maintaining her should he die or divorce her. He then has a right to her obedience and sexual and reproductive services. He also has the coterminous right to enter into up to three other similar contracts and the right to unilateral divorce. She has the right to be maintained and the duty to obey and provide sexual and reproductive services. She does not have a unilateral right to divorce and may seek it only in very limited circumstances. She cannot enter into another such contract coterminously, nor does she have any duty in regard to his support. Upon divorce, he has no further duty of support to her, though he must still maintain his children, to whose custody he is entitled. The contract bespeaks an implicit view of society as heavily gendered, with economic activity constituting the province of men.

With this as the outline of the *shari'a*-based law applied in the post-revolutionary religious divorce courts, many women were shocked to find themselves at risk late in their lives when their husbands unilaterally divorced them. Because of inflation or a marriage contract that had replaced the economic value of the *mahr* with some romantic conceit like a rose or a sigh, they could be left indigent with no resources at all, dependent on aged parents or grown children, and with little possibility of remarriage. Younger women who wished to divorce found it very difficult to leave a bad marriage without the consent of a spouse from whom they were alienated and were subject to being deprived of support if they separated.

Ziba Mir-Hosseini has richly described in her books and the film titled *Divorce Iranian Style* how these dilemmas made Qu'ranic exegetes of women who were challenged by this religious law to attain their goals in the context of unwanted divorce or marriage. Among the strategies they employed was an insistence on extracting the cash value of the *mahr* from a divorcing husband. Generally, payment of the *mahr* was deferred at the inception of the marriage, making the wife the first creditor on the husband's estate before its disbursal to successors after his death; in case of his unilateral exercise of *talaq*, she was then entitled to it, though many women did not understand their rights in this respect until they were educated by the women's press. Another use of the *mahr* was to waive its payment if the divorcing husband would give her custody of the children. Or she could buy her way out of the marriage by agreeing not to press her claim to the *mahr*.

But all these strategies relied upon the *mahr* retaining its value. In fact, however, inflation raged in Iran after the Revolution and during the Iran-Iraq War, making many *mahrs*, in the words of a woman member of the Iranian Majles, or parliament, "barely enough to pay a wife's taxi fare to the divorce court." Her only source of support after divorce, her potential means of obtaining a divorce or of keeping her children, might be completely valueless within a few years after the marriage.

The women's press took up this question and sought reform that would keep women from destitution after divorce or the destruction caused by a bad marriage. One solution, suggested by Khomeini, was the creation of a right for the wife, upon the husband's exercise of *talaq*, to half the property acquired by him during the course of the marriage.[16] Such a provision would be included in the boilerplate marriage contract[17] and could provide for the woman whose *mahr* had, at the time of divorce, declined dramatically in value because of inflation. But this solution only served women married after the new provision was added to the contract. It did nothing for the older women whose marriage contracts were made earlier than 1982 when Khomeini had the provision added.[18]

During the decade of the 1980s, women had been crucial to maintaining popular support for the Islamic Republic during the terrible Iran-Iraq War of 1980–1988. They lent both active and passive support to the IRI, on the one hand, filling roles as ambulance drivers, ammunition packers, health workers, and workplace substitutes for men at the front and, on the other, allowing their husbands and sons to go off to the devastating "human-wave" attacks that allowed Iran to use its population advantage to counter Iraq's weaponry advantage. By the end of the 1980s, issues of concern to women, including the laws applying to their marriages, divorces, and families, had become a focus of both administration and legislation. There had been a decade of attention to the "crisis of marriage" by women's organizations and in the women's press that had led to this outcome,[19] as both women and judges (who were, in the revolutionary aftermath, all men) sought ways to ameliorate the impact on women of the harsh strictures of classical marriage law.

But when the Majles took up this question, it did not at first provide a solution to this fundamental problem facing women, in part because it did not know how to do so. In finding a solution, it was aided by the demonstration in the women's press of the possibilities of new interpretive strategies when applied to religious law. The new "dynamic jurisprudence," or *feqh-e puya*, experimented with women-friendly interpretations of Qu'ranic text and *hadith* and was a product of the thinking devout and believing women and their allies had done about the situation of women in a religious state.

This position was advanced by the cleric Mohsen Sa'idzadeh, in the 1990s the author of a series of pseudonymous articles in the feminist magazine *Zanan* (Women), challenging traditional interpretations of *feqh* concerning women. Sa'idzadeh was apparently the first modern cleric to make "an overt attempt to reconcile feminism with Islam," believing that religion and gender equality are reconcilable. His starting point was the strong equality claims of Islam, which allowed him to conclude that gender is a social construction, "a relative matter [that] . . . has no place in the divine realm." Hence, those traditions that seem to mandate inequality are either misinterpreted or otherwise incorrect.[20] *Zanan* published these articles as explicit challenges to retrograde interpretations of the situation of women and in order to provide women with ammunition in legal actions regarding their own marriages.

At the same time, there were a number of women among members of the Majles who were interested in improving the legal situation of women and who were apparently attending to the discussion of *feqh-e puya*. They and their male allies took up the problem of the lack of support for divorced women and were able to suggest a religiously acceptable means of providing that support. The novel solution they proposed was drawn from accepted notions of religious jurisprudence reconceptualized in a post-revolutionary context.

Their solution was to turn to *mu'amalat*, the religious account of the duties people owed one another. Among them is the responsibility to compensate fairly those who labor in one's behalf, so long as that labor is volunteered, and not commanded. In that situation, the laborer is worthy of his or her hire, as another monotheistic tradition has it. The corresponding concept in Islam is *ujrat al-mithal,* meaning that a fair price should be paid for any commodity, including the labor of a free person.

Now, although the marriage contract commits the wife to compensate her husband with her obedience and sexual and reproductive services in return for his maintenance of her, it does not require her to keep house or nurse children. Yet most women do so. Thus, they are entitled to be compensated for this work, should they demand it, as they might do upon divorce. Such a provision was added to the 1991 divorce law at the end of 1992, as another judicially cognizable claim a divorced woman would have upon her husband.[21] This time, the Majles not only required that the form contract include the provision that the wife was due her wages in case of divorce but also made it possible for a woman married under the old form of contract to get wages for housework, implied into the old contract judicially, if a court found she had not agreed to contribute her work without pay.[22] Thus, even a woman married before the right to wages was made explicit in the form contract might be entitled to receive them, though there were limitations on this right that were a product of compromise.

The most complete answer to the problem of support for divorced women was in a sense both the simplest and the most faithful to the religious tradition. Recall that the marriage gift was intended to provide women with the assurance of support regardless of what happened to their husbands or their marriages. The *mahr* ceased to accomplish that function only because of inflation, which diminished the value of the marriage gift when stated in terms of currency. The obvious solution, and the one adopted by the Majles, encouraged by female parliamentarians within and women's organizations and the women's press externally, was to inflation-index the marriage gift.[23] Thus, whatever amount of gold the currency-denominated gift would have bought at the time of the marriage was understood to be the ongoing value of the gift at whatever time it might be demanded by the female spouse. In one simple amendment, then, the issue of support for divorced women was resolved. That amount which she and her family had believed would serve as a capital sum capable of supporting her for life would be available to her whenever the marriage ended, whether it ended by death or divorce.

All of this, occurring as it does even before the reformers take over in the elections of 1997, is surprising, given the standard narrative of women's situation in Iran, and begs, but does not defy, explanation. That explanation, in my view, lies in the events surrounding the Islamic Revolution, both its precursors and *sequelae,* and the activism of Iranian women in that context.

Here it is necessary to review a bit of history. Although Iranian women were supporters of national independence as far back as the Qajar dynasty at the end of the 19th century, they were not traditionally expected or encouraged to be politically active. The notion of female suffrage was first raised in the context of the Constitutional Revolution of 1905 but was soundly rejected by both clerics and laypersons. The founder of the Pahlavi dynasty, Reza Shah, ordered that women had to unveil in public and established girls' schools in major cities, but he did not otherwise seek their political support. After his forced abdication, in the 1940s, a popular front government introduced suffrage legislation, but once again it was defeated. With the overthrow of Prime Minister Mossadegh in 1953, Reza Shah's son, Mohammad Reza, undertook personal governance of the state. On the advice of his U.S. supporters, he sought to broaden his internal base of support by giving women the vote. It was, in fact, on this issue that Ruhollah Khomeini, then a relatively low-ranked cleric, first made known his public opposition to the Shah in 1963, denouncing women's suffrage as un-Islamic. And certainly at least in part because of his opposition, relatively few women voted in the Majles elections, which were, in any case, a sham, for the Shah brooked no opposition electorally or otherwise.

But the opposition to the Shah and his government had never declined since Mossadegh's overthrow, despite savage repression, and Khomeini, though sent into exile, continued as one of the public faces of that opposition, which contained secular, religious, and liberal figures of many political stripes. Khomeini's forces had an edge—as clerics, they were less repressible than were other groups, whose organization was perforce underground, whereas the clergy's was visible in every mosque and *husayniya* (a place of gathering where ceremonies commemorating the life and martyrdom of Imam Husayn are held). It was within the power of Khomeini and his organization to rally truly mass support for the anti-Shah movement. Nor did Khomeini scruple to include women within these forces.

Mary Hooglund (the well-known social anthropologist Mary Ellen Hegland) was conducting her thesis research in a small village near Shiraz in the summer of 1978, when the protests against the Shah entered their final and most populous stage. She describes how women became active in them. She notes first that the mosque was the "most important center of revolutionary activity" in the village and that women who regularly attended were "more likely to be influenced by the revolutionary ideas." Moreover, the seven young girls in the village who went to high school were taught by a mullah whose classes "became forums for learning revolutionary ideology." Both men and women experienced "horror, rage, and frustration . . . when witnessing or hearing of acts of violence against their fellow citizens."[24]

Nonetheless, village women, unlike their male counterparts, did not actually participate in demonstrations until January 1979. The demonstrations of the previous month had been enormous, and there was much bloodshed as the Shah's forces attacked the demonstrators. On a day appointed for mourning those killed in December, village women, on their own, came out of their houses and walked "a little ways up the alley," chanting slogans. "When the men heard their voices," Hooglund was told, "they came out too." This must have been a transformative moment for the village women, most of whom never left their houses socially except to clean off family graves in a group every few weeks. And these demonstrations continued and grew larger. "After the first evening of chanting, they began to feel that all was possible."[25] They began to travel to Shiraz to take part in the larger demonstrations for "independence, freedom and Islamic republic." This last was a characteristic demand of the Khomeini forces, as opposed to the more secular left, which sought simply a republic. Hooglund's informants explained their participation, so unusual for Iranian women, as justified by religious authority:

> The religious scholars and the ayatollahs have said that men and women must revolt together, they must demonstrate together for religion and for freedom for all. Islamic government is for everybody and the Islamic struggle is for everybody. Before women didn't do this. . . . If we don't speak, this government will go on for hundreds of years more.[26]

Indeed, Khomeini had sanctioned and called for women's participation on the streets, calling their involvement "one of the blessings of this movement."[27] His was a call that could not be denied even by men completely unaccustomed to seeing women in their family as political actors. As Homa Hoodfar writes, the "unconventional presence of women in political demonstrations, wearing traditional black chador, became the symbol of the popular revolution."[28] This evocation of women's agency by the leading cleric and most revered political figure in the country simply swept away the customary barriers to such action.

I have spent some time on the Aliabad experience because it so clearly indicates the radical break with the past that the Revolution created for women there, a break duplicated hundreds of thousands of times around the country. Once the Revolution succeeded, the women who had supported it so unconventionally had some claims upon it. Those claims were, in fact, enhanced by the need Khomeini felt to appeal to women for their support for the creation of the Islamic Republic itself in an election and referendum to decide the shape of the new republic. Khomeini, who had been so opposed to the Shah's 1963 offer of suffrage for women, did not maintain this position. He urged women to come out to vote, first for the constitution of the Islamic Republic approved in December 1979, and then in March 1980 for election of candidates who backed him. "Women in the Islamic Republic must vote. Just as men have the right to vote, women too have that right."[29] Indeed, Khomeini went further, commanding that for women, voting was a "religious, Islamic and divine duty."[30] This, as Parvin Paidar says, "was a total reversal of the history of clerical opposition to women's participation in the economy, politics and society."[31]

Nor did the creation of the Islamic Republic of Iran in 1980 call a halt to this new phase. Immediately after the Revolution, there were a variety of independent women's organizations and now-visible women's caucuses within the political formations that had been underground in the Shah's time. The leading women's group, the Women's Organization of Iran (WOI), headed by the Shah's sister, had been created in the wake of the extension of suffrage to women, a formal group recognized by the monarchy. This was disbanded in favor of Women in Support of the Islamic Revolution (WSIR), a group that replaced the WOI as the conduit to and from the government in respect to issues of concern to women. At the same time, control over publications of interest to women shifted from secular supporters of the Shah to Islamist women.

What looked to the West like antiwomen policies were interpreted by these Islamist women as antisecular ones. They first overcame their secular counterparts, who argued for gender equality regardless of the traditions of the *shari'a*, by espousing a version of difference feminism that "stressed that the Quran has given different rights and responsibilities to the different creations of God."[32] Though they agreed that women's primary roles were in the family, they also supported women who wanted or needed to work outside the home. In fact, they became advocates for interpretations of *shari'a* more open to the concerns of modernist women than those embraced by prerevolutionary traditionalists.[33]

In practice, Islamist women first mobilized women's support for the Islamic Republic, then became advocates for the improvement in their status and condition. This shift in emphasis required that women engage the religious establishment with "female-centered interpretations of Islam,"[34] becoming innovators in developing an "Islamic feminist theory of women's oppression and liberation."[35] They came to argue that true religious practice would not oppress women or make them lesser persons than men; thus, any practices or laws that did so were not Islamic but accretions that should be shed.

At the same time, while the new government may not have approved of self-conscious feminism, even in its Islamic mode,[36] it maintained its support among women by measures beneficial to the popular classes. These included literacy programs for adults, more widely available public education for both sexes, and accessible primary health care particularly focused on healthy mothers and children.[37] These were the kinds of policies helpful to women living in traditional families, who had rejected the state feminism of the monarchy's Women's Organization of Iran.

The war with Iraq that followed also required changes in women's roles; it evoked from the government a more conciliatory approach to women than had existed in the immediate post-revolutionary period when ideological rigor was at its peak and women judges were dismissed, some faculties were closed to women, and *hejab* was widely imposed. During the war, women were involved in assisting in battle areas; in providing food, transportation, and medical support; and in distributing arms. At home, they aided the wounded; participated in meetings, demonstrations, and conferences to support the war effort; and resettled refugees from the front. As a woman interviewed by Maryam Poya said of her activities during that period, "My husband couldn't disagree; it was all for God."[38]

And when men did not come home, or came home wounded, their mothers, wives, sisters, and children needed to be provided the means of living in order to ensure continued popular support for the terrible carnage. The impact on women's employment was substantial. More women had to work outside the home, either because their husbands were at the front or because the galloping inflation of the war years required families to have two incomes. Women who had never been employed outside the home were encouraged by the state to enter the workforce so that they could support their families.[39] While the early position of the Islamic Republic had discouraged women from working outside the home, this changed quickly. Labor practices favorable to working mothers—part-time jobs with significant full-time benefits,[40] for example, and requirements that workplaces provide day care[41]—were adopted to make work and motherhood compatible.

Once the war ended, women felt not only empowered but also obliged to discuss their status and establish the continuity of their participation in public life in both politics and employment. Women demanded and society agreed that the government should undertake the task of promoting women's social participation as one of its overt goals, rather than simply responding piecemeal to women's issues as it had during the war. One form this process took was institutional, with the creation of entities within the government that focused on women's issues directly. Until then, women's issues were the purview of government-sponsored quasi-nongovernmental organizations (NGOs) and the women's press. In 1987, under then-president Ali Khamenei (who later replaced Ayatollah Khomeini as supreme leader), the government created the Women's Social and Cultural Council as a formal means of providing recommendations on women's issues to the executive branch.[42] Its creation was, in effect, an admission by the conservatives in control of the executive branch that women's issues had an existence independent of those of society at large. Moreover, those issues had to be addressed not only through the mechanism of the Majles, whose female representatives might or might not raise particular questions, but in a direct and coherent fashion. Subsequently, the Bureau of Women's Affairs was created within the President's Office in 1991; after President Mohammad Khatami's election in 1997, it became the Center for Women's Participation; and after President Ahmadinejad's election, the Center for Women and Families.[43]

In short, women who were supportive of the Revolution became the first to undertake an institutional challenge to the Islamic government's attempt to restore unchanged a patriarchal tradition. They insisted that change for women would not come automatically with the mere existence of Islamic government but would require specific attention and action to women as a discrete group within the polity. Their success has demonstrated that democratic change is possible in the context of Islamic law. While the male-dominated reform movement did not succeed in such other legislative efforts as winning a free "press, stopping torture, [ensuring] free elections, regulating state-run Radio and TV, making [political] institutions . . . accountable to [the] Majles, or the fair trial of political crimes,"[44] women have experienced numerous successes regardless of the fate of reformers. Iranian women instigated change with respect to marriage and divorce laws even before the 1997 election of the reform-minded President Khatami: they have opened up schools, employment, and political office to women; and they have modified the legal regime to their benefit.

Such successes have not only substantive but also procedural, impacts. Each time women have moved in a new direction—seeking to enter previously barred occupations, taking part in sports in which women have not participated, running for offices that women have not yet held—they have evoked a response. Because the regime claims not only divine but also electoral authority, this response cannot be simply a pro forma negative. Explanations are demanded, interpretations offered, responses written, and arguments engaged in. Because a basis in religion is also claimed, texts are produced, authorities cited, and rationalizations proffered. Each can, in its turn, be the subject of debate. Like a public trial, such a conversation creates a process of public engagement, a space of discourse hitherto unknown, and contributes to the legitimization of multiple voices.

NOTES

1. World Bank, GenderStats; and United Nations, *Human Development Report*.

2. World Bank, GenderStats: Capabilities and Human Capital—Iran, Islamic Rep. http://genderstats.worldbank.org/.

3. Ibid.

4. Ibid. This is the only participation-in-education figure for which data from both 1980 and 2000 are readily available. The corresponding figure for young men also increased but not as dramatically. Males in school as a percentage of the eligible group went from 52 percent in 1980 to 85 percent in 2000.

5. United Nations Development Program, *Human Development Report, 2001*: Iran, Islamic Rep., available at http://hdr.undp.org/en/reports/global/hdr2001/. According to UNESCO, gender parity in literacy is "a significant indicator of the empowerment of women in society." Section for Women and Gender Equality of the Bureau of Strategic Planning, UNESCO, UNESCO's Gender Mainstreaming Implementation Framework 18 (2003), available at http://unesdoc.unesco.org/images/0013/001318/131854e.pdf.

6. Azadeh Kian-Thiebaut, "Women and the Making of Civil Society," in *Twenty Years of Islamic Revolution: Political and Social Transition in Iran since 1979*, ed. Eric Hooglund (Syracuse, NY: Syracuse University Press, 2002), 63.

7. Jaleh Shadi, "Officials Concerned about Controversy over Women's Employment and Housewifery," *Zanan*, no. 77, July 2001.

8. World Bank, GenderStats: Opportunity—Iran, Islamic Rep., at http://genderstats.worldbank.org/.

9. Capabilities/Iran, supra note 2. Life expectancy for females born in 2000 was 70, for males 68, up from 59.2 and 58.5, respectively, in 1986, according to Dr. Hamid Sadeghipour of Tehran University School of Medicine. Alvin Powell, "Iranian Primary Care Produces Big Results," *Harvard Gazette*, Jan. 21, 2003.

10. Farzaneh Roudi-Fahimi, *Iran's Family Planning Program: Responding to a Nation's Needs* (Washington, DC: Population Reference Bureau, 2002).

11. Ibid., 3.

12. The important women's newspapers include *Farzaneh* (editor Mahbubeh Abasgholizadeh), *Hoghugh Zanan* (editor Ashraf Geramizadegan), *Jens Dovom* (editor Nooshin Ahmady-Khorasany), *Nashriyeh Bonyad Pazhuheshhaye Zanan Irani* (editor Goli Amin), *Nimeye Digar*, 1983–2000 (editor Afsaneh Najmabadi), *Payam Hajar* (editor Azam Taleghani), *Zan* (editor Faeze Rafsanjani), *Zan Ruz* (various editors); and *Zanan* (editor Shahla Sherkat). Parvin Paidar, "Gender of Democracy: The Encounter between Feminism and Reformism in Contemporary Iran," United Nations Research Institute for Social Development:

Democracy, Governance, and Human Rights, Programme Paper 6 (Oct. 2001), available at http://www.onlinewomeninpolitics.org/beijing12/paidar.pdf.

13. Parvin Paidar, *Women and the Political Process in Twentieth-century Iran* (Cambridge: Cambridge University Press, 1995), 276.

14. Ziba Mir-Hosseini, "Women and Politics in Post-Khomeini Iran: Divorce, Veiling and Emerging Feminist Voices," in *Women and Politics in the Third World*, ed. Haleh Afshar (London: Routledge, 1996), 144–47.

15. The following paragraph is drawn from Ziba Mir-Hosseini, *Marriage on Trial: A Study of Islamic Family Law* (London: I. B. Tauris, 1993), 35–39.

16. In marriages occurring after 1982, the year when post-revolutionary marriage contracts were issued, the marriage contract contains a stipulation to which the parties consent by signing. This stipulation requires the husband to pay his wife, upon divorce, up to half of the wealth he has acquired during that marriage, provided that the divorce has not been initiated or caused by any fault of the wife. Ibid. at 57, 210 note 5.

17. Although both sides must agree, standardized provisions favorable to women provide some assistance in redressing the balance of this gendered transaction. Thus, "the burden is shifted to the groom who must negotiate to remove the clauses he disagrees with, giving the bride's party leverage to request additional conditions of their own." Homa Hoodfar, *The Women's Movement in Iran: Women at the Crossroads of Secularization and Islamization*, The Women's Movement Series, no. 1 (Grabels Cedex, France: Women Living Under Muslim Laws, 1999), 35, available at http://www.wluml.org/english/pubs/pdf/misc/women-movement-iran-eng.pdf.

18. Similarly, Khomeini also had approved of the adoption of an old strategy to restrain men from exercise of their polygamous rights. That strategy included a provision in the marriage contract delegating to the wife the power to act as her husband's agent in the exercise of *talaq*, his unilateral right to divorce, in the event that he took a second wife. In effect, this provision provided her the power to end her marriage. Khomeini also took other steps to protect women's interests in their marriages, including means to assure them continued custody of their children upon the death of husbands in the bloody and almost interminable Iran-Iraq War, although the traditional understanding was that their custody went to the husband's relatives after his death. Ibid., 34.

19. Throughout the 1980s, the women's press attacked male custody rights over children, polygamy, and inequitable division of property on divorce and argued for alternative understandings of religious prescriptions that seemed to support them. For example, the publication *Zan-e Ruz* [Today's Woman] carried articles with headlines like "With Polygamy, No One Adheres to Islamic Law," *Zan-e Ruz*, July 14, 1984, 8; "Women Have Grievances with the Lack of

Enforcement of the Orders of Family Courts, but We Don't Have Adequate Laws in This Regard," *Zan-e Ruz*, Dec. 2, 1989, 20 (discussing issues of custody and support); "Family Conflict Is the Primary Cause of Suicide," *Zan-e Ruz*, June 4, 1989, 5 (addressing the topic of women's suicide); and "A Wife Who Has Worked Hard in My House for Years Is a Partner in My Pension/Benefits," *Zan-e Ruz*, July 18, 1989, 6. See also Hoodfar, *The Women's Movement in Iran*, 33–34.

20. Ziba Mir-Hosseini, *Islam and Gender: The Religious Debate in Contemporary Iran* (London: I. B. Tauris, 2000), 249–50.

21. The Guardian Council did not approve that provision until 1993 and it went into effect then. Hoodfar, supra note 17, at 35.

22. "Determination of Wages for Work Done," *Zan-e Ruz*, Dec. 18, 1993.

23. Louise Halper, "Law, Authority and Gender in Post-Revolutionary Iran," *Buffalo Law Review* 54 (2007): 1137.

24. Mary Hooglund, "The Village Women of Aliabad and the Iranian Revolution," *Review of Iranian Political Economy and History* 4, no. 2 (Fall 1980): 27, 33.

25. Ibid., 37–38.

26. Ibid., 40.

27. Vanessa Martin, *Creating an Islamic State: Khomeini and the Making of a New Iran* (London: I. B. Tauris, 2000), 156.

28. Hoodfar, supra note 17, at 22.

29. Imam Ruhollah Khomeini, *The Position of Women from the Viewpoint of Imam Khomeini*, ed. and trans. Juliana Shaw and Behrooz Arezoo (Tehran: Institute for the Compilation and Publication of Imam Khomeini's Works, 2001) [hereinafter Khomeini], 58, available at http://www.iranchamber.com/history/rkhomeini/books/women_position_khomeini.pdf.

30. Nesta Ramazani, "Women in Iran: The Revolutionary Ebb and Flow," *Middle East Journal* 47 (1993): 409, 411.

31. Paidar, supra note 13, at 257.

32. Maryam Poya, *Women, Work & Islamism* (London: Zed Books, 1999), 6.

33. Hoodfar, supra note 17, at 20.

34. Ibid., 3.

35. Paidar, supra note 13, at 240.

36. Ibid.

37. Louise Halper, "Law and Women's Agency in Post-Revolutionary Iran," *Harvard Journal of Law and Gender* 28 (2005): 85, 113.

38. Poya, supra note 31, at 136–37.

39. Ramazani, supra note 30, at 411.

40. Paidar, supra note 13, at 328.

41. Ramazani, supra note 30, at 414.

42. Elham Gheytanchi, Appendix (to Nikkie Keddie) titled "Chronology of Events regarding Women in Iran since the Revolution of 1979," *Social Research Journal* 67, no. 2 (2000): 439, 445.

43. Nahid Motee, Population Council, Scientific and Cultural Exchange Program between Iranian and International Researchers, app. 4 (2000), available at http://www.iranngos.org/reports/SciCulExch/Women011ProfilesGovAgenResWo .htm.

44. Majid Mohammadi, "Iran's Way of Constitutionalism after 1996: Interpretations of Iran's Constitution by the Judiciary and the Reformers" (unpublished paper presented at the 2003 Annual Meeting of the Law & Society Association, Pittsburgh, June 5, 2003, on file with the author), 3.

CHAPTER 2

Gendered Space and Shared Security: Women's Activism in Peace and Conflict Resolution in Indonesia

Etin Anwar

This chapter investigates the ways in which men and women, irrespective of religious, cultural, and ethnic differences, disseminate activism for a shared concern of security as a public good in Indonesia. Women's involvement and activism in peace and reconciliation projects is gendered, since their participation is somewhat associated with accepted gender roles. In places where ethnic, political, and religious conflict erupted, such as in Sambas, Aceh, and Maluku,[1] women did not necessarily get involved in deciding how the peace and reconciliation process was resolved. The exclusion of women from the peace decision-making process should not come as a surprise, since such exclusion goes along with the expected social and cultural roles of women in private and public spheres. Although the peace agreements of ethnic and interreligious conflicts have been mostly resolved among men, women have the proclivity to contribute to peacemaking in those areas that are socially and culturally relevant to them.

This chapter echoes Charlotte Bunch's argument regarding war and peace as gendered activities because the rhetoric of war and peace is culturally specific and relates to gender constructs.[2] It also agrees with Ritu

Menon's view of how women's encounters with violence inspire them to engage in peacemaking.[3] Further, this chapter examines how social and cultural views of gender constructs correlate to gender activism in the peace and reconciliation process. Of particular interest is how masculine power and prestige rhetoric relates to peacemaking. Also investigated here is the impact of conflict on human security, especially women, and national security. In this chapter, finally, I proceed to formulate a pattern of women's activism in peace and conflict resolution carried out by women as negotiators and agents of peace.

GENDERED POWER: NEGOTIATING EQUALITY AND DIFFERENCE

This first section discusses whether culturally and socially gendered roles correlate to peacemaking. Indonesia, like many other archipelagos in Southeast Asia, is well known for sex complementarity attributable to the convention of bilateral kinship.[4] Despite some variations, there appears to be a greater equality of men and women and a substitutability of the roles of husband and wife. Shelly Errington argues that because women have "higher status" and high visibility in public, gender difference is downplayed and not always visible. Women's higher status appears to be more calculating, instrumental, and direct than men's and more controlling on practical matters and money.[5] The economic control in the family refers to the management of money mostly for daily expenses by the wives or mothers under the supervision of their husbands, whereas economic control in public refers to such activities as trade, labor, and banking. Women often occupy the position of treasurers in local, regional, and national organizations and government-owned institutions.

Although some women in Southeast Asian cultures are more direct, economically powerful, practical, active, and controlling, they are not automatically entitled to "power" and "prestige" in the way that men are because women are considered to lack "spiritual power and potency" and refined behavior.[6] This accepted gender construct implies that men have greater self-control and spiritual potency than women. The social expectation of masculinity cultivates masculine refined behavior and spiritual potency in the private and public spheres. Brennen contextualizes the masculine refined behavior and spiritual potency within Errington's framework of andocentric male power and prestige through the investigations of gender construct, especially among the Javanese, in Indonesia. The traditional Javanese ideology associates women with irrationality and emotionality and men with self-control and a superior capacity for reason.[7] Women's lack of reason makes them suitable for jobs associated with such so-called female natural tendencies as *dapur* (kitchen), *kasur* (bed), and *sumur* (well). It is often said that women have no need to advance in education because they will eventually spend the rest of their lives carrying out household duties.

Theologically, the feminine and masculine construct is rooted in the popular story of Adam and Eve, which produces the cultural gender prototype through the characters of Adam as rational and Eve (named Hawwa' in Arabic) as irrational. Even though the Qur'an does not discuss the way in which Hawwa' was created, the *hadith* (reports of what the Prophet Muhammad said and did in his lifetime) records the creation of Eve out of Adam's rib. Umar, a leading scholar in the feminist studies of the Qur'an, shows how the classical and contemporary exegetes continuously reiterate the delicate nature of women.[8] In the classical *Tafsir Ibn Katsir*, which is widely taught and read in Indonesian *pesantrens*,[9] it is said that "a woman is created out of a crooked rib. If you try to straighten it, it will break. But, if you leave it alone, it will continue to be crooked." The contemporary Indonesian exegete Quraish Shihab explains that the crooked rib should be understood metaphorically. It reminds men to be wise in dealing with female characters because of their natural difference from men and of their potency to drive men to improper behaviors. Men would not be able to change inborn female characteristics, and any changes would consequently break the crooked rib. The crooked nature of a woman functions as a reminder of the biological, social, political, and ethical difference between men and women. The combination of Javanese and Islamic notions of masculinity and femininity portrays men as potent, self-controlled, and in the possession of the higher mental and spiritual faculties that allow them to maintain order in their own lives and in the social and supernatural world.[10] Women, on the other hand, are depicted as spiritually impotent, less rational than men, and lacking in control. Such categorical statements about the nature of the sexes are well in keeping with the ideological system that places men at the center of the social, moral, and symbolic order.

The reiteration of the politics of difference between men and women is best reflected in everyday life. Not only are men expected to function as the center pillar (*sokoguru*) of the household, the ones who offer protection (*ngayomi*), security (*ngayemi*), basic needs for the household (*ngayani*), certainty (*ngantepi*), and advice (*ngandani*), but they are also assumed to carry their refined behavior and spiritual potency in public spheres.[11]

The masculine and feminine construct is not exclusive to the Javanese because the traditional role of the sexual division of labor not only endorses women as domestic beings but also encourages men to represent the family and to engage in social and political activities. The extent to which Javanese masculinity and femininity is embodied within the Indonesian mindset can be seen in the national plan for development during the 1970s. This development was a gendered process in that it socially, culturally, and politically expected women to conform to the endorsement, ruling, and plan of the masculine nostalgia of femininity. Although the government definitely encouraged women to partake in Indonesian national development, their roles were defined as secondary to their husbands because women were considered the supporters of men's devotion to the state. During the Suharto era, the sexual division of labor was instituted through the establishment of Dharma Wanita—an organization for the wives of civil servants at the local, regional, and national levels—and through the institution of Pembinaan Kesejahtraan Keluarga (PKK, Family Welfare Movement) for the masses.

The state also endorsed the institutionalization of motherhood and wifehood as virtues in keeping with the ideal domesticated roles of women. The state discourse on women as "mothers of nation" has been profoundly assimilated into the dualism of "private" and "public" spheres. This dualism was reiterated in the 1974 Marriage Law and has been inscribed in the marriage certificate. Women ought to be responsible for the family and household, whereas men ought to be responsible for the public sphere. The prevailing impact of such a division of labor is extended into opportunities that are available for women's occupation. Although the breadth of women's occupational titles has extended to the level of president, minister, executive, and manager, the majority of women are still caught up with jobs associated with their sexuality: teachers, nurses, traders, laborers, house helpers, and other low-paying jobs. Women internalize domesticity as their virtue to the extent that their being in the world is valued through the lenses of such domestic fulfillments as caring for the children and husbands, cooking, and managing household duties, even if they work outside the home.

Since the sexual division of labor requires women to downplay their potential agencies, the different roles of men and women, in the Indonesian mindset, do not always entail inequality. Equality in Indonesia is not defined based on the Western sense of rights, but it is understood in terms of obligations and commitments to oneself, one's family, and others. The idea of "equal but different" is echoed through the religious, cultural, social, and political apparatus emphasizing the masculine appropriation of feminine virtue. Male and female biological difference becomes the starting point for determining what is vicious and virtuous for women. While men and women succumb to their religious and cultural senses of duties and obligations, women's biological dispositions receive more gendered constructs and appropriations. Virtue is often associated with excellence in the household and less public exposure.

The "equal but different" mindset also coincides with the way power is constructed. Power derives from seniority or age, familial kinship, ethnicity, authoritative knowledge, sequence of birth, and sexuality. When it comes to women, power is mostly bestowed through the familial kinship that endows women with more opportunities, prestige, and respect. For women who are outsiders to powerful familial kinship and networking, affiliation with powerful men by virtue of marriage, organizations, educational institutions, or political parties is among the ways utilized to engender certain degrees of power. It should be noted, however, that women's entitlement to spiritual potency is not as promising as men's because of the duality of masculinity and femininity in the private and public spheres.

According to Suzanna Brenner, because women's perceived lack of self-control strips them from being equally endowed with masculine power and prestige, they negotiate their "lower status" through economic control in the family and the public spheres.[12] The exclusion of women from masculine power, along with a greater emphasis on a female role in finance, accords with a cultural stigma of how money connotes ambition and greed, which hinder spiritual power. The process of making money, especially in traditional markets, often involves a subset of such behaviors as deceit, high voice, and cunning that violates the virtue of humility, virility, and self-respect. For this reason, it is improper for men to engage in a daily life that is seen as naturally and culturally not fitting to them. At the very least, men doing women's dirty jobs, like cooking, washing dishes, and taking care of the children, are not socially and culturally well respected. Even if husbands were doing it for fun and being supportive of their wives, some tradition-oriented neighbors might make a fuss or gossip about it.

The duality of female economic power at the personal and familial levels and male refined behavior correlates to the peacemaking process. The performativity of masculine spiritual power and potency paves the way for more social and political roles for men than for women as seen in the life of a *tokoh*—a prominent figure whom people consult about daily, religious, cultural, social, and political issues. As a *tokoh* embodies prestige stemming from personal refinement and spiritual potency, the trust that the community has invested in the institution of tokohism has a significant role in the peace and conflict resolution process. For every major religious, ethnic, interreligious, and racial conflict, a few prominent figures (*tokoh*) emerged as heroes and heroines. Abdurrahman Wahid, the fourth president of Indonesia, has played an instrumental role in the peace and conflict resolution process within the Nahdlatul Ulama organization,[13] in intergroup dialogues with Muhammadiyah,[14] and other racial clashes and interreligious conflicts. Likewise, Megawati Sukarno Putri became a heroine after the Suharto regime cracked down on her organization during the 1996 riots. In this case, it is important to note that Megawati, who was a full-time mother prior to her political debut and spotlight, receives her power from her kinship connection to her father, Sukarno, the first

Indonesian president. At the provincial level, Hasan Di Tiro's prominent tokohism (leadership), for instance, is considered to be the father of the Acehnese independence movement. The importance of such prominent figures demonstrates how male dominance prevails in peacemaking at the communal, regional, and national levels.

Paradox of Masculine Refined Behavior and Violence

If the masculine traits of refined behavior and spiritual potency generate power and prestige in private and public spheres, where does the violence come from? Although the specificity through which the conflicts emerged is multidimensional and multilayered, the conflicts were driven not by male biology but by the imbalanced power relations among different groups and the stakeholders at the social and governmental levels. As violent conflicts and wars occur within a men-made world, they, in Michel Foucault's analysis of power, are driven by "a complex strategical situation in a particular society" in which "unbalanced, heterogeneous, unstable, and tense relations" collide.[15] Within the Indonesian context, the diverse ethnicities, languages, cultures, and religions are potent forces for unity and disintegration. The state often identifies the trajectory of *suku* (ethnicity), *agama* (religion), *ras* (race), and *antar golongan* (intergroup), collectively known as SARA, as the source of conflicts. While the politics of SARA shaped government policies in targeting interreligious and ethnic violence, the state also became the repressive power in eradicating Islamic-oriented organizations or parties, especially after the introduction of *Pancasila* (five principles) as the state's sole ideology in 1970s.

The Indonesian New Order led by Suharto from 1967 to 1998 issued a cultural policy called "Bhineka Tunggal Ika," which means "Unity in Diversity." This policy endorsed the homogeneity of Indonesian cultures with less recognition of differences by appointing Javanese officials for a number of important posts and encouraging the Javanese masses to migrate to unpopulated islands. The changing structures of society in Sumatra, Kalimantan, and Maluku influenced the economic, social, and political lives of the locals. When the locals felt threatened by the overwhelming migrants who were economically more powerful, tensions and unbalanced power relations became unavoidable. These tense relationships were often exacerbated by national policies that were not sensitive to local needs. The people of Aceh, for example, felt betrayed by the government's political and economic policies on Aceh,[16] whereas in Maluku, the social and cultural conflicts between Muslims and Christians were politicized as religious conflicts.

Apart from ethnic, religious, and economic conflicts, Stefan Eklöf offered a convincing interpretation of the political events in Indonesia by introducing "the hidden mastermind" (*auctor intellectualis*) or *dalang* (puppet master).[17] It was suspected that the conflicts in 1996 in Java were fueled by military and government elites struggling to maintain the status quo of Suharto's power in the presidency. Similarly, the conflicts that emerged in the years following the toppling of Suharto were known to be masterminded by the elites. Adding to the cultural and political tension was the unequal distribution of control of the economy among the central and regional governments (as seen in Aceh),[18] the natives (*pribumi*) and the Chinese,[19] and Madura and Dayak from 1996 to 1997 (Sampit, Kalimantan).[20] Some interreligious violence also occurred in Situbondo (1996),[21] Tasikmalaya (1996),[22] and Maluku (1999).[23]

All of the conflicts that emerged in Indonesia were perpetrated by men, nurtured by men, and reconciled by men. Why do men collaborate in violence? Is male aggression hormonal? Although the argument of how the "male hormone makes men more competitive, better at sports, go-getters in the business world, and ready to fight to defend their honor" sounds very seductive, the biological literature offers little evidence for that idea.[24] Anne Fausto-Sterling carefully investigated six studies that attempt to measure the correlation between human aggressiveness and the level of testosterone in the blood.[25] The findings show that social conditions affect hormonal levels and that attributing behavior to a single hormone misrepresents the "actual physiological events."[26] In addition, such studies cannot be used as a standard to measure and identify violent behavior as biological because of the interplay of three factors: inadequate control, inappropriate method, and the lack of an alternative paradigm for explaining findings that could have overridden the overall result.[27] Since there is not necessarily a biological basis for the correlation between male aggression and hormones, Fausto-Sterling attributes male aggressiveness to *"the particular context in which it occurs."*[28] What is interesting from Fausto-Sterling's study of the assumed correlation between the hormone testosterone and violence is the way the social, cultural, and political construct of gender informed the scientific endeavor of gender constructs.

If male aggression is culturally constructed, what kind of socialization process generates appropriated power relations between men and women, and what is their impact on women's activism? A. A. Mazrui characterizes the power relation between men and women as paradoxical. The paradox of gender refers to the propositions that "(1) among humans, the senior partner in the creation of new life is the female of the species (woman as mother); (2) among humans, the senior partner in the destruction of life is the male of the species (man as warrior); and (3) it is the power of destruction that has given the male of the species dominion over the female (man as ruler)."[29] Mazrui further explains that the origin of male

dominance lies in the military and the control of coercive means, not in
the economy. Male control over the power of destruction yields men the
power of domination over women. Thus the paradox of gender refers to
the pattern of the accepted roles of men and women in reproduction, but
the domestic roles of men and women do not engender equality of men
and women in every sense of the word. The institution of the family is the
sphere in which a woman is often most oppressed with the religiously
sanctioned sexual division of labor, sexual intimacy as obligatory, domesti-
cation of the female members of the family, and unequal share of the
economy. Male and female reproductive partnership is also considered
unequal for three reasons: "male superiority in reproduction, women's
intended purposes as reproducers, and the wives of the husbands' tilth."[30]

I concur with Mazrui's point that the notion of "men as rulers" generates male domination. Asma Barlas defines patriarchy as a politics of male
privilege based on sexual differentiation.[31] Patriarchy not only refers to the
rule of the fathers but also includes "a set of symbols and ideas that make
up a culture embodied by everything from the content of everyday."[32] In
Islam, the patriarchal elements of the existing local cultures to which
Islam was born and the diverse cultures in which Islam spread have been
assimilated to Islam. The antipatriarchal messages of the Qur'an and the
Prophet Muhammad gradually disappeared because Muslims conflated
the assimilation of local patriarchal cultures with Islam. The patriarchal
readings of the Qur'an along with the assimilation of such secondary sources as the literal interpretation (*tafsir*) of the Qur'an, the recorded account
of prophetic sayings, deeds, approvals, and disapprovals, and the customary praxis of Muhammad's life (*sunna*)[33] have cemented the systematic
production of patriarchal ideals, symbols, and institutions.

The institution of power and prestige derived from refined behavior is
not only a patriarchal construct of how men and women are socially, culturally, and politically appropriated; it also generates "a gendered person to
the idea of prestige and power systems."[34] Although the root of female-
sexed bodies can be traced to the changing logic of male *jahiliyyah* sexual
misconduct to women's misconduct, it is also partly cultural.[35] Chilla Bulbeck argues that unlike the Western construction of the self, which is separated from the community, the construction of the self in the non-
Western world varies and the self is constructed through association with
kin relationship, age, and other elements.[36] Gender construct is sanctioned through the embodiment of religious and cultural morality and
practices. As a person's identity is constructed on the basis of behavioral
and social attributes and interpersonal relationships within the networking
of power and prestige, the behavioral construct of gender is embodied
through the two distinct social performativities of masculinity and femininity.

Although the enactment of social and cultural roles of gender has less to do with conflicts and violence, it definitely correlates to the way in which women's activism in peace and conflict resolution progresses in conflict zones.

GENDERED PEACEMAKING AND SHARED SECURITY

Human security emerged in 1994 as an issue when then–Secretary General Kofi Annan introduced it as an important factor in the United Nations Development Program (UNDP) Human Development Report. The document demonstrates a greater interest on the part of the United Nations agencies to improve development, human rights, and peace building.[37] In the Indonesian experience, human security often comes second after national security because of the manner in which the state is involved in conflicts: masterminding them, crushing them, or politicizing them for the sake of Indonesian unity. The state has also deployed military forces to end conflicts, as seen in the case of the Gerakan Aceh Merdeka (GAM, Aceh Freedom Movement) and East Timor. Although these conflicts emerged when unbalanced, complex, and tense forced relations collided and were politicized by the competing parties, the conflicts were situated within a specific locality—time, place, race, ethnicity, class, religion, and the social construct of masculinity and femininity.[38] This is also true about women's relation to war and conflict and their responses in disseminating appropriate activism. Because each conflict is culturally located, each has a far-reaching effect on human security, especially the well-being of women and children, and on the security of Indonesia, the Unitary State of the Republic of Indonesia (Negara Kesatuan Republic Indonesia, NKRI). There follow examples in which human security in the Aceh and Maluku conflicts became less important in comparison with national security.

Suraiya Kamaruzzaman, a peace activist and founder of Flower Aceh, recorded the horrific, devastating stories of Aceh women during the military operation. She vividly reported the impact of the armed struggles between the GAM and the Indonesian military from 1976 to 2005 that have taken their toll on men, women, and children. By 2000, she wrote:

> Thousands of women were widowed, their husbands murdered or kidnapped. Children were orphaned. Some women faced sexual violence from soldiers, in part as a deliberate instrument of terror against their communities. The women became pariahs in their own communities, which did not want to associate with anyone dangerously tainted by GPK [Gerakan Pengacau Kemerdekaan (Security Disturbance Movement)] suspicions. These single women, with children to support, could no longer go out safely to work in the fields.[39]

Between the beginning and the end of the military operation from 1990 to 1998, the Coalition of Human Rights reported about 7,727 cases of human rights abuses. From January 1999 to February 2000, the coalition also reported 304 arbitrary detentions, 318 extrajudicial executions, and 138 disappearances, and 9 cases of "massacres" in which 132 civilians were killed and 472 wounded. From June to August 1999, the number of internally displaced persons in Aceh increased from 250,000 to 300,000. Two months later, the number increased by 4,110 refugees, "including 712 infants, 818 children aged less than five years, 52 pregnant women, and 112 women who were still nursing infants."[40] Kamaruzzaman lists the reasons for the increase of the refugees as follows:[41]

- The Indonesian military carried out frequent searches using forces and violent means such as beatings, forcible removals of individuals from home, and destruction of the property and villages.
- The armed contacts between GAM and the army in rural areas continued and threatened the security of people in the village.
- The military and civilian militia engaged in kidnappings and the latter were suspected of being supporters of GAM.
- Certain refugees were banned from returning to their village, even though the refugees themselves considered the situation safe.
- The camps were not always safe and the conditions of the camps were appalling with lack of facilities for pregnant women and children.

She further notes that women living in the camps experienced a "double burden" in that they were repressed both by the state and by the patriarchal social mechanisms. In Aceh, women are culturally and socially expected to stay in the house. Their economic activities outside the home, such as selling goods at the markets or working in informal sectors, are considered as secondary and as auxiliaries to that of their husbands.[42] Although women's domestic roles as caretakers of the family extend to life in the camps, the women did not necessarily have access to food and preparation materials. The food in the camps was a male business and a public and social matter to which men had greater access. Men were generally responsible for the decisions made in the camps. With less access to food, women often became depressed because the maintenance of food in the family related to their existential mode of being.[43] Since the male members of the family were absent from the female-led household, women lacked access not only to food but to other facilities as well. The poorest facility in which the women were housed was made up of camps built next to the mosques and made of plastics or coconut leaves with plaited mats covering the soil floors. Women lived, slept, and even gave birth in such places. Many women became ill as a result of a combination of the pouring rain, the blowing wind, and the striking heat. To alleviate illness, the members of Flower Aceh introduced acupuncture and natural medicine because no medical facilities, nurses, or doctors were available in many conflict areas.[44] With women lacking access to basic needs—food, water, health care, reproductive rights, and education—the conflict presented a threat to women's security and the security of all people involved.

Nunuk Murniati, a member of the National Commission on Violence against Women, reports on the abuses of women through the accounts of women's organizations in Aceh that documented violent actions against women. In 2003, Murniati recalls:[45]

> "Rumah geudong" (Geudong House) in Aceh is the symbol of violence against women. In that place, hundred of women and children were killed, tortured and raped by the military. Almost all the victims are women accused of being part of the family of GAM members. Their testimonies gave inspirations to uncover more facts.

Although some women related stories of suffering, many violent actions have gone unreported for the following reasons:[46]

1. Most victims of rape are [too] shy to tell their problems, because these kinds of tragedy are really embarrassing. Therefore, they always keep them as secrets.
2. The intimidation of the doers to not tell the cases to other people, because the doers were the armies.
3. The traumatic experience of violence that makes it too hard for them to inform other people.
4. There was an intimidation of certain people or institutions toward NGOs that offer advocacy to the victims.

The Aceh conflict is an example of how devastating an impact such a conflict has on women. This experience is not unique to Aceh women, for as Rubina Saigol writes: "Women also suffer from the militarization in indirect ways, e.g. when social services tend to be the worst hit. As a result, women's health, education, and basic services become low priorities for states engaged in combat."[47] Women of the Aceh conflict certainly have had no sense of security. Female sexualities became the contested sites that were regularly transgressed and tortured for political deployment. Suraiya Kamaruzzaman, an activist from Flower Aceh, and Raihan Diani, a member of Partai Rakyat Aceh (Acehnese People's Party), noted that the Indonesian military used rape as an instrument of torture to weaken the Acehnese rebels, whereas the Free Aceh Movement (GAM) utilized women as a mechanism to defend female honor and the land.[48] Many women in the conflict areas consequently suffered mental and physical hysteria because they lacked such basic necessities as food, health care, and water. Children growing up in this particular context learned to be violent by observing what adults, including military or GAM members, did to their families. The spiral of violence evolved and grew until the agreement to end the violence was made.

The human impacts of the Maluku conflict were also devastating. Although the Maluku conflict had morphed into a Christian-Muslim conflict, the weakened traditional social structures, horizontal inequalities between Christians and Muslims, and the legacy of the New Order, which emphasized using violence to defend nationalism and the integrity of the country, were among the structural causes of the conflicts.[49] Indonesia's economic crisis, the decentralization and democratization of the government, the security forces of the Christian and Muslim militias, the media bias that inflamed sentiments, the cycles of revenge, each played a role in escalating the conflicts. Among the human consequences of the conflicts were 7,000 deaths in addition to those injured and displaced. An estimated half million people were displaced, included Christians fleeing Muslim-majority areas, like Ternate and Bacan, and Muslims fleeing Christian-majority areas, like Tobelo.[50] The spiral of conflicts had a series of impacts on access to health and education, especially among the displaced people, and on the increase of poverty, especially among women and children.

The Aceh and Maluku conflicts were among the few conflicts that drew military deployment in the name of national security and the Unitary State of the Republic of Indonesia. Although the state has a legitimate concern in securing the country's national security, such security should have been considered in conjunction with the economic, social, and gender effects of a military deployment that tended to prolong conflicts. Often, the structural causes of conflicts and the stakeholders that could contribute to peacemaking are not adequately addressed. As for women, they were involved in the peacemaking through their making connections among the female victims. Women's agency as peacemakers generates economic, social, and political activism that alleviates the process of peace building for increased human and national security.

A PATTERN OF ACTIVISM IN PEACEMAKING BY WOMEN

According to United Nations Security Council Resolution 1325 on Women, Peace and Security, women have the equal right to participate in decision making and the maintenance of peacekeeping and peace building. The resolution also grants protection for women and girls during the conflicts and makes an effort to fulfill their needs. This resolution not only invites women to contribute to peacemaking and resolution of conflict but also emphasizes an equal-gender perspective in peacekeeping and peace building. As the gender component is fully integrated into the peace and resolution process, appropriate training in decision making, peacekeeping maintenance, and peace building becomes necessary for women. The UN resolution also urges women's participation "at all decision-making levels in national, regional, and international institutions and mechanisms for the prevention, management, and resolution of conflict."[51] This section examines a pattern of activism in peacemaking among women as peacemakers within Indonesian cultures.

Although women are commonly seen as direct or indirect victims of violence, Radhika Coomaraswamy proposes three models in which women play active roles in peacemaking and resolution.[52] First, essentialists use images of biological identities and feminine traits, like motherhood, to advance peace. Second, constructivists utilize women's psychological traits, such as those characterizing caregivers and nurturers, to promote peace. Finally, exclusivists refer to the way in which women utilize their agency as peacemakers by lifting their exclusion from public life and struggling to gain access to that sphere through activism that promotes peacemaking. Using these models, here I present the way in which women, along with men, express their activism in an effort to promote peacemaking. I particularly discuss male and female activism at the grassroots level, with less emphasis on state engagement on peace. Although each model is dealt with separately, they are all interconnected, since they were born out of women's realities within the conflict zones in Aceh and Maluku.

ESSENTIALIST ACTIVISM AND PEACEMAKING

Essentialist activism relies on the biological connection between women in promoting and maintaining the peacemaking process. Indonesian women are culturally and socially expected at certain points to fulfill wifehood and motherhood. This cultural expectation for some families is concurrent with the demand that women's place be relegated to the private sphere. In this view, it would only be natural for women in conflict zones to engage in peacemaking by connecting to other women through their biological connection as women. In both Maluku and Aceh, women suffered violence, became displaced, and were at constant risk of widowhood. As women told stories about their vulnerability to sexual, mental, physical, and psychological violence, they transformed their personal experience into the political. Women also connected with other women who lost husbands and sons and transformed themselves to become negotiators with the military and members of Free

Aceh Movement (GAM).[53] The biological connection among women became the common thread that moved them to go beyond their everyday roles as mothers, yet they utilized motherhood as a common cause for making peace in their cultural locations.

Gender activists and feminists responded to the ongoing violence in Aceh, for instance, through community-based organizing built on their connection as women. Flower Aceh supported women at camps and assisted women as victims of wars through community engagement and empowerment.[54] Relawan Perempuan untuk Kemanusiaan (RPuK, Women's Volunteers for Humanity), a group of women that assisted women and children war victims, reported that the court did not consider rape a crime against humanity because of the lack of evidence. Activists from PEKKA (the Female Headed Household Empowerment Program in Aceh) reported about the lives of widows who lost their husbands to kidnapping, arrest, or murder, about their traumatic and hysteric experiences, the disturbance of reproductive function, and the horrors suffered by their children.[55] Serikat ureung Inong Aceh (SeIA, Aceh Mothers Association or Aceh Women's Union) addressed women's socioeconomic problems at the grassroots levels. The group also cared for the victims of domestic violence. LBH APIK, a legal institution for women, also assisted women, especially an *inongbale* (a female GAM member) who was raped and tortured by the military.

In North Maluku, women make connections with women who have lost husbands to religious and ethnic conflicts. The Female Headed Household Empowerment Program (PEKKA) cares for women as widows or as the head of household and attempts a number of goals:[56]

> To build a vision and mission as well as a perspective of justice and equality in class and gender
>
> To increase the technical, managerial, and leadership capacity in the PEKKA personnel in their attitude to life
>
> To develop the PEKKA organization and network into a movement
>
> To conduct policy advocacy and to campaign the changes in values in order to build gender justice in the society
>
> To document and publish stories of the life, struggle and activities of the women-headed families

Similarly, women in Maluku and North Maluku received assistance from international organizations that focused on localized and small-scale projects and promoted economic sufficiency for women and children.[57] Economic self-sufficiency also included livelihood assistance programs, which provided equipment and training for fishing and farming, especially for internally displaced people (IDP) and current returnees.[58] Women in the postconflict

recovery period continue to express their concern and activism by connecting to others as women and peacemakers.

CONSTRUCTIVIST ACTIVISM AND PEACEMAKING

Constructivist activism uses such female psychological traits as nurturing
and caring in promoting peacemaking and peace building. This type of activism requires female peacemakers, victims, perpetrators of conflicts, and
stakeholders to get involved. Women as caring peacemakers reach out to
victims to negotiate peace in an indirect way. In areas of conflict situated
within Indonesian political, social, and cultural landscapes, these victims
are often family members divided by religion, ethnicity, political alliances,
race, or other factors. Women as victors and victims build bridges of communication out of the domestic need to prepare food for the family. In this
context, it is relevant to mention the sexual division of labor in terms of its
utility to promote peace. Because women are responsible for domestic
management, they have the opportunity to make contact with women in
their own community as well as the community of the enemy. Consequently, women bring stories home and interject the idea of the commonalities experienced among women in times of conflicts and wars. They are
thus able, finally, to suggest to male members of the family the necessity
of halting violence against the enemy. The communication process
between both sides generates communal healing among the divided community.[59] It should be noted, however, that this kind of healing process
was not possible within the Aceh conflict because the conflict was
between the military and the rebels. Any decisions for a Military Opera-
tional Area (Daerah Operasi Militer, DOM) in the 1980s and a "humanitarian ceasefire" (Jeda Kemanusiaan) on May 12, 2000, were decided by
the elites in Jakarta.[60]

Women's security certainly never crosses the mind of the elites. There
has been an emphasis on the part of the perpetrators, who are mostly
men, to sympathize with women by giving up violence. Giving up violence
is multilayered depending on what incites tense relations and violence in
the first place. A spiral of violence does not solve the existing problem; it
only advances the strategic propaganda that divides people in falsely setting up boundaries of "us" and "them." The logic of the Othering process
and the violent methods enacted to defend it lead to more violence. In
attempting to unfold the impact of violence and the misery it inflicts, perpetrators are given an incentive to give up violence, its tactics, its politics,
and its mediums. Giving up the tactics of violence means that perpetrators
halt the use of religion and the politics of ethnic and racial difference as a
means to an end. Similarly, the politics of violence is also based in such

things as social and economic injustices, separatist movements, a repressive government, the dysfunctional deflective violent movement generated by poverty, and spiritually sanctioned violent movements driven by faith.

The spiral of violence, according to Jack Nelson-Pallmeyer, is interconnected and overlapping.[61] The violence driven by social and economic injustice proceeds to become repressive violence when the state militarily crushes violence without necessarily solving unjust social problems. Similarly, social and economic problems could lead the people to rebel against the elites or the government, who are held responsible for their misery. The violence grows worse when the groups, races, or ethnicities in conflict resort to religion to justify their violence. Giving up the politics of violence and its medium requires all the parties involved in violent conflicts, including women, to strategically address ways in which to advance peacemaking and peace building.

Caring also includes the act of forgiving. While forgiving in itself could be a healing process, forgiving along with acknowledging the common need for human security and togetherness goes beyond the mere act of saying, "I forgive and move on." Individuals involved in perpetuating conflicts are persuaded by speech, according to Hannah Arendt, that "serves as a means to an end" and "to deceive the enemy or to dazzle everybody with propaganda."[62] However, just as speech can instill violence, it is also a powerful means through which to inspire peacemaking and conflict resolution. The act of forgiving situates human togetherness at the core of the peace and resolution process. The constructivist peacemakers utilize forgiving along with caring and nurturing to empower women who culturally perceive these feminine traits as theirs.

Although women in Maluku were involved in peacemaking through a greater access to economy and were connected to other women through economic need, women in Aceh engaged in conflict resolution through the promotion of peace. Using the word "peace" was for women a strategic choice because in doing so they could avoid the military's suspicion of being labeled GAM supporters for independence and GAM's perception of lacking adequate support from the locals. Women activists, academicians, and members of the community proposed "peace talks" because they were tired of the prolonged conflict and wanted the children to have normal lives, go to schools, and have access to the future.[63] As they socialized the promotion of peace, they exercised the virtue of caring for and nurturance of the self and the others.

EXCLUSIVIST ACTIVISM AND PEACEMAKING

Exclusivist activism utilizes restrictive gendered access to public spheres by expanding traditional female roles as homemakers. Women's primary roles in the conflict and in peaceful areas are culturally and religiously construed as that of homemakers who manage the familial finances and the everyday goings-on within the household. Ratna Megawangi argues that women's economic role reflects the traditional practice of "income pooling," in which the utility function of finance in a family revolves around women.[64] Certainly, the increasingly changing roles of women to workers outside the home and nurturers within the family provide more opportunities for women, yet many families maintain income pooling as an economic institution within the family. Women among the lower classes work out of necessity, whereas middle- and upper-class women work for personal fulfillment and interests by delegating their everyday roles as child nurturers to a nanny or babysitter and their household duties to a household helper or domestic worker. In any case, women's economic power in the household remains important to many women in Indonesia.

During the conflicts, women opted to go beyond the accepted norms and contributed to the peacemaking process by creating new spaces in the public sphere. Women in Maluku and North Maluku responded to the conflicts by moving into the economic roles from which they were formerly excluded. Maluku women seized the economic opportunity by taking on multiple roles as economic agents in addition to their traditional role as homemakers. By 2002, the gender-related development index (GDI) shows an increased participation in the labor force, from 33.1 prior to the conflict to 49.2. Although the conflict boosted the economic significance of women, it also saw an escalation of violence against women, which took many forms, including domestic violence at the displaced persons' camps, sexual harassment, and rape.[65] The United Nations Development Program (UNDP) Gender Thematic Assessment team in the Sayoan Internally Displaced Persons (IDP) camp on Bacan Inland reported complaints about the rape and the humiliation of women by security forces. Women in both provinces reported frequent harassment and sexual violence by security forces.[66]

Women of Aceh went beyond their traditional cultural limitations as mothers and wives by engaging in social activism and humanitarian efforts. Women had more access to the economy during the conflicts because men were not able to perform their economic duties and were oftentimes on the run.[67] Men's movements were also limited by their fear of being suspected as rebels, supporters of the GAM, or even GAM members. Women activists founded organizations that assisted female need as peacemakers and victims of wars. Relawan Perempuan untuk Kemanusiaan (RPuk, Women Volunteers for Humanity), as mentioned earlier, was established to assist the internally displaced women, widows, and housewives.[68] Women volunteers, along with international donors, institutions, and individuals, worked to meet the need of internally displaced people, distributing food, providing facilities for the sick, and supporting educational materials for children.[69] Working with Flower Aceh, women volunteers supported the economic self-sufficiency by providing loans for women.[70]

As women, especially in Aceh, helped each other in humanitarian activities, they demanded an end to violence and more active participation in decision making in the peace process. Women's collective desire to end the violence and their acknowledgment of human togetherness emphasize what Arendt calls "the disclosure of the agent in the act," without which any actions lose their specific character and meaning.[71] When competing parties use violence to achieve their objective, speech becomes a means to an end and functions to deceive the enemy who clouded the disclosure of the speaking subjects. Women of Aceh used words through prayers and demonstrations and met with the GAM commander to discuss establishing a peace zone for women.[72] In these situations, women's agency as peacemakers and activists strategically addressed a series of complex, unbalanced, and forcefully tense relations by acknowledging the common need for security for the everyday life of men, women, and children and the places in which they live.

CONCLUSION

This chapter has argued that the gender construct correlates not with the origin of conflicts, but with male and female activism in peacemaking. The Aceh and Maluku conflicts emerged not because of the violent nature of men, but because of unbalanced power relations within the community triggered by the political and economic injustices at the provincial and national levels. The conflicts surveyed here belong to a men-made world that has affected men, women, and children as well as national security. Although women have been affected most and are more vulnerable than men to sexual, physical, and psychological violence, they have utilized their agency as actors and activists in peacemaking, economics, and politics. They also share their stories of rape and violence as central to their struggles. Women transform the personal to the political, the private to the public, and the marginal to the center. Through these various agencies and their activism, women go beyond the traditional expectations of cultures that demand their conformity to the politics of masculinity and femininity.

Religiously, culturally, and politically gendered constructs, however, engender the ways in which peacemaking and conflict resolution proceed. The sexual division of labor in the private and public spheres, along with feminine and masculine virtues, produces peace building and activism that are gendered. Women are excluded from decision-making, yet women have chances to develop their economic prowess. Males with power and prestige have full access to decision making in the peace building and reconciliation process, whereas women as peacemakers resort to their feminine virtues as caregivers and nurturers. Women's togetherness as human beings transforms personal stories to political ones. In Maluku and North Maluku, conflict provided women with an economic role. Women were most involved and activists in the social, economic, and cultural sides of the conflicts while male stakeholders resolved the political aspect of the disputes. Despite the gendered peace and resolution process, women as peacemakers and activists have contributed to attaining the shared goal of security as a public good.

NOTES

1. For more information about the research on religion and conflict resolution, see Chandra Setiawan, ed., *Direktori Penelitian Agama, Konflik dan Perdamaian* (Jakarta: Komisi Nasional Hak Asasi Manusia and Institut Pluralisme Agama, 2005).

2. Charlotte Bunch, "Peace, Human Rights, and Women's Peace Activism: Feminist Readings," in *Peace Work: Women, Armed Conflict and Negotiation*, ed. Radhika Coomaraswamy and Dilrukshi Fonseka (New Delhi: Women Unlimited, 2004), 28–53.

3. Ritu Menon, "Doing Peace: Women Resist Daily Battle in South Asia," in *Peace Work*, ed. Coomaraswamy and Fonseka, 54–72.

4. Shelly Errington, "Recasting Sex, Gender, and Power: A Theoretical and Regional Overview," in *Power and Difference: Gender in Island Southeast Asia*, ed. Shelly Errington (Stanford, CA: Stanford University Press, 1990), 1–2.

5. Ibid., 7.

6. Ibid., 6–7.

7. Suzanna A. Brenner, "Why Women Rule the Roost: Rethinking Javanese Ideologies of Gender and Self Control," in *Gender in Cross-Cultural Perspective*, ed. Caroline B. Brettell and Carolyn F. Sargent (Upper Saddle River, NJ: Prentice Hall, 2000), 143.

8. See also Nasaruddin Umar, *Argumen Kesetaraan Gender: Perspektif al-Qur'ân* (Jakarta: Paramadina, 1997), 238.

9. *Pesantren* is a formal and informal educational system that teaches such fundamentals of Islamic knowledge as Arabic, the Qur'anic exegesis, and *hadith*.

10. Brenner, "Why Women Rule the Roost," 143.

11. Maria A. Sarjono, "Rekonsiliasi dalam Perspektif Gender: Suatu Refleksi atas Timpang antara laki-laki dan perempuan [Reconciliation from a Gender

Perspective: Reflection on the Gap between Men and Women]," in *Rekonsi-liasi, Menciptakan Hidup Damai dan Sejahtera: Tinjauan Perspektif Religiusitas*, ed. A. Widyahadi Seputra et al. (Jakarta: Kerjasama Sekretariat Komisi PSE/APP-KAJ, LDD-KAJ, Komisi PSE-KWI, and LPPS-KWI, 2002), 94.

12. Brenner, "Why Women Rule the Roost," 142.

13. The formation of Nahdlatul Ulama was a response to rigorous attempts to purify religion from indigenous belief by two modernist movements, Muhammadiyah and Persatuan Islam. The Nahdlatul Ulama usually refers to the unity of traditionalist *ulama* (the "learned" in religion) and their followers from the Shafi'i school of law. See, M. Nakamura, "Nahdlatul Ulama," in *The Oxford Encyclopedia of the Modern Islamic World*, ed. John L. Esposito (New York: Oxford University Press, 1991), 217–22.

14. The Muhammadiyah organization was founded at 1912 by a male activist, Ahmad Dahlan. The aim of Aisyiah was initially to train the wives and the daughters of the members of Muhammadiyah. Nowadays, Aisyiah has a branch in almost every city in Indonesia. For further discussion on the Muhammadiyah movement, see James Peacock, *Purifying the Faith: The Muhammadiyah Movement in Indonesian Islam* (Menlo Park, CA: Benyamin/Cumming Publishing, 1978).

15. Michel Foucault, *The History of Sexuality: An Introduction*, vol. 1, trans. Robert Hurley (New York: Vintage Books, 1990), 93.

16. Interview with Fuad Mardhatillah, one of the administrators for the Aceh Reintegration Board (BRA), June 14, 2009. I am indebted to Fuad and his family for allowing me to stay at their home during my stay in Aceh.

17. Stefan Eklöf, *Indonesian Politics in Crisis: The Long Fall of Suharto, 1996–98* (Copenhagen: Nordic Institute of Asian Studies, 1999), 60–63.

18. Thung Ju Lan et al., *Penyelesaian Konflik di Aceh: Aceh dalam Proses Rekontruksi & Rekonsiliasi* [Conflict Resolution in Aceh: Reconstruction and Reconciliation in Aceh] (Jakarta: Lembaga Ilmu Pengetahuan Indonesia, 2005).

19. For more information about the contexts of the riots in Jakarta, see Sai Siew Min, "'Eventing' the May 1998 Affair: Problematic Representations of Violence in Contemporary Indonesia," in *Violent Conflicts in Indonesia: Analysis, Representation, Resolution*, ed. Charles A. Coppel (London: Routledge, 2006), 39–57. As for the riots in Solo, see Jemma Purdey, "The 'Other' May Riots: Anti-Chinese Violence in Solo, May 1998," in *Violent Conflicts in Indonesia*, ed. Coppel, 72–89.

20. Eklöf, *Indonesian Politics in Crisis*, 65–68.

21. Ibid., 54–60.

22. Ibid., 68–74.

23. Gerry van Klinken, "The Maluku Wars: 'Communal Contenders' in a Failing State," in *Violent Conflicts in Indonesia*, ed. Coppel, 129–43.

24. Anne Fausto-Sterling, "Hormone and Aggression: An Explanation of Power," in *Myths of Gender: Biological Theories about Women and Men*, auth. Anne Fausto-Sterling (New York: Basic Books, 1985), 126 and 148.

25. Ibid., 127.

26. Ibid., 130–31.

27. Ibid., 136.

28. Ibid.

29. A. A. Mazrui, "The Black Woman and the Problem of Gender," in *Race, Gender, and Culture Conflict: Debating the African Condition: Mazrui and His Critics*, ed. Alamin Mazrui and Willy Mutunga (Trenton, NJ: African World Press, 2004), 221.

30. Etin Anwar, *Gender and Self in Islam* (London: Routledge, 2006), 72.

31. Asma Barlas, *"Believing Women" in Islam: Unreading Patriarchal Interpretations of the Qur'an* (Austin: University of Texas Press, 2002), 93.

32. Allan G. Johnson, "Patriarchy, the System: An It, Not a He, a Them, or an Us," in *Women's Lives: Multicultural Perspectives*, ed. Gwyn Kirk and Margo Okazawa-Rey (New York: McGraw Hill, 2000), 29–30.

33. Barlas, *"Believing Women" in Islam*, 63–66.

34. Errington, "Recasting Sex, Gender, and Power," 10.

35. Ibid., 50–52.

36. Chilla Bulbeck, *Re-orienting Western Feminisms: Women's Diversity in a Postcolonial World* (Cambridge: Cambridge University Press, 1998), 58.

37. Charlotte Bunch, "Peace, Human Rights, and Women's Peace Activism: Feminist Readings," in *Peace Work*, ed. Coomaraswamy and Fonseka, 33.

38. Ibid., 28.

39. Suraiya Kamaruzzaman, "Women and the War in Aceh: These Women Want to Silence All the Guns, Whether Indonesian or Acehnese," *Inside Indonesia*, no. 64, Oct.–Dec. 2000. See also Suraiya Kamaruzzaman, "Violence, Internal Displacement, and Its Impact on the Women of Aceh," in *Violent Conflicts in Indonesia*, ed. Coppel, 259 [Hereinafter "Violence, Internal Displacement"]. See also http://www.peacewomen.org/resources/Aceh/Suraiya WomenWarAceh2000.html (accessed October 13, 2008).

40. Kamaruzzaman, "Women and the War in Aceh," found at http://www .peacewomen.org/resources/Aceh/SuraiyaWomenWarAceh2000.html (accessed October 13, 2008).

41. Ibid.

42. Kamaruzzaman, "Violence, Internal Displacement," 263.

43. Interview with Suraiya Kamaruzzaman, June 15, 2009.

44. Ibid.

45. Nunuk P. Murniati and Komnas Perempuan, "Women in Aceh and Women's NGOs," *Asia Pacific Forum on Women, Law, and Development,*

Forum News 16, no. 2 (Aug.–Sep. 2003). See also http://www.peacewomen. org/resources/Aceh/acehindex.html (accessed October 13, 2008).

46. Suraiya Kamaruzzaman, "Country Report: Violence Action toward Women in Aceh," Asian Human Rights Commission, http://www.ahrchk.net/ pub/mainfile.php/torture2/60/ (accessed October 13, 2008).

47. Rubina Saigol, "Ter-Reign of Terror: 11 September and Its Aftermath," in *Peace Work*, ed. Coomaraswamy and Fonseka, 23.

48. Interview with Suraiya Kamaruzzaman and Raihan Diani, June 15, 2009.

49. Graham Brown, Christopher Wilson, and Suprayoga, *Overcoming Violent Conflict*, vol. 4: *Peace and Development Analysis in Maluku and North Maluku* (Jakarta: CPRU-UNDP, LIPI, and BAPPENAS, 2005), xi.

50. Ibid., 38.

51. United Nations Security Council Resolution 1325 on Women, Peace, and Security. See http://www.peacewomen.org/un/sc/1325.html (accessed October 13, 2008).

52. Coomaraswamy and Fonseka, eds., *Peace Work*, 6.

53. Interview with Suraiya Kamaruzzaman, June 15, 2009.

54. Interview with Zubaedah Johar, Acehnese gender activist, June 15, 2009.

55. Murniati and Komnas Perempuan, "Women in Aceh and Women's NGOs," http://www.peacewomen.org/resources/Aceh/acehindex.html (accessed October 13, 2008).

56. http://www.pekka.or.id/aboutus.html (accessed October 13, 2008).

57. Brown et al., *Overcoming Violent Conflict*, 56.

58. Ibid., 57.

59. I am indebted to Eti, a lecturer at Duta Wacana University, who shared her stories about her humanitarian effort in Maluku and brought up the issue of forgiving as healing. I also talked to Lahmudin, PhD, about his family experiences in Aceh during the Aceh War.

60. Interview with Fuad Mardhatillah, June 14, 2009.

61. Jack Nelson-Pallmeyer, *Is Religion Killing Us? Violence in the Bible and the Qur'an* (New York: Continuum International Publishing Group, 2003), 20–24.

62. Hannah Arendt, *The Human Condition* (Chicago: University of Chicago Press, 1998), 180.

63. Interview with Suraiya Kamaruzzaman, June 15, 2009.

64. Ratna Megawangi, *Membiarkan Berbeda: Sudut Pandang Baru tentang Relasi Gender* (Bandung: Mizan, 1999), 199.

65. Brown et al., *Overcoming Violent Conflict*, 47.

66. Ibid.

67. Interview with Musliah, an official of an NGO called Wanita Islam, in Aceh, June 12, 2009.

68. Kamaruzzaman, "Violence, Internal Displacement," 264.
69. Ibid., 265.
70. Ibid., 266.
71. Arendt, *The Human Condition*, 180.
72. Kamaruzzaman, "Violence, Internal Displacement," 267.

CHAPTER 3

Failures of Solidarity, Failures of the Nation-State: Nongovernmental Organizations and Moroccan Women's Activism*

Rachel Newcomb

I n one of the lower-middle-class suburbs of the Ville Nouvelle of Fes,[1] Morocco, set back from a busy street filled with taxi stands, drygoods stores, and discount clothing shops, the Najia Belghazi Center[2] was located in a small, two-storey apartment building, identical to the other buildings surrounding it. Throughout the day, women trickled in. They were lawyers rushing from the courthouse to offer free legal advice sessions, women arriving to ask questions about the type of evidence needed to secure a divorce from an abusive husband, or women coming to find out more about the Center's initiatives to teach divorced women with few resources a new trade. Frequent visitors to the Center often stopped by just to chat, to update the volunteers on the status of a case they were involved in, or just to share some hot doughnuts purchased from a street vendor outside.

The Najia Belghazi Center boasted notable successes, but there were also many interactions clients or volunteers deemed as failures. Sometimes clients arrived at the Center assuming volunteers would give them money, intervene in a family dispute, or offer shelter from an abusive husband. Volunteers were frustrated by assumptions that the Center had unlimited resources; but in addition to the challenge of getting clients to participate in the way the Center's organizers intended, they faced the added obstacle of community mistrust and suspicion. Many Fassis,[3] particularly in the middle class, did not recognize the nongovernmental organization (NGO) as a legitimate entity and suspected the NGO of offenses ranging from embezzlement of grant money to Western imperialism. This skepticism meant that Center volunteers spent considerable amounts of time defending their work as well as trying to recruit volunteers in a culture with a deep-seated belief that the family alone should be the sole source of altruism and that all other efforts of assistance took the form of patron-client relationships. The goal of achieving solidarity and promoting empowerment among Fassi women across class lines was ephemeral and momentary, usually accomplished during brief transactions rather than sustained within long-term social relations. Are these failures merely products of entrenched class differences, or do they indicate something more? What do these failures reveal about the viability of women's activist organizations in areas outside the cosmopolitan metropoles—Morocco, Casablanca, and Rabat—from which these initiatives typically emanate? This chapter explores the delicate positioning women's rights activists attempted to enact in order to convince various audiences that their intentions were legitimate. It is argued here that religion, local custom, and larger structural inequalities must be considered together in instances where the activists' efforts to foster social change failed.

Initially opened in 2000 to provide free legal advice for women in matters of marriage and divorce, the Najia Belghazi Center gradually came to deal with issues ranging from domestic abuse to job training. During my dissertation fieldwork in Fes, Morocco from 2001 to 2002, I spent many afternoons at the Center, observing the interactions between the Center's clients and its volunteers. The first of its kind in Fes, the Center was not directly associated with a political party or religious organization. The volunteers, mostly middle-upper-class female professionals and academics,[4] perceived their center as existing "outside civil society," asserting that in Morocco, the term "civil society" had been co-opted by male elites, both secular and religious. They were activists who attempted to mute their activism at the Center to show that they were within the law and would not overtly challenge it, particularly in matters concerning women's rights. They expressed their desire to transcend divisions of social class and forge links among all Moroccan women, hoping that the women who visited the Center would also be able to envision this possibility of solidarity. However, clients and volunteers were often at cross-purposes, and efforts to establish links across social classes that might lead to larger structural changes improving the status of women often failed. Sometimes these "failures" took the form of local resistance, exhibited in claims that the Center was "not Islamic enough" or that its volunteers were "attempting to import European customs." Volunteers anticipated these critiques and did their best to respond to them; so why, many wondered, did some Fassis continue to criticize them? These so-called failures cannot be attributed to insurmountable class differences or insufficient religiosity but must be considered in the light of the problematic role of the nation-state in an era of globalization.

A productive examination of the relationships of NGOs to their clients, the local community, and to the nation-state sheds light not only on specific processes of association but also on how domains of the national overlap with the global.[5] As in other regions of the Global South, globalization in Morocco has been accompanied by increasing market liberalization, involving deregulation, privatization, and an increase in consumption. International Monetary Fund–led structural adjustment programs (SAPs) of the 1990s have led to declines in government spending and high rates of unemployment, with no safety nets to assist those who fall deeper into poverty.[6] In response, the Moroccan government has encouraged the formation of NGOs to ameliorate resulting social problems, particularly those affecting women. Budget cuts in the health and education sectors hit women the hardest; for example, the school enrollment rate for girls declined 10 percent between 1985 and 1990.[7] The "feminization of poverty" one sees elsewhere in the developing world affects Morocco as well, and the majority of the clients who came to the Najia Belghazi Center experienced not only legal difficulties but also illiteracy, unemployment, poverty, and the loss of social ties brought about by rural-urban migration.

In an era in which globalization has supposedly rendered the nation-state impotent, NGOs represent one among many possibilities for community and solidarity. In Morocco, activism springing from women's NGOs has contributed to the increased visibility of women's concerns in the public sphere. However, if my research with the Najia Belghazi Center is indicative, NGOs are often overstretched and understaffed, in addition to facing resistance both from within and outside the larger community in which they are based. Women's activism in particular was viewed with suspicion by many Fassis insofar as the volunteers at the Center were perceived as attempting to undermine the boundaries of family, community, and religion by creating links among citizens that fell completely outside these areas.

These resistances and failures of solidarity demonstrate not that NGOs are not useful or necessary but that they are capable of doing only so much. The struggles of female activists at one NGO indicate that the supposedly "disappearing" nation-state is simply evading its responsibilities to its citizens. In the case of the Najia Belghazi Center of Fes, the NGO's attempt to assert a vision of community encompassing all women met with both local and class-based resistance. Much of this resistance stems from core structural issues that demand the intervention of the nation-state. The work of the activists at the Center touched upon sensitive political issues that, from 2000 to 2003, were hotly contested on a national level. While NGOs can certainly serve as agents of change, the assumption that NGOs can solve major social problems allows the state to evade its responsibilities for suffering brought on by cuts in government spending as a result of SAPs or by government laws and policies that legitimate discrimination against women.

NATIONAL CONTEXTS

The Najia Belghazi Center opened at a time of intense debate about the role of women in Moroccan society. Women's activism between 2000 and 2003 was largely focused on the issue of reforming the *mudawana*, the personal status codes that govern a woman's rights in marriage and divorce. In 2000, Prime Minister Abderrahmane Youssoufi, with approval from the new monarch, Mohammed VI, publicly set forth a plan to alter the *mudawana*, which met with mass demonstrations both in support of and against the plan.[8] Titled "the integration of women in development," the proposed reforms would have altered the existing *mudawana* in several areas, including giving women the right to a judicial divorce and substantially restricting men's unilateral freedom to repudiate their wives. Opponents argued that the plan was anti-Islamic, whereas those in favor claimed that the existing laws denied women their basic human rights and violated the 1979 Convention on the Elimination of All Forms of Discrimination Against Women (CEDAW), which Morocco had signed. The outcome of this debate was also viewed as a litmus test for King Mohammed VI's nascent rule, since the legitimacy of the Moroccan monarchy rests in part on divine sanction. The government's careful straddling of both sides of this debate reflects inherent contradictions in government policy, which has over the past several years attempted to placate "traditional conservative Islamist interests, while at the same time projecting a modernist progressive image."[9]

Although religion lies at the core of Moroccan family law and is frequently used in defense of its immutability, a society organized around patriarchal family structures provided the social context for the *mudawa-na's* initial codification in the 1950s. The *mudawana* was the only area of Islamic jurisprudence maintained when Morocco became independent in 1956—all criminal and business laws were modeled on European legal codes.[10] Although the *mudawana* had received some cosmetic changes in 1993 during the reign of King Hassan II,[11] it had remained largely unchanged since the time of independence from the French in 1956. Signaling its intentions to change these laws opened the current government up to considerable criticism, particularly from Islamist parties. After the demonstrations, King Mohammed VI appointed a commission to examine the *mudawana* reforms more closely; and for three years, the committee disappeared behind closed doors while the topic was debated endlessly in Moroccan society.[12]

Arguments for maintaining the law in its original form were not merely about religion but also about vestiges of male familial authority that some male elites wanted to maintain, although many in Moroccan society had long since lost the benefits and protections these laws might once have afforded. At the time of my fieldwork in 2001–2002, many of the difficulties reported by clients at the Najia Belghazi Center related specifically to laws that favored male authority above all other interests. However, many of the original safety nets that were designed to balance out the laws' uneven effects were missing, particularly for lower-class women. For example, in the past, a woman entering a marriage contract could count on a strong extended family structure to support her should the marriage fail. A sufficient dowry negotiated by a woman's family acted as insurance against a bad marriage, and the necessity of maintaining harmonious group relations among families led to greater pressure for the husband to treat his wife with dignity. If a couple divorced, the woman could usually return to her family, counting on male family members to wield sufficient influence to ensure that she left the marriage with all her dowry.

However, women in Morocco today, particularly from lower socioeconomic groups, are less likely to have this community support. From the 1960s onward, tribal models of production gradually came to be displaced by the impersonal demands of a capitalist economy, which frequently necessitated women's participation in a cash economy. Family structures deteriorated, particularly among the urban poor, though laws and local attitudes about women's rights and women's place in the public sphere remain conservative. For urban women, Moha Ennaji and Fatima Sadiqi have explained, this crisis was "a clash between an essential tribal superstructure and a production system whose economic logic was alien to the traditional communal mode."[13] Structural adjustment programs have further contributed to rapid modernization and a weakening of extended family structures, and the laws have made women the most vulnerable. The declining need for rural agricultural labor has led to mass urban migrations, high levels of unemployment, and as a result, the disintegration of local networks and familial resources that are a woman's first recourse in the event of a divorce. Women who came to the Center for help often lived far from their families, in addition to lacking the literacy to negotiate the law and the job skills to enable them to support themselves and their children once divorced. The activists who founded the Najia Belghazi Center initially felt that legal literacy would go a long way toward solving women's marital problems, but they soon found themselves attempting to respond to much larger issues. Structural causes of poverty, resulting from government policies, have led to a rise in marital problems, as well as to the community fragmentation that has resulted in women's loss of traditional forms of support. The Moroccan government has nonetheless placed its support behind the creation of nongovernmental organizations designed to tackle a range of problems from orphans to women's rights.

Movements of association have a long history in Morocco, although in recent decades, they have taken new forms and begun to deal with such issues as human rights. Feminism in Morocco was first associated with nationalism, and the origins of the feminist movement can be traced back to 1946, when the women's branch of the nationalist Istiqlal Party demanded greater representation in the public sphere and an end to polygamy.[14] Unveiling and nation building became part of the nationalist project when King Mohammed V unveiled his daughters in public, and as in other parts of the Middle East and North Africa (MENA) region, progress in the nationalist movement was measured by European standards concerning the treatment of women. Middle- and upper-class women entered the public sphere through education and high-status professions, and female journalists and writers in the 1960s and 1970s promoted ideas of equality through what Ennaji and Sadiqi call "feminist hagiography," that is, journalistic biographies of famous world feminists as a way to introduce feminism without directly implicating the writer.[15] During this period, women's progressive political parties (e.g., the Union Progressiste des Femmes Marocaines in 1962 and the Union Nationale des Femmes Marocaines in 1969) and women's professional organizations began to appear as well.

It was not until the 1980s that such national women's associations as the Association Démocratique des Femmes du Maroc (ADFM) moved outside the political parties. Not surprisingly, many of these associations were founded by women who felt their concerns had not been addressed in the political arena, particularly as politicians invoked "women's issues" more as a political device and less out of any real concern for the women themselves. *Mudawana* reform has been a primary goal of many of these groups, along with ending discrimination and violence against women. As of 1990, there were 29 formal women's associations in Morocco, 16 created in the past decade.[16] Since then, many more have appeared, although a recent government statistic lists 34 associations in 1997.[17] The creation of so many organizations since the 1980s has been attributed to a number of factors, including new political openness on the part of the monarchy and a growing awareness among citizens that existing societal structures are insufficient to address social problems among the poor and disenfranchised.[18]

Many Moroccan women's associations were and are concerned with the "promotion of the Moroccan woman," ameliorating social hardships as well as helping to obtain a better standard of living. Ennaji and Sadiqi distinguish between two "types" of feminist women's associations: the first concerned with ameliorating the effects of poverty and inefficient state structures, the second focused more on overt political activism and the insertion of women into the political process.[19] In addition to humanitarian, political, and feminist organizations, there are also professional associations for women in different high-status careers, including administration, law, and business. Some areas of activity among the organizations overlap; for example, both political parties and feminist groups offer such activities as literacy training, prenatal care, and legal awareness seminars. Other organizations focus on reforming the *mudawana* as well as sensitizing Moroccans to a variety of social issues. "Their objective," writes Aïcha Belarbi, "is not to integrate women into a system of production which rarely benefits them, but to increase awareness, to arm them to become active and effective agents in the dynamic of social transformations."[20]

SOLIDARITY WITH DISTINCTIONS: THE POSITIONING OF ONE WOMEN'S NGO

Often funded by governments and organizations throughout Europe and the United States, many Moroccan NGOs have a degree of independence from the state that allows them to operate without excessive recourse to bureaucratic procedures. The anthropological literature on NGOs reveals two general trends in the perception of their effectiveness: either NGOs are contributing to the workings of the nation-state in an era of neoliberal capitalism, or they work outside the state in processes that will, they hope, transform society.[21] To proponents of the first viewpoint, NGOs provide evidence of a strong civil society, one in which citizens are actively engaged in renegotiating the relationship between individuals and the state, and in the process, reimagining forms of community and creating new arenas to support those whom the system has failed. Some analysts have pointed to the importance of the role of NGOs in an era of neoliberal capitalism, whereby NGOs are expected to contribute more rapidly and efficiently to processes of "development" than governments.[22] Their presence is believed to offer evidence of democracy and in the case of women's associations, to indicate the participation of women in Moroccan society. Proponents of the second viewpoint argue that NGOs offer what Michel Foucault calls an "insurrection of subjugated knowledges," politicizing previously taboo subjects and demanding radical societal change.[23]

NGOs such as the Najia Belghazi Center fit neither of these paradigms perfectly. The presence of NGOs offers a positive international image for the Moroccan government, giving the appearance of a strong civil society in the absence of real democracy. However, while the Center promoted many initiatives related to the government's plan to integrate women in development, the Center was unable to efficiently solve the overwhelming number of problems brought by clients. In terms of its politicization, as this chapter will show, the Center felt compelled to tone down perceived "radical" elements in its discourse in order to try to gain acceptance by a locally conservative society.

The activists at the Najia Belghazi Center insisted that their goals were strictly apolitical.[24] Publicly, they wanted to stay outside the domain of politics while quietly working to "inform" women of their legal rights and, by implication, the inadequacy of those rights. They avoided directly addressing the issue of *mudawana* reform because, as one activist told me, most Moroccans were already polarized over the debates, and they would lose potential supporters who might decide the NGO was "against Islam." Instead, they took the theme of violence against women as their principal mission. They asserted that all Moroccan women were victims of violence: juridical, physical, or structural violence. This broad stance allowed them to assert solidarity across social classes with their clients, most of whom were lower class, economically disenfranchised, or illiterate. Rather than interacting in typical patron-client patterns, whereby clients received favors from volunteers but then owed them something in return, at the Center, volunteers and clients could meet on more neutral grounds, united by the shared theme of "violence" inflicted by patriarchal social interests. Legal, physical, and economic concerns were perceived as intertwined. With grant money received from foreign NGOs and even foreign governments, they created various programs aimed to train women with limited resources to work for themselves, frequently in nontraditional positions. With control of an income, female dependence on the quixotic whims of husbands would decline, women would become savvier about their rights,

and some of the social structures that continued to replicate this dependence on men would themselves dissolve, whether or not the laws themselves followed suit.

Despite volunteers' insistence that these concerns were not political,
to many Fassi Moroccans, they appeared to be explicitly so. Some of the
Center's failures were rooted in Fassi rejections of the Center's claims that
challenged entrenched notions of patriarchy, class, and social structure.
Seeking to create a distinctive space for women outside the confines of
civil society and the nation-state, the forms of solidarity the Najia Belghazi
Center attempted to forge were often fleeting, dissolving in the face of
other cultural and class-based pressures.

Nationally, public debates over changing the *mudawana* focused upon
law, Islam, and the permissibility of new interpretations of the religion.
Those against the plan claimed the reformists were attempting to change
Islam itself, particularly since laws were derived from the Maliki school of
shari'a jurisprudence to which Morocco belongs. Other feminist activists
argued not only that the *mudawana* conflicted with the CEDAW but also
that Islamic doctrines could be reinterpreted as long as the Qur'an itself
was not altered. However, activists at the Najia Belghazi Center did not
attempt to go on record about these debates but instead felt they were
working to effect change by encouraging clients to see themselves as sharing common concerns with all Moroccan women. Rather than criticizing
the *mudawana*, the volunteers at the Najia Belghazi Center argued that
within the existing laws, there was room to maneuver. In addition, the
Center's official position that all women were united by gendered experiences of legal, physical, or psychological violence led them to consider
women's legal rights as related to larger issues of inequality in Moroccan
society. This shared experience of what the Center's president called "juridical violence" and the attempt to make client-volunteer interactions as
equitable as possible were two examples of strategies employed to promote
solidarity among women. Volunteers spent a great deal of time explaining
to clients that they were not interested in perpetuating the patron-client
relationship, in which people seek a benefactor in exchange for services.

However, there were limits to these attempts to create solidarity. Activists at the Center distanced themselves from personal experiences of
physical violence, identifying with the more abstract notion of "juridical"
violence and with the sexual violence that comprised basic street harassment. Although volunteers often cited the statistic that domestic violence
crosses class lines, the volunteers were quick to point out that they themselves had never been physically victimized. Physical violence was perceived as a problem specific to lower-socioeconomic groups, a problem
that could be ameliorated with access to education and employment.

Bringing poor women to the Center to discuss physical and sexual abuse was touted as progress, as "lifting the veil of shame on this taboo subject," as one of the activists once said to me. Yet the subject of violence among the middle and upper classes remained a taboo among the educated volunteers, as if it were presumed not to exist at all. Similarly, clients who spoke of their experiences with physical abuse and domestic violence were almost always from the lower classes.

OBSTACLES TO SOLIDARITY: LOCAL, NATIONAL, AND GLOBAL

The volunteers' distinction among their experiences of violence (juridical) from those of the women who came to the Center (physical) contributed to the perpetuation of class divisions within the Center, while outside it, the majority of middle- and upper-class Fassis I interviewed still felt that marital problems should be resolved within families. Many of my middle-class informants considered it shameful that the women who visited the Center aired intimate details of their domestic life before an audience of strangers. To me, it seemed obvious that the women had no other resources upon which to fall back, but these Fassis insisted that the women "had no shame" and that they did not care about how they were embarrassing their families in the process. Furthermore, they doubted the honest intentions of the Center's volunteers and asserted that the volunteers must be pocketing their grant money.

Other criticisms leveled against the activists included the observation that they were following an imported code of morals and that they had created the NGO in the first place only to influence the *mudawana* debates. Driss, an English professor at the university, described the work of local NGOs to me as "cultural imperialism," equating it to "missionary work. They want to accomplish legal reform to give Moroccan women the same rights as European women," he told me. "But they're ignoring our traditions, and our heritage." This was also a common argument against altering the *mudawana*—that any changes to the existing laws somehow threatened to destroy Moroccan culture. Issues of violence and poverty, or more significantly, the structures of patriarchal social relations and patron-client ties, are effaced in favor of a view that sees Moroccan women as repositories of traditional culture. The accusation that activists were "destroying Moroccan culture" was almost as damning as the idea that they were flaunting religious dictates.

In addition, activists faced difficulties recruiting professionals interested in volunteering their time, which made the task of solving such a wide range of problems even more overwhelming. Volunteering in the Western sense of donating one's time to help strangers in an impersonal location with no expectation of personal gain did not fit in with standard notions of aid, many of which revolved around the mutually beneficial idea of patron-client relations. Fassis are accustomed to dispensing aid through preexisting social or kin-based networks, a practice unavailable to rural-urban migrants who typically arrive in the cities with no such networks in place.

In this respect, the comments of Khadija, a lawyer who had refused an invitation to volunteer at the Center, were telling.

"To be honest, I don't think I would benefit from helping them," Khadija told me. "The women who go there do not actually want help. They want money, or else a lawyer they do not have to pay for, and as soon as they understand that the Center is not going to give it to them, they will stop coming. If you have time, it is better to help someone you know, especially if they are in the family. You will see the results [of your assistance], and you can be sure they will be grateful."

In fact, in many of the interactions that I witnessed between clients and volunteers, clients did attempt to draw on this patron-client model. Women often recounted long and painful sagas of abuse, divorce, and expulsion from the marital home, ending with a plea for the Center to help them with a free lawyer or money. Occasionally, clients tried to offer their services as maids in exchange for a lawyer. Ideally, activists envisioned the Center as a place where women would gain a better sense of the path they needed to take in the judicial system; they might also take advantage of literacy or job-training classes and then promote themselves as entrepreneurs. However, upon hearing that the Center was not offering money or free lawyers, many women left the Center and never came back.

Class differences—here exemplified by the promotion of solidarity with distinctions, the sense among Fassis that only the poor and uneducated would air their marital grievances at an impersonal NGO, and the difficulties of convincing educated professionals to volunteer—mask a larger problem faced by women activists. This is that the Moroccan government itself has in some sense contributed to the creation of these problems; by encouraging NGOs to solve them, it is ignoring the larger structural causes. The structure of social relations has broken down as a result of rapid modernization brought on by economic policies; and the government, rather than developing social services to aid in the resulting societal transformations, has actually taken them away. Expecting one NGO to bear the burden for an entire city's problems with domestic violence, illiteracy, divorce, and abandonment and blaming these problems on a lack of education, poverty, or social class tend to abstract these issues from their true causes. The illusion of a flourishing civil society, in which impartial, uncoerced NGOs stand between the government and the population, allows the government to receive accolades from human rights groups for its openness, obscuring the true causes of human suffering.

As labor and global capital cross borders with increasing ease, unimpeded by such traditional regulations as tariffs or labor laws, the provocative idea of the "death of the nation-state" has often been asserted as a by-product of globalization.[25] According to this formulation, nations have lost their ability to legislate and are made irrelevant by powerful flows of global capital. Economic deregulation leads to higher corporate profits as companies relocate to areas in the Global South with weak unions, low wages, and the fewest restrictions on labor practices. Within Global South economies, IMF-led programs of structural adjustment promote globalization by offering loans on the condition that recipients privatize public assets and cut government spending. However, structural adjustment programs, rather than leading to economic growth and improvement, often result in economic recessions, greater unemployment, and poverty, particularly for women. The loss of public-sector jobs and an accompanying shift from formal to informal employment have increased women's work while failing to improve their decision-making power in the household. With less education and lower status than men, women find themselves in lower-paid, riskier, more labor-intensive jobs. Employment instability and job loss contribute to marital tensions and an increase in domestic violence. As the weakened nation-state is no longer able to offer services to combat issues related to the feminization of poverty, we see a rise in the number of non-governmental organizations devoted to addressing women's concerns.

Thus, the issue of Moroccan women's activism in response to the proposed revision of the *mudawana* laws paints a complex picture: of tribal customs masquerading as immutable divine law; of efforts to tackle the interconnected problems of abandonment, illiteracy, unemployment, and the feminization of poverty; and of the larger global issues that have, indirectly and directly, brought many of these problems into being. Yet globalization does not simply happen to passive, helpless actors, whether nations or individuals, and assertions about the death of the nation-state are perhaps premature. Saskia Sassen has observed that globalization requires active implementation on the part of nation-states to facilitate the movement of capital and labor; she asserts that globalization is, in fact, embedded in the national.[26] In Morocco, structural adjustment programs have led to an improved standard of living for some, but in other respects they have hurt many citizens. An IMF study of the effect of SAPs from 1980 to 1996 shows that Morocco did not improve in the rate of exports of goods and services or in its trade balance.[27] Debt rose in the 1990s, the rate of investment continued to be low, and most significantly, unemployment increased. As a result of cuts in social and educational programs, these economic effects are often even more deeply felt by women and children.

The efforts of the Najia Belghazi Center to address a wide range of social problems met with resistance from well-meaning volunteers, clients, and citizens. Although women's NGOs in other Moroccan cities may not face an identical set of issues as the Najia Belghazi Center, most NGOs are dealing with issues that stem from poverty, the deterioration of family and social structure in the process of rural-urban migration, and the cutting of government-based social programs that might previously have alleviated some of these difficulties. In addition, activists working in NGOs from 2000 to 2003 were also operating in the context of *mudawana* debates, which created a more politicized public sphere. Activists often had to hide their support for the reforms for fear of being labeled secularists who were against Islam and in favor of Westernization.

In activists' encounters with clients, their attempt to efface class differences often failed when some activists distanced themselves from the problems particular to the lower classes or when clients affirmed these differences by attempting to replicate patriarchal structures by forming patron-client relationships with the volunteers. Middle- and middle-upper-class Fassi observers who benefited from the patriarchal social structures in place to resolve marital differences within the family disapproved of the NGO's intervention in marital (and hence, familial) disputes. The activists' insistence that they were apolitical did not exempt them from accusations that through their very existence, they were affronting both Islam and Moroccan culture. The Moroccan government, it seems, offers the least resistance, since it allows the NGO to operate with considerably leeway, pursuing an agenda set by the activists themselves.

Yet blaming the failures of solidarity on the NGO's founders, volunteers, clients, or local citizens obscures the fact that many of these problems might not be so pronounced had the underlying economic causes not contributed to them. In 1983 the monarchy signed on to structural adjustment programs without consulting the people, and to this day economic reforms are a result of top-down, hierarchical state policy. The flourishing of NGOs conceals the absence of a strong democracy. Rather than disappearing, the nation-state still plays a very pronounced role in the lives of citizens. On a local level, NGO solidarity failed for two reasons: one, that divisions of social class created obstacles to solidarity; and two, that these class-based divisions often existed as a direct result of state policies that undermined the core issues the NGOs attempt to address. These policies included legalized inequality between men and women, structural adjustment programs leading to "official" unemployment rates as high as 25 percent, and finally, the failure of government to offer creative solutions to the feminization of poverty.

Women's associations in Morocco have made great strides toward incorporation into the political decision-making process, and women's activists have contributed in no small part to the fact that women's issues are taken seriously in the public sphere and are considered by many to be integral toward Morocco's development. Upon taking office in 1999, King Mohammed VI asked, "How can society achieve progress, while women, who represent half the nation, see their rights violated and suffer as a result of injustice, violence, and marginalization, notwithstanding the dignity and justice granted them by our glorious religion?"[28] However, as Moha Ennaji and Fatima Sadiqi point out, one of the primary challenges activists face is to continue "to push the state into revising its policies."[29] Nongovernmental organizations in the Global South, while making a valiant attempt to address these issues on a small scale, must not be seen as the sole recourse for marginalized citizens: the state must do its part to address the crucial issues that contribute to poverty, marginality, and disenfranchisement. These insights into the failure of solidarity at the hands of the state can be used to develop new strategies to create solidarity and bring about social change in North Africa and beyond.

NOTES

1. First established in 789 CE, Fes lays claim to being the oldest city in Morocco; and with a total population of 946,815 inhabitants, it is the third-largest city in the country. The "Ville Nouvelle" refers to the newer parts of Moroccan cities, constructed by the French during the Protectorate (1912–1956). In most large Moroccan cities, the Ville Nouvelle is contrasted with the *medina*, the Arabic term for the old cities built by Moroccans over the centuries. In Fes, the terms "Ville Nouvelle" and "*medina*" have come to bear the markers of social class, as the Fes *medina*, although once occupied by urban Arab aristocracy, is now inhabited primarily by poor rural-to-urban migrants.

2. All organizational and proper names used in this chapter are pseudonyms.

3. "Fassi" is the term that denotes a resident of Fes.

4. "Social class" is a problematic term with meanings ranging from a group's objective relation to the means of production to a social position determined by inequalities of race, education, or economic status. This is further complicated by the fact that theories about class formation cannot be applied uniformly to every society, since a variety of other "cultural" factors both affect and are intertwined with social position. Thus, I use "middle" or "middle-upper class" here with full acknowledgment of the complicated associations of this term. The growth of a substantial middle class in MENA societies is a

relatively recent phenomenon, stemming from increased access to education and economic development in the region, particularly since independence.

5. I define nation-state in its broadest sense, as sovereign territory ruled over by a government whose population is constituted as citizens. Morocco is a constitutional monarchy led since 1999 by King Mohammed VI after the death of his father, Hassan II, who ruled since 1960. The ruling Alaoui family has been in power since the 1600s; during the French Protectorate (1912–1956), the family maintained its legitimacy by associating with the Moroccan nationalist movement.

6. Karen Pfeifer, "How Tunisia, Morocco, Jordan and Even Egypt Became IMF 'Success Stories' in the 1990s," in *Middle East Report*, no. 210 (1999): 25 [Hereinafter "Success Stories'"].

7. Moha Ennaji and Fatima Sadiqi, "The Feminization of Public Space: Women's Activism, the Family Law, and Social Change in Morocco," *Journal of Middle East Women's Studies* 2, no. 2 (2006): 94.

8. The government-sponsored plan was announced by former prime minister Abderrahmane Youssoufi, who heads an elected parliament that does possess some decision-making capabilities. The government's stance on women's issues can be perceived as symbolic of its modernizing, Western-leaning approach, with women's participation in society used as an indicator of supposed progress toward democracy. But as Suad Joseph has pointed out, patriarchy is central to social organization in Middle East and North African societies, and women are almost always recognized as embedded in familial structures before they are considered as individuals (Suad Joseph, "Gender and Citizenship in Middle Eastern States," *Middle East Report*, no. 198 [1996]: 7). Family rather than the individual remains paramount in articulating the core unit of society.

9. Rabéa Naciri, *The Women's Movement and Political Discourse in Morocco* (United Nations Research Institute for Social Development, Occasional Paper 8, March 1998), i [Hereinafter *Women's Movement*].

10. For more on how a conservative *mudawana* legitimates patrilineal social organization and supports the authority of husbands and male-centered patrilineages over women's marriages, see Mounira Charrad, *States and Women's Rights: The Making of Postcolonial Tunisia, Algeria, and Morocco* (Berkeley: University of California Press, 2001).

11. The changes to the *mudawana* in 1993 were preceded by a two-year campaign by the Moroccan feminist organization Union de L'action Féminine to gather 1 million signatures in support of reforming the laws according to international standards of human rights. Islamist opponents immediately attacked the campaign as an act of apostasy aimed at completely Westernizing Moroccan society. See Laurie Brand, *Women, the State, and Political Liberalization: Middle Eastern and North African Experiences* (New York: Columbia

University Press, 1998). King Hassan II authorized only minor changes to the laws, including the requirement that two witnesses and the wife had to be present for a husband to initiate a divorce, that a woman could choose her own marital guardian (*wali*), and that a woman had to be informed if her husband took another wife. Some feminists perceived these reforms as significant evidence of a new willingness on the part of the monarchy to consider previously taboo topics, whereas others felt that the reforms were cosmetic changes only and had not gone far enough. For more on these reforms, see Leon Buskens, "Recent Debates on Family Law Reform in Morocco: Islamic Law as Politics in an Emerging Public Sphere," *Islamic Law and Society Journal* 10, no. 1 (2003): 70–131; or Brand, *Women, the State, and Political Liberalization*, 1998.

12. On October 13, 2003, King Mohammed finally announced that he would revise the *mudawana*, easing women's abilities to obtain a divorce, raising the age of marriage to 18, and placing restrictions on polygamy, including the approval of a judge and the first wife. The revisions further assert that men and women are equal in marriage and that the wife will no longer be considered a minor under the guardianship of her husband. Divorce will supposedly require mutual consent, unlike the prior practice of unilateral repudiation; and in the event of a divorce, the revisions encourage a fair division of property acquired after the marriage. Despite the enthusiasm that greeted the revisions, many women's and human rights groups asserted that the revisions did not accomplish as much as they had hoped, especially since polygamy was not banned and the question of equality in inheritance had not been addressed. Criticism was muted on both sides, undoubtedly because the King had announced that the reforms agreed with principles for interpreting the Qur'an, stating in his address to Parliament, "I cannot authorize that which God has prohibited, nor prohibit that which the Almighty has authorized." As for the two primary Islamist groups in the country, the PJD (Party of Justice and Development) and Al-adl wal-ihssane (Justice and Charity), both were said to have backed away considerably from criticism of the reforms since the terrorist attacks in Casablanca of May 16, 2003, which had led to a backlash against Islamist groups. Enforcing the new laws was expected to be difficult, especially among conservative judges or in far-flung locations. See *Le Journal hebdomadaire*, nos. 129 (Oct. 11–17, 2003) and 130 (Oct. 18–24, 2003), for a survey of reactions.

13. Ennaji and Sadiqi, "The Feminization of Public Space," 94.

14. Ibid., 96.

15. Ibid., 98.

16. Aïcha Belarbi, "Mouvements des Femmes au Maroc," in *La Societe Civile au Maroc*, ed. Noureddine El Ayoufi (Rabat: Imprimerie El Maârif Al Jadida, 1992), 187.

17. CERED, ed., *Population et Développement au Maroc* (Rabat: Centre d'Etudes et de Recherches Démographiques [CERED], 1997), 153.

18. Belarbi, "Mouvements," 187.

19. Ennaji and Sadiqi, "The Feminization of Public Space," 106.

20. Belarbi, "Mouvements," 192.

21. William F. Fisher, "Doing Good? The Politics and Antipolitics of NGO Practices," *Annual Review of Anthropology* 26 (1997): 445.

22. Ibid., 444.

23. Michel Foucault, *Power/Knowledge: Selected Interviews and Other Writings*, ed. C. Gordon (New York: Pantheon, 1980), 81.

24. This has been a common strategy of the women's movement in Morocco since the 1980s, since early efforts to politicize women's issues were suppressed by elites. Instead, women's associations have sought to become part of the domain of civil society while quietly working to draw attention to the state's duplicity in asserting its progressive aims while continuing to appease patriarchal interests in practice. See Naciri, *Women's Movement*, 1.

25. See, for example, Jean Guehenno, *The End of the Nation State* (Minneapolis: University of Minnesota Press, 1995), and Kenichi Ohmae, *End of the Nation State: The Rise of Regional Economies* (New York: Touchstone Press, 1996).

26. Saskia Sassen, "Spatialities and Temporalities of the Global: Elements for a Theorization," *Public Culture* 12, no. 1 (2000): 217.

27. Pfeifer, "Success Stories," 24.

28. Ennaji and Sadiqi, "The Feminization of Public Space," 105.

29. Ibid., 107.

PART II

Socioeconomics, Politics, and Authority

CHAPTER 4

Beyond Personal Belief? The Role of Religious Identities among Muslim Women Respect Activists

Narzanin Massoumi

S ince the war on terrorism, there is an increasingly suspicious gaze on Muslims in Britain, as in other Western societies. Moral panics are about not just Islamic terrorism but the clash of civilisations and the death of multiculturalism in Britain.[1] Islamophobia has become widespread with wild generalizations made about British Muslims through accusations of self-segregation, fanaticism, and the illiberal nature of religious practices. Muslim women are represented as oppressed victims of their religion, their religious identities subject to liberal and feminist critique.

This chapter aims to show that far from being victims, some British Muslim women are active agents of their own religion, participating in political life and forging alternative political communities and visions. Muslim women have become increasingly involved in social movements that have been in direct opposition to the war on terrorism. They have adopted leadership roles within the organizations, and some of them have joined in alliance with sections of the left to form a new political party, Respect. The Respect Party was formed in 2004 by a coalition of activists in the wake of the large antiwar movement against the wars in Iraq and Afghanistan. The party is a political alliance forged between socialists and peace activists, as well as sections of the British Muslim community. This chapter reflects an original empirical inquiry into a group of Muslim women political activists from the Respect Party.

Such an alliance between Muslims and the left is unique in terms of the history of British Muslim political activism. The politicization of Islam since the Rushdie affair has meant that British Muslims have come to privilege the religious aspect of their identity over other identities.[2] This has meant an increase in Muslim organizations that aim to represent the interests of Muslims as Muslims, by attempting to gain recognition within the public sphere. The women involved in the Respect Party, in contrast, have not been mobilizing in Muslim-only organizations but have instead formed a coalition with the mainly secular left. Thus, this raises interesting questions as to what has happened to the religious aspect of this identity in such a political alliance. How have these women found ways of negotiating between the two identities? Are religion and politics complementary, contradictory, or simply just disconnected in this process? Do these Muslim women political activists justify their political engagement using religious concepts, or do they simply draw on secular political values or ethics?

A NEW SPACE FOR BRITISH MUSLIMS?

The focus of academic understanding of British ethnic minorities was until recently predominantly focused on "race," leaving little space for developing an understanding of religious identities. "Race" is the state-sponsored category for cultural difference, backed by a series of race relations legislation.[3] Despite this focus, many Muslims have preferred to privilege their religious identity, creating a disjuncture between how Muslims self-defined and how they were understood in both legal and academic terms.

THE NEW POLITICAL COMMUNITIES OF ISLAM

Muslim preference for a public religious identity came to prevail since the Rushdie affair. However, since September 11 suspicion and doubt have been cast on the Muslim community as race relations and antiterrorism measures are becoming increasingly synonymous,[4] discrediting a political Muslim identity in the public sphere. Yet, race relations and antiterrorism measures are only two factors, albeit important ones, in a whole set of processes that have led to changes in the construction of a Muslim identity. Some observers have placed the development of a politicized British (or European) Muslim identity in the wider global processes of transnationalism.[5]

Peter Mandaville explores what happens to Islam when it "travels," looking at what happens to Islam when up to 40 percent of Muslims are living in situations where they are minorities. In the diaspora, Islam does not simply disappear but acquires new meanings. Islam takes the form of "a complex hybrid condition, one in which Islamic meanings shift, change and transmute, where things become something else."[6]

Mandaville's interest in Muslims living in the West stems from a high concentration of what he calls translocal spaces, particularly in such global cities as London, Paris, Bradford, and Berlin. These Western translocal spaces stand in contrast to the situation in many Muslim majority states where the ability to be critical and move away from the officially public doctrine is restricted. Many exiled intellectuals settle in these global cities, since such translocalities offer these aspiring Muslim intellectuals the opportunity to express and encounter alternative readings of Islam.[7] In being forced to hold a mirror up to themselves, Muslims become simultaneously more aware of their differences and as well have a greater capacity to communicate, interact, and bridge distances between each other.[8] As a result, a critical vision of Islam is emerging. This involves the relativization of Islam, which becomes inherently political through the act of questioning its own parameters.[9]

Islam has therefore become something political, not necessarily political Islam but a mode of contesting authority.[10] The significance of the emergence of this new political discourse taking place within Islam is the way in which important rereadings are taking place with regards to conceptions of politics and the political community. Many new Islamic intellectuals are asserting that all Muslims are vested with the ability to practice Islamic reasoning, *ijtihād*.[11] This reassertion of *ijtihād* (literally, an "intellectual effort or struggle") as a capacity possessed by all Muslims, and not just the elite group of the *ulama*, or religious scholars, has led to two important developments.

The first development is the way in which Muslims have come to understand their Islamic self with regard to their relationship with non-Muslims.[12] For example, in the Qur'an, Allah reminds Muslims that if he wanted to, he could have created one nation but instead created many people and nations so they could get to know each other (see Qur'an 16:93 and 49:13). This "knowing the other" is used as the basis of cultural pluralism in the global community of Muslims, dubbed the *umma*.[13] Tariq Modood and Fauzia Ahmad illustrate in their research on British Muslim perspectives on multiculturalism that there are two ways in which those interviewed acknowledged the legitimacy of cultural pluralism within Islam. One was to invoke such Qur'anic passages as the one just cited; the other was to refer to examples from Islamic history.[14] The stress on such cultural pluralism and opening dialogue with others enables a political space whereby Muslims can work in very close alliance with non-Muslims without a sense of religious and political compromise.

The second development is with regards to gender and opening up spaces for political participation of women in the public sphere. More Muslim women are found in public spheres of the diaspora, for example, in places of work and, in particular, in higher education.[15] Furthermore, more women have taken interpretations of Islam into their own hands. They are not holding back from criticism or rejection of practices or views that are seen to violate their terms of equality. This is done so often in the form of separating culture from religion, which is seen to constitute the "true" Islam. Muslim feminists are hence returning to the earliest sources to read into Islamic history a discourse on women's rights that was conveniently forgotten.[16] These ideas are not confined to Islamic feminist scholars but have become widespread in the development of a "common sense" feminist understanding, resulting in the formation of a gendered public space whereby women have been able to engage in political activity that was previously confined to men.[17]

These developments raise an interesting question with regards to the empirical inquiry undertaken in this research. To what extent can the political activity of the Muslim women Respect activists, in forming an alliance with the left, be understood as part of the process of such renegotiations? That is, to what extent are these women invoking the rearticulations of such religious concepts to justify their political actions?

COLONIAL FANTASIES, WESTERN FEMINISM, AND ESSENTIALISM

Gender plays a constitutive role in the construction of the "Muslim community."[18] Since the Rushdie affair in Britain, through to the riots in France and in Britain, and September 11, 2001, in the United States, the visibility of Muslims centers particularly on young men. These young men are seen as perpetrators of violence and aggressive fundamentalism.[19] This focus on Muslim men has led to a small but growing literature that focuses on how Muslim masculinities are constructed.[20] Interestingly, this concern for Muslim men has meant that the role of women can be overlooked, in particular, in terms of the part they play in the construction of their religion.[21] Such blindsiding can act to reinforce the popular misconceptions of Muslim women, represented through their victimhood and despair. Their religious identities are frequently subject to secular and feminist skepticism, leaving little space for the possibilities of empowerment through such identities.[22] Some observers have begun to address the ways in which Muslim women have constructed new femininities through their religious identities.[23] Muslim women are active in asserting their Muslim identity; for some, simply wearing the headscarf has become a political act whereby they are publicly branding themselves as Muslims at a time when Islamophobia makes them potentially vulnerable to hostility.[24] Despite this growing hostility, Muslim women are beginning to regard their religion as a resource. Rather than seeing it as a marker of oppression and exclusion, many of them use their religion to negotiate a discourse of rights[25] as a source of empowerment.[26]

Despite this new regard, there has not been any empirical research on Muslim women political activists in Britain; much of this type of research has been confined to Muslim majority countries.[27] Although there is in Britain a growing literature on Muslim women, such literature tends to focus on their dress,[28] their participation in the labour market,[29] and their involvement in higher education,[30] rather than their role in the political sphere. However, exploring the political role played by Muslim women has important political and theoretical consequences with regards to feminism, in particular challenging the liberal feminist conceptions of agency and freedom that are blind to women's involvement in religious movements.[31]

Some feminists have come to reject, not just religion, but multiculturalism per se on the basis that it reinforces gender inequality. The way in which feminists have targeted religious and ethnic minorities for practices that are deemed antithetical to women's equality has created a seeming polarity between multiculturalism and feminism.[32] It is argued here that the feminist critique of multiculturalism relies on essentialist binaries characteristic of Orientalist discourse. The attempt by some Western feminists to "save brown women" means that they end up subscribing to a masculine imperialist ideological formation that renders third world women as monolithic.[33] However, some observers have argued that this has meant that feminism is becoming prone to a paralysis of cultural difference whereby, in becoming anxious of cultural imperialism, a form of cultural relativism has prevailed rendering it difficult to criticize any cultural practice as oppressive to women.[34]

For other observers, the root of the problem lies in essentialism. The charge is that in reifying particular social groups, multiculturalism undermines marginal voices by maintaining internal power hierarchies. This philosophical position of antiessentialism problematizes the formation of a collective identity in achieving solidarities in any form of identity politics. In outlining here my own position with regards to antiessentialism and identity, I argue that attributing a social identity with some form of coherence does not necessarily rely on the assumption of essence. There is more than one type of essentializing, and a failure to recognize this is, in itself, essentialist.

"SAVING BROWN WOMEN": ORIENTALIST FEMINISM
AND MUSLIM WOMEN

In the West, the mainstream feminist movement is regarded as secular. Indeed, the relationship between religion and Western feminism has been historically problematic. In order to explore the relationship between feminism and religion, it is important to place it within the context of this problematic history.

Orientalism plays an important role in the identity of the West. The West uses images of the East in order to represent itself. Orientalist discourse offers a body of knowledge about the cultures and peoples of "Oriental" localities as a means of distinguishing between "the Orient" and "the Occident."[35] In doing so, "European culture gained strength and identity by setting itself off against the Orient as a sort of surrogate and underground self."[36] Colonial fantasies of Muslim women as the Other have been used in such constructions of the East.[37]

Not only is the mission of "saving brown women" an important part in colonialist ideology, but this logic is entrenched in white women's consciousness and resurfaces in Western feminist discourses on religion.[38] In the colonies, white women, although disadvantaged as women, benefited from their class and racial privileges, and they were far from innocent, using the supposedly backward image of the indigenous women to promote their own emancipation.[39] This scenario is mirrored in the current context whereby some Western feminists during (and some before) September 2001 focused on the women under the Taliban, constructing these women as "exoticized others" and paradigmatic victims in need of salvation by Western feminists and hence failing to consider these women as equal.[40] Similarly, with regards to freeing Muslim women from the veil, Western feminists are imposing their ideas of freedom and liberation on these women. In doing so, Western feminists can affirm their own identity as free, equal, and liberated women by presenting the women of the Orient, Muslim women, as the oppressed Other.[41] This can be characterized as Orientalist feminism.[42]

IS MULTICULTURALISM BAD FOR WOMEN?

Orientalist feminism is most evident in the work of Susan Moller Okin, who argued that multiculturalism within Western societies undermines the fundamental basis of gender equality. She criticizes the Western liberal tradition for recognizing value in the existence of cultural diversity, proposing an assimilationist model of the integration of immigrants.[43] Her claim is that all cultures are patriarchal; however, some are more patriarchal than others. In particular, she argues that cultural minorities claiming group rights or multicultural accommodation are often more patriarchal in their practices than the surrounding cultures.[44] Therefore, she argues, such women need rescuing from their own culture, adding that minority women who are "locked in a more patriarchal minority culture in a less patriarchal majority culture . . . may be better off if the culture in which they were born were either to become extinct or preferably . . . be encouraged to alter itself so to reinforce the equality of women."[45] In recent years, particularly in post-7/7 Britain, such ideas have become prevalent in British society, evident in discussions in the media around the question of Muslim veiling.[46]

The view that Muslim women need rescuing is particularly disconcerting, as is Orientalist feminism in its attempt to "save brown women," has ended up attacking brown men and colluding with the masculinist-imperial hegemony, complementing an aggressive foreign policy in the Middle East as well as the anti-Muslim racism that has flourished in Europe and North America.[47] Its central tenet is that Western values of gender equality are superior to the values of the developing world. This position assumes a binary relationship between the West and the Orient, such that the West is progressive and is the best place for women, whereas the Orient is backward and the worst place for women. Second, women of the Orient are assumed to be passive victims of oppression rather than active social agents of transformation.[48] This argument fails to recognize the ways in which women contest power hierarchies within cultural groups, as well as the extent to which women themselves value their cultural or religious membership.[49] Finally, such feminists assume that all societies in the East are homogenous, that all Muslim women live under the same conditions, and that these conditions are brought with women when they migrate to the West.[50]

FEMINISM, MULTICULTURALISM, AND ESSENTIALISM

Okin's position was unattractive to many feminists because of its implicit hierarchies of cultures and an arrogant assertion of one true path to gender equality.[51] However, for some feminists, this opposition to Okin's view ran the risk of abandoning universal values and normative criticisms of practices deemed oppressive to women. Anne Phillips cites Okin in arguing that claims made on behalf of culture are often the ones that benefit the interests of the powerful in that group, namely, men. For Phillips, this view is not one with which many feminists would disagree.[52] However, she considers it important to reject the racist Othering of other cultures, without feminists having to curb their criticisms to avoid reproducing such stereotypes. She perceives a need to reconcile the normative commitment to both gender equality and multiculturalism. For Phillips, the solution lies in rejecting essentialist notions of culture.

To essentialize is "to impute a fundamental, basic, absolutely necessary constitutive quality to a person, social category, ethnic group, religious community or nation."[53] This approach posits a false timeless continuity or boundedness ignoring the internal contestations and processes of change,[54] thereby obscuring the relational aspects of the group or culture by the failure to see the way in which particular groups evolve through dialogue.[55]

Such a philosophical position of antiessentialism is increasingly fashionable within the sociological literature on identity politics, which has grown since the postmodern turn in sociology. The antiessentialist rejection of coherent notions of identity, groups, community, or culture has implications for its use for both political and analytical purposes. Nira Yuval-Davis claims that in using essentialist categories, multiculturalism constructs all members of an oppressed group as homogenous and in doing so reduces all social locations to one. The political implications are that marginal groups within a particular social category are silenced.[56] In particular, she refers to the rights of women, arguing that multiculturalism can have harmful effects on women in particular, as "different" cultural traditions are often defined in terms of culturally specific gender relations and the control of women's behavior.[57] She cites the example of an Iranian woman who is denied asylum, when escaping from Iran, after refusing to wear the veil on the grounds that "this is your culture." She claims that in emphasizing external difference, internal differentiations between social identities and political values are ignored. This view conflates collective and individual identities, the implication being that simply being a member of a particular social category enables one to speak on behalf of all members of that category,[58] an assumption that is patently false.

Phillips argues that feminists, in becoming aware of the dangers of presuming that other women's experiences coincided with their own, began discussing cultural difference in a way that was similarly problematic, using such essentialist generalizations as "Western culture" and "non-Western cultures." She claims that such a portrait of culture is not only more convenient to conservative members of a cultural group but creates a more exaggerated notion of the otherness of groups different from their own.[59] Such a portrait of culture enables critics of multiculturalism to misrepresent cultural difference as a major source of political instability.

However, what is then to be done when groups themselves invoke identities in ethnic, religious, and racial terms? Rogers Brubaker, in his rejection of "groupism," suggests that simply because participants have understood processes in such vernacular terms does not mean that the analyst must do so too. He claims that this is what "ethnopolitical entrepreneurs" do, for "by invoking groups, they evoke them, summon them, call them into being."[60] He claims that this reification is a social process rather than an "intellectual bad habit."[61] It is central to the process of a politicized ethnicity and is what ethnopolitical groups are "in the business of doing."[62] To criticize ethnopolitical groups for doing so would be to make a category mistake. Rather, he claims, such reification of ethnic groups should not be reinforced through social analysis.[63] Thus, he is not denying that people define themselves in terms of ethnicity; rather, he suggests that what are sometimes assumed to be protagonists of ethnic conflicts are not actually groups but organizations that have a vested interest in having people see themselves in terms of such groups.[64] Thus, he says, "they may live 'off' or live 'for' ethnicity."[65] It is useful, rather, to think of "groupness as an event, as something that 'happens,'" and ethnicity as something that has been made in order to do political work.[66]

However, this chapter argues that using a sense of groupism, culture, or identity in social analysis does not have to lead to such consequences. This view draws on arguments made by Tariq Modood (1998, 2007). Using Wittgenstein's language games, Modood shows how groups can be seen to have what he calls family resemblances without assuming some kind of inherent essence. He suggests that one does not need an essence in order to believe that some ways of thinking and acting have coherence. The example that is used is a game, as everyone knows what a game is; however, there is not one essential feature that defines a game. Rather, there are a number of characteristics that most games share. Therefore, in sharing a variety of combinations of these different characteristics, games resemble each other the way in which family members do. In addition, games change over time; they are made through change, and different games have different levels of changeability.[67] Using such terms as religion, culture, ethnicity, or identity in such a way as an analytical category can be done without reinforcing the reification created by ethnopolitical groups.

Further, it seems that it is those who advocate such a strong sense of antiessentialism that end up denying the role of agency and silencing particular groups. Here, it is useful to invoke Pnina Werbner's useful distinction between types of essentializing. She argues that not all collective cultural representations and self-representations are essentializing in the same way, and she argues that critics of essentialism can, in fact, end up essentializing essentialism, whereby all forms of essentialism are treated as homogenous. She differentiates between two types of essentialism: reification and objectification. In doing so, she argues that reification is the exclusionary process used by racists and xenophobes that acts to distort representation, whereas the process of objectification is a "rightful performance or representation of multiple, valorised and aestheticized identifications."[68] This distinction is an important one. Reification enacts a politics of racism, extreme nationalism, and xenophobia, a violent politics whereby the reified communities "are not imagined situationally but defined as fixed, immoral and dangerous."[69] In demonizing groups, they are reifying them. On the other hand, objectification enacts a positive politics whereby self-essentializing is a "rhetorical performance in which an imagined community is invoked."[70] Such politics serve to construct a moral and aesthetic community imaginatively.[71] Despite the racism and increased antagonism and hostility toward the Muslim community, the events of the Rushdie affair and September 11 have led the Muslim community to mobilize around issues of representation and recognition within British society. In addition to such mobilization, the visibilization process has opened up a space for reflection about the possibility of meanings and the limits of a transnational Muslim subjectivity.[72] However, there is a failure to understand the importance of solidarities and the dialogic nature to which they are established. In particular, solidarities are achievements that tend to be transient and are not simply given. In criticizing the construction of community or culture, however, antiessentialists fail to recognize the importance of participants in moral debates of an imaginative belief in achieved solidarities.[73] The contingency of how such solidarities are achieved should be subject to empirical investigation.

THE RESEARCH METHOD

There has not been any empirical research on Muslim women political activists in Britain. Although a small group of women, these women represent a significant minority whose political activity runs counter to current representations of Muslim women in the media and academic discourses. Rather than producing a piece of work from which generalizations can be drawn to the population as a whole, the aim of my research has been to represent a group that has been neglected or misrepresented in current academic, policy, and media discussions. I have tried to avoid using an essentialist notion of identity. By focusing on the questions of identity within a movement that is not explicitly forged around a particular social category, this moves away from the assumption that these identities are given or assumed.

THE SAMPLE: RECRUITMENT AND REPRESENTATION

The sample consisted of seven Respect Party activists (six of which were members and one of which was more loosely related to the organization in a coalition). The profile of the participants can be found in Table 4.1 (including age, ethnicity, inside or outside London, political role or position, and occupation).

Table 4.1 Profile of Participants

Name	Age	Ethnicity	Political position	City
Aisha	28	Bangladeshi	Stood as a local councillor	London
Malika	25	Bangladeshi	Stood as a local councillor	London
Sahar	23	Kenya	Student union sabbatical	Outside London
Sofia	24	Pakistani	Stood as local councillor	London
Samiya	24	Pakistani	Student union Sabbatical	London
Shazia	30	Pakistani	Stood as local councillor	Outside London
Hana	21	Yemeni	Student union part time sabbatical	Outside London

This sample was a theoretically informed sample in that the individuals were chosen for the particular characteristics they had of being Muslim women Respect Party political activists. There are a small number of Muslim women Respect political party activists, and they are dispersed across the country. The study focused on women in two cities, one in London and one outside London (the exact location is concealed to sustain the participants' anonymity). A further aim was to get a balance between women involved in their local communities and women involved in student politics, although this distinction proved to be futile because women involved in the latter tended to also be involved in the former. In terms of their religiosity, I chose women who described themselves as "practicing" Muslims in order to get a sense of the relationship between religious and political ideas.

The sample was obtained using a snowballing technique, where initial contact with a few members of the population leads to further contact.[74] Two lines of contact were utilized: I attended a women-only conference organized by the Respect Party on women's issues where I met some of my participants for the first time. Through the women I met at the conference, I managed to recruit two more respondents. Also, to recruit the rest of the participants, I used contacts that I had made in the Stop the War Coalition and in Respect through my own previous involvement in the antiwar movement since 2003. This sampling strategy meant that the respondents trusted me, since I was seen to have credibility in my interest and in the intentions of my research.[75]

Islamic Feminism and New Conceptions of the Community?

Post-9/11 Muslim Identity: Increased Visibility and Internal Reflection

The presence of a distinctive Muslim identity among these Muslim women was unequivocal and most (five of the seven) gave this aspect of their identity primacy over others, described by Sofia as "I'm Muslim first, I'm everything else second." This response confirms that there is growing identification among British Muslims with the religious aspect of their identity. Although this aspect of their identity held privilege over their political identity, their understanding of their religion was inherently political in that politicization and increased dedication to their religion came simultaneously. The importance of their religion was established when there was what a few referred to as a wake-up call for Muslims, that is, a sudden realization of the importance of politics and religion in the wake of September 11 and the war on terrorism. They referred to the intensification of Islamophobia, which has for many Muslims created an urgent need for forming solidarities.[76]

Some study participants drew explicit parallels between the injustices in their own lives and international injustices:

> The funny thing, from when I started uni[versity], September 11 happened and all those things, war on Afghanistan, war on Iraq. Everything that was going on around the world and was running parallel to what I was going through at uni[versity] . . . I kept thinking god man this is my small little life and that's like the big wide world and it's the same thing, it's just injustice. (Sofia discussing her experience of racial discrimination at university)

A few referred to how they had started thinking more about their religion, moving from being merely "cultural Muslims" in the way that they had been brought up toward becoming "practicing Muslims" who questioned the habitual practices of their religion:

> I questioned my identity . . . the more it made me question who I am, where I am coming from, what's the purpose of my life. The more I questioned myself, the more I found roots in Islam and that's when I actually felt compelled. I knew who I was, I was accepting myself and for me, September 11 happened and everything else, but before that it was easy going every day without thinking, and once you start thinking, once you know what the answer is, there is nothing that stops you. (Malika in group interview)

> Basically, the way I had been brought up, basically I would pray five times a day and fast, do the sort of normal things without actually

thinking about why I am doing it, so I'd do it because it's a good thing, but not completely understanding why. (Samiya, individual interview)

As mentioned, the process of visibility of British Muslims, namely, through the Rushdie affair and now, September 11, has meant that these women are in the full light of the public gaze. This gaze has stimulated a process of self-reflection; however, September 11 is one factor in a wider set of processes. This form of self-questioning comes as a result of the conditions created in being part of a religious diaspora.[77] The context of religious pluralism coupled with the heightened visibility of Islam means that these women, as believers, are in a context wherein it is necessary to justify elements of belief to nonmembers.[78] As a result, they are compelled to justify their status with regards to their religion, particularly as these women are engaged in political activity with non-Muslims of a left-wing or socialist orientation.

Their rationalization for this identity was articulated through the Islamic conception of social justice, through which these women developed a coherent identity that "made sense." Their political and religious views merged into a coherent moral and ethical system of belief. However, the focus seemed to be less on the spiritual or supernatural aspect of their religious views and more on practical social action:

For me it was because it was an Islamic obligation to care, to fight for social justice, so that is kind of where [I am], I mean my political awareness kind of actually came at a time when I, like religiously, I was looking more into Islam as well, so it kind of came hand-in-hand with that, so when I started reading more about Islam this kind of took precedent [sic] with it. (Hana, individual interview)

Islam and politics go hand-in-hand because Islam is a way of life, not a religion, gives you politics, economics, social. Given us everything, everything in life, join in what's right, forbid what's wrong. The politics in this country today is a perfect way of trying to get involved and do something that is part of religion. (Sofia in group interview)

A few of these women refer to their religion as "a way of life," stressing the importance of social action as opposed to internal spiritual reflection. Islam has, for these women, become a political badge of opposition, the tool of contesting injustice and creating, as Samiya said, a "way forward" in intervention in politics. Their Islamic identity has moved beyond personal belief.[79]

In contrast to what seemed to be articulated as the consensual view evident in the collective voice found in the group interview, Shazia explicitly rejected the way in which other Muslims, particularly those who, like her, were "Muslim women activists," privileged their Muslim rather than their political identity in a climate of hostility:

> I think there's a problem because unfortunately when you get cornered, and I think that's what's happening in Britain, Muslims are feeling cornered and threatened, it does bring out that Muslim in you because that's what you've been threatened on, do you know what I mean? So you cling on to that more and in a sense I think it's a level of lack of confidence in a way, a lack of maturity for a lot of Muslim activists who see themselves at first as Muslim not as activists.

She rejected what she saw as identity-led identification with Islam imposed by external factors, namely, Islamophobia. She thought that this was accepting the terms being sold to them by "buying in to that agenda." In her view, by seeing themselves as Muslim activists, these women are selling themselves short, not taking themselves seriously as activists, because they are not seeing themselves as legitimate activists in general but have to be Muslim ones.

Sahar also defined herself in a way that does not fit with the majority view. Although she understands the rationale for bringing the two together, she suggests a complete separation between her politics and her religion. Instead, she stresses the importance of her personal identity, stressing that she is just being herself and is not concerned with reconciling seemingly contradictory aspects of her identity:

> It makes it difficult because a lot of the time I've been working for the union a lot of people would get used to me because I'm not that extreme, I'd be dead open minded and stuff like even guys like; people see me talking to guys and say bloody hell you're a Muslim, you're not supposed to be talking to guys and stuff but it's different for me. I don't know why, although I've got this on my head, my personality is totally different. I'm easy going and I've got a self-confidence in myself as well.

"AMBASSADOR OF OUR OWN RELIGION": ISLAMIC FEMINISM, SEPARATING RELIGION, AND CULTURE FOR A DISCOURSE OF WOMEN'S RIGHTS

The visibility of Muslim women is through Islamic dress as signifier of their difference.[80] Most women draw attention to the stereotypical way in which they are perceived as victims of oppressive patriarchal relationships with the men in their lives, particularly with regards to their decision to wear the headscarf. Sofia, Samiya, and Malika refer to how people asked them if they had married once they started wearing the *hijab*, mimicking the attitude that people have toward them for wearing the headscarf:

Samiya: "I got asked if I got married."
[All laugh.]
Sofia: "Are you married? Because once you got married, your husband made you."
Malika: "You poor thing, he must beat you up as well [!]"

The attitude toward Muslim women wearing the *hijab* is not perceived just in terms of their wearing of the headscarf but in other areas of their life—including having children, engaging in domestic labor, being involved in politics, and having the ability to make decisions in their own lives. One of the women stresses why this makes it important for them as Muslim women to be involved in politics in order to act as an "ambassador of our own religion":

I realized that we have to constantly interact with these people to make them realize that if they have dialogue with us, they will realize that we're not dumb, we're not stupid, and we're not tied to the kitchen sink. . . . We have got other roles and it's not like once you are married, what are you going to give up? I'm not going to give up anything; every-thing else comes in addition to that. The more people wear the *hijab* and get more involved, that's when people are gonna take us seriously. (Malika in group interview)

In becoming an "ambassador of their religion," with one exception they all invoke a sense of Islamic feminism:

There is something that I always campaign for, which is not feminism but Islamic feminism. But even that is in a sense I don't agree with. I've come to think about the term and thought, no, even the term Islamic feminism shouldn't really be used because if we look at Islam itself there are rights for women in there, so we wouldn't need a feminist move-ment. But in terms of simplifying things, I would say, yes, I'm an Islamic feminist. (Hana, individual interview)

Others have invoked Islamic feminism more implicitly in the sense that they have not directly referred to themselves as Islamic feminists but have drawn on the ideas made evident by Islamic feminist scholars, draw-ing on the early years of the Prophet's life and the role his wives played in society. Islamic feminism is not used in such a way that it is what drives the political movement in which these women are engaged. Rather, it is an attitude that highlights the role that gender plays in the organization of society. It is a tool that can be used for highlighting the injustice of particular situations that are derived from expectations and norms governing men and women's behavior:[81]

> I mean during the Prophet's time, the Prophet's wife, when it came to the battle, she was at the forefront of the battle. So we've seen in our Islamic history it was allowed for us and so it's always happened and it's just these *stupid cultured Muslim men* that take everything away and we have to identify our identity. (Malika in group interview)

By "cultured Muslim men," Malika is suggesting that the sexist ideas of the men are a product of culture rather than religion. Therefore, a discourse of women's rights is negotiated by separating religion from culture. This notion is articulated by other women:

> I mean, even Muslims themselves tend to merge Islam and culture, 'cos if you actually look at the Islamic teachings, there is nothing in there that women should be forced into marriage to someone back home or whatever. (Hana, individual interview)

> It actually says in the Qur'an that if your wife cooks and cleans for you she is doing you a favor for you, not that's her role (Sofia in group interview)[82]

> A lot of things are culture, Prophet helped his wife, it's not a woman's job, if a woman does it she is doing him a favor, it's not her role. (Samiya in group interview)

The separation of culture from religion in favor of a "true" or "pure" Islam can be seen in context of a development of new positions in which Muslim women have managed their faith and culture for an acquisition of women's rights.[83] This development is in line with new Muslim political communities, in which different conceptions of Islam are articulated and new critical capacities emerge.[84] Reflection in a situation whereby Muslim women are active in a political movement of mainly non-Muslims allows them to develop their own responses to challenges and situations they deal with as Muslims. By invoking a sense of Islamic feminism, they are not only allowing themselves to be "European without breaking with Islam,"[85] but they are also able to assume a public political role without compromising their religious beliefs.

The ability to develop their own responses as Muslims is important because these women are negotiating a gendered political space within their own community. There was an explicit struggle with the men in their community for acceptance of their right to participate in public life. This became evident when the study participants discussed their experiences of standing for election; in particular, Shazia, Malika, and Aisha referred to how some men were going around saying, "Don't vote for her, she's a woman, she won't do a proper job." Thus, it seems that by calling upon Islamic feminism, they are invoking what Werbner referred to as "commonsensical embodied truths"; and although these truths seem self-evident to them, they are denied by some males in their community.[86] In Werbner's research on Al Masoom Trust, she illustrated that this was part of a wider transformation in the Pakistani ethnic public arena during the 1990s whereby the authority of the Pakistani male elders became contested. One of the key processes in the transformation was the emergence of a gendered and familial Pakistani space of voluntary action.[87] Similarly, the invocation of Islamic feminism by the women interviewed in this research can be seen as part of a wider process in their communities of negotiating not only a gendered public space of political action but one that reimagines the whole community along gendered lines. In doing so, they can be seen to be engaged in acts of creativity,[88] acts whereby they have contested the hegemony of male leaders of the community in their monopoly over the political sphere in the community. This allows them, therefore, to challenge the binaries of "traditional" and "modern,"[89] whereby modern connotes those who reject religious values and essentially assimilate Western notions of how they should be liberated as women. It is often assumed that Muslim women who are successful in academic or employment terms reject their religion and culture.[90] Hence, Islamic feminism can be a useful tool for these women because they can use it to reject such binaries. Their success in entering the public sphere through their political activity does not have to result in a rejection of their religious values but can, in fact, act as a defense of them.

The only woman who did not invoke a sense of Islamic feminism was Sahar. Her personal identity was what seemed most important to her; unlike the others, she did not see her religious identity in similar political terms. Therefore she felt no need to negotiate a set of rights from her religion; she simply rejected those aspects she did not personally like, without having a desire for a consistent system of belief:

I think it's basically because it's a religion and it's all about men doing the hard work and women staying at home being housewives and things like that. Obviously this has always been the subject of debate; even in

the media and so on, they always say Muslim women are treated as stereotypes. But I don't know; I feel that I'm different and even my family
don't seem to control me. I just see myself as a free person. I don't want
to get myself involved in things that are limiting. I don't know, maybe
other women have a different perspective.

REPRESENTING THE COMMUNITY: NEW LABOUR, MUSLIM MEN, AND THE "UNCLES' CLUB"

As mentioned, the Muslim community is imagined in gendered terms. In
particular, there is a dichotomy between the aggressive male fundamentalist and the passive, gentle Muslim woman, subject to violence from the
male aggressor. However, some researchers have shown how gendered
divisions within Islam are distinct from what has been envisaged by the
protagonists on either side of the Islamophobic divide. In so doing, they
contrast the multiplicity of identities among the women they interviewed
within the boundedness of combative male political Islam in such organizations as Hizb-ut-Tahrir, which sees Islam as an antagonistic force in the
United Kingdom.[91]

Similarly, my interviews have shown that the gendered divisions within
the Muslim community are distinct from what is imagined in popular discourse. In particular, the dichotomy between the passive, well-behaved
Muslim women and the aggressive, "bad" Muslim men can be rejected.
These women envisage their political identity and what constitutes the
boundaries of a legitimate political community as a struggle against what
one refers to as the "uncles' club." For Muslim women, the uncles' club
represents those they see as their political antagonists, the men who have
worked very closely with New Labour and hold positions of power with
regards to state bureaucracy or large government-funded Muslim organizations. As politicians, mosque leaders, or leaders of Muslim organizations,
these "uncles" are seen to be claiming to represent the Muslim community; yet for these women, they represent a real sense of betrayal.

Three problems arise from the power that these men wield. First,
these men are perceived as holding Muslim women back from political
action:

It is very difficult for Muslim women to do anything, because firstly, the
whole society has difficulty in accepting them and then you have the
Muslims that you have to fight, and if you push the community too far,
they say ooh, she's a tart, she wants to associate with men. You are

constantly being attacked left, right, and center. Even though you are trying to fight for the community, it is often the community that holds you back. (Malika in group interview)

Second, the women rejected the way these powerful and influential men had devised distinct constructions of Muslim masculinity and made clear that these distinctions contrasted with the way they saw the men in their own lives, stressing that not all Muslim men were bad and that it was these corrupt individuals who gave them a bad name:

It's not the Muslim men, it is the corrupt Labour councillor.

I realized that all Muslim men ain't bad because my dad isn't and he's [one of] the ones that are pushing us to get involved [with politics]. And my brothers are the second guys I see around and they're always pushing us [to get involved with politics], "You should do this, you should do that," so for when people generalize all Muslim men, that's not what it's like for me because that's not what it's like in my house-hold. (Malika, individual interview)

The third issue was representation. For these women, the leadership of these powerful men leads to a representational deficit for Muslims, con-stituting one of the main reasons that these women were attracted to Respect. Muslim politicians were seen to "backstab the Muslim commun-ities that elected them" in that they were "dictatorial" and "corrupt," as well as unprincipled, in that they "vote blind like sheep."

Such Muslim organizations as the Muslim Council of Britain (MCB) and the Federation of Student Islamic Societies (FOSIS) were rejected on similar grounds. Only Aisha said something positive about MCB; that they were "generally a good thing"; but she added, "I don't like groups keeping themselves to themselves." The rest were much more overtly critical of such organizations for their pro-government stance. They are described as "self-appointed leaders of the Muslim community" (Shazia) and "Blair's version of moderate Muslims" (Sofia and Malika in group interview). Sahar was critical from personal experience with FOSIS, where she had been rejected from a meeting as a result of her political alliance with Respect and her gay candidacy for president of the National Union of Students (NUS). FOSIS refused to support her candidacy despite her being the black students officer for NUS and from a Muslim background.

A CONCRETE CONCEPTION OF THE UMMA?

As a result and in response to such exclusionary practices, it appears the Muslim women in my study have articulated alternative conceptions of *umma*, or Islamic political community. This concept of community seems to exist among all these women, and the question of the authentic author of that community is important to all of them. There are two dimensions to the way in which these women reconceptualize the political community: the community as "the movement" and the community as "locality." These notions run in direct contrast to the invocation of the Muslim political community as the universal transnational identity bringing together Muslims across all divisions. The concept of the political community for these women is asserted in far more concrete terms with respect to their political engagement on the ground rather than an appeal to an abstract global community.

THE COMMUNITY AS "THE MOVEMENT" AND "LOCALITY"

For Shazia the concept of community seems to be manifested in what she describes as "people on the ground," whereby the people who are legitimately representing the community are grassroots activists. When talking about selecting a candidate for local elections, she says:

> I really thought this, I will meet someone that can represent that community and then it dawned on me that actually Respect is different. It's not about having a figurehead, you can't go and say Respect is about activists and people on the ground and then think you're just gonna go and pull somebody in and say right, you're it.

This sense of an organic activist developing from the movement is for Shazia what gives her legitimacy. She says:

> I sometimes joke and say the only reason that I was selected is because I'm a Muslim and I wear the *hijab*, but I don't actually think that's why I got selected; I really think I saw myself *as representative of the movement*. (emphasis added)

Shazia's view of her own legitimacy stands in contrast to how she sees the MCB: "To me they are nonexistent, there's never been anyone I've recognized." She therefore contrasts what she sees as legitimate grassroots activists who have done a lot of Stop the War campaigning on the ground with these "self-appointed leaders" who are "nonexistent." They are irrelevant because they have not been fighting the struggle where it counts. This assessment also reflects how she and many others view Muslim MPs and councillors in their area. For example, she says what she liked about Respect was that its leaders were

> not real politicians in the sense of being politicians for the sake of being politicians, and that was the difference. They were already fighting for

stuff, and where have you seen a Lib or Labour candidate or any of them? These are people I already know doing stuff, and I think that was really it. I really saw it as something different, it wasn't having a position of power.

This view is not exclusive to Shazia, for others express similar sentiments. For example, Sofia says about losing her election:

I never really wanted to be a councillor, *I'm not a career politician.* For me it's not something I ever had the ambition to be, for me I was just a Respect Stop the War campaigner. From the whole time that I'd been involved in these things I had always wanted, I just wanted to be part of the movement really. (emphasis added)

Although Shazia's sentiment is evident in others, for them it seems to take a slightly different emphasis. Whereas Shazia's focus is on the movement and Stop the War, the others seem to stress the importance of helping the local community and addressing the issues of local people. They saw their politics as very much about having people come knocking on their door and providing them with services:

I don't feel like a real politician 'cos the way we work in Newham is very strange, it's like a *community project you're all working for a better community* [emphasis added]. (Malika, individual interview)

Basically, when I got involved in politics, even now, now that I'm more involved day-by-day, it's my religion saying *serve your community* [emphasis added], do something good for other people. (Aisha, individual interview)

Such locally based political action was contrasted against the emphasis many Muslims place on the international concerns of Muslims. The concept of the Muslim *umma* is often reinvented by many young British-born Muslims through romantic solidarities with Muslims as victims in Palestine, Kosovo, the Gulf, Chechnya, and Kashmir.[92] Malika, who works for an Islamic charity, contrasts her colleagues' emphasis on the concerns of Muslims internationally with her own focus on local matters:

I strongly believe that what I am doing in the community is the right cause of action because the way I see it, you can't help people abroad if you can't help people locally. So I mean you can think globally and act locally, but I don't think a lot of people see it like that. (Malika, individual interview)

Rather than invoking a sense of the *umma* by focusing on the charitable appeal of helping those abroad, Malika draws attention to the way those who invoke the *umma* neglect the community at home. Hence, she sees the key to helping such an *umma* through the serving of her local community. In the literature on British Muslims, there is little documentation of how the experience of the *umma* is actualized in lived experience, the focus being more on how it is imagined rather than concretely manifested.[93]

In summary, the consensus found among the Muslim women study participants through the group interview and individual interviews was that they made an explicit link between politics and religion. The increased public domain of their religion has led to increased internal reflection such that they have turned more explicitly toward their religion. In doing so, they have referred to the Islamic conception of social justice to justify the relationship between the two. However, the relationship between their politics and religion seemed to need further justification within their community, particularly with regards to the supposed contradiction between Islam and women's rights. Thus, these women have invoked a sense of Islamic feminism that allows them to reconcile their commitment to gender equality and their commitment to their religion. This reconciliation can be situated as part of a wider process of articulation and rearticulation taking place within Islam whereby there has been the creation of new conceptions of what constitutes the Muslim community.[94] Their use of Islamic feminism gives these women a gendered space to articulate such conceptions of their community. This community is not imagined as the Muslim *umma*, that is, a universal conception that transcends divisions of race, ethnicity, class, and gender. Rather, their conception is far less abstract, grounded in political action in the "movement" or "locality" in direct opposition to what they see as the dominant forces in the community. Far from being seen as one of unity, the community is imagined as working through antagonisms between them and those whom they see as betraying the community.

Therefore, the ways in which these women have negotiated their identity presents an interesting example of what Werbner refers to as an objectification process whereby certain meanings of identity or community are invoked in order to challenge the process of essentialism. This is a dialogic process whereby these solidarities are not given but develop "situationally in opposition to other moral and aesthetic communities."[95]

CONCLUSION: POSTCOLONIALISM, ISLAMIC FEMINISM, AND SECULARISM

This chapter has shown how a group of Muslim women have become political activists since September 11 and have engaged in negotiating a positive political role for themselves within their community. Their invocation of Islamic feminism has provided a challenge to the liberal and feminist skepticism of religious identities, particularly with regard to its relationship with gender equality. In recent years, the development of postcolonial theory has meant that there is an increased literature exploring the relationship between race, gender, and sexuality in the context of colonialism. However, little attention is paid to religion in the context of these debates.[96] There is now an established critique of liberal Western (white) feminism proposed by black feminists and more recently by postcolonial feminists of the ethnocentrism and imperial mentality of the liberal Western tradition of feminism. Black feminists highlight the ethnocentrism of Western feminism in prioritizing certain struggles over others, for example, abortion rights and critiques of the family. In doing so, there is a failure of such feminism to understand the experience or the struggles of women of color or of the third world. They critique the lack of political importance attributed to the antiracist struggle among Western feminism, which results in a failure to understand that black women are oppressed not only by men but also by whites.[97] Proponents of black feminism have begun to develop antiessentialist arguments around black subjectivity and identity as a political category in favor of more fluid notions and marginal perspectives.[98]

Similar arguments can be put forward with regard to religion; however, because of the absence of a religious category in understandings of racism, this has been neglected. Religion, unlike race or even ethnicity, is with few exceptions not given the same attention as a hybrid or fluid form of identity.[99] With regards to feminism, this neglect has meant that there are assumptions made about religion, particularly Islam, which are similar in nature to the way in which black identities were treated by liberal Western feminism prior to the development of the critique.

Yuval-Davis presents a clear example of this. Although accepting many of the critiques of black feminism and the postmodern critique of essentialist identities (in fact, she is one of the proponents of such critiques), she argues that there is nonetheless a tendency for them to assume an essentialist understanding of religion, that is, that religion is inherently bad for women. Such an assumption becomes problematic when women themselves use their religion as means of fighting for liberation. Yuval-Davis claims, however, that where there is a secular space available, political movements of liberation should assume a secular stance, arguing that "using Islam for your discourse of liberation only gives power to religious leaders who claim it as the only authority."[100] She claims that giving up feminism as a secular discourse results in accepting that there is an essential homogenous

"Islamic" position on women, whereby women's difference is constructed as their roles as wives and mothers. She claims that religion and culture creates racialized exclusions toward women who are not part of those collectivities and that hence there is a need for secular spaces.[101]

First, in claiming that Islamic feminism results in the exclusion of non-Muslims, one can easily argue that secularism results in the exclusion of Muslims. Such a claim rests on the assumption of the neutrality of secularism, where there is a traditional separation between private and public spheres with regards to matters of identity, one that was undermined by feminists and antiracists in the demand to be recognized in the public sphere.[102] The position of the assumed neutrality of secularism rests on age-old Orientalist arguments. In assuming that secularism is more neutral, one is led to assume that secularism is superior. This view relies on ideas of religion as inherently backward and irrational (a product of the East, or Orient), whereas secularism is considered to be progressive and modern (a product of the West, or Occident). Thus, the former is ultimately bad for women, and the latter can offer freedom. Such a claim essentializes religion and simply reproduces Orientalist binarisms. It fails to treat religion as something that is situated within particular social contexts and that hence is fluid in terms of how it can be developed and used. Furthermore, the debate around the question of Islamic feminism is often confined to discussions in Muslim majority countries.[103] The debate assumes that Muslim women who are in the secular West would never consider a religious feminist ideology. Although Islamic feminism began in Muslim majority countries, it has become increasingly more widespread in non-Muslim countries among women to whom both religion and gender equality are important.[104] As mentioned, this reinterpretation of their religion is part of a wider phenomenon of new political communities developing within Islam, where key concepts are being revised. Islamic feminism is invoked as a way of refusing particular boundaries that are drawn out for women. It is used to reject the claim that Islam is necessarily more traditional than other identifications and to argue that their commitments to gender equality are an expansion rather than a rejection of their faith. In doing so, they are linking their religious, political, and individual gender identities in order to claim simultaneously seemingly contradictory allegiances in their political activity.[105] Since there are multiple representations of Muslim women, they develop multiple critiques. This is a "multi-layered discourse that allows them to engage with and criticize the various individuals, institutions, and systems that limit and oppress them while making sure that they are not caught in their own rhetoric."[106]

NOTES

1. Tariq Modood, *Multicultural Politics: Racism, Ethnicity, and Muslims in Britain* (Edinburgh: Edinburgh University Press, 2005), 149.

2. Tariq Modood, "Anti-essentialism, Multiculturalism and the 'Recognition' of Religious Groups," *Journal of Political Philosophy* 6, no. 4 (1998): 378–99.

3. P. Statham, "Political Mobilisation by Minorities in Britain: A Negative Feedback of 'Race Relations'?" *Journal of Ethnic and Migration Studies* 25, no. 4 (1999): 606.

4. L. Fekete, "Anti-Muslim Racism and the European Security State," *Race and Class* 46, no. 1 (2004): 3.

5. R. Grillo, "Islam and Transnationalism," *Journal of Ethnic and Migration Studies* 30, no. 5 (2004): 861.

6. P. Mandaville, *Transnational Muslim Politics: Reimagining the Umma* (London: Routledge, 2004), 116.

7. Ibid., 135.

8. Ibid., 187.

9. Ibid., 136.

10. Ibid., 139.

11. Ibid., 88.

12. Ibid., 136.

13. Ibid., 140.

14. Tariq Modood and Fauzia Ahmad, "British Muslim Perspectives on Multiculturalism," *Theory, Culture and Society* 24, no. 2 (2007): 198–97.

15. See Fauzia Ahmed, "Modern Traditions? British Muslim Women and Academic Achievement," *Gender and Education* 13, no. 2 (2001): 137–52.

16. Mandaville, *Transnational Muslim Politics*, 142.

17. On the Al Masoom (Innocent) Foundation, see, for example, P. Werbner, "Public Spaces, Political Voices: Gender, Feminism and Aspects of British Muslim Participation in the Public Sphere," in *Political Participation and Identities of Muslims in Non-Muslim States*, ed. W. A. R. Shahid and P. S. van Koningsveld (Kampen, Neth.: Kok Pharos Publishing House, 1996), 53–70. Al Masoom was a charitable body based in Manchester in the 1990s. It was run by Muslim women focused on organizing aid to such embattled parts of the Muslim world as Kashmir or Bosnia.

18. See H. Afshar, R. Aitken, and M. Franks, "Feminisms, Islamophobia and Identities," *Political Studies* 53, no. 2 (2005): 262–83.

19. C. Alexander, "Imagining the Asian Gang: Ethnicity, Masculinity and Youth after 'the Riots,'" *Critical Social Policy* 24, no. 4 (2004): 534–35.

20. See ibid.; L. Archer, "'Muslim Brothers, Black Lads and Traditional Asians': British Muslim Young Men's Constructions of Race, Religion and

Masculinity," *Feminism and Psychology* 11, no. 1 (2001): 79–105; and M. Macey, "Class, Gender and Religious Influences on Changing Patterns of Pakistani Muslim Male Violence in Bradford," *Ethnic and Racial Studies* 22, no. 5 (1999): 845–66.

21. G. Sanghera and S. Thapar-Björkert, "'Because I am Pakistani . . . and I am Muslim . . . I am political': Gendering Political Radicalism: Young Femininities in Bradford," in *Islamic Political Radicalism: A European Perspective*, ed. T. Abbas (Edinburgh: Edinburgh University Press, 2007), 178.

22. Fauzia Ahmad, "Sign of the Times," *BBK Magazine* 15, 2003, http://www.bbk.ac.uk/news/bbkmag/15/signs.html.

23. See Sanghera and Thapar-Björkert, "'Because I Am Pakistani'"; Afshar et al., "Feminisms, Islamophobia and Identities."

24. Afshar et al., "Feminisms, Islamophobia and Identities," 262.

25. K. Brown, "Realising Muslim Women's Rights: The Role of Islamic Identity amongst British Muslim Women," *Women's Studies International Forum* 29, no. 4 (2006): 417–30.

26. Sanghera and Thapar-Björkert, "'Because I am Pakistani,'" 187.

27. See Saba Mahmood, *Politics of Piety: The Islamic Revival and the Feminist Subject* (Princeton, NJ: Princeton University Press, 2005).

28. See C. Dywer, "Veiled Meanings: British Muslim Women and the Negotiation of Differences," *Gender, Place and Culture* 6 (1999): 5–26.

29. See A. Brah, "'Race' and 'Culture' in the Gendering of Labour Markets: South Asian Young Muslim Women and the Labour Market," *New Community* 29 (1993): 441–58.

30. See Ahmad, "Modern Traditions?", 137.

31. Saba Mahmood, "Feminist Theory, Embodiment, and the Docile Agent: Some Reflections on the Egyptian Islamic Revival," *Cultural Anthropology* 16, no. 2 (2001): 203.

32. A. Phillips, *Multiculturalism without Culture* (Princeton, NJ: Princeton University Press, 2007), 1.

33. Gayatri Chakravorty Spivak, "Can the Subaltern Speak?" in *Marxism and the Interpretation of Culture*, ed. C. Nelson and L. Grossberg (Basingstoke, Hants, UK: Macmillan Education, 1988), 296, cited by Kwok Pui-lan, "Unbinding Our Feet: Saving Brown Women and Feminist Religious Discourse," in *Postcolonialism, Feminism and Religious Discourse*, ed. L. E. Donaldson and K. Pui-lan (London: Routledge, 2002), 64.

34. Phillips, *Multiculturalism without Culture*, 1.

35. M. Yeğenoğlu, *Colonial Fantasies: Towards a Feminist Reading of Orientalism* (Cambridge: Cambridge University Press, 1998), 15.

36. Edward Said, *Orientalism* (London: Penguin, 2003), 3.

37. See, for example, Leila Ahmed, *Women and Gender in Islam: Historical Roots of a Modern Debate* (New Haven, CT: Yale University Press, 1992).

38. Pui-lan, "Unbinding Our Feet," 63.

39. E. Midden, "Faith in Feminism: Rethinking the Relationship between Religion, Secularism and Gender Equality" (unpublished paper, 2007), 13.

40. I. Young, "The Logic of Masculinist Protection: Reflections on the Current Security State," *Signs: Journal of Women in Culture and Society* 29, no. 1 (2003): 19.

41. M. Yeğenoğlu, "Sartorial Fabrications: Enlightenment and Western Feminism," in *Postcolonialism, Feminism and Religious Discourse*, ed. Donaldson and Pui-lan, 84.

42. R. Bahramitash, "The War on Terror, Feminist Orientalism and Orientalist Feminism: Case Studies of Two North American Bestsellers," *Critique: Critical Middle Eastern Studies* 14, no. 2 (2005): 221.

43. See Susan Moller Okin, "Is Multiculturalism Bad for Women?" in *Is Multiculturalism Bad for Women?* ed. J. Cohen, M. Howard, and M. C. Nussbaum (Princeton, NJ: Princeton University Press, 1999), 7–26.

44. Phillips, *Multiculturalism without Culture*, 1.

45. Okin, "Is Multiculturalism Bad for Women?" 22.

46. See, for example, Deborah Orr, "Why This Picture Offends Me," *The Independent*, July 8, 2006, and Polly Toynbee, "Only a Fully Secular State Can Protect Women's Rights," *The Independent*, October 17, 2006.

47. Bahramitash, "The War on Terror," 223; L. Fekete, "Enlightenment Fundamentalism? Immigration, Feminism and the Right," *Race and Class* 48, no. 2 (2006): 12.

48. Bahramitash, "The War on Terror," 222.

49. Phillips, *Multiculturalism without Culture*, 26.

50. Bahramitash, "The War on Terror," 222.

51. Phillips, *Multiculturalism without Culture*, 2.

52. Ibid.

53. P. Werbner, "Essentialising Essentialism, Essentialising Silence: Ambivalence and Multiplicity in the Constructions of Racism and Ethnicity," in *Debating Cultural Hybridity: Multi-cultural Identities and the Politics of Anti-racism*, ed. P. Werbner and T. Modood (London: Zed Books, 1997), 228.

54. Phillips, *Multiculturalism without Culture*, 27.

55. Werbner, "Essentialising Essentialism," 228.

56. N. Yuval-Davis, "Intersectionality and Feminist Politics," *European Journal of Women's Studies* 13, no. 3 (2006): 195.

57. N. Yuval-Davis, "Ethnicity, Gender Relations and Multiculturalism," in *Debating Cultural Hybridity*, ed. Werbner and Modood, 201.

58. N. Yuval-Davis, "Human Rights and Feminist Transversal Politics" (lecture, University of Bristol series on Politics of Belonging, June 2004), http://www.bristol.ac.uk/sociology/ethnicitycitizenship/nyd2.pdf.

59. Phillips, *Multiculturalism without Culture*, 27.

60. R. Brubaker, "Ethnicity without Groups," *European Journal of Sociology* 43, no. 2 (2003): 166.

61. Ibid.

62. Ibid., 167.

63. Ibid.

64. Cited by Phillips, *Multiculturalism without Culture*, 17.

65. Brubaker, "Ethnicity without Groups," 166.

66. Ibid., 168.

67. Tariq Modood, *Multiculturalism: A Civic Idea* (Cambridge: Polity, 2007), 98.

68. Werbner, "Essentialising Essentialism," 229.

69. Ibid., 230.

70. Ibid.

71. Ibid.

72. P. Werbner, *Imagined Diasporas amongst Manchester Muslims: The Public Performance of Pakistani Transnational Identity Politics* (Oxford: James Currey, 2002), 108.

73. Werbner, "Essentialising Essentialism," 240.

74. S. Arber, "Designing Samples," in *Researching Social Life*, ed. N. Gilbert (London: Sage Publications, 2003), 63.

75. Ibid.

76. Afshar et al., "Feminisms, Islamophobia and Identities," 276.

77. S. Vertovec, "Three Meanings of 'Diaspora', Exemplified among South Asian Religions" (working paper, Oxford University, 1999), 11, http://www .transcomm.ox.ac.uk/working%20papers/diaspora.pdf.

78. Ibid.

79. P. Werbner, "Theorizing Complex Diasporas: Purity and Hybridity in South Asian Public Sphere in Britain," *Journal of Ethnic and Migration Studies* 30, no. 5 (2004): 906.

80. Brown, "Realising Muslim Women's Rights," 418.

81. m. cooke, "Multiple Critiques: Islamic Feminist Rhetorical Strategies," in *Postcolonialism, Feminism and Religious Discourse*, ed. Donaldson and Pui-lan, 143.

82. This view is not actually found in the Qur'an, so it is not entirely clear where she has learned this.

83. Brown, "Realising Muslim Women's Rights," 421.

84. Mandaville, *Transnational Muslim Politics*, 110.

85. Ibid., 134.

86. Werbner, "Public Spaces, Political Voices," 57.

87. Ibid., 58.

88. Ibid., 55.

89. See Ahmad, "Modern Traditions?"

90. See K. Bhopal, "How Gender and Ethnicity Intersect: The Significance of Education, Employment and Marital Status," *Sociological Research Online* 3, no. 3 (1998): para 9.1. http://www.socresonline.org.uk/socresonline/3/3/6.html.

91. See Afshar et al., "Feminisms, Islamophobia and Identities," 262.

92. Modood, *Multicultural Politics*, 160.

93. Grillo, "Islam and Transnationalism," 868.

94. Mandaville, *Transnational Muslim Politics*, 132.

95. Werbner, "Essentialising Essentialism," 230.

96. For an exception see Donaldson and Pui-lan, eds., *Postcolonialism, Feminism and Religious Discourse*.

97. F. Anthias and N. Yuval-Davis, *Racialised Boundaries: Race, Nation, Gender and Class and the Anti-Racist Struggle* (London: Routledge, 1992), 101.

98. bell hooks cited by Anthias and Yuval-Davis, *Racialised Boundaries*, 102.

99. See Mandaville, *Transnational Muslim Politics*.

100. N. Yuval-Davis, "Is There a Space in Religion for Feminists?" in *Women Against Fundamentalism Journal*, 1996, http://waf.gn.apc.org/.

101. Yuval-Davis, "Ethnicity," 124.

102. See T. Modood, "Muslims and the Politics of Multiculturalism in Britain," in *Critical Views of September 11: Analyses from Around the World*, ed. Eric Hershberg and Kevin W. Moore (New York: New Press, 2002), 193–207.

103. See, for example, Valentine Moghadam, "Islamic Feminism and Its Discontents: Towards a Resolution of the Debate," *Signs: Journal of Women in Culture and Society* 27, no. 4 (2002): 1135–71.

104. See Afshar et al., "Feminisms, Islamophobia and Identities"; Werbner, "Public Spaces, Political Voices."

105. cooke, "Multiple Critiques," 145.

106. Ibid., 151.

CHAPTER 5

In Search of Faithful Citizens in Postcolonial Malaysia: Islamic Ethics, Muslim Activism, and Feminist Politics*

Azza Basarudin

Religion is an important part of us and our identity. We cannot deal with the conflict between the realities of our lives and somebody telling us that the religion doesn't support the fact that we are educated, we have our own mind, we are financially independent, we can make decisions, and we can be leaders. People are saying all this is un-Islamic and it doesn't make sense. We could have made the choice to reject religion, but we made the choice to study the religion. This is why I always say

*This chapter is primarily, though not exclusively, based on field research conducted from July 2006 through March 2007 on Sisters in Islam (SIS) in Kuala Lumpur, Malaysia. My field research was made possible by the Wenner-Gren Foundation Dissertation Field-work Grant, the Social Science Research Council International Dissertation Field Research Fellowship (SSRC), and the National Science Foundation Doctoral Dissertation Research Improvement Grant (NSF). I am grateful to Nora Murad and Nik Norani Nik Badlishah for their clarification on the Malaysian legal system. My deepest gratitude is reserved for the members of SIS who have shared their personal and professional lives, opened their hearts and minds to me, and confided their hopes and dreams for a just Muslim society.

that it is a liberating experience to find verses and words in the Qur'an
that speak of justice, compassion, and equality. The message was so
strong and it gave us the courage to stand up and make public our voice
because we know what we stand for is rooted in the teachings of Islam.

Suhana, Sisters in Islam[1]

Not only have the sacred texts always been manipulated, but manipulation of them is a structural characteristic of the practice of power in
Muslim societies.

Fatima Mernissi[2]

To seek secular answers is simply to abandon the field to the fundamen-
talists, who will succeed in carrying the vast majority of the population
with them by citing religious authority for their policies and theories.
Intelligent and enlightened Muslims are therefore best advised to remain
within the religious framework and endeavor to achieve the reforms that
would make Islam a viable modern technology.

Abdullahi An-Na'im[3]

MAPPING FAITH-CENTERED FEMINIST POLITICAL ENGAGEMENT

Questions of gender justice and social transformation in Islamic tradition have
generated some of the most highly contested and contentious discourses in
the contemporary moment of globalization.[4] Across the Muslim world from
Saudi Arabia to Indonesia, Islam's faithful, particularly women, are calling for
innovative ways to balance their religion with the demands of a rapidly changing world.[5] While current scholarship provides salient feminist, legal, and
theological insights into discourse on the role of faith-centered struggles in
shaping women's choices and lives, a significant portion of this research is predicated on textual reinterpretation. Muslim women's[6] praxis, particularly the
hopes, possibilities, and challenges that accompany this scholarly textual reinterpretation, remains under-researched.[7] This chapter responds to this la-
cuna by grounding theories in empirical research within the everyday
social practices of Malaysian Sunni Muslims. Within the transnational
political context of the war on terrorism, my position as a Muslim feminist scholar inspired by Chandra Mohanty's vision of feminist solidarity[8]
informs and colors this research as I straddle spaces of Islamophobia
and conventional Muslim hegemony in exploring this particular feminist
political engagement.

The chapter studies the research and advocacy of Sisters in Islam (SIS hereafter), an organization of Malaysian Muslim women professionals dedicated to promoting and advancing Muslim women's rights through societal and legal reforms. By paying attention to their strategy and the meaning of their intervention in conventional Islamic discourse, this chapter argues that their intellectual activism is a contested site of alternative knowledge production in (re)claiming their faith to (re)imagine a transformative Muslim *umma* (community) inclusive of women's concerns, experiences, and realities. In doing so, I analyze an indigenized feminist vision of social transformation conceptualized by local activists that calls for Muslims to move away from privileging *taqlid* (blind imitation) because it precludes them from the ability to exercise *ijtihad* (critical independent reasoning) and from recognizing a politics of possibility engendered by hermeneutics of Qur'anic *tafsir* (exegesis). Situating their intellectual activism within the transnational discourse of Muslim feminists and Islamic feminisms demonstrates how members of this organization struggle to cultivate an ethical and moral Islam in their community.

The strategy of SIS, understood as faith-centered intellectual activism, engages sources of Islamic tradition[9] alongside international human rights principles and national laws and policies to seek rights through "reform from within," or what Abdullahi An-Na'im has conceptualized as "cultural mediation."[10] This approach consists of identifying and recognizing that the notion of rights-based struggles is conditioned by culture and context and that Muslim reformist projects are carried out with attention to this understanding. Norani Othman, a sociologist and one of the founding members of SIS, builds on An-Na'im's conception to suggest a middle-ground space by working within religious and cultural paradigms in pursuit of women's rights in Muslim societies.[11] My analysis of SIS builds on An-Na'im's concept to explicate this organization's strategy as a marriage of local cultural elements and transnational ideas and practices in shaping their organizational subculture and in influencing their ability to engage effectively in the public sphere. This strategy, which affirms investment in their faith and its ability to accommodate a rapidly globalizing 21st century, is deemed as morally familiar and culturally acceptable to the Muslim majority in Malaysia. It reflects miriam cooke's aptly termed "double commitment" in describing Muslim women's engagement with religion: to a "faith position on the one hand, and to women's rights both inside and outside the home on the other."[12]

To circumvent "overprivileging Islam" and "Islamic determinism," I locate Muslim practices within the specificity of geographical, social, and political milieus in the entanglement of gender power relations, Islamic authoritarianism, and feminist aspirations.[13] My interpretation of Muslim

women's agency and faith-centered intellectual activism is situated within
the context of Islamic revivalism in postcolonial Malaysia and is predicated
upon the dynamics of the (re)assertion of Islam into citizens' lives and of
the debates on the proper role of religion in politics. I hope to complicate
liberal-secular feminist understandings of faith-centered recovery projects
and knowledge production and of the linkage between faith, power, and
agency by highlighting the intricate ways a postcolonial state compels Muslim women to seek holistic methods to structure their intellectual activism.
This chapter is very much a project-on-the-move, its primary aim being to
engage with and contribute to the vibrant conversations and scholarship on
the subject of Muslim women as active interpreters of their faith.

LOCATING THE POSTCOLONIAL DEBATE: POLITICAL ISLAM AND GENDER RELATIONS

Malaysia is renowned as a stable nation with one of the fastest-growing
economies in Southeast Asia. Home to the former tallest buildings in the
world, the Petronas Twin Towers, modern Malaysia is a regional financial,
telecommunications, educational, and high-tech manufacturing hub.
Between the 11th and 16th centuries Arab, Chinese, and Indian traders
brought Islam to the Malay Archipelago.[14] With a population of 27 million, this multicultural and multiconfessional nation consists of the majority ethnic Malays and the minority populations of ethnic Chinese, Indians,
Sikhs, and indigenous people.[15] While Islam is the official religion of the
Malay Federation, the constitution recognizes the limited rights of minorities to profess and practice their religion; the state monitors propagation
of religion other than Islam to Muslims and places restrictions on aberrant
Sunni Muslim practices and Shi'ism.[16] The political system has been
described as "neither authoritarian, nor democratic," indicating that such
structures of democracy as the electoral process are present yet authoritarianism is strongly entrenched in practice.[17] In the process of developing
Malaysia from a little-known backwater into a prosperous nation, its leaders have projected a vision of democratic governance that embraces human
rights principles but in practice only pays it lip service, particularly through
the preventive detention law of the Internal Security Act (ISA). The politicization of Islam in Malaysia, as well as the role and sustainability of SIS,
must be understood within the dynamics of the decolonization processes
and the ways in which state and Islamist politics, although in opposition
on many levels, collude on the "woman question."

Malaysia has parallel legal justice systems—the common law and
Islamic law. All citizens are bound by common law, but Muslims are bound
by both common law and Islamic law. Common law governs matters related

to the constitution, crime, property, and contracts whereas Islamic law governs matters related to Muslims under the Islamic family law (IFL).[18] Although non-Muslims are not subject to Islamic law, they may be implicated, particularly in cases of conversion to Islam and matrimonial obligations, since IFL covers matrimonial law (marriage, divorce, guardianship, custody, and maintenance), charitable endowments, inheritance, adoption, *khalwat* (close proximity cases between unmarried male and female), and some religious-based offenses. The jurisdiction of common law falls under federal control, whereas matters related to Islamic law fall under the jurisdiction of each state; the 13 states and 3 Federal Territories (Kuala Lumpur, Labuan, and Putrajaya) have their own set of laws and are given the authority to legislate them through enactments or ordinances. As such, the states' laws and federal jurisdiction result in 14 sets of IFL. When the IFL (Federal Territories) was designed in 1984, it was a model for Islamic law enactments and ordinances and one of the most progressive of its kind in relation to provisions for polygamy and divorce. The federal government has taken initiatives toward standardization using the Federal Territory model, but the move has been resisted by individual states and rulers. Variations in implementation and legislation from state to state have created complexity for not only citizens but also policy makers, particularly in the case of polygamy.[19] The conventional amendments in the IFL Act of 1994 repealed positive reforms and signaled the discomfort of the *ulama* (singular: *alim*)[20] with a reformist trend.[21]

Launched in the aftermath of the 1969 Malay-Chinese riots, the New Economic Policy, which aimed to mediate the British colonial legacy of economic divide, ethnic distrust, and political discontent, is one of the many factors that led to Islam's politicization in the public sphere. It influenced a new generation of Malays, who saw Islam as "the solution" for the economic disparity and the disintegration of Malay moral and religious beliefs and as a rallying point to uplift the status of the *Bangsa Melayu* (Malay race) and to solidify *Ketuanan Melayu* (Malay supremacy). Simultaneously, the Islamic revivalism that swept across the Muslim world in the 1970s reshaped the urgency for "authentic" ways of living and practicing Islam, which witnessed the race for Arabization of Malaysian Muslims through modes of consumption and politics of behavior. The revivalism took shape in a number of ways: many Malay Muslim students educated in the West banded together under the banner of Islam for self-preservation and returned home with a heightened racial, ethnic, and religious consciousness; accelerated modernization and urbanization spiritually alienated many rural Malays; and state-imposed restrictions on students' political movements compelled them to turn to religious associations.[22] Thus, for example, the Muslim Youth Movement of Malaysia (ABIM) was established during this period to provide young Muslims with an avenue to pursue *dakwah* (missionary work and proselytization) in the Islamization process. Wazir Karim has argued that Malay *adat* (concepts, rules, and codes of behavior) acts as an "equalizer" between patriarchal revivalist ideologies of Islam and egalitarian Malay gender relations. Through *dakwah*, *adat* has come to be contested in revivalist rejections of capitalism and Westernization in favor of Arabized notions of living and practicing Islam, particularly through restructuring gender power relations. While Karim does not allude to Islamic revivalism as anti-*adat* or as successful in eroding the role of *adat*, her analysis highlights an attempt to redefine rigid and hier-archical Malay gender relations through a transnational connection of the Muslim *umma*.[23]

Islamic cultures and practices in Southeast Asia have long been rele-gated to the periphery of normative religious knowledge production for a variety of reasons, one of which is because the region has often been per-ceived as lacking the intellectual rigor and originality of Islamic discourse in the Middle East.[24] As the heartland of the religion, Muslim cultures and practices in the Middle East are held in high regard by a majority of Malaysians and are generally understood to be the most superior manifes-tations of Islam. The historical linkage between Malaysia and the Middle East was facilitated through education, religious pilgrimage, print publica-tions, and trade; since the opening of the Suez Canal in 1869, Malaysian students have descended upon such centers of learning as Al-Azhar Uni-versity in Cairo for religious and political education.[25] Nationalist move-ments against colonial enterprises in the Middle East also served as an inspiration to understand the role of Islam in religious practices, daily behavior, and politics. Furthermore, the *ulama* who studied in the Middle East are revered and perceived to be in a better position to instruct and mold a "good Muslim."[26] Despite Southeast Asia's marginalization, given its diversity, history, and culture and the plurality of Muslim practices and religious activism, Robert Hefner suggests, contemporary Islamic revival characteristics in the region are "marked not only by theological totalism or strident authoritarianism, but by a remarkable combination of pluralism, intellectual dynamism, and openness to dialogue with non-Muslim actors and institutions."[27] In turn, these characteristics have generated an oppor-tunity to better understand Muslim politics, particularly in relation to the debates on gender and Islam.

Under the leadership of former prime minister Mahathir bin Mohamad, state-driven policies directed toward becoming an industrialized nation have witnessed the expansion of education and employment sectors and provided an avenue for women's integration into the development agenda. While the state embraces policies of modernization, personal status law has been left in the hands of the religious establishment, and conventional Islamic perceptions of gender power relations remain unchallenged in society. Although women are increasingly entering educational institutions and labor markets, they do so by juggling normative expectations of gender dynamics and womanhood and by balancing career and family life. To negotiate cultural norms, "feminist" struggles are substituted as "women's" struggles, and demands for rights are grounded within the communitarian realm, particularly within the discourse of state, family, and religion.[28] During Mahathir's era, his state-defined Islam was hailed as "modern" and "moderate," where multiculturalism and Islamic religiosity thrived in a *demokrasi terpimpin* (guided democracy).[29] His version of Islam shares a comfortable space with nationalism, secularism, and capitalism.

Mahathir's successor, Abdullah Badawi, promulgated a vision of Islam *Hadhari* (civilizational) that has been hailed as the foundation for promoting a progressive interpretation and legislation of Islam by accommodating a multiconfessional state. Despite Badawi's vision, Islam *Hadhari* has come under heavy criticism by intellectuals and civil society groups, given the disengagement between his vision and its implementation, particularly with the rising trend of the totalizing discourse of conventional Islam. This discourse includes an assault on alternative views of Islam; a declaration by the deputy prime minister that Malaysia is an Islamic state; the outlawing of mainstream media from reporting on Islamic state debate; the banning of books and movies that are "insensitive for religious and moral reasons"; and the reserving by the state of the word "Allah" exclusively for Muslims by claiming it refers to the "Muslim God." Furthermore, religious agencies have increased moral policing by raiding entertainment clubs and detaining Muslims, specifically women, for "indecent dress and promoting immoral behavior."[30]

A form of conventional political Islam is embodied by Parti Islam Se-Malaysia (PAS) (All-Malaysia Islamic Party), the main Islamic opposition to the ruling Barisan National (National Alliance).[31] Aspiring to capture federal state power, PAS lobbies for the implementation of *hudud* laws[32] to create an Islamic social alternative by promoting policies of gender segregation and veiling. In response to rising Islamic conventionalism à la PAS, during Mahathir's era, the state embarked on its own trademark of Islamization through such projects as Islamic banking, insurance (*takaful*), a work ethics program for state employees, and rehabilitation centers to (re)educate Muslim apostates. Additionally, in the 1990s, a wide range of IFL was amended to further erode women's rights.[33] The state's Islamization processes have intensified not only ethnic but also gender differences. Various initiatives have called for a return to family values, which subsume women's rights under the discourse of the family and national development. Aside from Jabatan Kemajuan Islam Malaysia (JAKIM, Department of Islamic

Development), a central agency that manages Islamic affairs and is responsible for disseminating and monitoring the "authentic" understanding and practice of religion, the state also sponsors Islamic social organizations to support its Islamization policy. While these organizations benefit from state financial assistance, this dependency also carries an expectation that they will support state policies on Islam and provide an avenue for the state to deflect public criticism on its Islamization project.

Since independence from British colonial rule in 1957, the state and Malaysia's citizenry, including opposition political parties, nongovernmental organizations (NGOs), and civil society groups, have grappled with the role of identity-based politics as a vehicle to mobilize political strategies. The struggle for the hearts and minds of the Muslim electorate has played out in the form of the politicization of faith, with both the ruling National Alliance and its opposition parties engaged in a self-righteous race for the "official" brand of Islam. Politicians and political parties have claimed exclusivity over the meaning and practices of Islam and have attempted to silence alternative voices on religious discourse. This effort is anchored by a majority of Malaysian Muslims who still subscribe to the practice of *taqlid*. In the struggle for political hegemony, Islamic homogeneity and Malay intercommunal privileges converge and are deployed as a highly contested site where racial, ethnic, and religious boundaries (re)inscribe normative societal behavior and expectations, and where gender power relations are patrolled through patriarchal predilection. As Muslim women are considered the repository of culture and religion, they are "entrusted" with protecting the "purity" of Malay culture and Malaysian Islam. This arrangement results in containing the boundaries that separate men from women, the licit from illicit, and the moral from the immoral and have become tools to authenticate religiosity and morality. Within this terrain, the polemics of political parties, particularly the National Alliance and PAS on the "woman question," are not always on opposite ends of the spectrum, hence reinforcing gender inequality in society.[34] Amid a booming liberalized economy, cosmopolitan consumption, and modern skyscrapers, Malaysia celebrated its 51st Independence Day in 2008 under the shadow of racial, ethnic, and religious tension, factionalist politics, and state repression. It is against this particular sociopolitical landscape that I situate the faith-centered intellectual activism of SIS in researching and promoting rights for Muslim women.

SISTERS IN FAITH: RETURNING TO THE FUNDAMENTALS OF ISLAM

If Islam is a just religion and we were all brought up with the idea that Islam is just, that God is just, why is there so much injustice occurring in the name of Islam? . . . First we focused on the legal aspect but we realize looking at the law alone is not enough to solve the problem. We have to look at the root of the problem to find out for ourselves whether the religion really promotes the injustice and that was when we decided to read the Qur'an. (Suhana)

The decision to return to textual reinterpretation of the Qur'an for guidance to dismantle the layers of injustice marked the inception of the internationally renowned Sisters in Islam. This organization began as a loosely based consciousness-raising group in the mid-1980s when a group of professional women concerned over the discrimination and injustices Muslim women were experiencing under the IFL Act of 1984 came together to address this problem under a *shari'a* subcommittee of the Association of Women Lawyers (AWL). Many were lawyers, journalists, academics, analysts, and activists and were either close friends or colleagues. They met to discuss gender issues, to examine current events in relation to the law, and to deepen their understanding of the law. The AWL gathering was conceived as a space for critical listening, analysis, and strategizing to improve the condition of women's lives.

It was from this subcommittee that three of the eight founding members of SIS emerged. Suhana, a founding member, recalled complaints from women who went to *Shari'a* Courts to settle cases of custody, polygamy, and domestic violence only to discover the judicial system proclaiming men as superior to women because the law dictates "*hak dia sebagai suami*" (his right as a husband). These rights included obedience to wifehood and family, polygamy as a man's God-given right, and wife-beating as sanctioned in Islam. Unsettled by the patriarchal attitude of court officers, the implication of the role of religion in eroding women's rights and the number of women buying into the ideology of the "rights of husbands," this group of friends found themselves asking similar troubling questions: Does Islam discriminate between men and women? Are women inferior to men in Islam? Does Islam justify discrimination and cruelty toward women?

The injustice of the *Shari'a* Court officers and the ways in which religion is employed to support patriarchal projects was the impetus behind Nur's desire to better understand the religion she was born into and the faith she values:

I have always wondered why *Shari'a* Courts are biased towards women . . . Is it Islam? Why aren't Muslim women getting a fair deal? It was so difficult to get a divorce, maintenance, custody, etcetera. There were so many problems that Muslim women faced, and I felt angry about the injustice. . . . [W]e decided that law was not enough and began to read the Qur'an. We found beautiful passages in the Qur'an, it was amazing—about equality, justice. . . . [W]e discovered a lot of things that we didn't even know existed.

As the founding members realized focusing on *shari'a* law alone is insufficient in understanding the role of religion in forming the basis of laws and policies, the group evolved to create private study sessions where the members met to deepen their understanding of Islam under the guidance of Dr. Amina Wadud, a theologian whose groundbreaking scholarship engages hermeneutics of Qur'anic exegesis from a pro-faith perspective. At that time, Dr. Amina was teaching at the International Islamic University (IIU) in Kuala Lumpur and had completed her dissertation, which later became the critically acclaimed book *Qur'an and Women: Rereading the Sacred Text from a Woman's Perspective*. Rabiah, also a founding member, invited Dr. Amina into this group of friends to guide them in (re)discovering the Qur'an. Although no longer a member of SIS, Amina Wadud remains as a consultant to their projects, including *Musawah*, a global movement calling for equality and justice in the Muslim family. Rabiah reminisces about their study sessions:

Amina would go through verses in the Qur'an and she would tell us what it means. It was amazing. Within a month of just learning with her, we realized that this was something that can work. We realized that if we can get this right, this would be the liberating factor for women, to look at the Qur'an from this perspective, which is an alternative way of looking at the Qur'an but nevertheless just as right as others.

Amina Wadud's hermeneutics of Qur'anic exegesis in guiding SIS members argues for the contextualization of revelation and the understanding of Qur'anic Weltanschauung and the grammatical composition of the text in order to understand contemporary discourses of gender in Islam. This position argues that Qur'anic accommodation of various social and cultural structures in the 7th-century Arabian Peninsula cannot be viewed as implying support for those structures. Continuous interpretation of the Qur'an is a necessity if Muslims are to realize the principles of Qur'anic justice in their daily lives. Her approach focuses on the significance of gender as a category of thought in interpretive methodology and the role of language in *tafsir*. Moving away from a "gender-distinct language," she argues that the Qur'an does not recognize or reflect human categorization of male/female and man/women. Rather, the Qur'an emphasizes a single *nafs* (soul) constituting a pair in the creation process and stresses that the distinction in individuals lies in their *taqwa* (piety).[35]

Through studying with Amina Wadud, this group of friends acquired concrete tools to address how injustice toward Muslim women is incompatible with the spirit of compassion and justice in the Qur'an. In addition, this group of women also studied with An-Na'im and Fathi Osman, both reformist legal scholars, and learned many different ways to approach Islamic sources. They realized that though the Qur'an is divine, *fiqh* is not, as it is a body of law devised by jurists of medieval Islam and that therefore embarking on *ijtihad* is necessary for reform. As this group of women read the Qur'an alongside Islamic history, law, and politics, for them a different picture of Islam began to emerge—an Islam of "ethical egalitarianism" put forward by historian Leila Ahmed.[36] Ahmed suggests that there are two distinct voices in the understanding of gender in Islam, one expressed in the pragmatic set of laws for society and the other in the articulation of an ethical vision. The ethical vision, according to Ahmed, is why "Muslim women frequently insist, often inexplicably to non-Muslims, that Islam is not sexist. They hear and read in its sacred text, justly and legitimately, a different message from that heard by the makers and enforcers of orthodox, androcentric Islam."[37] This ethical message is precisely the element SIS founding members excavated through their recovery project.

As this group of friends acquired sophisticated understandings of the historical development of the methods of inquiry and the role of human agency in Qur'anic *tafsir*, the disconnection between the revealed text and Muslim practices began to unravel. This realization infused their urgency to rectify the divergence by providing a competing interpretation that affirms their conviction in an Islam that encourages and promotes gender justice. The patriarchal interpretation of the Qur'an and its implication on Muslim women's roles, status, and rights has been well documented and argued for by such scholars as Ziba Mir-Hosseini, Fatima Mernissi, Riffat Hassan, and Asma Barlas, all of whom call for Muslims to turn inward and (re)evaluate commonly held assumptions of gender power relations and the rights and privileges of men. Given the social and cultural context of where the Qur'an was revealed, women's exclusion from interpretative communities and the codification of laws and policies are hardly remarkable; Bouthania Shaaban suggests there are very few women interpreters of the Qur'an in the history of Islam because women are seen to be the "subject of the Islamic *Shari'a* and not its legislators"; Barlas stresses, "The teachings of the Qur'an are radically egalitarian and even antipatriarchal," but this aspect has largely been buried through incorporation of oppressive cultural elements by some classical interpreters through the hermeneutical moves of privileging *ahadith*; and Mernissi has written extensively on the need to question the authenticity of *hadith* and points to patriarchal selectivity and biases in Islamic history and collective memory.[38]

The foregoing types of recovery projects by contemporary scholars in
the excavation of the ethical and moral spirit of Islam form the backbone
of SIS's research and advocacy. Aside from their own research, the members of SIS draw on such scholarships to formulate and support their argument that it is the patriarchal monopoly of religious knowledge production
from within cultural frameworks that has rendered Muslim women's rights
a highly contested subject. This transnational circulation of ideas and
knowledge feeds into localized initiatives on the ground; in turn, the
grounded practices provide the foundation to sustain scholarly textual reinterpretations. Their intellectual activism is distinct because it brings textual reinterpretation scholarship to bear on the ground through their legal
clinics, workshops, study sessions, public talks, conferences, and publications in the hope of cultivating an *umma* of enlightened citizens who are
able to critically engage their faith. Their vision of responsible citizenry is
formulated along the lines of An-Nai'm's articulation of human agency,
that is, "to call on people to take responsibility for the relevance and meaning of their religious beliefs to their own lives, instead of perceiving themselves as passive objects of manipulation by forces beyond their control."[39]
The intellectual activism of SIS is a part of the vibrant Islamic tradition of
tajdid (revival) and *islah* (reform)—processes that continue to be constituted and reconstituted through various modes of expression and mobilization and are products of a particular historical and social formation.
Within the particulars of Malaysian Islam and the larger context of Southeast Asian modernist reform initiatives, this organization is "repackaging"
religion by asking fellow Muslim citizens to engage on an intellectual and
activist level with their faith so that Islam remains pertinent and Muslims
may participate in the globalization process without sacrificing their religious beliefs.

IN THE PATH OF FEMINIST *JIHAD* (STRUGGLE): GENDER JUSTICE AND SOCIAL TRANSFORMATION

We uphold the revolutionary spirit of Islam, a religion which uplifted
the status of women when it was revealed 1,400 years ago. We believe
that Islam does not endorse the oppression of women and denial of their
basic rights of equality and human dignity. We are deeply saddened that
religion has been used to justify cultural practices and values that regard
women as inferior and subordinate to men and we believe that this has
been made possible because men have had exclusive control over the
interpretation of the text of the Qur'an. . . . Our mission is to promote
an awareness of the true principles of Islam, principles that enshrine the

concept of equality between women and men, and to strive towards creating a society that upholds the Islamic principles of equality, justice, freedom and dignity within a democratic state.[40]

The foregoing mission statement describes SIS, one of the first NGOs in Malaysia to engage the question of women's rights in Islam in the public sphere. This organization produces booklets, working papers, and scholarly books; it issues press statements, writes letters to newspaper editors, and submits memoranda to the state to influence public opinion, national laws, and policies.[41] The organization's booklets have been translated into numerous languages (e.g., Pashtun, Mandarin, and Arabic), indicating that SIS's faith-centered intellectual activism transcends national boundaries. Many NGOs in Malaysia are situated in urban areas, particularly in such cosmopolitan cities as Kuala Lumpur, and are led mainly by upper-middle- and middle-class individuals. Sisters in Islam operates an office in a well-established older neighborhood of Petaling Jaya, Selangor. The organization's founding members, with the exception of three, share a similar social class and educational backgrounds: they are middle-class Malays with high upward mobility. The social locations of the founding members, their upbringing, and the type of worldview they espouse enable them to build an organization focused on transforming gender power relations. Despite the social class of the founders, SIS has actively been recruiting a younger generation of employees having diverse social strata, experience, and educational background. The staff and founding members are all females, but the organization currently has two male associate members. Structured as a nonmembership organization to protect their research and advocacy, SIS has recently broadened their national support base by creating a category of "Friends of SIS," which consists of Muslim as well as non-Muslim supporters. For a small fee, these members are invited to events and informed of the organization's activities.

The Sisters in Islam's evolved strategy of engaging Islam in the public sphere is framed within the larger context of postcolonial Malaysian pluralism and the spirit of *muhibbah* (goodwill) by considering the role of civil society actors in nation building; in facing the challenges of democratization, globalization, and modernity; in Islamic revivalism; and in securing civil liberties. In this vein, the struggle for Muslim women's rights can be sustained only through active collaboration with other organizations to ensure that civil society remains a domain of public interest for citizens' responsible participation. Reflecting SIS's broader mission of struggling for social justice, their first initiative was a symposium in Kuala Lumpur in 1992 on "The Modern Nation State and Islam." They worked closely with An-Na'im, whose scholarship focused on the historical evolution of Islamic legal theory and its relationship with international human rights principles. This scholarship was the guiding principle in understanding the role of religion in modern nation-states. The blending of a faith-centered intellectual activism, international human rights principles, and national laws and policies has since characterized SIS's approach.

Aside from national and regional consulting and networking with progressive scholars, research centers, and women's groups, as well as participating in conferences and meetings, the members of SIS receive regular international invitations to conduct workshops with lawyers, judges, and religious leaders. The demand for their expertise and their esteemed image internationally have led to criticism that SIS privileges the international at the expense of the local. In addition, criticisms are also focused on funding from international donor agencies, often cast as promoters of "hyperliberal" Islam. Mariam, a former board member, dismissed the criticism and suggested that transnational networking is crucial because it enables SIS members to "learn from other activists and groups working for Muslim women's rights about *shari'a* law, particularly from our Moroccan counterparts on their progressive *Moudawana* (Family Code)—this is a model to reform Malaysia's family law." Aside from learning and sharing strategies for gender justice, transnational networking also ensures international visibility and creates a "safety net" in the event that the state decides to clamp down on the organization. Rabiah voiced her concerns on state crackdowns of groups working for Islamic reform across the Muslim world and feels better knowing the international reputation SIS has cultivated will serve the organization if such an event occurs.

Here, the focus is on SIS's core advocacy of the IFL through the polygamy-monogamy campaigns and religious freedom and moral policing initiatives to explicate their intellectual activism as a process of challenging conventional religious knowledge production. Since its establishment, SIS has maintained a vigilant watch on discriminatory legislation of the IFL, and this has forced the state to be more cautious in its amendments and administration. Sisters in Islam operates pro bono legal clinics from its office and recently launched a Telenisa helpline to provide legal counseling. This organization also manages a legal column in the mainstream Malay newspaper *Utusan Malaysia*.

Polygamy: Between Desire and Rights and Responsibility

I am against polygamy. The way I see it, the interpretation that men have the right to four wives comes with a lot of conditions, and God knows that men are not able to fulfill these conditions. (Nadia, SIS staff)

The first SIS project, before this group of friends officially registered as SIS, came in 1990 through a letter to local Malay- and English-language newspapers discussing the contentious debate on polygamy. In the case of *Aishah Abdul Rauf v. Wan Mohd. Yusof Wan Othman*, the Selangor *Shari'a* Appeals Court denied Wan Yusof the right to take another wife because he had not fulfilled all the conditions set by the Selangor Family Law Enactment (1984).[42] The court ruled that the *shari'a* judge considered only the financial aspect of the contract and ignored whether the proposed marriage was both just *and* necessary and whether the husband had the capacity to treat both wives equally. The ruling generated heated protest in many Malay-language newspapers because it was seen as denying God-given rights to Muslim men.[43] This reaction prompted SIS to write a letter to the newspaper editors in support of the court's decision. In "Polygamy Is Not a Right in Islam,"[44] SIS argued that the theory and practice of polygamy is "a responsibility and not a right" in Islam. The letter was intended to unsettle three conventional conceptions of polygamy: (1) polygamy is a God-given right enshrined in the Qur'an; (2) polygamy is the ideal solution to men's alleged insatiable sexual drive; and (3) a woman who allows her husband to take a second wife is assured a place in heaven. Constructing an argument from a faith-centered paradigm by utilizing hermeneutics of Qur'anic exegesis acquired in their study sessions, SIS members laid out a step-by-step argument as to why the spirit of compassion and justice in Islam necessitates monogamy as the preferred condition of marriage.

The overarching framework of SIS's intervention on the polygamy debate requires understanding the contextual specificity of Qur'anic revelations pertaining to polygamy and to marriage. Bolstering SIS's claim that God intended to "restrict polygamy" was the historical narrative of the tragedy of the battle of Uhud.[45] After that battle, given the unprecedented number of men killed in a community still at its infancy, the remaining men of Medina were advised to treat the orphans and women with fairness. In the aftermath of war and chaos, God could have endorsed unlimited polygamy but instead constrained the number of wives to four. Furthermore, this revelation came with an additional restriction—namely, the practice is permissible so long as a man can support and treat all his wives equally. In their letter, SIS members encourage a rereading of the text as they "urge our sisters and brothers in Islam to go back to the Qur'an and read its words carefully. To allege that the recent judgement of the Selangor Syariah Appeal Court is against Hukum Syarak [*shari'a*] is a gross denial of the true intent and spirit of justice so insistently enjoined by the Qur'an." Building on the Qur'anic verses of An-Nisa 4:3 and 4:129,[46] members of SIS suggest that the main concern of polygamy was protection of and justice for those left behind after the battle and not to satisfy men's unlimited sexual lusts and desires.

In the letter, SIS members also evoke the relationships of the Prophet Muhammad to the women in his life, arguing that he was monogamous for 25 years during his marriage to Khadija. If a Muslim follows the Sunnah of the Prophet, one would surely only marry once during one's lifetime. With the exception of Aisha, none of the Prophet's wives were virgins, and subsequent marriages were contracted mainly for political purposes.[47] They also cite an authentic *hadith* where the Prophet contested his son-in-law Ali's wish to marry another woman unless Ali divorced the Prophet's daughter, Fatima. In relation to polygamy issues that have surfaced since 1990, SIS has been actively advocating against the fundamental misunderstanding and unjust practices of polygamy through letters to newspapers, memorandums to the state, campaigns, and research projects.[48] In each initiative, SIS continues to reiterate the contextual specificity of Qur'anic verses by arguing for gender justice for women, family, and society; a responsibility-based framework in contrast to a rights-and-privilege-based framework; the importance of preserving human dignity and the sanctity of marriage; and the morality of piety and self-control.

As the Secretariat of the Coalition of Women's Rights in Islam in 2003,[49] SIS launched the Monogamy, My Choice campaign to promote monogamy as an ideal state of marriage in Islam. Launched by the late wife of Prime Minister Badawi, this campaign also sought to educate women on their rights in polygamous marriages. The aim was to popularize Qur'anic verses related to their interpretation of the restrictions on polygamy through a creative avenue by producing three bumper stickers bearing such slogans as "*Jika kamu khuatir tidak akan berlaku adil, maka berkahwinlah* SATU *sahaja. 4:3*" (If you fear you cannot be fair, then marry only ONE. 4:3), "*Monogami Pilihanku*" (Monogamy, My Choice), and "1 *Suami* = 1 *Isteri*" (1 Husband = 1 Wife). According to SIS, the majority of Malaysian Muslims are unaware of or ignore the second part of An-Nisa 4:3 (in italics): "If you fear that you shall not be able to deal justly with the orphans, marry women of your choice, two, or three or four; *But if you fear that ye shall not be able to deal justly (with them), then only one . . . That will be more suitable, to prevent you from doing injustice.*" This lesser-known part of the verse, SIS argues, if read in conjunction with other verses in the Qu'ran (i.e., An-Nisa 4:129), supports their interpretation that polygamy is restricted.

In collaboration with academics of two national universities, in 2006 SIS launched a polygamy research project intended to examine the complexity of polygamous institutions on the macro and micro levels. The five dimensions of the research were familial relationships, the psychological well-being of family members, social relationships of family members, and financial conditions and legal remedies that protect the interests of family members. To generate local funding for this initiative, SIS organized a charity premiere of *Berbagi Suami* (Love for Share), an award-winning Indonesian film that complicates polygamy through the lenses of love, security, and dignity. Realizing that embarking on monogamy campaigns alone is insufficient, SIS decided to undertake a project that would make a stronger impact on state and society by combining qualitative and quantitative research. They hoped to strengthen their argument that the Malaysian practice of polygamy, which puts the "rights of men" above the "responsibility of men," not only contradicts restrictions laid out in the Qur'an but also contributes to immense social problems (e.g., neglected children). Their polygamy research and campaign is consistent with their mission to move away from practices of *taqlid* in order to create civic-minded Muslims who embody Qur'anic ideals of reciprocity between the two genders and emphasize the importance of *ijtihad* in cultivating a just and responsible communalism.

BELIEVING MUSLIMS, MORAL POLICING, AND MULTIRACIAL CITIZENRY

"Let there be no compulsion in religion."

Qur'an, Al-Baqarah 2:226

Shamala and Jeyaganesh, a Hindu couple, contracted a civil marriage under the Law Reform (Marriage and Divorce) 1976 Act. Jeyaganesh later converted to Islam, and he also converted the couple's minor children without his wife's knowledge or consent. While Shamala initiated a custody order from the High Court, he obtained an ex parte *Hadanah* (custodial order) from *Shari'a* Court. Once he initiated a divorce proceeding at the *Shari'a* Court, Shamala was summoned to the *Shari'a* Court for *Hadanah* and divorce proceedings. As a Hindu, she is not subject to *shari'a* jurisdiction; but given her failure to appear in *Shari'a* Court, a warrant was issued for her arrest. It was later stayed on the order of a High Court judge.[50] The High Court awarded joint custody to both parties but stipulated Shamala's guardianship is dependent on the condition that she refrained from imparting Hinduism to her children.

Shamala's case reflects the competing jurisdiction of common law and Islamic law in the parallel justice systems. It also marks the controversial public intervention of SIS in the racially and emotionally charged debate over conversion (to Islam), apostasy (from Islam), and protection of ethnic and religious minorities. Although minority groups are protected under civil law, when one spouse converts to Islam, the nonconverting party experiences complicated and discriminatory legal processes, particularly in relation to matrimonial matters. Haunted by a string of highly publicized and controversial cases, in late December 2007, the Federal Court decided that the civil court under the Law Reform (Marriage and Divorce) 1976 Act has exclusive jurisdiction over marriage and custody disputes in the event one spouse converts to Islam.[51] In April 2009, the recently elected prime minister, Najib Razak, announced that children cannot be converted without the consent of both parents, yet it remains to be seen if and when the law will go into effect.[52] Nora, a former legal officer, explains that SIS's involvement in this case began when the group was approached by the Women's Aid Organisation (WAO), where Shamala sought assistance. The WAO needed SIS's expertise on the IFL:

> We got involved because of Shamala. Her husband converted to Islam while they were still married. She remained Hindu. It started with Islamic family law issue—the question was on whether he has the rights to convert underage children and divorce his Hindu wife in *Shari'a* Court. It was our concern that a Muslim should not take advantage of Islam or the judicial system in relation to custody and dissolution of a marriage contracted under civil law. Where is the right of the mother in this? Who is going to protect her rights? During Shamala's case the Article 11 group was formed and we lobbied for her. At that stage, our concentration was IFL. After Shamala came other cases such as Lina Joy,[53] which received more prominence and publicity in the media. That was when the freedom-of-religion argument exploded. IFL started the whole ball rolling.

Sisters in Islam assisted WAO and Shamala's lawyers with legal advice, translation of letters into Malay, and press statements. According to Nora, SIS was the only Muslim group providing support on this case. Their legal advice focused on alternative positions of Islam to provide Shamala and her lawyers with knowledge of diverse Islamic thought and Muslim practices. As such, SIS members promote their reading of Islamic sources and generate a better understanding of the administration and legislation of *shari'a*.

The Article 11 coalition (Art 11 hereinafter) is an umbrella of NGOs, lawyers, academics, and activists formed to uphold the supremacy of the constitution, a move that is seen by many conventional Muslims as posing a threat to the preeminence of Islam and Malays. The involvement of SIS was premised on the grounds that Islam should not be a tool to inflict injustice on Shamala and that the rights of a Muslim majority should not be held above those of other ethnic and religious groups. The SIS organization argues that Jeyaganesh's seeking remedy in *Shari'a* Court to deny his wife the right to parent her children is not in line with Islamic teachings of equality, compassion, and reciprocity. They also suggest that legal mediation should reflect the broader multiracial context of citizens' rights to be protected under the constitution regardless of gender, religion, and ethnicity.

In 2007, SIS issued a press statement calling for the protection of religious minorities and the supremacy of the Federal Constitution by stressing that all Malaysian citizens deserve equal protection and respect under the law. Drawing on their interpretation of the Qur'anic verse of Al-Maidah (5:8), SIS encouraged Muslims and Muslim organizations to speak up against injustice perpetrated against their fellow non-Muslim citizens ("O ye who believe! Be steadfast witnesses for Allah in equity, and let not hatred of any people seduce you that ye deal not justly. Deal justly, that is nearer to your duty. Observe your duty to Allah. Lo! Allah is Aware of what you do").[54] On the broader issue of religious freedom, particularly on apostasy, which has reinforced ethnic and religious tensions, the members of SIS tread cautiously while staying true to their beliefs and the mission of their organization. Based on their three-pronged strategy of Qur'anic *tafsir*, national laws and policies, and international human rights principles, along with evoking Prime Minister's Badawi's vision of Islam *Hadhari*, SIS urged the state to approach this increasingly salient matter to ensure justice is served in accordance to Islamic teachings and Malaysia's reputation as a progressive Muslim country. Based on Qur'anic verses Al-Baqarah, 2:256—"Let there be no compulsion in religion"—and Yunus 10:99—"If your Lord had willed, all the people on the earth would have come to believe, one and all. Are you going to compel the people to believe against their will?"—SIS argues that the fundamental aspect of Islam, which means submission to God, underlies one's status as a believer and is nonenforceable.[55] To force someone to believe is to violate the precepts of the religion.

The Art 11 coalition has organized public forums to explain their objectives, clarify misconceptions, and discuss religious freedom in a communal manner. However, the response was mixed, for there was heated opposition and interruption by protesters at their forums. A most recent attempt to discuss non-Muslim conversion to Islam in relation to matrimonial matters organized by the Bar Council ended abruptly after Muslim NGOs and political parties issued threats and engaged in frenzied protests, which included the use of Molotov cocktails.[56] In a press statement, SIS condemned the violence committed in the name of Islam, labeling it "terrorist actions" that serve to reinforce perceptions that equate Islam and

Muslims with violence. Given the highly charged identity-based politics, SIS's involvement as secretariat for Article 11 is seen as controversial by many conventional Muslims despite the organization's low-profile membership in the coalition. Many Muslims believe that SIS as an organization should advocate exclusively for the rights of Muslim women, which does not include speaking out on issues of apostasy, and that speaking out against a conventional interpretation of Islam is speaking out against Islam. Many Muslims also fail to understand the interconnectivity of a pluralistic nation that compels their involvement; the struggle for the rights of Muslim women is entangled in the struggle to preserve the supremacy of the Federal Constitution, uphold respect for religious and ethnic minorities, and secure a democratic space for civil society debates. An enlightened citizen cannot advocate for the protection and rights of one ethnic and religious group while abandoning responsibility to the larger societal context that forms and informs the vein of the nation.

Sisters in Islam has long been critical of the state's attempt to set a "moral standard" to monitor the behavior and practices of Malaysians, particularly Muslims, through the police, various state agencies, and the Volunteer Reserve Corps (RELA). The *Shari'a* Criminal Offences Enactment regulates the boundaries of Muslim morality in public spaces through provisions that include indecent dressing and behavior, sodomy, apostasy, drinking alcohol, neglecting Friday prayers (men), eating during Ramadan (fasting month), and *khalwat* (close proximity of the opposite sex in a secluded space). The state's attempt at policing its Muslim citizens' morality through self-appointed "moral police" ranges from arresting a Muslim woman participant of a beauty contest and a transgender in a private house, launching "snoop squads" to spy on youths and couples, to raiding a nightclub, which subsequently led to the detention and humiliation of approximately 100 Muslims, mostly women.[57] Aside from humiliation, abuse, and intimidation at the hands of the moral police, self-appointed vigilante groups have also engaged in harassment of Muslim women who do not wear the *tudung* (headscarf), mix with non-Muslims, and are present in nonsegregated settings.[58] Ethnic and religious minorities are also concerned with this form of policing, given recent discussions to extend punishment for *khalwat* to non-Muslims.[59]

Women are particularly vulnerable to verbal and physical sexual abuse during moral policing raids. Faridah, a former SIS member, tells the story of RELA members and religious officers of the Federal Territory Islamic Affairs Department (JAWI) humiliating Muslim women detained after a nightclub raid by hurling lewd remarks about their skimpy attire and profession of choice. One of the detainees requested a restroom break but was denied. She was forced to relieve herself in the RELA truck where one of the RELA members took photos of her during the act. Under the coalition of Malaysians against Moral Policing (MAAP), SIS issued letters to newspaper editors, and its members attended seminars and panel discussions to raise awareness about criminalizing morality. By arguing against un-Islamic and unconstitutional methods of constructing behavioral boundaries, SIS demonstrates that the control of Muslim citizens' morality goes against injunctions laid out in various verses in the Qur'an (Al-Hujurat 49:12; An-Nur 24:27, 28).[60]

ON LIBERATING FAITH: YEARNING AND COURAGE FOR ISLAM

Despite the care and strategizing SIS has taken to avoid controversy, the group has come under intense scrutiny since its establishment. The personal lives of its members and their choices are debated in public, their religious beliefs and practices contested, and their sincerity to reform Islam and transform the condition of women's lives questioned. They have also been tagged as agents of the "secular West" and the Israeli Mossad seeking to infiltrate Malaysian Islam with liberal-secular ideas. In my interviews with religious state agencies, activists, academics, leaders of political parties, and a variety of Islamic NGOs, the most common criticism of SIS relates to the monopoly of religious knowledge production and the social capital of the right to speak on Islam. Responding to my question on his perception of SIS intellectual activism, a high-ranking JAKIM officer expressed his views:[61]

> If Sisters in Islam wishes to be effective, their advocacy must include the community of *ulama*. Reform without *ulama* is bound to fail; any religious reform must be guided by *ulama*. This is something that this organization does not acknowledge. They also do not understand religion—none of the members can read or write Arabic or read the holy text in its original form. Using rationalization to explain religion is a weak argument and blasphemous at best.

Most recently, in June 2009, a controversy erupted when PAS called on the Malaysian National Fatwa Council to investigate SIS for its advocacy of "liberal Islam" and "putting the faith of the Muslims in danger" and proposed a ban on the organization if its "activities are found to be contrary to the Islamic teachings and principles" in addition to the "rehabilitation" of SIS members.[62] The president of PAS was quoted as saying, "They [SIS] are ignorant about Islam. We have tried to engage them by sending Dr [Siti] Mariah Mahmood[63] to one of their events but they talk not from their knowledge . . . If you are not a fisherman, you cannot talk about fishing. It's the same with SIS, if you do not have knowledge about Islam, you cannot talk about Islam."[64] Furthermore, an elected member of Parliament suggested SIS drop the word "Islam" from its name and rename its organization "Association of Cosmopolitan Women" (*Ikatan Wanita Kosmopolitan*) in line with his understanding of SIS's "non-Islamic"-oriented intellectual activism. Among other reasons, he further cited SIS's support for religious freedom debates, the organization's IFL campaigns, particularly in relation to questioning men's rights to polygamy and inheritance, and the unmarried status of its members as reasons for the organization to be investigated and for legal action be taken against SIS under the Syariah Criminal Enactment.[65] While PAS has consistently called into question the legitimacy of the intellectual activism of SIS since the organization's establishment, this is the first time that the former prime minister, Mahathir bin Mohammad, and the minister of Women, Family and Community Development, Shahrizat Abdul Jalil, publicly supported the group. Mahathir wrote on his blog, "I don't always agree with the views of SIS, but they have not negated Islam. . . . In most instances they cite verses of the Quran and Hadith to support their views. If we don't agree then give the reasons why we don't agree . . . to resort to banning is draconian," while Shahrizat chastised PAS for the party's inability to negotiate with dissenting voices.[66] While Mahathir's and Shahrizat's declarations of support for SIS is welcomed by many, it is also unprecedented and calls the role of factional politics in relation to Islamic discourse and the "women question" into question, particularly given the current juncture in the country's political history.

Although those individuals knowledgeable about SIS and the larger debates on gender and Islam can counter accusations and criticisms, there are also many Malaysian Muslims who do not look beyond them. Therefore, such detractors, without knowing or understanding SIS's advocacy, recycle and promulgate these criticisms in a guided attempt to silence the cacophony of voices in Islam. During my field research, I was consistently told that members of SIS who do not wear *tudung* and are not married cannot possibly be an authority on religion when they ignore one of the most important tenets of the religion (marriage). Given my physical appearance (sans *tudung*), during my interviews with a few Islamic NGOs and religious officials, I was often mistaken for a member of SIS and accused of being a member sent to solicit information about religious authorities' perceptions of the organization, even as I explained that I was carrying out research on the organization for my doctoral degree. The religious officials and those who view themselves as the authority on Islam evoke the legitimacy card to silence those speaking publicly about religion and cultivate a culture of fear in Malaysia, particularly among the rising racial and religious divisions and the climate of the transnational war on terrorism.

Suhana argued that those who set themselves up as the authority on Islam, evoking fear to silence other voices, are employing a "bankrupt tactic" because the detractors are not engaging the real issues that form the core of SIS's advocacy. In their own defense, SIS members note that the criticisms strengthen their resolve to ensure that diverse Islamic interpretations are cultivated in Malaysia. Nur explains:

> We don't make statements out of thin air. We do research and consult with experts. For many people, it still is an issue that we cannot read the Qur'an in Arabic. God says in the Qur'an that the book is revealed in the language of the people so they can understand it. I take it to mean that if I want to understand the Qur'an, I need to do so in my language. If God had given it to the Malays, if the Malays were as bad as the Arabs back then, than the language will be the Malay. This part is still a big deal—you don't speak Arabic, you don't go to Al-Azhar, you don't have a degree in Islamic studies or *shari'a* law, so how can you speak about Islam? But every Muslim has the right to speak about Islam, speak up against injustice. We are not like the Christians, who need the pope or the clergy to tell us what to do. These *ulama* want to be like the clergy.

Although conventional jurists require that persons exercising *ijtihad* possess such qualifications as having memorized the Qur'an, being pious and moral, or being expert in the Arabic language and having an extensive knowledge of Islamic history, An-Na'im has argued that these requirements and methods of containing the boundaries of knowledge production are problematic for the modern context. In the case of memorization of the Qur'an, modern technology provides access to "indexed sources, computerized access and cross-references"; and "personal piety and moral standing can hardly be verified by formal qualification," an approach that was perhaps possible in the "small and close-knit community of scholars in the few leading centers of learning of the Middle East in the eighth and ninth centuries."[67] Furthermore, Barlas asserts, a majority of Muslims believe that only males have the right and authority to produce religious knowledge; in fact, "people who do not belong to a well-recognized interpretive community (most of which tend to be conservative) are likely to face censure for undertaking certain kinds of scholarship."[68] In reflecting on the monopoly of religious knowledge production and the delegitimization of the faith-centered intellectual activism of SIS, it is crucial to consider the interconnectedness between the text, interpretive community, meaning making, and authority.[69]

Nur, as with other members of SIS, believes they have the right to speak about Islam because given their experiences as Muslim women living under Islamic law. They have informed knowledge rooted in an ethical and moral understanding of Islam. This knowledge is anchored by a politics of possibility in the ethical egalitarian vision of Islam. They are claiming the right to speak, not in vacuity, but from an engaged positionality of Muslim women who truly reflect and believe in the spirit of justice in Islam. Indeed, through an alternative feminist method of engaging religion, SIS is (re)creating power dynamics by "fracturing" conventional Islamic hegemony. "Fracturing" is used here to indicate the discursive process of claiming public space, denoting how SIS's intellectual activism is seeping through the cracks to rupture the delicate relationships of power. While a comprehensive discussion on the impact of the organization's intellectual activism is beyond the scope of this chapter, my field research indicates that SIS's influence is possibly limited because mainstream Malaysian Muslims perceive their advocacy as elitist and controversial.[70] However, since the conclusion of my field research in 2007, SIS has actively been reaching out through collaboration with grassroots organizations by conducting workshops and legal training on Muslim women's rights across Malaysia. In relation to focusing on expanding their advocacy, more importantly, SIS needs to reevaluate questions of constituency and accountability to the larger cause of gender justice, particularly in sustaining a process of religious and cultural reforms that are capable of expanding critical debates on the promotion and protection of rights-based struggles.

The intellectual activism of Sisters in Islam is not an isolated 21st-century form of engaging religion, for their strategy is situated within the broader recovery projects of Muslim feminists and Islamic feminisms. Scholars such as miriam cooke, Margot Badran, and Omaima Abou-Bakr have engaged the transnational scope of these recovery projects and the debates over the politics of naming such projects. cooke views Islamic feminisms as a contextualized speaking position and a "double commitment," as discussed earlier in this chapter; Margot Badran shares cooke's view in addition to understanding it as a radical form of feminism that functions as a bridge to unite religious and secular Muslims, as well as East and West, while redefining the meaning of feminists and feminism;[71] and Omaima Abou-Bakr differentiates between two types of Islamic feminisms—the first as a hegemonic form of categorizing the "other" and the second as a form of self-definition by Muslim women who are developing alternatives to reclaim Islam from internal corruption.[72] As such, SIS's faith-centered intellectual activism is located within the transnational struggles of Muslim women because it illuminates the local and global as bounded and shared geographical spaces that subscribe to historical specificities yet simultaneously connect women's diverse experiences of negotiating Islam. In taking this view, I follow the feminist vision of Mohanty (2003) to articulate women's agency and to frame feminist solidarity as interconnected across national borders and cultures.

The recovery projects have been critiqued for moves that preclude integration of secular-liberal frameworks and the cyclical competing interpretations of Islamic sources. Scholars have engaged the case for and against claiming rights through cultural mediation by highlighting the complexities of this strategy and its sustainability.[73] Although the concerns are well founded, in the case of pluralistic postcolonial Malaysia, the discursive hermeneutics of Qur'anic *tafsir* is a strategy born of necessity and the unwavering belief in the unfulfilled promise of gender egalitarianism in Islam. This method of claiming rights offers Malaysian Muslim women strategic access to participate in religious discourse; in a state where Islam is the battlefield for national laws and public policies, to not partake in this battle is to leave women's lives and realities vulnerable to co-optation by those who seek to preserve Islamic exclusivity. In this light, we have to critically consider the relationship between modes of Muslim women's agency and the implication of Islamic gatekeeping, which is tangled up in the larger matrix of the struggle between those who believe in dogmatic understanding of religion and those who believe in Islam's contextuality of historical specificity.

In their search for equality and justice, the members of Sisters in Islam have (re)discovered the moral and ethical spirit of Islam. In the recuperation of their faith, these Muslim women have embarked on a liberating political and spiritual experience to produce alternative religious knowledge that values their lived experiences as Muslim women. In grounding their claims for rights by engaging sources of Islamic tradition alongside national laws and policies and international human rights principles, SIS is struggling to (re)imagine a transformative *umma* that protects the rights of both its Muslim and non-Muslim citizens. While the organization's faith-centered intellectual activism may continue to command controversy and may be limited in its scope, given the marginalization of Muslim women in the public discourse of religion, this indigenized feminist intervention cannot be underestimated. Through a faith-centered intellectual activism, SIS is "fracturing" conventional Islamic hegemony and is (re)creating a (sub)religious community of the faithful by asserting that for Islam to have meaning in the lives of Muslims, the practice of privileging *taqlid* can no longer find justification in this globalized world.

NOTES

1. All the names of my interlocutors, except for Dr. Amina Wadud and Nora Murad, are pseudonyms. The information about their lives and backgrounds has been altered to protect their privacy.

2. Fatima Mernissi, *The Veil and the Male Elite: A Feminist Interpretation of Women's Rights in Islam* (New York: Perseus, 1991), 8.

3. Mahmoud Mohamed Taha, *The Second Message of Islam*, trans. Abdullahi An-Na'im (New York: Syracuse University Press, 1987), 28.

4. This discussion is restricted to the Sunni branch of Islam because it is the largest denomination in Malaysia. The majority of Malaysians follow the Shafi'i school of *fiqh* (jurisprudence). Approximately 85 percent of the world's Muslim population follows the Sunni branch.

5. The term "Muslim world" indicates countries where the majority of the population is Muslim.

6. To avoid the pitfalls of a monolithic and singular subject in the construction of "Muslim women," I heed Chandra Mohanty's critique that universalism and essentialism erase particular politics, knowledge production, and social locations. Thus, I follow Shahnaz Khan's deployment of "Muslim women" as a negotiated "starting point" in complicating notions of identity and women's faith-centered political engagement. See Chandra Mohanty, *Feminism without Borders: Decolonizing Theory, Practicing Solidarity* (Durham, NC: Duke University Press, 2003), and Shahnaz Khan, *Muslim Women: Crafting a North American Identity* (Gainesville: University Press of Florida, 2000).

7. There have been numerous empirical studies on the engagement of gender and religion concentrated on *Shi'a* Islam, particularly in Iran. See Lara Deeb, *An Enchanted Modern: Gender and Public Piety in Shi'i Lebanon* (Princeton, NJ: Princeton University Press, 2006); Ziba Mir-Hosseini, *Islam and Gender: The Religious Debate in Contemporary Islam* (Princeton, NJ: Princeton University Press, 1999); and Nayereh Tohidi, "The Global-Local Intersection of Feminism in Muslim Societies: The Cases of Iran and Azerbaijan," *Social Research* 69, no. 3 (2002): 851–88. For recent research on Sunni Islam in Indonesia, see Pieternella van Doorn-Harder, *Women Shaping Islam: Reading the Qur'an in Indonesia* (Chicago: University of Illinois Press, 2006). See also Amina Wadud, *Inside the Gender Jihad: Women's Reform in Islam* (Oxford: Oneworld Publications, 2006).

8. Mohanty, *Feminism without Borders*.

9. Sources of Islamic tradition are the Qur'an, which Muslims believe to be the word of God, Sunnah and *hadith* (practical traditions and oral sayings attributed to the Prophet Muhammad), *fiqh* (jurisprudence), and *shari'a* (code of law).

10. Abdullahi An-Na'im, "The Cultural Mediation of Human Rights: The Case of Al-Arqam in Malaysia," in *The East Asian Challenge for Human Rights*, ed. Joanne Bauer and Daniel Bell (Cambridge: Cambridge University Press, 1999), 147–68.

11. Norani Othman, "Grounding Human Rights Arguments in Non-Western Culture: Shari'a and the Citizenship Rights of Women in a Modern Islamic Nation-State," in *The East Asian Challenge for Human Rights*, ed. Bauer and Bell, 169–92. Othman has written extensively on SIS. For instance,

see Othman et al., "Malaysia: Islamization, Muslim Politics and State Authoritarianism," in *Muslim Women and the Challenge of Islamic Extremism*, ed. Norani Othman (Selangor: Vinlin Press, Sdn, Bhd, 2005), 78–108. See also Zainah Anwar, "Sisters in Islam and the Struggle for Women's Rights," in *On Shifting Ground: Muslim Women in the Global Era*, ed. Fereshteh Nouraie-Simone (New York: Feminist Press, 2005), 233–66.

12. miriam cooke, "Multiple Critique: Islamic Feminist Rhetorical Strategies," *Nepantla: Views from South* 1, no. 1 (2000): 91–110; 93.

13. Sondra Hale, *Gender Politics in Sudan: Islamism, Socialism, and the State* (Boulder, CO: Westview Press, 1996), and Victoria Bernal, "Gender, Culture, and Capitalism: Women and the Remaking of Islamic 'Tradition' in a Sudanese Village," *Comparative Studies in Society and History* 36, no. 1 (1994): 36–67.

14. Malaysia's (formally known as Malaya) strategic maritime route, particularly the port of Malacca, was important to such colonial enterprises as those of the Portuguese (1511–1640) and the Dutch (1641–1785). Later, the availability of such raw materials as tin and rubber made the country lucrative for the British (1786–1957). Then, Japan occupied Malaya during World War 11 (1941–1945), and the British reasserted their colonial rule after the surrender of Japanese troops. For a detailed country history and contemporary politics, consult Barbara Watson Andaya and Leonard Y. Andaya, *A History of Malaysia* (Basingstoke, Hants, UK: Palgrave, 2001), and Anthony Reid, *Southeast Asia in the Age of Commerce, 1450–1680: Expansion and Crisis* (New Haven, CT: Yale University Press, 1993).

15. Ethnic Malays, some indigenous tribal groups (Orang Asli) in peninsular Malaysia and in Sabah and Sarawak are known as *Bumiputra/Bumiputera* (sons and daughters of the earth). The Federal Constitution dictates that Malay is "a person, who professes the religion of Islam, habitually speaks Malay language, conforms to Malay customs" (Article 160, 2). The formulation of Malay-Muslim identity must be viewed through the imbrication of religion, political and electoral arrangement, legal system, and nation-building strategies. For source materials, see Tim Harper, *The End of Empire and the Making of Malaya* (Cambridge: Cambridge University Press, 1999); Hussin Mutalib, *Islam and Ethnicity in Malay Politics* (New York: Oxford University Press, 1990); Judith Nagata, "What Is a Malay? Situational Selection of Ethnic Identity in a Plural Society," *American Ethnologist* 1 (1974): 331–50; Timothy Barnard, *Contesting Malayness: Malay Identity across Boundaries* (Singapore: Singapore University Press, 2004); Reid, "Understanding Melayu (Malay) as a Source of Diverse Modern Identities," *Journal of Southeast Asian Studies* 32 (2001): 295–313; A. B. Shamsul, "A History of an Identity, an Identity of a History: The Idea and Practise of 'Malayness' in Malaysia Reconsidered," *Journal of Southeast Asian Studies* 32 (2001): 355–66;

and Mahathir Mohamad, *The Malay Dilemma* (Kuala Lumpur: Federal Publications, 1995).

16. Article 3 (1) states, "Islam is the religion of the Federation; but other religions may be practiced in peace and harmony in any part of the Federation." Article 11 (1) states, "Every person has the right to profess and practice his religion and, subject to Clause (4), to propagate it." Clause (4): "State law and in respect of the Federal Territories of Kuala Lumpur and Labuan, federal law may control or restrict the propagation of any religious doctrine or belief among persons professing the religion of Islam." "Constitution of Malaysia," Part I, 3 (1). The federal government banned the Al-Arqam movement in 1993, citing the group's teachings as "cultish" and "dangerous." See An-Na'im, "The Cultural Mediation of Human Rights." In addition, Malaysian Shi'as have also been detained without trial under the Internal Security Act (ISA) and sent to detention centers for spreading "deviant Islamic teachings." See Anil Noel Netto, "Malaysia-Religion: Crackdown of Shiah Muslims Puzzles Many," *Inter Press Service,* November 11, 2007.

17. Harold Crouch, "Malaysia: Neither Authoritarian nor Democratic," in *Southeast Asia in the 1990s: Authoritarianism, Democracy and Capitalism,* ed. Kevin Hewison, Richard Robison, and Gary Rodan (Sydney: Allen & Unwin, 1993).

18. The 1988 amendment under Article 121 (1A) prohibits civil courts from interfering with the jurisdiction of *Shar'ia* Courts, although this amendment has only amplified the competing jurisdictions between the two systems. For a discussion of background on Islamic family law in Malaysia, consult Muhammad Hashim Kamali, *Islamic Law in Malaysia: Issues and Developments* (Kuala Lumpur: Ilmiah Publishers, 2000); Ahmed Mohammed Ibrahim, *The Administration of Islamic Law in Malaysia* (Kuala Lumpur: Institute of Islamic Understanding Malaysia, IKIM, 2000), and "The Administration of Muslim Law in Southeast Asia," 13 *MLR* 124, 1971.

19. In general, under the IFL (Federal Territory) Act 1984, there are five conditions that must be fulfilled before a judge would sanction a polygamous marriage to evaluate a man's credibility and protect women's rights within the family: just and necessary; financial means; consent of existing wife; equal treatment of wives; proposed marriage causes no harm to existing wife or wives. The states of Perak, Kelantan, and Terengganu do not stipulate the five conditions in evaluating a man's financial, moral, and religious standing; and so often times, men cross state lines to contract polygamous marriages. See Kamali, *Islamic Law in Malaysia.*

20. *Ulama* refers to scholars who are knowledgeable about religious sciences and Islamic jurisprudence and are central to the religious education of communities. They are interpreters of the Qur'an, transmitters of *hadith,* and jurists of Islamic law. See Muhammad Qasim Zaman, *The Ulama in*

Contemporary Islam: Custodians of Change (Princeton, NJ: Princeton University Press, 2002).

21. See Kamali, *Islamic Law in Malaysia*.

22. Zainah Anwar, *Islamic Revivalism in Malaysia: Dakwah among the Students* (Kuala Lumpur: Pelanduk Publications, 1987); Chandra Muzaffar, *Islamic Resurgence in Malaysia* (Kuala Lumpur: Fajar Bakti, 1987); and Judith Nagata, *The Reflowering of Malaysian Islam: Modern Religious Radicals and Their Roots* (Vancouver: University of British Columbia Press, 1984).

23. Wazir Jahan Karim, *Women and Culture: Between Malay Adat and Islam* (London: Westview Press, 1992). Othman and Aihwa Ong have also written on the impact of Islamic revivalism on Malaysian gender relations. See Othman, "Islamization and Modernization in Malaysia: Competing Cultural Reassertions and Women's Identity in a Changing Society," in *Women, Ethnicity and Nationalism: The Politics of Transition*, ed. Rick Wolford and Robert Miller (London: Routledge, 1998), 170–92; Ong, "State versus Islam: Malay Families, Women's Bodies and the Body Politics," in *Bewitching Women, Pious Men: Gender and Body Politics in Southeast Asia* (Berkeley: University of California Press, 1995), 159–94.

24. Refer to Mona Abaza, "Images of Gender and Islam: The Middle East and Malaysia, Affinities, Borrowing, and Exchanges," *Orient* 39, no. 2 (1998): 271–84; A. H. Johns, "Perspective of Islamic Spirituality in Southeast Asia: Reflections and Encounters," *Islam and Christian-Muslim Relations* 1, no. 12 (2001): 5–21; and Robert Hefner and Patricia Horvatich, eds., *Islam in the Era of Nation States: Politics and Religious Renewal in Muslim Southeast Asia* (Honolulu: University of Hawaii Press, 1997).

25. See William Roff, "Indonesian and Malay Students in Cairo in the 1920s," *Indonesia* 9 (1970): 73–87, and "Patterns of Islamization in Malaysia, 1890s–1990s: Exemplars, Institutions, and Vectors," *Journal of Islamic Studies* 9, no. 2 (1998): 210–28.

26. Ibid.

27. Hefner, "Politics and Religious Renewal in Muslim Southeast Asia," in *Islam in the Era of Nation States*, 7.

28. Rohana Ariffin, "Feminism in Malaysia: A Historical and Present Perspective on Women's Struggles in Malaysia," *Women's Studies International Forum* 22, no. 4 (1999): 417–23.

29. Mahathir was praised by many international observers as one of the Muslim world's moderate voices for his ability to reconcile religion and modernization projects, although he recently claimed that the label "moderate Muslim" is an oxymoron. See "No Such Thing as a Moderate Muslim," *Bernama*, February 24, 2007. A controversial and enigmatic leader, Mahathir followed a political trajectory synonymous with judicial tempering, removal of the royal veto and immunity from prosecution, excessive cronyism, and arbitrary

detentions of those opposed to his policies. See Khoo Boo Teik, *Paradoxes of Mahathirism: An Intellectual Biography of Mahathir Mohamad* (Oxford: Oxford University Press, 2003); Diane Mauzy and R. S. Milne, "The Mahathir Administration in Malaysia: Discipline through Islam," *Pacific Affairs* 56, no. 4 (1983–84): 617–48.

30. Refer to the following media reports: "Malaysia Not a Secular State, Says Najib," *Bernama*, July 17, 2007; "Ministry Bans Islamic State Debate in Media," *Malaysiakini*, July 19, 2007; "Ministry Bans 18 Books," *Bernama*, June 15, 2006. Among banned movies are *The Prince of Egypt* ("Malaysia Bans Spielberg's Prince," *BBC News*, January 27, 1999) and *The Passion of the Christ* (*The Guardian*, "Malaysian Censors Say That Passion Is Only for Christians," July 30, 2004); "Malaysian Church, Weekly Newspaper Sue Government for Banning Use of Word 'Allah,'" Associated Press, December 28, 2007; "Singer Draws Ire of Religious Police," *The Star*, July 6, 2007; and "Malaysia Club Raid Sparks Row," *BBC News*, February 18, 2005.

31. The majority of National Alliance seats are held by three major race-based political parties: United Malays National Organization (UMNO), Malaysian Chinese Association (MCA), and Malaysian Indian Congress (MIC). The prime minister is always elected from the Malay political party (UMNO) and Mohd. Najib Tun Abdul Razak was sworn into office as the new prime minister in April 2009. A shift in the political landscape began with the *Reformasi* movement headed by supporters of the ousted deputy prime minister Anwar Ibrahim on sodomy and corruption charges during Mahathir's years. This movement has grown into a political party that formed Pakatan Rakyat, a coalition of People's Justice Party (PKR), Democratic Action Party (DAP), and PAS, which performed well in the general election on March 8, 2008, whereas Barisan National failed to secure a two-thirds majority in Parliament. For a social and political analysis of the result, see Bridget Welsh, "Election Post-Mortem: Top 10 Factors," *Malaysiakini*, March 12, 2008; Ooi Kee Beng, Johan Savaranamuttu, and Lee Hock Guan, *March 8: Eclipsing May 13* (Singapore: Institute of Southeast Asian Studies, 2008); and Ioannis Gatsiounis, *Beyond the Veneer: Malaysia's Struggle for Dignity and Direction* (Singapore: Monsoon Books, 2008). As of June 2009, the country is embroiled in political turmoil concerning corruption, constitutional crisis, sexual scandals, and a flagging economy, among others. For example, refer to "Malaysia Political Tension Ratchets Up," *Asia Sentinel*, May 6, 2009; "Malaysian Opposition Media Banned," *BBC News*, March 23, 2009; and Anil Netto, "A Battle of Wills in Malaysia's Perak," *Asia Times Online*, February 11, 2009 at http://www.atimes.com/atimes/Southeast_Asia/KB11Ae01.html.

32. *Hudud* indicates fixed punishment for such severe crimes as theft, adultery, and slanderous accusation. Salbiah Ahmad writes, "*Hudud*, in its legal sense, means a punishment which has been prescribed by God in the

reveled text of the Qur'an or the *Sunnah* (of the Prophet), the application of which is the right of God (*haqq* Allah)." See Salbiah Ahmad, "Zina and Rape under the Syariah Criminal Code (11) Bill 1993 (Kelantan)," in *Hudud in Malaysia: The Issues at Stake*, ed. Rose Ismail (Kuala Lumpur: SIS Forum Bhd, 1995), 20.

33. Examples of amendments include allowing polygamous marriages contracted outside the jurisdiction of the courts to be registered with a minor fine or jail sentence and permitting the registration of divorces pronounced outside court. See Maznah Mohamad, ed., *Muslim Women and Access to Justice: Historical, Legal, and Social Experience in Malaysia* (Penang: Women's Crisis Centre, 2000).

34. The culture of "blame the victim" in relation to sexuality and sexual violence is demonstrated by both PAS and the state. The leader of PAS stated that women who are victims of rape deserve their predicament for their choice of "skimpy clothes" ("Malaysian Minister in Rape Row," *BBC News*, October 9, 2000), and a high-profile Malaysian cleric proposed that women should be fitted with chastity belts to prevent rape ("Shocked Groups Slam Chastity Belt for Women Proposal," *The Star*, February 17, 2007).

35. See Amina Wadud, *Qur'an and Women Rereading the Sacred Text from a Woman's Perspective* (Oxford: Oxford University Press, 1999).

36. Leila Ahmed, *Women and Gender In Islam: Historical Roots of a Modern Debate* (New Haven, CT: Yale University Press, 1992).

37. Ibid., 66.

38. Bouthania Shaaban, "The Muted Voices of Women Interpreters," in *Faith and Freedom: Women's Human Rights in the Muslim World*, ed. Mahnaz Afkhami (Syracuse, NY: Syracuse University Press, 1995), 61; Asma Barlas, *'Believing Women' in Islam: Unreading Patriarchal Interpretations of the Quran* (Austin: University of Texas Press, 2002), 93; Fatima Mernissi, *The Veil and the Male Elite: A Feminist Interpretation of Women's Rights in Islam*, trans. Mary Jo Lakeland (New York: Perseus Books, 1991).

39. Abdullahi An-Na'im, "The Future of Shari'a and the Debate in Northern Nigeria," in *Comparative Perspectives on Shari'a in Nigeria*, ed. Philip Ostien, Jamila Nasir, and Franz Kogelmann (Ibadan, Nigeria: Spectrum Books, 2005), 327–57; 337.

40. Mission Statement, Sisters in Islam.

41. Examples of memoranda to the state are the Kelantan *Shari'a* Criminal Bill (1993), Domestic Violence Bill (1994), Islamic Family Law on Polygamy (1996), *Shari'a* Criminal Law and Fundamental Liberties (1997), equal right to guardianship for Muslim women (1998), and Syriah in Malaysian language Court Proceedings on Matrimonial Issues (2000). Sisters in Islam letters to the newspapers cover issues of polygamy (1990, 1996, 2002), equality (1991), dress and modesty in Islam (1991, 1997, 2001), the Hudud law (1993–94, 2002),

domestic violence (1996), women and work (1999), punishment for apostasy (1999, 2000), incest (2000, 2001), rape (2000), and freedom of expression in Islam (2002). Sisters in Islam also organizes workshops, forums, and public lectures, for example, Equality: Women and Islam (1996), Islam, Reproductive Health and Women's Rights (1998), Islamic Family Law and Justice for Women (2001), Sexuality Rights (2001), and Rights at Home (2003). Some of the public lecture series are Islam and Modernity (1995), Islam, Qur'an and the Female Voice (1996), Political Islam and Challenge of Democracy (2000), and Women in Islam: What Identities? Whose Interest? (2002).

42. For discussion of this case, see Nik Norani Nik Badlishah, *Marriage and Divorce under Islamic Law* (Kuala Lumpur: International Law Books Services, 1998).

43. See Nazri Abdullah, "Undang-undang Kekeluargaan Islam: Siapa yang Keliru?" [Islamic Family Law: Who Is Confused?], *Berita Minggu*, August 5, 1990; "Sejauh manakah undang-undang boleh halang poligami?" [How Far Can the Laws Restrict Polygamy?], *Mingguan Malaysia*, August 5, 1990; "Noorkumalasari Appeals to Trader's Wife," *The Star*, August 4, 1990.

44. This letter appeared under different titles with minor content variations in the local English- and Malay-language newspapers: "Polygamy Is Not a Right Enshrined in the Quran," *New Straits Times*, August 20, 1990; "Betulkan Salah Anggap Lelaki Tentang Hak Berpoligami" [Correct Men's Assumptions about Their Rights to Polygamy], *Utusan Malaysia*, August 18, 1990.

45. This was the second battle fought by the newly established Muslim community of Medina (Yathrib) after fleeing religious persecution from the Meccans. Led by Abu Sufyan, the Meccan army defeated the Medinan army.

46. An-Nisa 4:3: "If you fear that you shall not be able to deal justly with the orphans, marry women of your choice, two or three, or four; but if you fear that you shall not be able to deal justly (with them) then only one." An-Nisa 4:129: "You are never able to be fair and just between women even if that were your ardent desire."

47. In accordance with the customs of his time, Muhammad had concubines (according to Islamic tradition, he had two, cited in al-Tabari, 9:141). His favorite was Mariyah, a Coptic Christian slave who was sent as a gift from the Muqawqis of Egypt. She bore him a son, Ibrahim, who died in infancy. The Prophet's attraction and attention toward Mariyah started a rebellion in his household after one of his wives, Hafsah, found the Prophet in bed with Mariyah on the day designated for her. See Maxime Rodinson, *Muhammad* (London: Penguin Books, 1971); Montgomery W. Watt, *Muhammad: Prophet and Statesman* (London: Oxford University Press, 1961); Karen Armstrong, *Muhammad: A Biography of the Prophet* (San Francisco: Harper San Francisco, 1992).

48. For instance, in 1996, the Jabatan Agama Islam Selangor (JAIS) (Selangor Islamic Affairs Department) suggested accelerating petitions for polygamy without the consent of existing wife or wives; in 2002, debates on relegalizing polygamy for non-Muslim communities materialized, and SIS chastised the Muslim community for not leading by example to ban and abolish the practice. In 2003, SIS objected to the initiative in the state of Malacca to provide subsidized housing for polygamous men and applauded the Selangor state's moved to tighten the procedure for polygamy by requiring the consenting parties to be present in court before permission can be granted for a polygamous marriage to be contracted. See "Ideal State of Marriage in Islam," *The Star*, 1996; "Controversy on Polygamy," *New Straits Times* and *The Sun*, 2002; "Misunderstanding of the Prophet's Sunnah on Polygamy," SIS, 2002; "Tightened Procedure for Polygamy," *The Star*, 2003; "Deception and Dishonesty in the Practice of Polygamy," SIS, 2005; "How Polygamy Impacts the Family," *The Sun*, 2006; and "Poligami Dalam Hukum Islam" [Polygamy in Islamic Law], SIS, 2007.

49. Organizations under this coalition are All Women's Action Society (AWAM), Persatuan Isteri dan Keluarga Polis (Perkep), Persatuan Suri dan Anggota Wanita Perkhidmatan Awam (Puspanita), Perseketuan Pertubuhan-Pertubuhan Wanita Malaysia (NCWO), Persatuan Pekerja Wanita (PERWA-NIS), Wanita Perkim Kebangsaan, Wanita Inovatif Jayadiri (WIJADI), Women's Aid Organisation (WAO), Women's Candidacy Initiative (WCI), Women's Centre for Change (WCC), and Wanita Ikram.

50. Civil court judge Faiza Tamby Chik, in his judgment of September 11, 2003, for the originating summons (S8-24-3586-02) filed by Shamala, responded: "On 27 March 2003 the same Syariah Court issued a warrant of arrest against the plaintiff/wife for failure to attend the said Syariah Court. I cannot understand why the said Syariah Court whose jurisdiction is territorial and over matrimonial disputes involving Muslim marriages only can issue such a warrant. I am of the opinion that it is unconstitutional for the said Syariah Court to issue the warrant of arrest against the Plaintiff/Wife. In any event, the order for Warrant of Arrest has been stayed by the court on 17 April 2003 pending the outcome of Saman Pemula No. S8-24-297-2003." Cited from Rizal Chek Hashim, "Justice and Jurisdictions: The Shamala Sathiyaseelan v. Dr Jeyaganesh C Mograrajah (Muhammad Ridzuan) Custody Case," *Aliran Monthly* 7, 2004.

51. See "Apex Court Rules on Jurisdiction in Civil Divorce Involving Muslim," *Bernama*, December 2, 2007.

52. "Malaysia Tackles Child Conversion," *BBC News*, April 23, 2009.

53. Azlina Jailani was born a Muslim and changed her name to Lina Joy after embracing Christianity. She was baptized; and in an attempt to live her faith and life publicly, Lina petitioned the National Registration Department (NRD) to change her name and religious status. The name change was

approved but not the religious status. She is unable marry her Christian fiancé unless her legal status is recognized. Lina appealed to the High Court in 2001 to legally recognize her religious status, but in 2004 the Court of Appeal dismissed the case on the basis that her renunciation of Islam was not verified by the *Shari'a* Court. In 2007, the federal court rejected her appeal on the grounds that the jurisdiction in conversion lies solely with the *Shar'ia* Court. See *Lina Joy v Majlis Agama Islam Wilayah Persekutuan & 2 Ors* 2005 [CA], The Malaysian Bar; "Lina Joy Loses Appeal," *The Star Online*, May 30, 2007; Jane Perletz, "Once Muslim, Now Christian and Caught in the Courts," *New York Times*, August 24, 2006. For a recent summary of contentious cases on freedom of religion, see Johan Abdullah, "The Slide in Ethnic Relations," *Aliran Monthly* 26, no. 6, 2006.

54. SIS press statement, "Regarding Inter-religious Issues," April 2007.

55. SIS press statement, "Exercise Wisdom and Compassion on Freedom of Religion Issues," May 2007.

56. See "Media Room" section of the Article 11 coalition Web site: www .Article11.org.

57. SIS, *The State Has No Role in Moral Policing* (Petaling Jaya, 2005).

58. See Othman et al., *Malaysia.*

59. "Punishing Non-Muslims for Khalwat against Constitution," *The Star Online*, April 4, 2008.

60. SIS, *Moral Policing Violates Qur'anic Spirit and Fundamental Rights* (Petaling Jaya, 2005).

61. I have incorporated only partial criticisms of SIS for the purpose of this discussion.

62. See Sa'odah Elias, "PAS Wants Sisters in Islam Probed," *The Star Online*, June 7, 2009; Adib Zalkapli, "PAS Wants Sisters in Islam Banned," *The Malaysian Insider*, June 8, 2009; and Deborah Loh and Shanon Shah, "PAS Wants Sisters in Islam Investigated," *The Nut Graph*, June 7, 2009.

63. Dr. Mariah is one of the former Central Working Committee members of PAS who spoke out against PAS's resolution on SIS. On June 7, 2009, she stated, "I don't agree with banning them because I believe everybody needs to be able to speak their minds. . . . People think they are wrong, but I think their thoughts are rarely heard in Malaysia, and people tend to misunderstand them. . . . So if they invite me to their functions, I will go, because I don't have any problems with them." See Loh and Shah, "PAS Wants Sisters in Islam Investigated." She later issued the following statement on PAS's suggestion that the National Fatwa Council investigate SIS: "If [SIS] is found not to go against Islamic beliefs, then that is a certificate, or clearance, that their activities are based on Islamic struggles." See Zedeck Siew, "PAS Muslimat Oppose Unity Govt," *The Nut Graph*, June 18, 2009. In my personal interview with her in November 2006, she stated that although she sometimes disagrees

with SIS's viewpoints, she looks forward to their events and to continued engagement with SIS members.

64. Syed Jaymal Zahiid, "Hadi: SIS Know Nothing about Islam," *The Malaysian Insider* June 12, 2009. However, on the same day, the spiritual leader of PAS disagreed and was quoted saying, "I have met SIS leaders before and have no problems meeting them again. We should have more discussions and not simply ban the group." See "Enlighten Group Members Instead, says Nik Aziz," *New Straits Times*, June 11, 2009.

65. Zulkifli Noordin Blogspot, Ahli Parlimen Kulim Bandar Baharu, 18. www.zul4kulim.blogspot.com/2009/06/sisters-in-islam.html. Translated from Malay by author.

66. Dr. Mahathir Mohamad Blogspot, "Sound Bites" section, www.chedet .co.cc/chedetblog/2009/06/sound-bites-2.html#more; and "Shahrizat Defends Sisters in Islam," *The Star Online*, June 8, 2009.

67. Abdullahi An-Na'im, "Mahmud Muhammad Taha and the Crisis in Islamic Law Reform: Implications for Religious Relations," in *Muslims in Dialogue: The Evolution of a Dialogue*, ed. Leonard Swidler (Lewiston, NY: Edwin Mellen Press, 1992), 39.

68. Azza Basarudin, "Interview with Asma Barlas," *Islamic Institute for Human Rights*, 2002.

69. See Khaled Abou El Fadl, *The Authoritative and Authoritarian in Islamic Discourses* (Riyadh: Taiba Publishing House, 1997) and *Speaking in God's Name: Islamic Law, Authority and Women* (Oxford: OneWorld Publications, 2001).

70. Malaysian scholars Patricia Martinez and Saliha Hassan have made similar observations. See "Malaysia and Singapore: Early 20th Century to the Present," in *Encyclopedia of Women & Islamic Cultures*, vol. 1: *Methodologies, Paradigms, and Sources*, ed. Suad Joseph (Leiden: Brill, 2003), 222–27; Saliha Hassan, "Islamic Non-governmental Organizations," in *Social Movements in Malaysia: From Moral Communities to NGOs*, ed. Meredith Weiss and Saliha Hassan (New York: Routledge, 2002).

71. See Margot Badran, "Between Secular and Islamic Feminism/s: Reflections on the Middle East and Beyond," *Journal of Middle Eastern Women's Studies* 1, no. 1 (2005): 6–28; "Islamic Feminism: What's in a Name?" *Al Ahram*, no. 569, January 17–23, 2002; "Toward Islamic Feminism: A Look at the Middle East," in *Hermeneutics and Honor* ed. Asma Afsarudin and Anan Ameri (Cambridge: Harvard University Press, 1999), 159–88.

72. Omaima Abou-Bakr, "'Islamic Feminism? What's in a Name?' Preliminary Reflections," *Middle East Women's Studies Review* 15–16 (2001): 1–2.

73. Valentine Moghadam, "Islamic Feminism and Its Discontents: Towards a Resolution of the Debate," in *Gender, Islam, and Politics*, ed. Theresa Saliba (Chicago: University of Chicago Press, 2002), 15–52.

PART III

Body, Mind, and Spirit

CHAPTER 6

Muslim Women's Scholarship and the New Gender Jihad*

Roxanne D. Marcotte

Muslim women have always been active advocates and promoters of change when economical, social, political, and even religious conditions have affected them negatively. From at least the middle of the 19th century, Muslim women's movements, organizations, and the women's press have not ceased being active, as women have endeavored to improve their lives, whether from a secular or a religious perspective.[1] Throughout the 20th century, more and more Muslim women became literate with increased access to public education. A few eventually ventured into academia and chose to become advocates of change. Academia empowered a number of these women and provided them with opportunities to merge their spirituality, scholarship, and activism on the gender front, from where they could challenge and critically reevaluate their Islamic tradition. This is what Amina Wadud called "gender jihad."[2] In many instances, Muslim women's own personal experiences provided the catalyst that brought spirituality, scholarship, and activism together. Glimpses of these personal experiences provide some insight into what sparked their scholarly activism. These are individuals Gisela Webb likes

*I extend warm thanks to Prof. Martina Rieker, Director of the Cynthia Nelson Institute for Gender and Women's Studies (IGWS) at the American University in Cairo (April 26, 2009), for having provided me with an opportunity to discuss some of the ideas presented in this chapter at one of IGWS's research seminars, as well as Zayn R. Kassam for her kind invitation to contribute to this volume.

to call "scholar-activists,"[3] a useful term to designate Muslim women who struggle for the empowerment of women within the patriarchal Islamic tradition and Muslim society.

At the end of the 19th century and the beginning of the 20th century, Muslims were heralding modern reforms, but it was not until the end of the 20th and the beginning of the 21st centuries that Muslim women began themselves to herald the banners of gender reforms. For more than 30 years, Muslim women have been reevaluating normative Islam, going as far as challenging traditional leadership roles. More women are proposing new "feminist" yet quite Islamic understandings of the religious tradition, for example, Riffat Hassan; of the Qur'an, for example, Amina Wadud and Asma Barlas; of the legal tradition, for example, Etin Anwar and Kecia Ali. All these women have undertaken what might be labeled "feminist" critiques, by providing a variety of hermeneutical, philosophical, sociological, and religious readings that open new discursive spaces for thinking new possibilities for change.

This chapter explores this particularly interesting intersection of spirituality, activism, and scholarship in the lives and works of a few Muslim women. These scholar-activists have developed exceedingly sophisticated feminist arguments for gender reforms as means to counter dominant patriarchal discourses on women in Islam. The interplay of spirituality and scholarly activism in the lives of scholar-activists can be illustrated by appealing to narratives of the personal experiences that have triggered their lifelong interest and study of the place, status, roles, and rights of women that Islam offers them. The interplay can also be illustrated by looking at the works of Muslim women who live in Muslim countries and contrast those with the works of Muslim women who live in the West and Western women who have converted to Islam. Incursions into the nature of diasporic environments and the new discursive spaces they create can equally be helpful to shed some light on their work.

FEMINIST READINGS OF THE ISLAMIC TRADITION

Scholar-activists are driven by some sense of inadequacy or the perception of wrongs or injustices that need to be redressed. Their capacity of indignation often drives them to be quite critical of the injustices that take place in the name of their Islamic tradition. This often leads them to be more critical. It can take place within Muslim countries, as is the case with individuals like Fatima Mernissi (Morocco), or with groups like Sisters in Islam,[4] a group of professional Malaysian Muslim women committed to promoting women's rights within the framework of Islam.[5] Critical voices can also emerge from outside Muslim countries, as is the case with the activities of many scholar-activists who live in the West or with groups like the international solidarity network Women Living Under Muslim Laws (WLUML).[6]

Approaches that center on women and women's perspectives can be said to be feminist approaches. In the Islamic context, however, what constitutes an Islamic feminism? Muslim women do take feminist stances in their reinterpretations, but the idea of Islamic feminism remains, nonetheless, much debated, as is its politics.[7] One should, therefore, attempt to distinguish, as Badran does,[8] two different understandings of the term "Islamic feminism." One understanding of the term applies to what might constitute an explicit project for the betterment of women's situation within the framework of Islam. As such, the term becomes a useful analytical tool for shedding some light on Muslim women's writings and activities. A second understanding of the term consists of an identity that individuals consciously claim for themselves. While many Muslim women would not endorse the use of the term "Islamic feminism" to describe themselves and what they do, many of their writings and activities, nonetheless, aim at the betterment of women in Islam and can thus be understood in the first sense of the term. Islamic feminism, therefore, remains a valuable analytical category that can equally be applied to women who struggle for greater social or political roles for women within Islam, in spite of the constraints of their orthodox[9] or traditional[10] religious understandings and views.

Muslim women have been reclaiming the Islamic tradition in a number of ways, some through literary productions[11] and others through their work with various women's organizations. But at the heart of the projects of scholar-activists lies the process of reinterpretation, what June O'Connor identifies as "rereading, reconceiving, and reconstructing traditions."[12] Rereading women in Islam requires a reexamination of texts and traditions with a special attention to "women's presence and absence, women's words and women's silence, recognition given and denied women . . . Understanding the place of women, the contributions they have made and the ways they have been excluded,"[13] something Leila Ahmed has attempted to do in her *Women and Gender in Islam* (1992). Reconceiving women in Islam seeks "the retrieval and the recovery of lost sources and suppressed visions," what is also the project of "reclaiming" women's voices and heritage,[14] something Fatima Mernissi has done with her *Forgotten Queens of Islam* (1993). Reconstructing women in Islam is the reconstruction of the past "on the basis of new information and the use of historical imagination," together with "new paradigms for thinking, seeing, understanding, and valuing" that past, in order to rethink a whole tradition.[15] Anne Roald prefers to reduce these three steps to two: "namely the reselection or the rehierarchisation of source material, and the reinterpretation" of those sources, the former pertaining to the material to select (reselection), the latter to selected interpretative outlooks (reinterpretation).[16]

Reselection and reinterpretation are what a number of Muslim women—among them Amina Wadud, Asma Barlas, Etin Anwar, Kecia Ali, and Riffat Hassan—are undertaking with their writings. While their works employ various approaches (and agendas), they all fall under what we could label "progressive" interpretations of Islam.[17] More important, however, is the fact that these women's spirituality informs their project, as all of them have chosen to remain within the fold of Islam and none has thought of venturing into what Amina Wadud has called the suicidal "post-Muslim" position.[18] Their projects may be seen as their personal intellectual endeavors to engage with the religious tradition.

MUSLIM WOMEN LIVING IN MUSLIM COUNTRIES

Few Muslim women scholar-activists have gained the reputation of Moroccan sociologist Fatima Mernissi. Pursuing her academic career in Morocco, she criticized prevalent understandings of gender relations in the Muslim world with her sociological analyses of gender in Moroccan society,[19] record of the lives of Moroccan women,[20] attempts at a feminist theological critique of the "traditions" or *hadiths*,[21] homage to a number of prominent female Muslim leaders of the past,[22] and her political critique of democracy in Arab society.[23]

At times, banal incidents greatly impact an individual's life trajectory. Mernissi recounts what led her to write her *Women and Islam: An Historical and Theological Enquiry*. When asked if a woman could be the leader of Muslims, her dismayed grocer spontaneously replied, "I take refuge in Allah"; one customer murmured, "May God protect us from the catastrophes of the times!"; while another cited a *hadith* (a report attributed to the Prophet Muhammad): "Those who entrust their affairs to a woman will never know prosperity!" The authority of that *hadith* had settled the matter. Mernissi had to come to grips with the fact that the "political aphorism" was "as implacable as it [was] popular" and that

> silenced, defeated, and furious, I suddenly felt the urgent need to inform myself about this Hadith and to search out the texts where it is mentioned, to understand better its extraordinary power over the ordinary citizens of a modern state. . . . Revealing the misogynistic attitude of my neighbors, it indicated to me the path I should follow to better understand it—a study of the religious texts that everybody knows but no one

really probes, with the exception of the authorities on the subject: the mullahs and imams.[24]

With the help of Moulay Ahmed al-Khamlichi, a religious scholar and teacher of Islamic law at Mohammed V University in Rabat, and Ali Oumlil, a philosopher, she set out to investigate the authenticity of this particular political aphorism reported by Abu Bakra, one of the companions of the Prophet. Appeals to such *hadiths* perpetuate what she called a "tradition of misogyny."[25] While Bint al-Shati' was the first Muslim woman exegete of the Qur'an, she never really applied her exegetical skills to gender issues.[26] Mernissi, on the other hand, may have provided one of the first revolutionary feminist critiques of *hadiths*. Her journey back in time, what she called her "narrative of recollection," was not without posing certain pitfalls, as "delving into memory, slipping into the past, is an activity that these days is closely supervised, especially for Muslim women. A passport for such a journey is not always a right,"[27] adding that "it is not just the present that the imams and politicians want to manage to assure our well-being as Muslims, but above all the past that is being strictly supervised and completely managed for all of us, men and women. What is being supervised and managed, in fact, is memory and history."[28]

Mernissi's historical and theological critique provided one of the most incisive feminist critiques of *hadiths*, questioning the authenticity attributed to the two misogynist reports of Abu Bakra and Abu Hurayra that have both come to be included in authoritative collections of *hadiths* that are still used to derive religious interpretations. She relied on traditional Islamic exegetical principles to examine the misogyny of those two *hadiths*. Mernissi did not question the divine nature of the Qur'an, as revelation, but she took issue with the quasi-sacredness that *hadiths* have come to possess. In doing so, she provided greater Islamic legitimacy to her internal critique. Her Islamic critique was such that some of the staunchest critics of feminist approaches from among the ranks of the Islamists, such as Heba Raouf Ezzat, have appealed to her work.[29]

Much remains to be done, however, to present the local and indigenous voices of scholar-activists who live in the Muslim world. Noteworthy among those voices are Fatima Zahra-Zryouil and Amel Grami, who each in her own way has provided gendered critiques and feminist interpretations. Moroccan Fatima Zahra-Zryouil has, since the mid-1980s, written more than half a dozen works on women in Islam and on women in Muslim countries,[30] while Tunisian Amel Grami has recently published *Difference in Arabo-Islamic Culture: Gender Studies* (2007). Many more Muslim women who tackled the complex issue of women and gender in Islam live, however, in the West.

THE NEW DISCURSIVE SPACES OF DIASPORIC ENVIRONMENTS

In many Muslim countries, women's critical engagement with religious traditions and with Islam in particular is difficult, controlled, curtailed, and often censured. Liberal voices have been silenced in the most dramatic ways. Egyptian Nasr Hamid Abu Zayd was found guilty of apostasy in 1996 and thereafter forced into exile; more tragically, Sudanese Mahmoud Mohamed Taha was executed in 1985 for the same crime. During the last 30 years, the most fertile environments for Muslim women's critical engagement with Islam has undoubtedly been diasporic contexts where they have been able to reevaluate more freely the often traditional and cultural understandings of religious norms prevalent in Muslim countries. In non-Muslim contexts, Muslim women who were raised in Muslim countries, second- and even third-generation Muslims living in the West, or Muslim converts can engage in new creative dialogues with the religious tradition. New diasporic discursive spaces allow them to explore, through their scholarship and their activism, new understandings of gender equality in Islam by claiming for themselves the right to interpret the Islamic tradition and Islamic religious texts and beliefs in a manner that becomes meaningful to them as Muslim women.

Diasporic environments appear to be, by their nature, often conducive to the emergence of a variety of novel discourses. The term "diaspora" does not merely encompass any group of expatriates or individual migrants but alludes to the importance of the maintenance of community identities in diasporic environments based on a relationship with the homeland and all that it represents.[31] While typologies of diasporas can be quite complex, most highlight the "deep symbolical (and at times organizational) relation individuals and communities have to the 'homeland'—be it an independent nation-state or set in quasi-mythological distant past."[32] The symbolic relation is "maintained by reference to constructs of common language, history, culture and—central to many cases—to religion."[33]

In its early stage of introduction, Islam in diasporic environments remains an Islam of the peripheries, on the outskirts of the heartlands of the Islamic world whose epicenter has often been the Middle East (e.g., Mecca, Baghdad, and Damascus) and, at times, the Indian subcontinent. While "a 'homeland' orientation is widely perceived to be *the* major element that distinguishes a diaspora from ordinary immigrant expatriate communities," the complexity of "*homeland* orientation" should not be underestimated.[34] Immigrant communities often revolve and grow in symbiosis with their religious communities. Martin Baumann noted the importance of the maintenance of religious identity for the cohesion of the community,[35] and Gary Bouma reminded us of the importance of religious

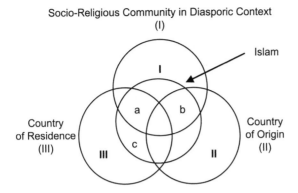

Figure 6.1
Three-Directional, Reciprocal Relations

settlements and the role of places of worship.[36] The importance of the religious element remains undervalued for both groups and individuals. Religion helps maintain cultural specificity and identity. Moreover, religious traditions remain essential for the construction of identities as individuals negotiate the complex relationships they have with religious, cultural, and ethnic communal identities in new minority contexts.[37] George Marcus noted that diaspora communities maintain multiple relationships.[38] These relationships shape their identities that do not consist of an "either-or," but they are more frequently "both-and," or partial and overlapping identities.[39] Baumann identified what he called the "tripolar interrelatedness" of the diasporic socioreligious community, the country of origin, and the country of residence.[40]

Baumann's "three-directional, reciprocal relations" model, illustrated here with a Venn diagram (Figure 6.1), remains useful to locate various discursive spaces immigrant Muslim women and Muslim converts inhabit. If we add on a fourth concentric circle in the middle to represent the Islamic tradition and its multiple relationships to the three different contexts (I, II, III), then one can envisage that a scholar-activist (a) engaged with her host country (III) and her socio-religious community (I) can remain committed to her Islamic tradition and yet operate a distinction between her new diasporic identities and the "culturally" determined religious understanding of the Islam of her country of origin (II). This would not be the case for an immigrant (b) who would choose not to interact with her host country and, therefore, be less inclined to take a critical stance regarding the "cultural" elements of her understanding of the Islam prevalent in her country of origin (II). A woman living in the West who converts to Islam (c) would, on the other hand, not necessarily possess personal experiences of Islamic understandings prevalent among diasporic socio-religious communities (I) or of "cultural" Islam associated with understandings prevalent in Muslim countries (II) unless she were to spend some time in either (or both) of them. Scholar-activists, it must be noted, can inhabit any of these positions. On the whole, insights provided by studies of diasporic religious and community identities can thus be said to provide useful heuristic tools and models for explaining the evident disparity between the production of new gender discourses in greater numbers in the Muslim world and the one occurring in the West.

IMMIGRANT MUSLIM WOMEN LIVING IN THE WEST

Greater access to higher education has also meant that, especially in the last twenty years or so, an increasing number of Muslim women have been actively claiming the right to interpret both the Islamic tradition and its sacred text(s). Some scholar-activists were raised and educated in their country of origin before they immigrated to the West, often to pursue higher education in a variety of disciplines, among them gender studies (Leila Ahmed), religious and Islamic studies (Riffat Hassan), international studies and journalism (Asma Barlas), and philosophy (Etin Anwar). Raised in Muslim countries, many scholar-activists now work as academics or researchers in the West, others may be second- or third-generation Muslim women, and still others are converts to Islam (Amina Wadud, Kecia Ali, and Aminah McCloud).

Like Mernissi, American Egyptian-born scholar Leila Ahmed has written what has become the standard reference work for many Western Muslim women with her *Women and Gender in Islam*. Originally intended as a historical survey of the lives of women in the Middle East, the focus of the work quickly shifted to the changing ways in which women and gender were discussed, especially in the wake of the resurgence of Islamic calls that "urge the reinstitution of the laws and practices set forth in the core Islamic discourses" and "shape and are shaped by specific moments in specific societies."[41]

In her autobiography, Ahmed notes that the idea of looking into Muslim women's history first began after a lecture on women in Islam while she was still a student in the Gulf region. One of the women sitting beside her objected to the lecturer's neglect of the strong women leaders and warriors in Islamic history, for he focused solely on "women whose virtues were as good wives and mothers."[42] The incident strengthened Ahmed's resolve to study Muslim women's lives (in the United States).

Leila Ahmed alluded to the existence of a "textual Islam," which she equated with men's Islam.[43] Male elite religious scholars produced this textual Islam that bears the hallmark of patriarchy and, as Fatima Mernissi demonstrated, was even, at times, misogynistic. Others, like Kecia Ali, have, however, noted that the same textual Islam could sometimes be more protective of women's rights than cultural practices.[44] This textual Islam does not, however, reflect the experiences of all Muslims, especially Muslim women's experiences, as Islamic discursive texts and their interpretations were written by male religious scholars and jurists. Asked whether there would ever "be a bridge between the living Islam of Muslim women and the official Islam," Ahmed replied,

> If you consider that today there are more than six millions [sic] Muslims in America, and that we're in the process of witnessing the development of an Islam that, for the first time in history, is unfolding in a country where the freedoms of thought and speech are guaranteed political rights, then the possibilities are quite different.[45]

The possibilities for the blossoming of a more egalitarian Islam envisioned by Ahmed are truly quite different from the limited ones available to Muslims living in the "countries where Islamic 'fundamentalism' is entrenched or growing," as in Egypt. Those are the possibilities that scholar-activists living in the West are exploring.

Another scholar-activist who struggled for more than 30 years to critically analyze the issue of women in Islam is Riffat Hassan. A Pakistani by birth, born to a Sayyid family of Lahore, she has spelled out the theological assumptions that lay at the heart of gender distinctions and discrimination in Islam. The event that led her to write "almost by accident and rather reluctantly" about Islamic feminist theology occurred more than a quarter century ago, in the mid-1970s. As the nominated faculty adviser to the Muslim Students' Association at the university where she was teaching, Hassan was invited to address the association's annual seminar, where Muslim women were themselves not allowed to attend, to read a paper on women in Islam. Members of the Muslim Students' Association believed that "it would have been totally inappropriate to expect a Muslim woman, even one who taught them Islamic studies, to be competent to speak on any other subject pertaining to Islam." Although she "resented what the assigning of a subject meant" and she had not previously been interested in the subject, the event was of great importance:

> I do not know exactly when my "academic" study of women in Islam became a passionate quest for truth and justice on behalf of Muslim women. It began, perhaps, when I came to understand the impact so-called Islamic ideas and attitudes regarding women had had on my own life. What began as a scholarly exercise became an Odyssean venture in self-understanding. But "enlightenment" does not always lead to "endless

bliss." The more I saw the justice and compassion of God reflected in the Qur'anic teachings regarding women, the more anguished and angry I became seeing the injustice and inhumanity to which Muslim women in general are subjected in actual life. I began to feel strongly that it was my duty, as a part of the microscopic minority of educated Muslim women, to do as much consciousness-raising regarding the situation of Muslim women as I could. The journey which began in Stillwater has been a long and arduous one.[46]

Hassan's reflective account of the impact the "quest for truth and justice" had on her outlook on Muslim society eloquently illustrates the coming together of spirituality, scholarship, and activism in her own personal life, a convergence that has become the hallmark of many Muslim women intent on improving theirs and other Muslim women's lives.

Hassan set out to identify and analyze fundamental theological assumptions responsible for patriarchal and even misogynist readings of the Islamic tradition. She identified three major assumptions that have determined negatively religious understanding and interpretation of the scriptures: namely,

> (1) that God's primary creation is man, not woman, since woman is believed to have been created from man's rib, hence, women are derivative and secondary ontologically; (2) that woman, not man, was the primary agent of what is generally referred to as "Man's Fall" or man's expulsion from the Garden of Eden, hence, "all daughters of Eve" are to be regarded with hatred, suspicion, and contempt; and (3) that woman was created not only *from* man but also *for* man, which makes her existence merely instrumental and not fundamental [italics in text].[47]

Hassan indicated that the theological and ontological constructions of women's inferior status were derived from the biblical story of Eve's creation from man's rib, a story that is not Qur'anic. On the contrary, the Qur'anic creation story posits one undifferentiated primordial being from which all of humanity derived, including Adam and Eve, thus affirming an original and ontological equality imparted to woman and man, on account of their equal shares of this primordial being.[48] Muslims must, therefore, revert to egalitarian Qur'anic principles and ethics. Only then will the feminist project of changing society, mentalities, and relationships between individuals have any chance of transforming the Islamic tradition and Muslim societies.[49]

Another scholar-activist, Asma Barlas, elected to examine the Qur'an in an attempt to identify and elucidate the nature of existing Qur'anic principles of equality that Muslims have historically been unable to put into practice. Born and raised in Pakistan, Barlas completed a BA in English literature and philosophy in Lahore, where she also obtained an MA in journalism from the University of the Punjab. Forced to flee Pakistan at the beginning of the 1980s, she eventually obtained political asylum in the United States, where she pursued her education, completing an MA and a PhD in international studies at the University of Denver. Her recent work titled *"Believing Women" in Islam: Unreading Patriarchal Interpretations of the Qur'an* was the outcome of a course she taught in Middle East politics.[50] She mentioned that during the process of redaction and of developing her arguments, she came to appreciate more fully her own faith.[51]

Barlas's work aimed at elucidating the nature of a text many accuse of being patriarchal, by "unreading" patriarchal interpretations of the Qur'an, noting that "more and more Muslims . . . are beginning to reclaim their interpretive rights."[52] For Barlas, the recovery of the scriptural basis for sexual equality between men and women is possible because Qur'anic epistemology upholds "the principle of the ontic equality of the sexes" upon which it is possible to "theorize radical sexual equality from the Qur'an's teachings."[53] Both woman and man came into existence from one single entity, thus both partaking in the same primordial being upon which the principle of equality rests.

Barlas's feminist project for recovering the Qur'anic principle of equality necessitated a new gender-critical rereading of the Qur'an with which she could then reconceive and, ultimately, reconstruct Islamic interpretations that rest on what she calls the "principle of ontic equality of the sexes." She wrote *"Believing Women" in Islam*

> in the hope that it will be among those egalitarian and antipatriarchal readings of Islam that will, in time, come to replace misogynist and patriarchal understandings of it. . . . As a Muslim woman, I have a great deal at stake in combating repressive readings of the Qur'an and also in affirming that Islam is not based in the idea of male epistemic privilege, or in a formally ordained interpretive community, or clergy. This means that "all Muslims may qualify" as interpreters of religious knowledge or *mujtahid* . . . [who] is thus, before all else, a believer imbued with a sense of God-consciousness, and a believer's right to interpret religion derives not from social sanctions (permission from clergies or interpretive communities), but from the depths of our own convictions and from the advice the Qur'an gives us to exercise our own intellect and knowledge in reading it.[54]

Like other scholar-activists who struggle for gender jihad, Barlas claimed the right to produce, as a woman, religious knowledge. No longer can this be the sole prerogative of Muslim men. As did Muslim reformers before her, Barlas also claimed the right to practice *ijtihad*, or independent rational investigation of the religious tradition and its sacred text, what was once the privilege of male religious scholars (*ulama*) and jurists (*fuqaha*) who were specialists of Islamic law. Muslim women's new *ijtihad* becomes gynocentric as it attempts to deconstruct patriarchal and anti-egalitarian readings of Islam and to examine their negative impacts on Muslim women's lives. Muslim women have embarked on a process of revisiting, reconceiving, and reconstructing the Islamic tradition, and *ijtihad* becomes the means to proceed forward. A new gynocentric *ijtihad* is emerging as a novel methodological approach for rethinking Islamic hermeneutics, a development that is bound to shape the future of gender jihad. Once more, we see how spirituality, scholarship, and activism have become the backbone of Barlas's engagement with the religious tradition and her efforts to envision the possibility of a truly egalitarian Islam.

Like most scholar-activists, Barlas believed that gender inequality and discrimination in Islam are not derived from the Qur'an but that they originate in *hadiths* and religious commentaries (*tafsirs*). There exists, therefore, a need for the reevaluation of this literature and for a systematic critique of methods used by Muslims to produce religious interpretations. An egalitarian reading has not yet been possible, however, because of hermeneutical and theological failures, Riffat Hassan having highlighted the latter. Barlas wrote that "Muslims have yet to derive a theory of equality from the Qur'an."[55] The elaboration of such a theory will depend on how Muslim women position the Qur'an and themselves in relation to the sacred text. Barlas's rereading of the Qur'an was part of this project, whose approach allowed her to think of equality and justice as an intrinsic component of the nature of the divine by focusing on what she called "divine ontology" and the idea of God's self-disclosure.

Barlas, first, understood God's absolute sovereignty as one that is not transferable to human beings, for "no theory of male (or popular) sovereignty that pretends to be an extension of God's Rule/Sovereignty, or comes into conflict with it, can be considered compatible with the doctrine of *Tawhīd*,"[56] or the unity of God; stating otherwise would only be "theologically unsound." She could then argue that the most central and pivotal concept of Islam—the doctrine of unity (*tawhid*)—directly undermines "theories of father-rule/right."[57] She then focused on God's justice, such that God's speech cannot be oppressive on any individual and, by extension, cannot be misogynist or teach misogyny or injustice, because divine justice "is self-circumscribed by respect for the rights of humans as moral agents," both women and men.[58] And finally, she discussed the notion of incomparability, which precludes any such anthropomorphic terms as "father" (male), which, for example, occurs in Christianity. As such, Islam cannot be patriarchal in the same sense: "Not only should we recover the liberatory potential of Islam's rejection of a patriarchalized God, we should also make it the hermeneutic site from which to read the Qur'ān's antipatriarchal epistemology."[59] She could then conclude that "the liberatory nature of Qurānic epistemology inheres in the very nature of God's Being,"[60] whereby only one reading of the Qur'an is possible, a reading that is "holistic," one that she found in the Qur'an itself (Q 3:7; Q 15:89–93). Barlas's own reading of the Qur'an sought to be a holistic hermeneutics.[61]

Her project aimed at liberating Muslim women through the "rereading" of the Qur'an, in order to provide and establish the Islamic legitimacy of her "liberatory readings" and thus ground them in the Islamic tradition because change will not come from, or be legitimized by, secular approaches.[62] Others, like Abdullahi An-Na'im, have similarly argued that "people are more likely to comply with standards of human rights when they accept norms and values underlying those standards as valid or legitimate from the point of view of their own culture,"[63] thus providing them with greater Islamic cultural legitimacy, which, in turn, may foster greater commitment and implementation. In a similar fashion, Barlas sought to provide Islamic legitimacy to her readings by grounding them in the "liberatory aspects of the Qur'an's teachings."[64] This liberatory project remains greatly political, for it seeks to guarantee women rights by using the Qur'an to argue for those rights.[65]

Scholar-activists employ a variety of gender-critical approaches. Etin Anwar, for example, explored the intersection of gender studies and philosophy in an attempt to create a new discursive space for her philosophical discussions on *Gender and Self in Islam* (2006). She located her approach within the critical discourses of Muslim feminists who are social and political activists and who work for the empowerment of Muslim women. Her perspective was grounded in her *santri* identity (class and religion) as a Muslim who, like many, tries to "embody Islam in their everyday lives, best exemplified in the culture of the *madrasah* and *pesantren* (Islamic boarding schools)."[66] Arguing against the reduction of Muslim women's experiences and discourses to one particular type of Islam, she appealed to the specificity of cultural Indonesian and South Asian Islam and to the need to recognize the existence of a variety of Islamic understandings and practices.[67] She grounded her perspective in her own experiences of Indonesian Islam that, she argues, exhibits greatly inclusive features. She could thus point to the existence of more "liberal" interpretations of "cultural" Islam, the latter generally denounced as patriarchal.

Noteworthy is the fact that Anwar did not provide any clue as to the events that might have led her to explore issues of gender in Islam. She only noted that she does not propose a treatment of the legal aspects of gender and self. Nonetheless, she identified what she calls the inclusive nature of *shari'a*, an element she deemed important for any discussion on gender and Islam.[68] Anwar attempted to rethink the place of *shari'a*, rather than to discard it. Others, like Ziba Mir-Hosseini, provided detailed analyses of legal developments within Shi'i Islam.[69] Anwar believed *shari'a* presently embodies only a "partial Islam" with respect to gender. In order to bring about a fully developed Islam, the production of an egalitarian gender system remains a need.[70] Hence, she aimed at "uncovering" the roots of Islam's hierarchical gender system and its "oppressive" effect on the "self-becoming" of Muslim women as agents. She wrote:

> Muslim women have for centuries lived within a social, cultural, and religious "system" that is not friendly to them. This structure systematically alienates women's worth as human beings. However, Muslim women do not recognize the alienation of their selves as a problem because the system in which they live their lives is so powerful and is sometimes alleged to be the system that women themselves unquestionably support.[71]

Anwar's work provides, however, yet another example of a scholar-activist who now lives in a diasporic context from where she can propose her feminist critique of the religious tradition Muslim majority countries might not deem appropriate.

For Anwar, Muslims will produce an egalitarian gender system only by returning to the scriptures and by deconstructing hierarchical perceptions of gender-minded Muslims as legitimate sources of knowledge, of authority, and of power.[72] Both provide a means to highlight the two levels of the "construction of the self": a first level of Qur'anic ontological inclusiveness of the self—the idea of the creation of the first undifferentiated "one self" (*nafs*)[73] with which an ontological equality, given that both male and female possess the same origin, can be envisioned—and a second level of embodied or material self that emerges out of social, political, and religious constructs. This second level is particularly important because the "mythologizing of the divine role of women as a partner in reproduction (with all its attendant household responsibilities) is seen as ideal for women" and is "reiterated through numerous institutions ranging from family, society, and state regulations, and are often magnified and politicized by the Islamist movements."[74] This mythologized vision is one reason why "it is 'safer' for a Muslim woman growing up in the Muslim community to embody the fixity of the material self" that requires the presentation of timid, docile, and obedient behaviors, as opposed to assertive and talkative women associated with "disobedient and unruly women,"[75] a reminder of Deniz Kandiyoti's patriarchal bargain.[76] From the vantage point of the periphery, however, Muslim women can disregard socially, culturally, and politically constructed popular authoritative male interpretations of religious teachings.[77]

Epistemic and ontological reforms required to establish the new egalitarian gender system in Islam will need an "ethical transformation" through the embodiment of this new egalitarian Islam in the daily lives of Muslims at both individual and social levels.[78] For this purpose, Muslims need to appeal to an "ontological *tawhid* (the Oneness of God) as a means to promote an inclusive humanity," unity (*tawhid*) being at the heart of Muslim theological thinking.[79] Anwar noted that "the self-personal experience can become political when women altogether voice their concerns of social, cultural, psychological, and political realities that oppress them and care for transforming the current conditions by bringing women into the front-page of humanity." These changes would be more effective if initiated from "within its locality," thus allowing feminists to find the best way to transform their condition "without much suspicion from the hierarchical gender-minded Muslims."[80] Such theological perspectives have the potential of being quite disruptive of traditional religious authority.

CONVERTS TO ISLAM LIVING IN THE WEST

Raised and educated in the West, some Muslim women converts have become active re-readers of the Islamic tradition. These women, who were completely socialized in Western societies, have, for any number of reasons, chosen to convert to Islam. Their personal experiences have, nonetheless, led some of them to be at the forefront of scholarly activism. How can one account for their feminist stances, as converts, when it is often assumed that new converts, whose identities as new Muslims need to be strengthened and reaffirmed, would not generally adopt critical stances on the religious tradition and not be unsatisfied with "canonical" interpretations of Islam?

One should not forget that Islam, its values and principles, is detached from any initial process of "inculturation"—that is, the acquisition of the behavioral characteristics of a particular culture or group by a person—into any particular Muslim society. Converts come to Islam from a different perspective, even while they may be in contact with Muslim diasporic communities. Cultural interpretations of Islam are not automatically part of their understanding of Islam. In fact, there is an undeniable convergence of interpretations between North American Muslim women (immigrants and second generation) and some Muslim women converts like Amina Wadud and her Islamic studies perspective, Kecia Ali's Islamic jurisprudence perspective, or Anne Sophie Roald's social sciences perspective.[81] Both groups of scholar-activists explore, propose, and uphold new religious interpretations that they feel are closer to egalitarian Qur'anic ideals.

Many scholar-activists insist on relying solely on the Qur'an for their feminist interpretations and do not appeal to *hadiths* or to the Islamic intellectual tradition, seen as equally patriarchal. On the other hand, American Kecia Ali, who converted to Islam in college and was educated at Stanford University and Duke University, preferred to revisit the religio-legal tradition, rather than discard it too hastily. She believed the emphasis on the interpretative tradition can avoid the "rupturing of traditional Islamic authority" that comes about from the reformist (*salafi*) insistence on the primacy of the Qur'an and the *sunna* (e.g., Basheer Nafi and Suha Taji-Farouki) and that does not always open up any "democratic intellectual space," as noted by Khaled Abou El Fadl, but also from the Qur'an-only approaches of Muslim feminists like Amina Wadud and Asma Barlas.[82]

Ali elected to place the question of the "structures of authority and the shifting and competing models of authoritativeness" of contemporary debates at the heart of her feminist reflections on Qur'an, *hadith*, and jurisprudence in order to revisit classical understandings of gender issues in Islam with her work titled *Sexual Ethics and Islam: Feminist Reflections on Qur'an, Hadith, and Jurisprudence*.[83] She admitted that as a Muslim "who considers herself progressive,"[84] she reflected on her "journey" into Islam and acknowledged that she was not a jurist, a Qur'an scholar, nor an ethicist and certainly not "doing" jurisprudence.[85] She noted, however, the need of "assessing customary practices and, rather than implementing them unquestioningly, modifying them as necessary," to avoid servile imitation, thereupon embarking on her own gender critical rereading of the religious tradition.[86]

Ali remained rather critical of approaches that focus solely on the Qur'an, for "much is lost when Muslims—Qur'an-only feminists and pro-*hadith* Salafis—choose to bypass the scholarly tradition for a literalist approach to source texts." She believed "a legal methodology offers legitimacy for a flexible approach to the Qur'an and the Prophet's Sunnah as revelation that emerged in an historical context" and thus preferred to focus on Islamic law as an ethical system.[87] Her concerns, as an American, are with Muslims living in what Abdal-Hakim Murad called the "post-traditional contexts"[88] of diasporic communities. Ali writes:

> Living in a nation where Islamic law has no coercive power, regardless of its moral weight for individual believers, I write as one with the luxury of deciding whether and how to apply religious doctrine in my own

life—whether to arrange my affairs to follow the dictates of one or another school of jurisprudence, or the regulations of the Qur'an, or to follow civil law. The entirely voluntary nature of all types of religious observance means that the urgent questions for Muslims living under civil laws in North America and Europe in particular are ethical or moral rather than narrowly legal.[89]

Living in minority contexts where Islamic law has no state-sanctioned coercive power, Muslims are faced with the challenges of rendering *shari'a* injunctions relevant to their lives. The shift from the narrowly legal to the broader ethical or moral becomes of great importance for Muslim women who have often relied on these Qur'anic ethical and moral injunctions to argue for greater gender equality in Islam. One of Ali's concerns remained the interpretation and application of Islamic law in diasporic contexts where, in the end, only the moral or ethical weight of Islamic law will have a grip over individual lives. In such a context, Muslims have tended to rely and "focus on 'authentic' texts" for guidance, "making engagement with the tradition necessary."[90] The need emerges for a truly constructive engagement with the texts to address new issues that are particular to diasporic environments.

Like Barlas, Ali has called for believers to claim the right to interpret the religious tradition. She also questions the nature of the various and so-called authoritative voices of Islam in the diaspora whose credentials, as religious scholars, often leave much to be desired. The unfilled void leaves Muslims in need for guidance, since "in the West, there is no such class of individuals to serve as an anchor or foil for Muslim public and private discussions of these complicated issues."[91]

The right of interpretation is taken up by Ali with her study on sexual ethics and her search for interpretations "in the direction of a just ethics of sex."[92] Sexual ethics, as she understands it, revolve around two main issues:

[These issues are] meaningful consent and mutuality, both of which I believe to be crucial for a just ethics of sexual intimacy, are structurally impossible within the constraints of lawful sexuality as defined by the classical Muslim scholars, whose views—drawing from and building on Qur'an and *sunnah*—permeate all Muslim discourses. It is possible to rethink Islamic sexual ethics to accommodate these values and there are resources within Muslim texts, both revealed and interpretive, for doing so. . . . We need, instead, a serious consideration of what makes sex lawful in the sight of God. The obvious response of "marriage" does not really answer the question.[93]

Ali's project for more egalitarian interpretations of gender relations and understandings of sexuality and sexual ethics in Islam proceeds from Muslim women's experiences in diasporic contexts in order to then explore classical Islamic interpretations to find new solutions. Contrary to those who only seek in the Qur'an answers to contemporary queries, Ali preferred to review classical texts and then to proceed with her gynocentric *ijtihad* to address a number of issues related to sexuality. She sets out to evaluate classical interpretations for their relevance for today's Muslim woman:

> My way of framing the question presupposes that Muslims will undertake this process of reflection primarily as individuals, for ourselves and in dialogue with those close to us. That does not mean that religious authorities do not matter; there are thinkers whose ideas have wide currency in the West as well as in Muslim-majority societies, and for those of us lucky enough to have a respected and thoughtful *imam* or other spiritual figures at our mosque or in our community, he—or perhaps, she—may be a trusted resource.[94]

Ali's world of possibilities certainly seeks to broaden Muslim women's roles. She alluded to their being potentially able to become spiritual guides and even imams. The "unthought"[95] emerges on the horizon of what she considers future possibilities. Ali appeared willing to entertain the idea of some sort of "feminized" Islamic authority, as has gradually been the case, for example, within the Jewish and Anglican traditions that gradually ordained women as rabbis and priests or bishops. Might Ali be envisioning that the Islamic (Sunni) tradition could, one day, be more progressive than the Catholic tradition and allow women to become imams and religious leaders? Much revolves around the nature of religious authority in diasporic environments. Ali noted:

> A limited conversation began in 2005, sparked by the controversies over female prayer leadership, but it has not yet developed into the kind of broader debate necessary for full exploration of the key questions surrounding Muslim religious authority and institutions in the United States. . . . Muslim feminists have become part of the Islamic intellectual tradition and, in doing so, have begun to push at its boundaries and reshape its contours.[96]

Like a number of scholar-activists who are acting on the "Frontier of Religious Ceremony," Ali became the *nikkah*, or marriage, celebrant.[97] In so doing, she filled in the shoes of what has always been traditionally the role of imams or of respected male members of the community. Far from being bent on disregarding the stipulations of traditional jurists regarding the required conditions for the fulfillment of an Islamic *nikkah* contract, Ali took extra precautions to make sure that none would be able to question the validity of the *nikkah* contract. Such innovations, however small they might be, are slowly showing the way for praxis to be rewritten.

In their quest for change, scholar-activists who live in the West can become rather potent disruptive forces with their scholarship and their activism. The quest for new contemporary interpretations does not preclude possibilities of going beyond the letter of the sacred text and its literal meaning, as Muslims have now been accustomed to do with respect to issues related to slavery. In a similar fashion, Muslims need to go beyond certain specific regulations that are no longer relevant regarding issues related to sexual ethics. Guidance is no longer mere reading of the sacred text and being guided by the letter of the text. Guidance must come from God's orders that Muslims "combat injustice and oppression," such that "the only possible response is to suggest that the Qur'anic text itself requires Muslims to sometimes depart from its literal provisions in order to establish justice."[98] As reformers before them have done, Ali and other Muslim women give precedence to the Qur'an's broad principles of justice over Qur'anic passages that would go against such principles. Ali summarized this hermeneutical process thus:

> How, though, can a feminist think about sexual intimacy within the constraints of God's revelation to humanity without becoming limited by patriarchal notions that deny women's lived experience and potential as fully human, fully moral, and fully sexual beings? It is easy to find revelatory support for women as fully human and fully moral; it is more challenging, but not impossible, to see women as fully sexual in a way that recognizes their status as moral agents. One must seek out and privilege these elements in the tradition, and justify one's choices. Appealing to timeless principles rather than historical specifics is a crucial interpretive strategy. But one must be prepared to define and defend the principles chosen and promoted in this way.[99]

Muslim women need to find Islamically grounded ways to reclaim their sense of agency as self-becoming human beings, something Ali's work shares with Anwar's philosophical project. Both women seek to challenge male-dominated and patriarchal discourses by identifying contradictions and limitations of those discourses and their negative impacts on Muslim women's lives and their self-becoming. Theirs may, in fact, be only the first step toward reconceptualization and, more important, reconstruction of more gender-amiable and equalitarian interpretations of the Islamic tradition. The next stages are the more crucial and difficult reconceptualization and reconstructive steps that Barlas has attempted to imagine. Scholar-activists often take nontraditional stances or roles as part of their willingness to explore new practical engagements in their reconceiving and reconstruction of the religious tradition. Ali, for example, occupied the unusual position, that is, for a Muslim woman, of officiant at a Muslim wedding, a much less controversial position than that of Amina Wadud.

During the last 20 years, spirituality has also informed the work of scholar-activist Amina Wadud. An Afro-American convert, Wadud spent six years researching how women were conceived and depicted in the Qur'an, a study that culminated in 1992 in the publication of her *Qur'an and Woman: Rereading the Sacred Text from a Woman's Perspective*.[100] She aimed at demonstrating that the eternal message of Qur'anic revelations could not go against principles of justice and equality by rereading the Qur'an, a project not dissimilar to, and indeed preceding, the one of Barlas. The Qur'anic message is not responsible for the inequalities and injustices suffered by Muslim women throughout the world. Responsibility falls on patriarchal and misogynist interpretations of those who have interpreted the Qur'an throughout history.

Indeed, Wadud noted that "the critical questioning of the functions and responsibilities of each gender has only recently been asked. . . . Once the question arose, a sound method of answering that question needed to be developed within the field of Islamic scholarship."[101] This is the task she set out to accomplish by analyzing the place of woman in the Qur'an in order to show how this text is still relevant once reinterpreted.[102] She wrote that if the Qur'anic concept of woman "had been fully implemented in the practical sense, then Islam would have been a global motivating force for women's empowerment."[103]

Wadud's own personal experience and indignation at the level of humanity ascribed by some Muslim men to Muslim women led her to explore issues of woman in the Qur'an:

> A significant part of the motivation behind my consideration of this subject was to challenge some of the attitudes and the resulting interpretations given with regards to the subject of woman and the Qur'an. I explicitly challenge the arrogance of those men who require a level of human dignity and respect for themselves while denying that level to another human, for whatever reason—including simply because she is a woman. In particular, I reject the false justification of such arrogance through narrow interpretations which ignore the basic social principles of justice, equality, and common humanity.[104]

Six years later, in the 1998 preface to the second edition of *Qur'an and Woman*, Wadud replied to criticism leveled against her work, remaining determined to struggle for justice:

> In the battle for gender parity, those who stand guard at the gate posts of Muslim status quo have sometimes reacted vehemently against claims for justice. The trenches are deep and the fighting often unfair, but the motivation for my entry into the struggle is nonnegotiable. One of the special merits of Islam as *din*, or, way of life, is that establishing and re-establishing orthodoxy sets an agenda for Islamic praxis. One cannot stand on the sidelines in the face of injustice and still be recognized as fully Muslim, fully *khalifah* [trustee on Earth]. I have accepted the responsibility and continue to struggle.[105]

Wadud's general project of rereading, reconceiving, and reconstructing Islamic interpretations based on the scripture was critical not only of traditional Islamic interpretations but also of scholarship written on Islam that often purports to provide progressive views on Islam while remaining generally silent on the issue of women.[106] Her ceaseless struggle has been the hallmark of her many writings, having, for example, provided insights into possible gendered interpretations of social justice, based on the Qur'anic text's perspective on the elimination of oppression and social injustice, and the need to "emphasize a shared privilege in access to divine will and a mutual responsibility in experiencing transformation and in discussing meaning," whereby women's Islamic experiences need to become an intrinsic part of this new shared Islamic knowledge.[107]

Wadud's gender activism within the Muslim community took a dramatic twist in 2005 when she led a very public, mixed-congregation Friday prayer in New York. What followed was almost unanimous condemnation by Muslim religious scholars from all over the world, but this has not prevented a few Muslim women to continue to occasionally lead Friday prayers. More determined than ever, Wadud titled her recent (2006) work *Inside the Gender Jihad*. Remaining one of the most critical voices from within academia and the Muslim community, Wadud continues to pursue gender jihad, which remains her battle for greater "egalitarian praxis" in Islam.[108]

Translocalities, Liminalities, and Hybridities

Scholar-activists living in the West all provide, therefore, good examples of how Muslim women are becoming producers of new Islamic gendered knowledge. In order to shed some light onto this phenomenon, we can explore the potentially fruitful ideas of translocalities, liminalities, and hybridities. In a diasporic environment, Muslims are able to dissociate Islam, as a religious tradition, from a variety of prevalent cultural understandings. A similar dissociation has been identified, for example, among young South Asian Muslims living in Britain, some of whom gradually distinguish between "religion" and "cultures" that shape particular understandings of Islam.[109] While there is a need for the preservation of one's religious identity,[110] Baumann noted, there is both "preservation and transformation"[111] of religious traditions in diasporic contexts, since the norms of diasporic communities differ from those of the community of the homeland and those of the countries in which Muslims have settled.[112] A novel "two-way process of negotiation" occurs whereby one of the major issues remains the degree of preservation of "some or all of what was previously held as normal, or to capitulate and adopt the new normal of the new homeland."[113] In fact, there exists a "diasporic duality of preservation and change" whereby identity, culture, tradition, and religion change and transform, even when fundamental perpetuation is explicitly presupposed.[114]

Peter Mandaville used the term "translocality" to illustrate the new dynamics of globalized Islam. Translocality is "theorised as a mode, one which pertains not to how peoples and cultures exist *in* places, but rather how they move *through* them."[115] He was mainly concerned with the capacity of translocality to disrupt traditional constructions of political identity and to give rise to novel political spaces, when Muslims are disembedded from their original contexts.

Translocality can equally disrupt religious identities, for identity constructions now become "configured across and in-between such spaces . . . what flows through localities rather than what is 'in' them."[116] Muslim feminist discourses similarly move between these translocalities that become spaces in which critical feminist interpretations that purport to renew and reform religious dogma can blossom. As new lay intellectuals, Muslim women now claim the right to reflect on their religious tradition and "to make moral choices based on responsible and rational readings of Islam's textual sources."[117] Some critics believe that the absence of authority in the Muslim minority context of North America, where individualization of Islam is growing, has allowed Wadud-like activism; whereas Mandaville noted how translocality, in fact, allows for an

> objectification of religion which occurs as Muslims move through and dwell in translocal space (i.e., their capability to externalize and critique Islam) has opened up new avenues for rethinking and reformulating Islamic thought . . . [which] enables Muslims to focus on a different type of hegemony—namely, power asymmetries *within* Islam. . . . Muslims

develop an increased capacity to recognise, account for, and debate the difference within their religion . . . and translocality provides them with the intellectual environment in which to develop counter-hegemonic discourses [italics in text].[118]

Scholar-activists criticize both cultural and traditional understandings of Islam that reiterate the hegemonic discourses of patriarchal and even misogynist interpretations of Islam. These women strive to emphasize the greater universality of the egalitarian message of the Qur'an. While diasporic environments do offer new critical discursive spaces for Muslims, they can, nonetheless, become fertile grounds for the spread of more conservative interpretations through the introduction, the reproduction, and the promotion of more conservative or ultra-orthodox normative forms of Islam that belong to the countries of origin. In minority contexts, however, Islam is no longer the dominant and overruling discourse. New dissenting Muslim women's voices are able to emerge in these translocalities of contestation, where even the forbidden, the taboo, and the unthought become voiced (e.g., Ayaan Hirsi Ali and Irshad Manji).

Contemporary Islam has not been impervious to some erosion of traditional religious authority, a situation made more prominent in minority context where the weight of tradition no longer takes the same hold on individual lives and the community. While some acknowledge the disruptive potential of faiths on host countries through the social-movement activism of diasporic communities,[119] the academic works of scholar-activists on women in Islam possess similarly disruptive qualities, but now from within the Islamic tradition. Like insiders writing about their religious traditions,[120] scholar-activists in diasporic contexts take risks and need to take responsibilities for their endeavors because they are not immune from criticism that emerges from Muslim communities. The disruptive potential of their Islamic feminist critiques on Islam in the periphery can, at times, be quite subversive. One only needs to remember Wadud's leading of the Friday prayer in 2005 that questioned 1,400 years of tradition.[121] In an age of greater globalization, mass media, and computer-mediated communication, translocality does not provide sanctity or immunity. Wadud's action was condemned throughout the world and especially in the Muslim world. Barely a few days elapsed before *fatwas* (legal pronouncements) condemning the event were issued, quickly translated into English, and posted on the Internet.

While the erosion of traditional authority in diasporic contexts may have contributed to the advent of a Muslim woman leading a Friday prayer, such events are not merely symptomatic of the erosion of religious authority. They are, in fact, indicative of the emergence of a novel

Muslim women's self-reflective and critical Islam, one that is slowly affirming its existence, something Mandaville noted when writing that there are

> ways in which translocal encounters modify how "authoritative" and "authentic" meanings are found in transnational religion—that is, the ways in which a system of symbols and laws is made relevant or acculturated to groups of people in particular places and times. Translocal spaces and the traveling theories and hybridities which inhabit them, I have argued, are the forums in which complex negotiations of Muslim identity take place today.[122]

Diasporic environments are, therefore, uncontested loci of hybridity, what Homi Bhabha has called the hybrid "third space" that makes up cultures of ("travellin") identities, of "mélange" and "*métissage/mestiza*" or the mixing of cultures.[123] Hybridity becomes pivotal for the construction of self-identity in an age of traveling cultures and religions and is also responsible for setting up new structures of authority in these new translocalities.[124] Pnina Werbner, for example, studied how Islam in Britain has become "hybridized discourse" among lay preachers and radical Muslims, as understandings of Islam, particularly *shari'a*, undergo new types of social construction.[125] Qudsia Mirza provides a discussion of this hybridization of the laws of marriage in Britain.[126]

Baumann also proposed a useful typology of five phases through which immigrants pass as they adapt to their new environments and form diasporic communities.[127] His third phase[128] is often associated with the beginning of the creation of new religious interpretations. Not only do diasporic communities wish to pursue their own cultural and religious worldviews, beliefs, and practices, but some of their members wish to reappropriate their religious traditions, some venturing novel critiques and interpretations that lead to the emergence of the "dilemma of the diaspora." While the creative nature of this third phase where hybridity occurs operates in various ways in diasporic environments as a whole, it can be argued that Muslim women, the historically "silent" voices of many Muslim communities, occupy the forefront of these new creative diasporic spaces. Not only do diasporic environments offer new critical discursive spaces to Muslims to explore and propose new Islamic feminist interpretations, they become environments where a variety of Islamic understandings and practices can emerge, develop, evolve, and interact.

By the same token, Muslim women who inhabit this hybrid "third space" can be said to be going through what Victor Turner (d. 1983) would call a "liminal" stage, a concept developed to describe the "betwixt and between" or "threshold" period individuals inhabit during a transitional state between two phases. The stage of liminality constitutes an unstructured experience with unfamiliar surroundings. For our purpose, we can imagine the initial separation to be the one undertaken by Muslim women who have left their homeland and its culture. The separation is followed by a liminal period, a time of trial and seclusion from the original community, but one where its members form an unstructured liminal communitas of diasporic communities, distinct from the normative communitas from which they were separated. In this liminal stage, all members become equal through this shared liminal experience.[129] It is possible to conceive of this threshold phase as a creative phase for Muslim women who embark on the reevaluation of the Islamic tradition, a phase that offers them endless possibilities, even opening up political horizons.

This liminal stage is usually followed by a stage of reentry or reassimilation into the original community. In the context of Muslim women living in minority contexts, however, this is not a reassimilation into the original community but a more personally meaningful reentry into the diasporic environments in which they live. We would like to think of Turner's notions of liminality and communitas as useful ideas to shed some light on the process that makes possible the emergence of Muslim women's academic activism in diasporic contexts. One could even suggest that Muslim feminists who engage in rereading the religious tradition, even theologically, are building a new "ideological" communitas—in the most positive sense of the term—that aims at transforming the gender consciousness of Muslims. It is thus not surprising that many Muslim women who partake in the "multiple critique" undertaken by progressive Muslims live in the West.[130]

Scholar-activists are, therefore, constructing these new Islamic, peripheral, and gendered consciousnesses with their scholarship. Multiple translocalities and the liminal hybrid spaces they open up provide Muslim women with a variety of opportunities to reflect critically on their own experiences and to question both religious interpretations and traditional hegemonic discourses on which the former depends. This is what Figure 6.1 attempted to illustrate with examples of Muslim immigrant and convert scholar-activists living in the West. Adoption of critical stances is unquestionably always more difficult in such Muslim countries as Saudi Arabia, Somalia, and Iran, where dominant and officially sanctioned state interpretations of Islam shape hegemonic discourses. Away from Muslim majority environments, the Foucauldian "disciplinary power" of the traditional hegemonic discourses of schools, media, religious institutions, and government policies—which "quietly coerce people into forms of behavior and attitudes of mind amenable to the interests of these disciplinary institutions and the larger societies they helped to constitute"[131]—no longer exert the same influence on individuals they exert in countries where Islam remains the dominant religion. Mandaville noted the existence of change in the structures of authority and its impact:

> What was religious becomes "political" as soon as Muslims begin to question the authority of those who have previously been recognized as legitimate sources of knowledge (e.g. the *ulama*). New intellectuals, university students and lay Muslims—men *and* women—can to some degree all be seen as sources of *ijtihad* and purveyors of authentic Islam. Their debates and critiques, I want to argue, constitute a dramatic widening of the *Muslim public sphere*. . . . [This sphere serves] a crucial political function insofar as it offers a discursive space in which Muslims can articulate their normative claims (i.e. "Islam') from a multiplicity of subject positions [italics in text].[132]

Gendered interpretations obviously question traditional religious authority. They embody the spirit of Muslim women's struggles within the Islamic tradition. These new Islamic feminist discourses may be seen as mere pleas by individual Muslim women that are not representative of the larger Muslim community and that have no real impact on the lives of ordinary Muslim women in most Muslim communities. Nonetheless, these voices are no longer silent. They are, one could argue, the beginnings of the foundations upon which a different Islamic gender understanding can be built. More important, these voices, like the activism of ordinary Muslim women who struggle for change at the grassroots level, certainly do become political.

In conclusion, we might note that almost 20 years ago, Judith Plaskow and Carol Christ[133] compiled a work on new patterns of feminist spirituality that did not have Islam in its purview. The few works of scholar-activists surveyed in this chapter demonstrate, however, that Muslim women do create new Islamic knowledge based on their experiences, their voices, their readings, their analyses, and their exegeses. In fact, they are now producing their own texts and their own feminist interpretations. They have become themselves producers of new Islamic knowledge that is bound to open up ways of thinking and will shape Islam for centuries to come. Amina Wadud, Asma Barlas, Riffat Hassan, Kecia Ali, and many more Muslim women are laying down the foundations of what will eventually develop into a Muslim "the*a*-logy," or a feminist theological reconstruction of Islam, upon which contemporary understandings of the Islamic tradition will be built.

NOTES

1. See Beth Baron, *The Women's Awakening in Egypt: Culture, Society, and the Press* (New Haven, CT: Yale University Press, 1994); Margot Badran, *Feminists, Islam, and Nation: Gender and the Making of Modern Egypt* (Princeton, NJ: Princeton University Press, 1995); Camron M. Amin, *The Making of the Modern Iranian Woman: Gender, State Policy, and Popular Culture, 1865–1946* (Gainesville: University Press of Florida, 2002); Hammed Shahidian, *Women in Iran* (Westport, CT: Greenwood Press, 2002).

2. See Amina Wadud, *Inside the Gender Jihad: Women's Reform in Islam* (Oxford: Oneworld Press, 2006).

3. See Gisela Webb, *Windows of Faith: Muslim Women Scholar-Activists in North America* (Syracuse, NY: Syracuse University Press, 2000).

4. www.sistersinislam.org.my/.

5. See Zainah Anwar, "Sisters in Islam and the Struggle for Women's Rights," in *On Shifting Ground: Muslim Women in the Global Era*, ed. Fereshteh Nouraie-Simone (New York: Feminist Press at the City University of New York, 2005), 233–47.

6. www.wluml.org/english/index.shtml.

7. See Valentine Moghadam, "Islamic Feminism and Its Discontents: Towards a Resolution of the Debate," *Signs* 27, no. 4 (2002): 1135–71, and Shahrzad Mojab, "Theorizing the Politics of Islamic Feminism," *Feminist Review* 69 (2001): 124–46.

8. See Margot Badran, "Islamic Feminism: What's in a Name?" *al-Ahram Weekly*, January 17–23, 2002. Available online at http://weekly.ahram.org.eg/2002/569/cu1.htm. See also "Islamic Feminism Revisited," *Countercurrents .org*, February 10, 2006. Available online at http://www.countercurrents.org/gen-badran100206.htm.

9. Roxanne D. Marcotte, "What Might an Islamist Gender Discourse Look Like?" *Australian Religion Studies Review* 19, no. 2 (2006): 141–67.

10. See Pieternella van Doorn-Harder, *Women Shaping Islam: Indonesian Women Reading the Qur'an* (Urbana: University of Illinois Press, 2006).

11. See miriam cooke, *Women Claim Islam: Creating Islamic Feminism through Literature* (New York: Routledge, 2001).

12. June O'Connor, "Rereading, Reconceiving and Reconstructing Traditions: Feminist Research in Religion," *Women's Studies* 17 (1989): 102.

13. Ibid., 102–3.

14. Ibid., 103–4.

15. Ibid., 104.

16. Anne Sofie Roald, *Women in Islam: The Western Experience* (London: Routledge, 2001), ix.

17. See Omid Safi, "*The Times Are A-Changin'*—A Muslim Quest for Justice, Gender Equality and Pluralism," introduction to *Progressive Muslims on Justice, Gender, and Pluralism*, Omid Safi, ed. (Oxford: Oneworld, 2003), 10–11.

18. Wadud, *Inside the Gender Jihad*, 81–82.

19. See Fatima Mernissi, *Beyond the Veil: Male-Female Dynamics in Modern Muslim Society*, rev. ed. (Bloomington: Indiana University Press, 1987).

20. See Fatima Mernissi, *Doing Daily Battle: Interviews with Moroccan Women*, ed. Fatima Mernissi and trans. Mary Jo Lakeland [reprint of 1988] (New Brunswick, NJ: Rutgers University Press, 1989).

21. See Fatima Mernissi, *Women and Islam: An Historical and Theological Enquiry*, trans. Mary Jo Lakeland (Oxford: Blackwell, 1991). Also published under the title *The Veil and the Male Elite: A Feminist Interpretation of Women's Rights in Islam*, trans. Mary Jo Lakeland (Reading, MA: Addison-Wesley).

22. See Fatima Mernissi, *The Forgotten Queens of Islam*, trans. Mary Jo Lakeland (Minneapolis: University of Minnesota Press, 1993).

23. See Fatima Mernissi, *Islam and Democracy: Fear of the Modern World*, rev. ed., trans. Mary Jo Lakeland (Cambridge, MA: Perseus, 2002).

24. Mernissi, *Women and Islam*, 2.

25. Ibid., 49–81.

26. Roxanne D. Marcotte, "The Qur'ān in Egypt: Bint al- Shati' on Women's Emancipation," in *Coming to Terms with the Qur'an: A Volume in Honor of Professor Issa Boullata*, ed. Khaleel Mohammed and Andrew Rippin (North Haledon, NJ: Islamic Publications International, 2008), 179–208.

27. Mernissi, *Women and Islam*, 9.

28. Ibid., 10.

29. Roxanne D. Marcotte, "Identity, Power, and the Islamist Discourse on Women: An Exploration of Islamism and Gender Issues in Egypt," in *Islam in World Politics*, ed. Nelly Lahoud, Anthony H. Johns, and Allan Patience (London: RoutledgeCurzon, 2005), 67–92.

30. See Alain Roussillon and Fatima Zahra-Zryouil, *Être femme en Égypte, au Maroc et en Jordanie* (Paris: Aux lieux d'être; Cairo: Cedej; Rabat: Cjb, coll. Documents, 2006).

31. William Safran, "Deconstructing and Comparing Diasporas," in *Diaspora, Identity and Religion: New Directions in Theory and Research*, Waltraud Kokot, Khachig Tölölyan, and Carolin Alfonso (London: Routledge, 2004), 10.

32. Kokot, Tölölyan, and Alfonso, eds., *Diaspora, Identity and Religion*, 2–3.

33. Ibid., 3.

34. Ibid.

35. Martin Baumann, "Conceptualizing Diaspora: The Preservation of Religious Identity in Foreign Parts, Exemplified by Hindu Communities outside India," *Temenos* 31 (1995): 28–29.

36. Gary D. Bouma, ed., *Many Religions, All Australians: Religious Settlement, Identity and Cultural Diversity* (Kew, Australia: Christian Research Association, 1996), 7.

37. John W. Berry, "Immigration, Acculturation, and Adaptation," *Applied Psychology: An International Review* 46, no. 1 (1997): 5–35, 56.

38. See George E. Marcus, "Ethnography in/of the World System: The Emergence of Multi-sited Ethnography," *Annual Review of Anthropology* 24 (1995): 95–117.

39. Michael Kearney, "The Local and the Global: The Anthropology of Globalization and Transnationalism," *Annual Review of Anthropology* 25 (1995): 558.

40. Martin Baumann, "Diaspora: Genealogies of Semantics and Transcultural Comparison," *Numen* 47 (2000): 327–28; Martin Baumann, "A Diachronic View of Diaspora, the Significance of Religion and Hindu Trinidadians," in Kokot, Tölölyan, and Alfonso, eds., *Diaspora, Identity and Religion*, 173.

41. Leila Ahmed, *Women and Gender in Islam: The Historical Roots of a Modern Debate* (New Haven, CT: Yale University Press, 1992), 2.

42. Leila Ahmed, *A Border Passage: From Cairo to America—A Woman's Journey* (New York: Penguin Books, 1999), 290.

43. See ibid.

44. Kecia Ali, *Sexual Ethics and Islam: Feminist Reflections on Qur'an, Hadith, and Jurisprudence* (Oxford: Oneworld, 2006), xx.

45. Ahmed, *A Border Passage*, 9.

46. Riffat Hassan, "Challenging the Stereotypes of Fundamentalism: An Islamic Feminist Perspective," *The Muslim World* 91, no. 1/2 (2001): 56–57.

47. Ibid., 59–60.

48. Ibid., 60–62.

49. Ibid., 64–68.

50. Asma Barlas, *"Believing Women" in Islam: Unreading Patriarchal Interpretations of the Qur'an* (Austin: University of Texas Press, 2002), xvi.

51. Ibid.

52. Ibid., xii.

53. Ibid., 203–4.

54. Ibid., 209–10.

55. Ibid., 4.

56. Ibid., 13.

57. Ibid., 14.

58. Ibid.

59. Ibid., 15.

60. Ibid.

61. Ibid., 13–25.

62. Ibid., 2–4.

63. Abdullahi An-Nai'm, "The Application of Shari'a (Islamic Law) and Human Rights in the Sudan," in *Islamic Law Reform and Human Rights, Challenges and Rejoinders: Proceedings of the Seminar on Human Rights and the Modern Application of Islamic Law, Oslo, 14–15 February 1992*, ed. with an introduction by Tore Lindholm and Kari Vogt (Copenhagen: Nordic Human Rights Publications, 1993), 141.

64. Barlas, *"Believing Women" in Islam*, 3.

65. See Margot Badran, *Feminism in Islam: Secular and Religious Convergences* (Oxford: Oneworld, 2009).

66. Etin Anwar, *Gender and Self in Islam* (London: Routledge, 2006), 6.

67. Ibid., 6–7.

68. Ibid., 8–9.

69. See Ziba Mir-Hosseini, "The Construction of Gender in Islamic Legal Thought and Strategies for Reform," *Hawwa* 1, no. 1 (2003): 1–28; and Ziba Mir-Hosseini, *Islam and Gender: The Religious Debate in Contemporary Iran* (Princeton, NJ: Princeton University Press, 1999).

70. Anwar, *Gender and Self in Islam*, 13.

71. Ibid., 5.

72. Ibid., 114.

73. Ibid., 70–71.

74. Ibid., 115.

75. Ibid.

76. See Deniz Kandiyoti, "Bargaining with Patriarchy," *Gender and Society* 2, no. 3 (1988): 274–90.

77. Anwar, *Gender and Self in Islam*, 115–16.

78. Ibid., 144–45.

79. Ibid., 142.

80. Ibid., 139.

81. Roald, *Women in Islam*, x–xiii.

82. Ali, *Sexual Ethics and Islam,* xxi–xxiii.

83. See Ali, *Sexual Ethics and Islam.*

84. Ibid., xix.

85. Ibid., xxviii.

86. Ibid., ix.

87. Ibid., xx–xxi.

88. Abdal-Hakim Murad, "Boys Will Be Boys" http://www.masud.co.uk/ISLAM/ahm/boys.htm.

89. Ali, *Sexual Ethics and Islam*, xx–xxi.

90. Ibid., xxiii.

91. Ibid., 152–53.

92. Ibid., xxviii.

93. Ibid., 151.

94. Ibid., 152.

95. See Mohammed Arkoun, *The Unthought in Contemporary Islamic Thought* (London: Saqi in association with the Institute of Ismaili Studies, 2002).

96. Ali, *Sexual Ethics and Islam*, 152–53.

97. See Kecia Ali, "Acting on a Frontier of Religious Ceremony: With Questions and Quiet Resolve, a Woman Officiates at a Muslim Wedding," *Harvard Divinity Bulletin* 32, no. 4 (2004). Available at http://www.hds .harvard.edu/news/bulletin/articles/ali_ceremony.html.

98. Ali, *Sexual Ethics and Islam*, 55.

99. Ibid., 154.

100. Amina Wadud, *Qur'an and Woman: Rereading the Sacred Text from a Woman's Perspective* [1992] (New York: Oxford University Press, 1999).

101. Ibid., xxi.

102. Ibid., 95.

103. Ibid., xxi.

104. Ibid., 96.

105. Ibid., xviii–xix.

106. Wadud, *Inside the Gender Jihad*, 72–75, 191.

107. Amina Wadud, "Towards a Qur'anic Hermeneutics of Social Justice: Race, Class and Gender," *Journal of Law and Religion* 12, no. 1 (1995–96): 49.

108. Wadud, *Inside the Gender Jihad*, 191.

109. Martin Sökefeld, "Religion or Culture? Concepts of Identity in the Alevi Diaspora," in Kokot, Tölölyan, and Alfonso, eds., *Diaspora, Identity and Religion*, 150; see also Kim Knott and Sadja Khokher, "Religious and Ethnic Identity among Young Muslim Women in Bradford," *New Community* 19, no. 4 (1993): 593–610.

110. Sökefeld, "Religion or Culture?" 149.

111. Baumann, "Conceptualizing Diaspora," 22–23.

112. See James Clifford, "Diasporas," *Cultural Anthropology* 9, no. 3 (1994): 302–38.

113. Gary D. Bouma, *Mosques and Muslim Settlement in Australia* (Canberra: Australian Government Publishing Service, 1994), 87–97, 102.

114. Sökefeld, "Religion or Culture?" 149.

115. Peter Mandaville, *Transnational Muslim Politics: Reimagining the Umma* (London: Routledge, 2004), 50.

116. Ibid., 50.

117. Ibid., 132.

118. Ibid., 179.

119. See Christian Smith, ed., *Disruptive Religion: The Force of Faith in Social-Movement Activism* (New York: Routledge, 1996).

120. See Tazim Kassam, "On Being a Scholar of Islam: Risks and Responsibilities," in Safi, ed., *Progressive Muslims*, 128–44; and Tazim Kassam, "Balancing Acts: Negotiating the Ethics of Scholarship and Identity," in *Identity and the Politics of Scholarship in the Study of Religion*, ed. José I. Cabezón and Sheila G. Davaney (New York: Routledge, 2004), 133–61.

121. Christopher Melchert, "Whether to Keep Women out of the Mosque: A Survey of Medieval Islamic Law," in *Authority, Privacy and Public Order in Islam: Proceedings of the 22nd Congress of l'Union Européenne des Arabisants et Islamisants*, ed. Barbara Michalak-Pikulska and A. Pikulski (Leuven, Belgium: Peeters, 2006), 59–69.

122. Mandaville, *Transnational Muslim Politics*, 107.

123. See Homi Bhabha, *The Location of Culture* (London: Routledge, 1994).

124. Homi Bhabha in Jonathan Rotherford, ed., "The Third Space: Interview with Homi Bhabha," in *Identity: Community, Culture, Difference* (London: Lawrence and Wishart, 1990), 211.

125. See Pnina Werbner, "The Making of Muslim Dissent: Hybridized Discourses, Lay Preachers, and Radical Rhetoric among British Pakistanis," *American Ethnologist* 13, no. 1 (1996): 102–22.

126. Qudsia Mirza, "Islam, Hybridity and the Laws of Marriage," *Australian Feminist Law Journal* 14 (2000): 15–21.

127. Baumann, "A Diachronic View of Diaspora," 173–81.

128. Ibid., 176–78.

129. See Victor W. Turner, *The Ritual Process: Structure and Anti-Structure* (Chicago: Aldine, 1969).

130. Omid Safi, "Introduction: *The Times Are A-Changin'*," in *Progressive Muslims*, ed. Safi, 2–5.

131. Geoff Danaher, Tony Schirato, and Fen Webb, *Understanding Foucault* (St Leonards, NSW Australia: Allen & Unwin, 2000), 100.

132. Mandaville, *Transnational Muslim Politics*, 186.

133. See Judith Plaskow and Carol Christ, eds., *Weaving the Visions: New Patterns in Feminist Spirituality* (San Francisco: Harper and Row, 1989).

CHAPTER 7

New Expressions of Religiosity: Al-Huda International and the Expansion of Islamic Education for Pakistani Muslim Women

Khanum Shaikh

READING THE QUR'AN

Growing up in Lahore, Pakistan, my sister and I learned to read the Qur'an through studying with our *maulvi sahib* (Qur'an teacher) for about half an hour each afternoon. *Maulvi sahib* rode his bicycle to our house, six days a week, to teach us how to read and properly enunciate each Arabic word in the Qur'an. Sitting outdoors in the usually intense afternoon heat, we both remember *maulvi sahib* nodding off and sometimes falling asleep in his chair as he listened to us recite our designated section of each day's lesson. Maybe it was the afternoon heat that rocked him to sleep, or perhaps the monotonous sight of our fingers sliding slowly over each word as we struggled to keep our accents thick and our focus intact. I don't know the reason, but I do remember that as soon as we were sure he was deeply asleep, both my sister and I would skip ahead a few pages in our lesson. By the time his nodding head would startle him awake, we had already moved much closer to the end of the assigned section, and to our goal, which was to get out of class early so we could get to the more fun parts of the day.

At the private girls' school I attended, I remember studying *Islamiyat* (the study of Islam) as a compulsory subject. To this day I can recite verses we learned in Arabic or their Urdu translations. Interestingly, the verses I remember most clearly are the ones having to do with rather graphic descriptions of what will happen on the Day of Judgment. Even though learning the Qur'an and understanding our faith was considered important in my family, neither of these avenues—Qur'an lessons with *maulvi sahib* or *Islamiyat* class in school—offered much of a meaningful space for engagement with religious texts. In my early Islamic education Allah remained a distant, daunting, and fear-inducing figure, and the Qur'an a text in Arabic that we treated with the utmost reverence without knowing the meanings of the words we considered divine.

But that was at least 20 years ago. I argue that in recent decades, there has been an expansion of avenues for women and girls who wish to pursue a more in-depth study of Islam and there has been a related proliferation in expressions of certain types of religiosity among various segments of Pakistani society. This chapter highlights one such space that has emerged as a premier center for women's religious education in Pakistan, a women's nonprofit organization by the name of Al-Huda International that has had phenomenal success among women of middle- to upper-class urban backgrounds. I argue here that through its emphasis on reform through religious education, Al-Huda has contributed to the proliferation of a certain type of religiosity among certain groups of Pakistani Muslim women. Between 2006 and 2007, I conducted ethnographic research with students, teachers, and critics of Al-Huda based in Lahore, Pakistan. This chapter explores how and why this group has had such phenomenal success in mobilizing primarily middle- to upper-class women in the field of Islamic education. It also touches on the new types of subjectivities that are emerging through participation in Al-Huda and considers critiques that have emerged around the politics of gender that are mobilized through Al-Huda's discourses.

THE BACKDROP: MADRASSAS FOR WORKING-CLASS GIRLS

By the early to mid-1990s, *madrassas* (religious seminaries) for girls from poor and working-class backgrounds had mushroomed in various cities across Pakistan.[1] In an article published in 1994, Pakistani feminist Khawar Mumtaz highlighted one such *madrassa* based in Lahore that was working to "rectify the neglect of women's spiritual education" to counter, in the words of their brochure, "Westernization that has affected women, who, under the pretext of emancipation and liberation are in reality spreading obscenity and immorality."[2] At the time Mumtaz conducted her research, this particular *madrassa* housed 300 to 500 students and offered simultaneous programs in coursework lasting from two to four years. A large number of the girls who were enrolled came from small towns and villages across Pakistan, and the age group of students ranged from 11 to 15 years. Mumtaz concluded her article by asking what the implications of this growing trend toward *madrassa*-based education might be for future generations of Pakistani women. Interestingly, it was the same year that Mumtaz's article was published that Al-Huda International came into existence as a space for Pakistani Muslim women to study the Qur'an and its *tafsir* (exegetical commentary). While the *madrassas* that Mumtaz's study refers to targeted poor and working-class girls, Al-Huda, the subject of my study, found its primary base and support among middle- to upper-class urban Muslim women in Pakistan. Let me begin by providing some background on this organization.

AL-HUDA INTERNATIONAL

According to their most recent brochure, Al-Huda International Welfare Foundation, whose name Al-Huda literally means "place of peace," is a registered nongovernmental organization (NGO) working to promote Islamic education and social welfare since 1994. Its stated objectives are "to promote purely Islamic values and thinking on sound knowledge and research, free from all kinds of bias and sectarianism" and "to plan, and work for, welfare of the deprived classes (i.e. the needy, and calamity-stricken people) of society."[3] To achieve these goals, Al-Huda is pursuing a range of activities in the fields of education and training, mass communications, and social welfare both in Pakistan and abroad. My research focuses exclusively on the religious education component of Al-Huda that comprises a sophisticated transnational network of predominantly female students and teachers who come together in diverse geographic locations (both physical and virtual spaces) to create communities of religious study.

Al-Huda is the brainchild of Dr. Farhat Hashmi, who founded it within her own home in an elite neighborhood in Islamabad. While she was growing up, Hashmi's parents were members of Jamaat-e-Islami (JI), the most prominent religio-political party in contemporary Pakistan that was originally founded by Maulana Maudoodi.[4] Hashmi pursued a master's degree in Arabic from Punjab University, Lahore, in 1980, and while she was a student at the University she became an active member of the student wing of Jam'iat.[5] Eventually she left Pakistan to pursue a doctorate in Islamic studies with an emphasis on Hadith (sayings of the Prophet) sciences from the University of Glasgow, Scotland. When she returned to Pakistan, she began working as an assistant professor at the International Islamic University (IIU) in Islamabad.[6] Simultaneously, she was also conducting informal *dars* (religious instruction) for women in her neighborhood, most of whom came from affluent family backgrounds.[7] For many of these women, this was their first exposure to studying the verse-by-verse translation and *tafsir* (contextual interpretation) of the Qur'an. Transformed by their new modes of engagement with the Qur'an under Hashmi's guidance, these women became catalysts for the expansion of Hashmi's teachings through providing both funds and forums for growth. Pretty soon what began as informal *dars* sessions from within Hashmi's home branched out into a formal institute offering one- to two-year courses for women and girls at the Al-Huda Academy, branches of which were soon to spring up in such urban cities as Islamabad, Lahore, and finally Karachi and eventually to spread to geographic areas beyond the borders of Pakistan.[8]

PERMEATING URBAN LANDSCAPES

In an interview published in 2001 in *Newsline* magazine, Dr. Hashmi states:

> I teach and like a river runs through whatever channel it finds, in the same way what I teach spreads in whatever way it can. Ultimately my goal is to reach as far as I can through those who come to my classes.[9]

And, indeed, her influence has spread like a river. As of January 2007, I was told, Al-Huda operates schools in 28 cities in Pakistan, in various rural areas, and in urban slums, and it has even gone into women's prisons to do *dawah* (religious outreach or the call to Islam).[10] Even more remarkable are the ways in which the organization has traveled beyond the boundaries of the Pakistani nation-state—both through various modes of technology and through former students who relocate to other countries and begin offering religious study courses from within their homes or local community centers. Currently, one may find both formal and informal spaces for religious study that use Al-Huda materials in various places around the world, for example, in Dubai, London, and the United States and in a formal institute in Mississauga, Canada, that was established by Hashmi herself in 2005.

To understand how Al-Huda in Pakistan operates, let me briefly map out its sophisticated organizational network. The main branches in each city are referred to as Institutes of Islamic Education. In Lahore, where my research was mostly based, the main branch is located in an upper-class area called Gulberg. The Institutes of Islam Education offer diploma and post-diploma courses, as well as what is referred to as a Supervised Education Program. Courses that are taught include *tarjuma* (translation of the Qur'an), *tafsir* (Qur'anic exegesis), *Uloom-ul-Qur'an* (Qur'anic sciences), *tajweed* (Qur'anic recitation), *Uloom-ul-Hadith* (*Hadith* sciences), *Fiqh-ul-Ibaadat* (Islamic jurisprudence), *usool-ul-fiqh* (rulings regarding Islamic jurisprudence), Muslim heroes, Arabic grammar, *Dawah* (inviting others to learn about Islam), and Islamic calligraphy.[11] Students can earn a one- or two-year diploma course depending on the module they pursue; and although the fees are not high, financial assistance is available to students who cannot afford to pay out of pocket. This is where a majority of the coursework and administrative work is housed. Beyond the main branches, there are Schools of Islamic Education, which are essentially smaller branches. In these branches former students teach courses from within their own homes, the houses of others who have donated rooms within their homes to Al-Huda, or other venues, for example, a hall in a local library. The benefit of these branches is that students can enroll in diploma courses and pursue studies within their own neighborhoods rather than having to travel to a potentially far main branch.[12] The third avenue for religious study exists in the form of the informal *dars* sessions. These are offered from within homes of women—once again, usually former graduates of Al-Huda. Attending *dars* requires less stringent commitment and more flexibility, and doing so is not geared toward earning a time-specific diploma. Finally, there are Cassette Courses. For these courses, women get together on an informal basis to listen to Dr. Farhat Hashmi's audio recordings on various topics. For example, if a group of women wishes to collectively study Qur'anic *tafsir*, they can request copies of the audiotapes of Dr. Hashmi's line-by-line *tafsir*. Rather than having a live teacher, students collectively listen to the voice of Dr. Hashmi on prerecorded audiocassettes and follow along in their lesson. Al-Huda teachers from the main branches may occasionally visit these Cassette Courses to provide guidance or administrative support to groups of women assembled in these courses.[13] The dispersed nature of the organization helps tremendously in making it easy for women in sprawled-out urban cities like Lahore to easily access spaces of religious study without traveling much distance.

Here, it is critical to point out that there are a few factors that make this organization unique in the context of Pakistan. First, in Pakistan Islamic education has been widely available across classes, but it is the male *ulama* (religious scholars) and *mullahs* (religious clerics) who have been responsible for the production and dissemination of religious education.[14] It is unprecedented for a female religious scholar to have come into such a high level of visibility and influence in Pakistan. Second, it is the first time that adult women of middle- to upper-class backgrounds have become prominent actors in a movement for religious reform through education. Third, Hashmi is not a product of the *madrassa*-based education system that teaches the *dars-e-nizami* curriculum,[15] completion of which is a requirement for anyone to become an *alim* or *alima* (female religious scholar) in Pakistan. In other words, her credentials of having earned a doctoral degree from the University in Scotland are often considered inadequate and suspect by those who have completed their studies through pursuing the more traditional route, that is, at religious seminaries in Muslim countries. These factors, combined with the phenomenal success that Hashmi has had in the field of religious education, have brought Hashmi and her organization into the limelight and made both a subject of much controversy among different members of Pakistani society.

But what are the reasons behind Al-Huda's success? This chapter argues that the primary factors that have made this organization a prominent player in the field of Islamic education in Pakistan include technological sophistication, pedagogical philosophy, accessibility, *dawah* as a strategy for outreach, and a funding base. Let me review each of these areas in more depth.

TECHNOLOGIES

Scholars have written about the ways that diversely located Muslims are utilizing various forms of technology to expand spaces for participation in the production and dissemination of Islamic discourses.[16] One strategy that has greatly facilitated Al-Huda's expansion into a transnational movement for religious reform has been the organization's creative uses of various modes of technology. Audiocassettes, printed matter, and video materials produced by Al-Huda have been circulating in diverse national and transnational contexts, contributing to what Dale F. Eickelman and Jon W. Anderson have referred to as the expansion of a new sense of public and a slow erosion of traditional centers of religious authority.[17] As such, this organization follows a larger pattern of Muslim women's growing participation in the production of discourses on Islam.[18] Dr. Hashmi has recorded countless lectures on a range of topics pertaining to Islam.[19] Some examples of popular titles of her audio recordings include the following, among others: "Song and Dance in Islam," "What to Do in Times of Chaos," "Why Is a Woman's Testimony Half That of a Man's?," and "Time Is Ticking Away." The audio recording of her Qur'anic *tafsir* is widely available both in religious bookstores in and beyond Pakistan, as well as on their

Web site at www.alhudapk.com.[20] She has also utilized mass media extensively and has often appeared on radio and television shows in Pakistan.
For example, a variety of programs on translation and brief explanations,
as well as on specific topics, have aired on FM radio stations in Karachi
and Islamabad. A few shows have also appeared on popular television
channels, including ARY digital and Pakistan Television (PTV). Al-Huda
is also savvy at using the printed word to disseminate all types of information; the organization sends out fliers, pamphlets, and instructional
handouts, for example, on how to celebrate holidays in an Islamically
appropriate manner. Many of these materials are also available in
the form of e-mail fliers and in downloadable formats on Al-Huda's
Web site.

Virtual spaces are another venue through which Al-Huda leadership
and members have been able to create communities of study and dialogue
that exceed the boundaries of the nation-state. Their extensive Web site
provides a forum for exchange of knowledge and information for Muslim
women by means of a Listserv, chat rooms, matrimonial links, and advice
and counseling for Muslims living in predominantly non-Muslim environments.[21] One can see how Al-Huda's extremely sophisticated Web site
allows for "dissolving prior barriers of space and distance and opening new
grounds for interaction and mutual recognition."[22] Testimonies of men
and women from countries as far flung as India, Australia, Malaysia, and
the United States, among others, are posted on the Web site. In these testimonies, individuals share stories about how deeply their lives have been
touched and transformed by the materials that Hashmi has made widely
available for purchase and/or download. It is this ability to harness various
technological tools with great skill that has contributed to Al-Huda's success in reaching members of the Pakistani Muslim community in diverse
transnational locations.

PEDAGOGICAL PHILOSOPHY: MAKING ISLAM EASY

The second reason that Al-Huda has been so successful as an organization has to do with the pedagogical practices that leaders have employed
in their teaching. When I asked my interviewees what it is about
Dr. Hashmi's approach that speaks to them, most responded with a single line, namely, "She [Hashmi] makes Islam easy." Rather than presenting an inaccessible and obscure version of Islam that is both contextually
and temporally removed from the immediate contours of students' lives,
Hashmi's approach is to help relate the divine to the contemporary
and mundane realities of women's lives. In the few classroom sessions
I observed, one thing that stood out quite clearly to me was the

pedagogical praxis of emphasizing the connection between lived realities
with concepts in the religious texts, rather than insisting on a rather
unbridgeable separation between the mundane concerns of contemporary
women's lives and the absolute perfection embodied by divine texts. I
asked teachers at Al-Huda about their pedagogical philosophies and
approaches during my research. Miss Sobia, a senior teacher in Karachi,
responded by saying that "Dr. Hashmi's interpretation considers modern-
day vocabulary. It is a practical approach that can be applied to contemporary day-to-day life—this is why people are drawn to it."[23] She drew on
an example from a class she had taught earlier that day to elaborate her
point. Miss Sobia shared a story of how the discussion in class had been
about Shaitan's (Satan) arrogance in first refusing to obey Allah and then
his subsequent insistence on justifying his mistake. She had narrated this
story to create a point of reference for the students to reflect on their
own behavior in their daily lives. To make this connection more concretely, Sobia generated an exercise where she asked students to first
reflect on, and then make a list of, the ways they embody and enact this
type of arrogance in their daily interactions. When the students came
back to class, many had gained profound insights on their own behaviors,
which they were eager to share with their classmates. One student, for
example, professed that she had always felt that her sense of fashion and
style was superior to those around her. It was through the exercise Sobia
assigned that she had come to realize that her perception of herself in
relation to others had been shaped by arrogance. Prior to these reflections on arrogance, she had believed that her sartorial taste was simply
superior to that of most others. However, being in Sobia's class had propelled her to consider for the first time that her attitude in this arena
might, in fact, be a manifestation of arrogance rather than humility—and
humility should be the desired trait. It was the story of Shaitan's refusal
to obey Allah that became the catalyst for this process of self-discovery.
Sobia went on to explain:

> The Qur'an is all about developing self-awareness—through discussion
> and debate we bring these issues to the surface in our teaching . . .
> these techniques help learn the application of tafsir. This way one is able
> to evaluate one's day-to-day obstacles and issues. Students share their
> problems. This is what clicks with people . . . perhaps what was lacking
> before this is that there was more of a monologue—no one was allowed
> to question, to expose, to discuss—this two-way discussion between the
> layman and the scholar makes all the difference. I learned from Dr.
> Hashmi myself and I have learned that giving people the freedom helps
> people realize that they are not being forced.[24]

This reflection is echoed in the document titled "About the Founder," which states,

> The driving force behind all of this, Dr. Farhat Hashmi's untraditional style of teaching and vast knowledge, aided by informative and stimulating lectures by other scholars which presents an altogether different view of Islam and the Qur'an *making it practical and relevant to today's world and the key to success* [italics added].[25]

I would add that Al-Huda makes Islam particularly relevant to the lives of women who were raised in fairly elite urban environments and educated in English-medium schools. Rather than impose an entirely different worldview that would require drastic changes in behavior, the environment at Al-Huda resonates on some levels with the lives that these women are used to living. Many of the teachers are from urban middle- to upper-class backgrounds as well, a factor that accords well with students in their classrooms. Saleema *Apa*,[26] for example, had been both a student and a teacher at Al-Huda in the past and had then gone on to join a more traditional *madrassa* in Karachi. During our interview, she pointed out another aspect of this phenomenon. She suggested that the environment in Al-Huda classrooms is much more suitable for women from elite classes because they are less rigid in enforcing certain codes of dress and behavior. The *madrassa* that she was currently attending, for instance, has a strict segregation of spaces based on gender so that male instructors teach an all-women's class from behind a curtain to maintain what they consider appropriate rules of *purdah* (seclusion and concealment of women). This is different from Al-Huda, where an occasional male instructor may teach a classroom full of women without enforcing such strict understandings of *purdah* between men and women. Similarly, she noted, the dress codes and other behavioral norms enforced at the *madrassas* create an environment that many from middle- and upper-class backgrounds would find rather alienating.

Accessibility

Flexibility and accessibility are embedded in the very structure of the Al-Huda organization. To accommodate women with different life circumstances and schedules, Al-Huda provides a broad range of formats for learning. For example, there are evening courses designed for professional women, weekend classes for students, and daytime classes for housewives. In some courses the language of instruction and communication is Urdu, whereas other courses are taught entirely in English. This variety ensures that women with different linguistic fluencies are able to attend classes. In some of the interviews I conducted, young, urban, upper-middle-class girls who have attended English-medium schools and are more conversant in English than in Urdu, as well as some diasporic Pakistanis I interviewed who are not fluent in Urdu, noted that the English classes were instrumental in their decision to join and stick with religious study at Al-Huda.[27] Indeed, one of the reasons Al-Huda has been able to mobilize this particular segment of society is because it is able to repackage Islamic education in a language and style that speaks to and accommodates members of the upper classes as well. This is a significant factor, since historically Islamic education has been associated with *mullahs* (religious clerics), who hail from lower-middle-class backgrounds and are not often conversant in English.[28]

DAWAH

Dawah can be loosely translated as inviting or summoning others to understand and come toward Islam. Students in Al-Huda classrooms are strongly encouraged to engage in the practice of *dawah* in their daily lives. Before graduating from the diploma course, students take a course on *dawah* that includes practical exercises on how to invite friends, family members, classmates, and professional colleagues to learn about Islam. Specific exercises may include organizing a family picnic and playing one of Dr. Hashmi's audiotapes when family members are assembled, or inviting people at work to pray together, or gathering fellow college students to discuss religious issues relevant to their lives on campus environments.

A typical story of how *dawah* has helped recruit members in different venues can be seen in a story of a dynamic young woman by the name of Nadia who had successfully recruited a large number of girls from elite backgrounds in Lahore. Nadia herself had studied in the United States and had come back to Pakistan to fulfill her desire to study Islam. Once she completed her course of study at Al-Huda, she started a religious study circle on the campus of an elite girls' college in Lahore. It was the month of Ramadan and students walking by were intrigued by the sight of this young woman teaching the Qur'an to others. While some laughed at this unusual spectacle, others worried that the atmosphere on campus was becoming too religious. There were some who occasionally sat down to listen to what Nadia had to say. Two of the women I interviewed had become active in Al-Huda through listening to Nadia and other Al-Huda members who conducted informal lessons on campus. Rozeena, for example, shared the story of how her sister was walking by when she saw Nadia leading a religious study session under a tree. She decided to sit down and listen just momentarily, but once she started listening to Nadia's words,

she felt compelled to come back the following day, and every day thereafter. Over time, the growing religious activism on campus began to worry
the administration, which tried to ban religious study circles from the college campus. But banning the groups only generated a feeling of being
under attack among the girls involved. Why, they asked, should religious
study be banned from a college campus? Subversively, these girls began
meeting in secret places, on roofs, and in empty classrooms to continue
their study circles and to reach new girls through their strategy of *dawah*.

Rather than offering a righteous, rigid, or confrontational style of
dawah, Hashmi instructs her students to lead through example, to interact
with others in compassionate and kind ways that invite others to learn
more about Islam. In her own words, "Present yourself and your behavior
so beautifully that people come onto this path on their own."[29] Such an
emphasis ensures that the message continues to travel. In the case of Al-
Huda, it is interaction with the Qur'an and an understanding of one's duty
as a Muslim, as well as consideration of the rewards in the afterlife, that
may provide the motivation to engage in *dawah*. Mehreen shared her experience as follows:

> Reading the Quran with *tarjuma* and *tafsir* changes your thinking. It
> makes you want to spread the message. . . . For instance, I wanted to
> spread what I had learned amongst other Muslims as well. I found a
> new sense of motivation to do this work. One also realizes that whatever
> obstacles we face in doing this work are obstacles that can [or] should
> be overcome because we are working toward a larger cause.

In the event that such a desire is born, Al-Huda has been able to effectively
provide channels for this desire to manifest itself. It is these channels that
have fueled the rapid growth and success of Al-Huda in and beyond
Pakistan.[30]

FUNDING BASE

Finally, it is the class of women targeted that provides the funds needed
for the expansion and sustenance of the organization. In informal conversations I had with people about Al-Huda, many expressed suspicions about
the sources of funding for such a huge operation. Since Dr. Hashmi was
once a member of the Jamaat-e-Islami, many speculate that the funds for
her organization may have links to Saudi Arabia, since the JI is known to
have received funding from there since the 1970s. In my interviews, I pursued this line of questioning and was told repeatedly that the funds come
entirely from donations. Nabila, a former student at Al-Huda, for example,
narrated a story about how she had witnessed women take off their gold

bangles and donate them spontaneously in classes because of how moved they had felt. Many of the houses that I went to for interviews also had specific rooms, or even entire sections, reserved for religious study.[31] Of course, the fact that this movement began among women of elite backgrounds has much to do with their financial ability to help sustain the organization. When asked why Dr. Hashmi had targeted the upper classes, she was very clear in her response:

> Well, some of the ladies who attend my classes previously spent their time at coffee and lunch parties. At least now they are coming here. That is the first step. The next step is to go out and help those less fortunate.[32]

Hashmi goes on to elaborate her theory for social change, which seems to resemble a trickle-down model for economic development. That is, educate the upper classes, and the impact will trickle down to the lower classes. Of course, the upper classes also provide funding for the enterprise to flourish. Giving in the name of Allah is also a means to secure one's position in the afterlife, which is why such an enterprise can flourish through private donations.

NEW RELIGIOUS SUBJECTIVITIES, GENDER POLITICS, AND CRITIQUES

I would like to emphasize that Al-Huda has managed to make a profound impact on a certain type of public religiosity among women, particularly urban women, in contemporary Pakistan. But what types of subjectivities are being articulated by women whose primary source of Islamic education has been Al-Huda classrooms? Simply put, engagement with Al-Huda generates a gendered form of moral agency that, rather than challenging normative societal roles, is firmly anchored in them. This anchoring is in contrast to feminist constructions of agency and activism that have historically worked to transform status quo relations of power that locate and confine women to hetero-normative social roles. In the interviews I conducted, many women consciously distanced themselves from "feminism," arguing that their goal was not to challenge normative prescriptions of gender and sexuality but, in fact, to inhabit these roles and transform the world *through* inhabiting them. Hence, references to motherhood and wifehood featured prominently in the interviews I conducted. Mothers are reminded of their responsibility to nurture religiously sound environments in their families and to raise children with a solid foundation in religious education. The primary argument that is put forth is that Islam sanctions gender complementarity rather than gender equality; furthermore, unlike the roles sought by Westernized women, who insist on sameness, gender roles in Islam are premised on essential difference. By extension, women's roles are primarily located in the domestic realm within a heterosexual familial context; although unlike some *ulema* who believe that women's entry into the public realm should be largely prohibited, Hashmi suggests that women may work outside of the house as long as they are not neglecting their household responsibilities. In her interview published in 2001, Hashmi claims:

> I have no agenda to take away women's rights. Al-Huda holds evening classes specially for working women. But, peace in the home depends on the woman and that aspect should not be ignored at the cost of working outside the home. A woman's role as a home-maker should not be sacrificed at the altar of ambition.

Contrary to stereotypical representations that cast Islam as being forced onto Muslim women, in the case of Al-Huda, many women face strong opposition from family members when they decided to take classes at the organization. Husbands, children, and even parents of some women began to express frustration as these women, affected by their newfound sense of religiosity, begin to take concrete steps to create what they see as more Islamically aligned environments in their homes, attires, ways of moving through space, or life choices in general. Resistance from family members is most intense for elite urban women who come from Western-educated backgrounds and where religion may not be such a primary source of identification. Some of the younger women I interviewed shared stories about struggles they had dealt with in their own familial and social networks. Single women who wear the *abbaya* talked about how difficult it has been to get marriage proposals, as most young urbanized men from this particular class do not want a wife who is fully covered. They spoke about the willpower and religious commitment required for them to resist pressures to unveil to secure good marriage proposals. As Aliya, a young woman in her twenties explained:

> One of the greatest challenges was that when I first started wearing *abbaya* I was 19, I think, so I used to get lots of marriage proposals. People liked me but they objected to my wearing an *abbaya*. I mean it's not as though girls who don't do *hijab* get married right away either, but it is a problem. This got stressful for my parents, and my mother started saying why are you doing this, it is becoming a hindrance to your marriage.

Another difficulty some of the women shared was how to get their husbands to become more religiously observant, to pray more regularly, to fast, and to stop listening to secular music, among other behavioral changes. Aliya shared a story about getting married recently to a man who is not that religiously observant. This is how she described her dilemma:

> In the beginning I was really concerned about *namaz* [prayer] because my husband wouldn't say all his prayers. I used to feel really bad and ask him to pray with me—it is *farz* [obligatory] you know, so I didn't like it. You can say that I kind of used to impose on him as well. So I discussed this issue with my teacher, and she said that you shouldn't insist so much that he gets put off all together. She discouraged me from insisting all the time.

Aliya went on to share how her teacher at Al-Huda advised the students to not take such rigid stances on enforcing piety in their homes because, after all, Islam wants homes to be sustained rather than broken. Following this advice, she shared with me how she had struggled with "picking her battles" on where to push her husband to become more pious and where to compromise and remain silent. One woman remarked that her teachers at Al-Huda had recognized this struggle but had advised the young girls that this, too, is part of their responsibility as Muslims. That is, if all the religious girls will marry religious boys, then who will speak to and affect the nonreligious ones? In a sense, we see the elevated role of these young women who view themselves as responsible for cultivating piety among other family members, be they children, husbands, siblings, or friends.[33]

One of the most notable outward transformations that women of Al-Huda undergo is a change in their modes of dress. Consequently, over the last 15 years, the visual landscape in much of urban Pakistan is sprinkled with women wearing an Arab-style *abbaya* (long, flowing, cloak-like garment worn over clothes) with a large *hijab*, or head covering. This trend is not unique to Pakistan and is, as some have noted, part of a larger trend that involves an "adaptation of certain 'universal' Islamic cultural forms and practices, notably changes in dress code."[34] This trend was not the case in the past, since many women of lower-middle-class backgrounds have historically worn a *burqa*, a tight-fitting long black shirt with a separate head piece that allows you to cover the face either fully or halfway. But this is distinctly different from the style of *purdah* observed by urban Al-Huda women, though not just limited to them. Hashmi herself wears a full, long black *abbaya* and covers her head and her entire face except her eyes. This particular shift in modes of dress has been particularly noteworthy for two reasons: (1) in the past, veiling in Pakistan has not been associated with the urban elite; and (2) this particular style of *purdah* is not indigenous to Pakistan but is an import of a style worn by many women in parts of the Arab world. Given that part of Al-Huda's main mission is to excavate a pure version of Islam through combing out cultural distortions, many critics find this switch from what is defined as "cultural" to what is defined as "religious" as a purist move that diminishes the rich cultural adaptations of Islam in Pakistan.[35] Noting this shift, some observers have argued that what Hashmi is promoting is a form of purist Wahhabi Islam. Many critique Hashmi for placing too much emphasis on covering for women. In the case of Al-Huda, all the women I spoke with had, since joining religious study, begun dressing in what they considered more modest attire in line with Islamic prescriptions of dress for women. Most of the women wore *abbaya*s when they left their homes, whereas a few loosely draped *duppatta*s over their hair but refrained from wearing the revealing Western clothes (tight, see-through, or sleeveless shirts; tight jeans, etc.) that many of them used to wear in the past.[36] However, it is clear that in Hashmi's teachings, a strict form of *purdah* that includes covering the face along with the body is also presented as the highest level of piety to which one should aspire. A few of the young women that I interviewed struggled with this issue, stating that even though they wished to embody this level of piety in their mode of dress, they had not yet been able to implement *purdah* of the face because of either internal resistances or external social pressures. Sometimes these changes in how women chose to dress were seen as so drastic by outsiders that during my research I often heard ridiculing or sarcastic remarks toward Al-Huda women who have gone from wearing a "sleeveless *shalwar kameez*" to a "full *abbaya*." Many people refer to Al-Huda women in a derogatory way as "ninjas" because of the fully covering long, black, and flowing outfits they wear. Others critique them for continuing to wear diamonds and decadently fashionable outfits, but covering up their elite tastes with a cloak of modesty to justify lavish tastes and habits of consumption. What is interesting is that many of the women who decide to wear the *abbaya* also encounter fierce resistance from their own family members, since many of them come from non-*purdah*-observing family backgrounds.

CRITICAL PERSPECTIVES ON AL-HUDA

Over the years, both Hashmi and her institute have come under much scrutiny from various segments of Pakistani society. There are numerous critiques of the type of religious ethos that this movement is helping to cultivate among women. Of particular interest to my study is the politics of gender that is being articulated in Al-Huda's discourse and the critiques that have emerged around this. One of the strongest critiques of Hashmi in this respect has come from feminist theologian Dr. Riffat Hassan, professor of religious studies at the University of Louisville, Kentucky. Hassan critiques Hashmi for adopting an approach that is reminiscent of Laura Bush's "compassionate conservatism." She claims that contrary to her own project of working to recover the gender egalitarian message inherent in the Qur'an, Hashmi's approach in fact echoes the patriarchal interpretations that have been advanced by orthodox male *ulema* in Pakistan for years. Focusing specifically on the issue of *purdah*, for example, she critiques Hashmi for advocating a certain interpretation of Qur'anic verses that suggests that Muslim women aspiring to cultivate the highest form of piety must observe an extremely strict form of *purdah*, one that requires covering the body in addition to the face. According to Hassan, the Qur'an requires both men and women to dress modestly but does not require women to observe such a strict form of *purdah*. As such, she believes that Hashmi is misguiding her students and advancing a perspective that is in line with traditional patriarchal discourses on gender that have been articulated by the predominantly male *ulama* for centuries.[37]

Another critique that Hassan raises is that Hashmi seems least concerned with issues of social justice or human rights (which include women's rights). Hassan argues that it is principles of justice that are, in fact, the most prominent overarching principles in Islam and that any progressive reading of Islamic texts must be done in relation to such principles. In Pakistan, she suggests, Islamic injunctions have become extremely distorted through centuries of patriarchal monopoly over interpretive processes, and these distortions are routinely used to justify various forms of violence against women. However, Hashmi's choice to not engage with these distortions that enact extreme forms of violence against women indicate her lack of concern with issues of justice that Islam is based on. In her own work, Hassan has tried to demonstrate that specific Qur'anic verses that have been used to discriminate against Muslim women lend themselves to different interpretations that can, in fact, be used to strengthen women's position in Muslim societies. She has argued that one must be cognizant that many words in Arabic words are derived from multiple root words and lend themselves to a multiplicity of meanings. It is the selective appropriation of meanings that articulate with and serve hegemonic structures of power that much of Hassan's work has sought to unmask.[38]

Fawzia Afzal-Khan, another Pakistani feminist, has suggested that the role Hashmi is playing in the field of Islamic education is a dangerous one that presents a "latent authoritarianism and exclusionary, apocalyptic, vision, with the role of women, 'liberated' through Al-Huda's 'proper' Quranic teachings, to serve as role models who could help shape the Muslim *ummah* into a united front against western-style decadence and depravity."[39] She goes on to write, "As usual the *hijab* emphasizes the behavior of women, not of men, and in focusing their energies on it, Pakistani *dars*-going followers of Farhat Hashmi not only signal their acceptance of the misogynism that would reduce woman to her body, but also divert their attention from the real problems faced by Pakistani women."[40] Even others have referred to this movement as one that is promoting the "Talibanization of Pakistani society,"[41] as a movement that is "orthodox icon,"[42] and as a movement that draws its ideological impetus from "Wahhabi Islam."[43] Eman Ahmed, writing in the context of Canada, writes that Hashmi's "brand of Islam is as retrogressive as the *mullahs*, but she is educated, speaks out against the religious right and is a woman, other women find her teachings acceptable and legitimate."[44] Another critique that merits attention comes from Sadaf Ahmed, who has, in her ethnographic study of Al-Huda, argued that the organization promotes a hegemonic discourse on Islam that seeks to impose an exclusionary approach and forecloses possibilities for the articulation of difference and diversity in modes of practice. More specifically, she argues, Al-Huda articulates an approach to Islam that resonates with the religio-nationalist perspective that has been normalized through various state and nonstate actors in the history of Pakistan.[45] She argues that Hashmi is propagating a monolithic form of Islam as truth in the context of Pakistan.

Hashmi herself has issued statements that project her as having a "liberal" approach to Islam, one that believes in and advocates *ijtihad* (independent reasoning), and does the crucial work of releasing Islamic interpretations on various issues from the orthodox and male-dominated clutches of the mullahs in Pakistan. She claims that there has been too much rigidity in the ways that Islam has been interpreted and disseminated among people in Pakistan, which has resulted in a narrow emphasis on the "do's and don'ts" rather than a comprehensive and holistic understanding of what Islam means.

When asked why she is known for propagating an approach to Islam that does not elevate the status of women, Hashmi responded:

> I am not propagating my personal views; I'm only conveying what is written in the Quran. As far as the Taliban are concerned, I have heard that they are against the education of women. When I myself have done my Ph.D. and gone to a foreign land to study, how can I tell others not to do the same? My point of view is that a woman's primary responsibility is her home; after she has fulfilled that, it is up to her to go into whatever field suits her best. I have no agenda to take away women's rights.

In other words, Hashmi claims that all she is doing is spreading the word of Allah and that if people have a problem with what she is doing, then it is really Islam that they have a problem with. This sentiment was echoed in many of the interviews that I conducted where my questions about the politics embedded in the interpretive strategies and approaches that Al-Huda uses were met with a concise assertion that all that teachers at Al-Huda are doing is exposing people to what is in the Qur'an and *hadith*. Here we see a problematic assertion of a direct, unmediated relationship to the divine text and a subsequent denial that for centuries there has been a diversity of approaches to reading and interpreting the Qur'an and *hadith*. It was this denial of the politics of the production of Islamic knowledges that was, indeed, one of the obstacles I confronted in my research.[46]

CONCLUSION

This chapter began with my suggestion that the spaces for women to engage with the Qur'an have expanded over the last few decades in Pakistan, a phenomenon of which Al-Huda International provides one of the most profound examples. These spaces for engagement have, in turn, made ways for Pakistani Muslim women to articulate new expressions of religiosity that have made a significant impact on the contemporary urban landscape in Pakistan. In conclusion, however, I argue that engagement with Al-Huda generates a gendered form of moral agency that, rather than challenging hetero-normative societal roles, is firmly anchored in them. Al-Huda has profoundly expanded the spaces for women to participate in the production and dissemination of Islamic knowledge. However, rather than expanding normative gendered roles of women in society, its discourse draw upon notions of essential difference in order to reinforce a dominant paradigm that places women squarely in the domestic realm and men in the realm of the public arena. While Hashmi's teachings make women aware of their God-given rights as wives, mothers, and daughters in the domestic realm, they are largely focused on propelling women to become agents of societal reform through transforming themselves and their families first.

NOTES

1. Khawar Mumtaz, "Identity Politics and Women: 'Fundamentalism' and Women in Pakistan," in *Identity Politics and Women: Cultural Reassertions and Feminisms in International Perspective*, ed. Valentine Moghadam (Boulder, CO: Westview Press, 1994).

2. Quoted in Mumtaz, 239.

3. Al-Huda International's official Web site, http://www.alhudapk.com/ (accessed August 1, 2007).

4. For a more detailed history of the Jamaat-e-Islami in Pakistan, see Seyyed Vali R. Nasr, *The Vanguard of Islamic Revolution: The Jama'at-i-Islami of Pakistan* (Berkeley: University of California Press, 1994).

5. Beginning in the early 1980s, the Jamaat-e-Islami began to organize on university campuses and recruit new members. Through their powerful organizing, they were able to mobilize large numbers of students and exercise influence on both administration and the general ethos on campuses. For more details, see ICG Asia Report 36, *Madrassas, Extremism and the Military*, July 29, 2002, Pakistan, 12.

6. See http://www.iiu.edu.pk/ for more information on the International Islamic University in Islamabad.

7. At this time she was using Maulana Maudoodi's exegetical commentary titled *Tafheem-ul-Qur'an* [Understanding the Qur'an] as a primary source of *tafsir* in her *dars* sessions.

8. Sadaf Ahmad, "The Story of Islamic Revivalism amongst Urban Pakistani Women" (unpublished PhD diss., Syracuse University, NY, 2006), 21.

9. Quoted in Samina Ibrahim, "Interview with Dr. Riffat Hassan," *Newsline*, 2001.

10. In Lahore alone, the list of places where women can go to enroll in coursework included the following: the main facility or Institute of Islamic Education in Gulberg, 5 branches or Schools for Islamic Education (2 in Defense, 1 in Model Town, 1 in Cavalry Grounds, and 1 in Shadman), 12 residential addresses where Qur'an classes are being offered three or four times a week, and 53 more addresses of residences where Qur'an classes are being offered two or three times per week.

11. *Al-Huda Aik Nazar Mein* [Al-Huda at a Glance] brochure.

12. The difference between the two is that the former is an entire facility that is operated by Al-Huda teachers and administrators, whereas the latter is usually comprised of branches operating from the homes of women who have either graduated from Al-Huda and wish to teach courses themselves or those who support the cause and donate portions of their home for religious study.

13. There are other miscellaneous forums: Al-Huda also offers a multitude of short courses, including the following: a three-month course for girls from rural areas, six- to eight-week courses for girls with a 10th-grade education, summer courses for children, and a course for men. Finally, they offer a Community Education Program that includes such weekly programs as "Colors of Islam" or special lectures and programs on specific occasions or topics. For example, there may be lectures on how to celebrate Eid-ul Fitr according to the Sunnah, or there may be provided special training for people who are planning to go on *hajj* or *umrah*. Under the Community Education Program there are also lectures on such social issues as the following listed on their brochure: "Happiness and Grief: information, training and guidance is provided for

certain occasions, such as weddings, birth, deaths and more." Listed also on their brochure are programs to provide religious education to girls from rural areas and *kachi bastis* (urban slums), as well as in prisons. As part of their community service, Al-Huda members also offer a Hospital Program, which is a "program for the moral uplift of aggrieved and despairing women patients."

14. For a detailed account of Islamic education in Pakistan, see Muhammad Qasim Zaman, *The Ulema in Contemporary Islam: Custodians of Change* (Princeton, NJ: Princeton University Press, 2002).

15. For more on the *dars-e-nizami* curriculum, see Jamal Malik, Introduction to *Madrassas in South Asia: Teaching Terror?* ed. Jamal Malik (London: Routledge, 2008), 4–5; and *Zaman, The Ulema in Contemporary Islam,* 68–69.

16. miriam cooke, *Women Claim Islam: Creating Islamic Feminism through Literature* (New York: Routledge, 2001); Peter Mandaville, *Transnational Muslim Politics: Re-imagining the Umma* (London: Routledge, 2001).

17. Dale F. Eickelman and Jon W. Anderson, "Redefining Muslim Publics," in *New Media in the Muslim World,* 2003, 1.

18. See, for instance, Saba Mahmood's 2005 study on the piety movement in Egypt.

19. cooke writes that until the 1990s, it was mostly men whose sermons were taped and circulated among the public; but in the last few decades, women preachers are utilizing this forum as an effective means to disseminate their teachings on Islam as well.

20. This collection is used in what are referred to as Cassette Classes and by individuals who are interested in pursuing independent study from within their homes.

21. Al-Huda International Web site, www.alhudapk.com.

22. Eickelman and Anderson, "Redefining Muslim Publics," 3.

23. Interview with Sobia, Karachi, January 2007.

24. Interview with Sobia, Karachi, January 2007.

25. "About the Founder Dr. Farhat Naseem Hashmi," 3, http://www.alhudapk.com/home/about-us/About%20the%20Founder.pdf.

26. *Apa* is a term of respect used for women older than oneself. Many of the students referred to older teachers by adding the term *Apa* at the end of their first names.

27. Formats for the courses are designed to meet diverse schedules of different women. For example, whereas some students enroll in full-time coursework at the main branch of the academy for six hours of study a day over the course of a year or two, others are able to attend more loosely structured classes offered by Al-Huda graduates within their homes in different neighborhoods. Yet others are able to enroll in evening courses—a module created specifically for working women who cannot attend during the day—while some attend Cassette Classes, where women gather together in a home to

listen to and discuss *tafsir* (exegesis) of the Qur'an recorded in the voice of Dr. Hashmi.

28. Ahmad writes: "One of the reasons why middle and upper class urban people have kept religious discourse at some distance from their lives is because of its association with the clerics or *maulvis* of Pakistan. They are generally perceived by the masses in general, and women in particular, as uneducated, unkempt, misogynist, and extremist. Islam had largely been associated with them, and therefore, it too became infused with a specific meaning i.e. that of being 'out of date' and 'backward' through mere association. It became something that these women, who prided themselves on being "modern," did not associate with." "The Story of Islamic Revivalism," 84.

29. Ibid., 27.

30. Some interviewees mentioned that they were afraid of graduating because they are not sure exactly how they will pursue the work they have begun at Al-Huda.

31. Ahmad points out that some of the people that have invited Farhat Hashmi to give *dars* in the past include the mother and wife of Farooq Leghari, who was the president of the country in the early 1990s, as well as the Saudi royal family. It would be fair to assume, Ahmad speculates, that Hashmi has been well compensated for these efforts. Ahmad, "The Story of Islamic Revivalism," 29, footnote 14.

32. Samina Ibrahim, "Interview with Farhat Hashmi," *Newsline*, May 2001.

33. I suggest that it is precisely in the strategy of *dawah*, which recasts women as prominent actors who fulfill their respective roles in society while using these very roles to transform the consciousness of those around them, that Al-Huda's success lies.

34. In the context of Turkey, Nilüfer Göle has pointed out that even though traditional ways of covering oneself change from one Muslim country to another in terms of the form of "folk" dresses, the contemporary Islamist outfit is similar in all Muslim countries. See Nilüfer Göle, *The Forbidden Modern: Civilization and Veiling* (Ann Arbor: University of Michigan Press, 1996).

35. This can be seen as part of a phenomenon that Suroosh Irfani has referred to as the "Arabized shift" in expressions of Islam in Pakistan, which has lent itself to less tolerance toward diverse practices of Islam that manifest in growing sectarian violence. See Suroosh Irfani, "Pakistan's Sectarian Violence: Between the 'Arabist Shift' and Indo-Persian Culture," in *Religious Radicalism and Security in South Asia*, ed. Satu P. Limaye, Robert G. Wirsing, and Mohan Malik (Honolulu: Asia-Pacific Center for Security Studies, 2004).

36. It was interesting to hear some students say that the environment in Al-Huda classrooms is such that one feels uncomfortable if one is not properly

covered while attending classes. Others, however, pointed out that they were never pressured to change their ways of dressing but came to this decision on their own as they read the Qur'an and its *tafsir* in their classes.

37. Riffat Hassan, "Islam and Human Rights in Pakistan: A Critical Analysis of the Positions of Three Contemporary Women" (2004). Published on Islamic Research International Foundation (IRFI) Web site: http://www.irfi.org/articles/articles_101_150/islam_and_human_rights_in_pakist.htm.

38. See, for instance, Riffat Hassan, "The Issue of Woman-Man Equality on the Islamic Tradition," in *Eve & Adam: Jewish, Christian, and Muslim Readings on Genesis and Gender*, ed. Dristen E. Kvam, Linda S. Schearing, and Valerie H. Ziegler (Bloomington: Indiana University Press, 1999); Riffat Hassan, "Brief Comment on Feminist Misunderstandings," *Journal of Women's History* 13, no. 1 (2001); Riffat Hassan, "Challenging the Stereotypes of Fundamentalism: An Islamic Feminist Perspective," *The Muslim World* 91, no. 1 (2001): 55.

39. Fawzia Afzal-Khan, "Betwixt and Between? Women, the Nation and Islamization in Pakistan," *Social Identities* 13, no. 1 (Jan. 2007): 23.

40. Ibid., 28.

41. Ibrahim, "Interview with Farhat Hashmi," 2001.

42. Shiamala Matri Dawood, "Will the Real Pakistani Woman Please Stand Up?" *Newsline*, March 2005.

43. Eman Ahmed. "Not the Only Way," February 2008, http://www.awid.org/eng/Issues-and-Analysis/By-AWID-Initiative/Library/Not-the-only-way.

44. Ibid.

45. Ahmad, "The Story of Islamic Revivalism," 27.

46. Through meticulous study, scholars have shown that the processes surrounding the production of religious knowledge are far from unbiased and transparent. See, among others, Asma Barlas, *"Believing Women," in Islam: Unreading Patriarchal Interpretations of the Qur'an* (Austin: University of Texas Press, 2004); Amina Wadud, *Qur'an and Woman: Rereading the Sacred Text from a Woman's Perspective* (Oxford: Oxford University Press, 1999); and Fatima Mernissi, *The Veil and the Male Elite: A Feminist Interpretation of Women's Rights in Islam* (New York: Perseus, 1991).

CHAPTER 8

"Women's Spirit" and "Spiritual Matter(s)": Gender, Activism, and Scholarship in an Ethiopian Eco-Spiritual System

Patricia H. Karimi-Taleghani

The scholarly intersection of gender, activism, and spirituality seems unquestionable when the subject is African womanhood. While patriarchal systems of male dominance have challenged African women's control of certain spheres of knowledge and social practice, it is largely in areas of gender-specific epistemologies that feminist scholarship explores women's lived existences. Yet, a trend that has recently emerged in the research literature is concerned with not only a gender perspective but also the spiritual dimension of women, men, and children's lives. This academic trend I have termed an *eco-spiritual systems and gender approach.*[1] I argue here that women, men, and children, as gendered individuals, live and act within specific ecosystems. Within most African societies, these communities or ecosystems are inextricably shaped by spiritual concerns. Hence, African women's lives and their activism are informed, in part, by spirituality.

It is in both private and public arenas that gender, spirituality, and scholarship combine to create dynamism within specific African and global

185

women's communities. From *within* the parameters of African women's spirituality, we as researchers should begin informing how we express our knowledge and practice of African gender scholarship. Toward this end, an eco-spiritual and gender approach will be used here as a framework for exploring women's activism and scholarship in one African nation, Ethiopia.

This discussion provides, first, an undercurrent critique of feminist scholarship that is drawn from various social science paradigms. These social science paradigms currently form the basis for research on gender issues in Africa. Because such scholarship is predicated on Western epistemologies, these paradigms often neglect the role of African women's spirituality in their activism, particularly because that activism pertains to daily existence within urban African contexts. Throughout, this chapter interweaves the themes of Ethiopian women's spirituality, material existence, and gender struggles for social and economic justice within the context of globalization, colonialism, and neocolonialism.

Second, this chapter briefly describes select cultural features of indigenous sub-Saharan African societies that are reflected in "traditional" Ethiopian society, especially social constructs that affect women's ability to affect their economic situations within contemporary Ethiopia. Such cultural aspects as indigenous African spirituality point to a unity of ontology, if not ideology, that provides Ethiopian and other African women with the organizing principles that are so necessary for creating collective spaces for transforming their local economic, political, and social conditions.

Third, the relationships between scholarship, women's development issues, and activism are explored within the framework of indigenous organizations employed by Ethiopian women social activists. These women are affecting, if not transforming, their own socioeconomic and political environments in ways that benefit not only individual Ethiopian women, men, and children but local communities as well. The civil society organization that is described in the later half of this chapter places Ethiopian women's life issues, activism, and eco-spirituality firmly within the context of other African women's life issues, activism, and eco-spirituality.

INTERLOCUTORY DISCUSSION ON THE STUDY OF GENDER AND WOMEN IN AFRICA

Since the mid- to late-1970s and early 1980s, African women's issues have come to the forefront of research on Africa. This is especially the case for feminist research on Africa. In the third millennium CE, feminist scholars realize that within the feminist paradigm there are myriad theoretical frameworks,[2] as well as sociopolitical and cultural contexts within which they operate.[3] Western feminist scholarship is particularly critiqued from within the growing field of African gender and women's studies. This is happening across the various disciplines and across local and transnational boarders. Feminist scholars are now, more so than ever, turning the analytic lens onto themselves and their scholarship that focuses on African women's lives.

While many feminist women scholars are questioning the very nature of conventional scholarship, that is, the mechanics and interpretations of gender studies concerned with current socioeconomic and political realities in Africa,[4] what compels most scholars, especially African women scholars, is the need to study, research, and write with clear epistemological objectives.[5] Hence, the study of gender relations in Africa emerges as a much more complex area of inquiry. Within this complexity there arises the problem that concerns how we, as activist scholars, Western and African, can support African women activists in their attempts to surmount the concrete objective realities they face on a continuous basis. Many African women meet head on devitalizing forces that plague parts of the African continent: the daily onslaught of war, famine, environmental degradation, state-sanctioned public and private gender violence, disastrous foreign and domestic development policies (under the auspices of "globalization" and "privatization"), HIV/AIDS, and genocide and femicide.[6] Wars and internal conflict limit women's ability to undertake economic activities that are life sustaining for themselves, their children, and their extended families. African women respond to such crises and pressing concerns in varied and intricately multifaceted ways. They do so within the composite of their own religiosity, social justice, and gender expressions. For scholars, then, the following question is of critical importance: From what knowledge base and from whose perspectives do we inform our interpretations of the variety of life expressions that are experienced by African women?

What knowledge base and whose perspective is a prominent theme discussed in the introduction to Obioma Nnaemeka's thought-provoking anthology *Female Circumcision and the Politics of Knowledge: African Women in Imperialist Discourses* (2005). The anthology features essays by prominent women scholars of Africa and of African descent. Nnaemeka's anthology provides African women—and I inject into her statement *"and other women who are concerned about these questions"*—spaces where they can "participate as producers of knowledge,"[7] especially the production of knowledge concerned with African societies. Locality then becomes a central concern in the study of gender, race, and class in African contexts.

As scholars venture to explore innovative ways to research and write about African women's experiences, they must also heed the reservations of their African sisters. Researchers on African women,[8] and in particular African women researchers, have for decades voiced their concerns regarding conventional Western feminist academics and the manner in which they study and represent African women's issues.[9] Ifi Amadiume, in her seminal work on gender and sex in Igboland, *Male Daughters, Female Husbands* (1987), sees the works of many feminists located in the West as a new form of imperialism.[10] Since the 1960s, there have been gross misinterpretations within gender and women's studies. What most of these works reflect in terms of misinterpretations is the complexity of the "imperialist gaze." Here is where locality plays a crucial role in understanding or misunderstanding and misconstruing the cultures and concerns of African women as viewed from outside, by outsiders. As Chimalum Nwankwo suggests, the writings of some women of color not only mirror the arrogance of European colonial anthropologists but also juxtapose African women in subordinate positions.[11] African women scholars are putting to rest the misconceptions that portray them and their lives in subordinate terms. African women are serious about researching and writing their own gender studies from the locale of their particular countries, regions, cultures, and historical perspectives. They also read, understand, and critique the works that others write about them.[12]

As feminist scholars, we cannot put words into each other's mouth, but we can offer a scholarly platform upon which we can begin to analyze and dialogue. The objective of this chapter is an effort to do just that—to offer a scholarly platform for dialogue and analysis of some of these issues.

GENDER IDEOLOGY IN AFRICA

One readily ascertains the workings of ecology, production, and gender philosophy in and on the lives of women in rural and urban Africa. What may not be so apparent, however, is how ecological niches in urban and rural Africa gave rise to male reinterpretation and manipulation of gender ideologies. Just how much does ecological deprivation affect ideological control of scarce resources, especially in times of war, food crises, fuel shortages, and urban overpopulation?

Production has been historically a gendered activity in Africa in rural as well as in contemporary urbanized areas. The division of labor is a gender construction whereby males have various amounts of control over women's access to land, labor, and the products of that labor. But this control is determined by the ecological environment and sanctioned, ideologically, through ritual.[13]

Ecological environments determine the types of crops that can be grown in certain areas. In some regions of Africa, for example, males dominated in areas of production that required more specialized skills. In the precolonial past, within the various ecological environments, the amount of labor that went into producing certain crops determined the cultural value of the crop and the gender of the producer. In societies where agricultural land or ecological niches were not fertile, there tended to develop gender ideologies that had as their focus the control of fertility of land and women's productive activities. Under these various circumstances, males may have come to dominate in specific areas of *indigenous knowledge*,[14] that is, the knowledge necessary in particular areas for crafting or producing certain crops or products, thereby engendering their control over these and other vital local natural resources. In some traditional societies of western Africa, males cultivated what some writers have termed prestige crops,[15] whereas women cultivated crops that were considered less prestigious in that they were less labor intensive. Although women's crops and their indigenous knowledge of cultivation technology may have been viewed, by some groups, as less prestigious, they were crucial to the survival of the kinship unit.

During the colonial period (1890s–1990s Namibia and South Africa, the last two African colonies to gain independence), it was through African male heads of household that the colonial states were able to produce cash crops for European metropolitan markets by appropriating some of the lands that women traditionally used to produce crops for their families and for local consumption. The crops that women produced did not have the monetary value on the international market that African males' cash crops did. Consequently, women's access to essential natural resources, especially land, became increasingly limited.

As women have less access to the resources necessary for maintenance of their families, women and their children are thrust into poverty. For example, in colonial Africa, many African males used and even manipulated traditional religions, customary laws, and especially colonial laws to dominate and control women's productive work and movements.[16] This tendency to use the legal system to control women continues into the present in various areas of Africa.[17] As well, African males in colonial southern Africa controlled women's access to such critical natural resources as land and even technology. These and related types of dynamics become part of what is to be considered as we delve into the study of gender scholarship, activism, and spirituality in Africa.

The focus of many contemporary African feminist scholars is to research and write from the vantage point of gender transformations and also to elucidate the politics of knowledge. When the foregoing types of issues are included within African women's studies, the investigation of African women's organizing and leadership increasingly reveals an underlying thread, namely, African women's indigenous spiritualism. Current research points to the need for those who study African women's activism to include in their analyses how African women use their spiritual traditions as they strive toward fundamental economic, political, and social transformations in their societies.

THE RESEARCHER AS CULTURAL-POLITICAL INSTRUMENT

The background of any researcher bears on the research. Consequently, it is important to ask and answer two specific questions: "Who am I, and what business do I have talking about African women?"

This chapter is written from the vantage point or locale of a woman of African descent. My voice, my perspective, is only one of a variety of views on gender and spirituality in Africa. Uniquely situated in the United States, my ancestors were African; they were grains of sand taken from the shores of Africa to toil on the plantations of the so-called New World. With them came their memories of epistemological systems based on mother societies, cultures, religions, and languages.[18] These memories or epistemological systems formed the base for much of their social, political, and economic resistance within the United States from the early 17th century to the present. Such scholars as Robin D. G. Kelley (2002) and Cedric J. Robinson (1983) view this type of resistance as "surrealism." Kelley argues that much of the activism of enslaved and colonized Africans stem from an awareness that "any serious motion toward freedom must begin in the mind."[19] While historical memories actually formed the epistemological basis for the activism of African Americans, it also provided a spiritual connection to Africa. Some of these historical memories revolve around the spiritual world, and some of these they passed on to me. These memories, handed down to me through my kinfolk (mostly women), create a spiritual bridge to other African women. This spiritual connection, or bridge, as I like to think of it, links me to the experiences of African women in ways that are not always recognized in the West. It is the trajectory of *my socialization*, within my family and community, that forms the knot that ties me spiritually to women of African descent. What I have just said does not mean that women of different socialization cannot study the gender or activist context in Africa. Obviously, they can and do. What this does mean, however, is that the presence or absence of historical sensitivities, including African spiritual retentions, may influence such things as perspective, focus, values, and depth of research explorations. Let me illustrate by using myself as an example:

- Being the first generation out of the African American rural South, my parents instilled in us a respect for nature. Our worldview was shaped by instructions about not only this tangible world of humans, plants, and animals and the environment but also the non-tangible world of the spirit and how this unseen world worked in and on our lives.

- As is common in Africa, what I was taught did not recognize a dichotomy between our physical and metaphysical environments. Each of these areas of existence has impact on the other. The relationship is symbiotic.

- I was raised with the knowledge that the spirit world exists in the same space that I inhabit and is as tangible as the chair on which I am seated. For example, my paternal grandmother often paraded me through her home because, she said, I could *"feel"*[20] when *"spirits"* were present. She would take blessed water and sprinkle it where I had walked, thereby cleansing and chasing the undesired spirits out of the house.[21] This she did to restore harmony and balance to our physical world through spiritual actions.

- Stories about a male relative who attracted spirits whenever he wore white at night, and how this forced him to have to continually step aside to allow the spirits to pass, were commonplace in our household.

- The concrete connection to Africa was explained to me very early in my childhood when I asked, "Where do we come from?" My grandmother answered very simply, "Africa."

- Growing up in an economically poor, segregated section of a large city in southern California during the 1960s and 1970s and being aware of our isolation from white society, when I ventured to ask, "Why do they [white people] hate us?" My grandmother answered, "We were brought here from Africa, and because they worked us as slaves, this is how they see us."

- My interdisciplinary training in African studies and Yoruba culture and language provided the backdrop for my early interest in cross-cultural analyses of African religious retentions in the New World, but specifically Jamaica. In my master's thesis, I examined the ontological and metaphysical beliefs surrounding death and burial among the Yoruba of Nigeria and compared them with those beliefs held by Kumina devotees in Jamaica during the 1950s.

- Presently, my scholarly focus has shifted from western Africa and the New World to Ethiopian political economy and educational history. Within this academic niche, gender and development issues have become a central concern of my scholarly work. I am literate in Amharic, an Ethiopian language, and have lived in and conducted research in Ethiopia. The data for this chapter were gathered in Addis Ababa, Ethiopia, during July and August of 2006.

My socialization, subsequent formal academic training, and social commitment enable me to enter Africa in different ways, to hear differently and to report differently because I have experienced differently. My socialization, as well as my formal, interdisciplinary training in African history, particularly Ethiopian history, influences how I as a scholar address and characterize the pressing concerns of the African women about whom I write. In essence, my particular eco-spiritual background influences how I apply my scholarly training, what I come to understand, and how I interpret African women's and, more specifically, Ethiopian women's life experiences.

SELECT FEATURES OF THE AFRICAN CONTEXT

"Who is to say if the key that unlocks the cage might not lie hidden inside the cage?"

Arvind Sharma, *Feminism and World Religions* (1999)

Before we move on to examples from Ethiopia, several additional key features about the general African context are important to understand. First, in most traditional African societies—and Ethiopia is no exception—there has never been an acute dichotomy or delineation between the spiritual world and the material world. The intrusion of global capitalist economic, social, and political structures and their inherent counterpart, patriarchal ideology (i.e., male-dominated religion and Western education), has been the root cause for the observed contemporary delineations between the spiritual and material worlds.[22] Under the "triple yokes" of racialist colonialism, intellectual chauvinism, and capitalism, gender binaries became etched in marble. Hence, in much of Western scholarship, African women's social, spiritual, economic, and political existences are viewed in fragments. These aspects of their lives were once integrated into parallel and symbiotic gender systems, or "dual-sex" social systems,[23] which are now submerged under the effects of Western imperialism.

A skewed view of African women's lives was further validated within much of the early scholarship of Western feminist literature. This can be seen in Western literature centered around such African social and cultural practices as female husbands and more recently female circumcision (which many in the West refer to as female genital mutilation, or FGM). Omofolabo Ajayi-Soyinka describes this tendency as "double-patriarchy." Ajayi-Soyinka explains that African women are negated and subordinated twice, once by their own cultural patriarchies, and again by "white-based and male-focused feminist theories."[24] The continuing debate around female circumcision is an especially sensitive issue in northeastern Africa and the Horn of Africa among Ethiopian, Eritrean, and Somali women.[25]

Second, there is the problem of oversimplification. Can we speak of such broad overarching concepts as "African feminist" or "African women," or is it more appropriate to examine gender relations[26] from the particular socioeconomic, spiritual, and political dimensions of localized ethnic, class, and cultural vantage points within Africa? Given the recent historical events taking place in Ethiopia, it is certainly problematic to use a general term such as "Ethiopian women."[27] African people of various cultural and social backgrounds exist within the confines of particular African polities (e.g., within the nations of Egypt, Ethiopia, Sudan, and Somalia). Whether or not they personally identify with this polity, these identifications are to be respected.

Third, rural and urban African women experience the interconnectedness of gender, ideology, and social structures within their respective societies and the impact that state policies have had on these areas. African women also encounter "domestic-public"[28] roles within gender sites that are often reshaped by such exterior relations as contemporary global social, economic, and political pressures on African states and the policy directives connected to these pressures. As their cultures, economies, and political structures are changed by external relations, so too are their gender relationships. These newer externally induced relationships are layered on top of older indigenous African cultural foundations. This layering aspect of transformations and social change has been too often overlooked in the conventional Western-based literature on African societies.

African women's history has revealed that the older indigenous gender relationships were parallel and complementary, and they were always amenable to manipulation.[29] It is most important to understand that "traditional" African women perceive maleness as a power relationship and not merely as a sexual or biological determination. In addition, in most African societies, this gender relationship is strongly sanctioned by ritual. Therefore, as in the past, African women have had ways for redressing and even strongly confronting female subordination through female kin institutions. Within these female institutions, women have abilities to assert ritual arbitration, political power, and personal wealth to effect changes in their and other women's lives.

Power, then, is understood by traditional women to be a cultural attribute associated with maleness. Through such female-centered spiritual institutions as *zar*[30] (spirit possession and healing) in Ethiopia and female husbands, male daughters, and female kings (unique to specific African societies), women manage their physical environments with metaphysical tools.

AFRICAN WOMEN'S SPIRIT MATTERS

What are traditional African perceptions of spiritual realities? Are these perceptions of spiritual reality conceptually gendered? Do African women's experiences differ from men's at the very basic level of spiritual beliefs? If African men's and women's experiences are different, how are they different? Lebisa J. Teffo and Abraham P. J. Roux, in "Metaphysical Thinking in Africa," explain that *"our perceptions of reality are influenced by our expectations, beliefs and emotions, but also by our conceptual schemes, our histories and social circumstances, and the language we talk."*[31] They explain these particularities of individual or group worldviews without interjecting gender as an essential element of that discussion. Teffo and Roux's exclusion of gender as a factor in perceptions of reality suggests that African metaphysics is not a gendered concept. We may infer from Teffo and Roux's analysis that African women's ritual position and understanding of the spiritual world differs little from that of African males' ritual position and understanding of the spiritual world within local cosmologies. Therefore, African women's conceptions of the spiritual world and their ritual positions within it are often neglected in much of the scholarship on African societies.

Nwando Achebe's pioneering history of Nsukka women farmers, traders, warriors, and kings (*Farmers, Traders, Warriors and Kings: Female Power and Authority in Igboland,* 2005) contradicts Teffo and Roux's view and infuses the feminine principal into the historical literature.[32] Achebe has pointed the way to articulating, organizing, and evaluating Igbo women's history "in ways that deviate from traditional historical writing."[33] Achebe's work describes women's position within Nsukka cosmological structure and places the spiritual world at the center of Nsukka women's history. Achebe asserts that it is the invisible world that her work highlights. She does not concentrate on the human world exclusively. This approach fits into the worldview of the Nsukka people. It is how their world is organized and understood.[34]

New research conducted on and by African women scholars and activists is revealing that the organizational abilities of African women are unique in relation to other areas of the female world, and an integral component of their organizational strategies has spirituality at the core. Diedre Badejo's work "Authority and Discourse in the Orin Odún Osun" demonstrates how the sacred and secular meld as feminine "cosmic authority" provides the impetus for social action among contemporary Yoruba women devotees of Osun.[35] According to Badejo, in 1982, as political rifts throughout Nigeria translated into intense religious strife, in Oshogbo, female Osun devotees used such traditional Yoruba idioms as ritual songs to voice their dissatisfaction with the situation and offer indigenous solutions. During early periods of European colonization of Africa, in the 1920s, whenever women in various parts of Africa felt their livelihoods or culture threatened by colonial governments, they were able to organize both rural and urban women to effectively resist. In Owerri Province, Nigeria, it was possible for them to organize large numbers of women across stratified and diverse communities; hence, the "women's war."[36] Bonds of "female solidarity,"[37] especially apparent during the colonial period, remain a powerful tool for women's political activism in many African societies even today.

Writers like Janet M. Bujra (1986) even suggest that such concepts as female solidarity need to be more deeply analyzed within the framework of an emerging working class in Africa. Her work points to the intricate balance between politics of gender and class activism among women in African societies—especially, Bujra points out, as some upper-strata African women who advocate local poor women's issues may be promoting actions that further their own class interests and not the interests of those communities with which they purport solidarity.[38] Another consideration is that African women's solidarity may have little to do with conventional Eurocentric forms of activism. As Bujra points out, female solidarity is a by-product of African women's organizing. African women organize around issues that bear on their continued existence and the survival of their communities.

What Bujra does not take into consideration is that many upper-strata women in Africa promote the issues of poor women and children for other than material reasons. While it is imperative that class be considered in the actions of African women's political and social activities, we should also investigate the links between African women's activism and their spirituality regardless of their class backgrounds. Also, it must be acknowledged that age and gender hierarchies have been salient features of African societies for many millennia prior to foreign penetration into Africa. Even in contemporary African societies, spirituality has provided the impetus for collective female action across class and religious designations. For example, in 2003, the collective actions of Sierra Leonean and Liberian women's movements brought an end to the chaos and violence of civil war. The actions of these women created the cultural and political context for peace in their respective societies. Liberian women, Muslim as well as Christian, were the moral force that galvanized Liberians and placed pressure on delegates of the African Union to encourage Charles Taylor to relinquish power. Their struggle has been documented in a film entitled *Pray the Devil Back to Hell*.[39] Three years later, in 2006, Liberian women again organized for political inclusion and successfully elected the first female president in Liberia, Ellen Johnson Sirleaf.

In sum, while such multiple hierarchies as gender, ethnicity, and regionalism are all powerful forces in African political and social realities, spirituality plays a significant role in the organization and activism of many elite African women. Elite women's ability to align themselves with other women across differing social and economic strata and toward collective action is democratizing their societies. They are creating political spaces where women are able to challenge male power and privilege in the realms of the political, economic, and social.

ELEMENTS OF AFRICAN INDIGENOUS TRADITIONS THAT BEAR ON ECO-SPIRITUAL AND GENDER SYSTEMS

Here I offer several key examples and insights into some of what I have already discussed. Various aspects of female solidarity in contemporary African societies, as well as conceptions of gender and power, rest upon older ideological strata. Traditional aspects of gender and power in Africa were more fluid compared to what is commonly portrayed about Africa today. Deepening changes within many indigenous African gender and power structures are largely attributable to the effects of capitalism, colonialism, and neocolonialism.

Western academic writing contains many misconceptions concerning African female socioeconomic subordination, domesticity, and ideological, ritual, and political powerlessness. Much of this misdirection has been inherited from the early writings of the European colonial era.[40] For instance, to clarify one common misconception, gender in many traditional African societies did not always correlate with sex. In Igbo societies, for example, one could be a male daughter or a female husband. These roles reflected power relationships, not physical or biological determinations. This type of traditional conceptualization of gender is expressed linguistically as well. It appears in aspects of many African cultures. For example, in "Igbo grammatical construction of gender, a neuter particle is used in Igbo subject or object pronouns, so that no gender distinction is made in reference to males and females in writing or in speech."[41] This linguistic tendency to blur gender lines also shows up as a reversal of gender indicators in Amarinya, an Ethiopian Semitic language. While male and female gender markers are an aspect of the grammatical makeup of Amharic, when a young male child speaks to an older woman in order to indicate respect, he may use the male form (*anta*, you m.) for addressing her. Likewise, I have witnessed young men referring to one another with the feminine indicator (*anchi*, you f.), especially if they are close friends. This gender aspect of the Amharic language has yet to be fully explored. Once this dimension of Amharic is fully understood, it may yield a body of knowledge that helps to explain the relationship between language usages, gender, and power systems in Ethiopia.

A second common misconception involves patrilineal rules of descent. Patrilineal rules of descent are quickly becoming dominant over earlier matrilineal and bilateral forms of descent.[42] Traditionally, the latter two forms of kinship organization were instrumental in offering alternative rules and regulations for gender relations, especially in terms of inheritance[43] and sociopolitical and economic obligations within kinship systems. Among the Amarinya and Tigrinya speakers of Ethiopia and Eritrea, for instance, women traditionally inherited usufructory rights through both maternal and paternal lines. Aristocratic women, such as the Ethiopian empress Tayitu,[44] were also able to amass wealth, prestige, and political power through kin affiliations, strategic marriages, and military service to the state.[45] In traditional Africa, integrated gender systems were embedded within agrarian societies and "corporate kin-groups."[46] These gender systems were based firmly on principles of age, consanguinity, and ritual. Parallel gender systems were also apparent in metaphysical and political components of African leadership. For instance, the role of the Queen Mother in ritual obligations associated with kingship and governing in Ashante, Buganda, and Ethiopian societies is illustrative of this tendency.

In more contemporary times, we are able to witness and experience the powerful influence of strong metaphysical (ideological) and corporate kinship ties in private and public arenas in Africa. These arenas include political aspects of indigenous society that are highly charged with parallel gender role expectations. Parallel gender role expectations are present in productive and reproductive relationships within households, family and marital responsibilities, customary and state laws, and religious duties. Traditionally, these parallel gender systems have offered women avenues for creating feminine spaces, contiguous to male institutions, leadership roles, and political niches. In the case of Ethiopia post-1941, such institutionalized religions as missionary Christianity, Islam, and state-sponsored organizations have tended to marginalize women's position to a greater degree than in the past. This tendency raises another issue, that is, to what degree have Ethiopian women been included or excluded from leadership roles and political participation within state and local structures?

One of the concerns in this chapter is to begin to understand the degree to which urban and rural women in Ethiopia are included or excluded from power sharing with men because of their gender and class.[47] If women are excluded, how does this inability to share power affect Ethiopian women's ability to organize and advocate for their "gender as a class"?[48] Does residing in a hierarchical and patriarchal society like Ethiopia mean that women must rely more heavily on female institutions and organizations as avenues for change rather than rely on state-sponsored programs that target female populations? In addition to women's having their female institutions and organizations, do women's spirituality and spiritual institutions offer women the mechanisms they need to alter and even transform their environments in order to satisfy their own and their family's needs? Answers to these questions will illuminate how connected the spiritual and material are and show the degree to which these realms are governed by gender ideology.

Such spiritual concepts as the goddess or female deities that are commonly evoked when studying women's political leadership roles in western Africa are little touched on in scholarship that focuses on Ethiopian women's religiosity. For instance, no one has studied such indigenous female deities as Etete or Maryam of the Ethiopian Orthodox Christians and how these might influence women's activism around issues of social, economic, or political development.[49] These are essential areas that are briefly touched on later in this chapter.

In Africa, Ethiopia in particular, one cannot account for complexity in gender relationships within the environmental, political, socioeconomic, and cultural interactions of human communities without also recognizing that all these systems are intrinsically connected to, and often rooted in, the specificity of local spiritual systems. Thus, we cannot study Ethiopian women as agents of economic and social change without being aware of their eco-spiritual systems. If we look at Ethiopian women's activism, it is almost always within the context of the foregoing framework.

THE CASE OF ETHIOPIA

The study of gender relations in Ethiopia is in its infancy compared with gender studies in other areas of Africa.[50] This state of affairs is not because women's roles in Ethiopia are static or uncomplicated. Nor is it that Ethiopia lacks rich cultural and historical relevance. Quite the contrary, Ethiopia can boast of over 3,000 years of indigenous rule, excepting a brief 5-year foreign occupation (1935–1941 CE). It is in Ethiopia where human history begins to unfold over 4 million years ago. In fact, one of our oldest common female ancestors was unearthed in Hadar, Ethiopia, in 1974.[51] Ethiopia is the home base for the African Union (established in 1963 as the Organization of African Unity) and houses the United Nations Economic Commission on Africa, which has had a gender component since the 1960s.

Many Ethiopian women were powerful actors in this history. Taddesse Tamrat mentions a 10th-century queen, believed to be of Sidama origin, who led a revolt against Christian Ethiopian rulers and won her society's independence.[52] As well, such 19th- and 20th-century women as Tayitu and Zewditu and countless other unnamed women were mothers, sisters, daughters, and "warriors and kings." Shawaragad Gadle, who played a crucial role in the liberation of Ethiopia from Italian colonialism in 1941, illustrates Ethiopian women's involvement in anti-colonial struggles.[53]

During the 1930s, Empress Mennen, Senadu Gebru, and Ennis Ford[54] pioneered the establishment of women's education in Ethiopia. These women were actively engaged in advocating for women's causes.

Influential Ethiopian women helped to shape the political and cultural environment that is Ethiopia today. In the 1950s and 1960s, Western-educated Ethiopian women were actively engaged within the state apparatus as officials within ministries. They have been administrators and diplomats. In contemporary Ethiopia, internal political struggles against the Mengistu regime produced women fighters whose political influence is shaping gender policy in Ethiopia today. From the 1990s to the present, such women of Ethiopia as Nestanat Asfaw of the Ministry of Information have worked in the Ethiopian political arena to bring about equitable changes in government policies that affect the judicial, social, and economic lives of women in Ethiopian society.

In the area of harmful cultural practices that affect women and girls in contemporary Ethiopia—for example, female circumcision—activist Dr. Bogalech Gebre formed the Kembatta Women's Self-Help Center in 1997. In an attempt to discourage female circumcision and help in the prevention of the spread of HIV/AIDS, her organization works to provide women and girls in Kembatta with information on reproductive health rights. The Kembatta Women's Self-Help Center also makes available vocational and business training and instructs women in practices that ensure ecological preservation. Dr. Bogalech's work extends to establishing a legal aid clinic devoted to offering women instruction in their legal rights as stipulated in the Constitution of the Democratic Republic of Ethiopia.

Throughout the entire specter of history in modern Ethiopia, the state's sociopolitical relationship to gender issues in general and women's issues in particular has always been complex and contradictory. The pre-1991 state's gender policy, or lack of concrete gender policy implementation, colored the manner in which gender is researched and written about in Ethiopia. However, what is certain is that as elsewhere, the direction for any changes in gender roles in Ethiopia and in other parts of Africa has been influenced by patriarchal African states, "parasitic . . . capitalism,"[55] and European imperialism in all its varied manifestations.

Therefore, the absence of an extended period of European colonialism does not mean that Ethiopia experienced no form of foreign economic and intellectual domination. One need only look closely at Ethiopia's present economy and educational system to understand the effects of externally driven capitalism and its ideological component, Western education. Western ideological and economic systems have become the basis upon which Ethiopians and other Africans measure their own social, economic, and political development.[56]

Within the context of internal cultural hegemony, Ethiopia has a complex social history. Historically, Ethiopian Orthodox Christianity forms the basis of the dominant political elite in Ethiopia. Many of the internal acculturative processes that have taken place in modern Ethiopia—that is, in the 19th and 20th centuries—have occurred in the context of Amhara culture and language in conjunction with its ideological component, Ethiopian Orthodox Christianity. During the 1950s, to this cultural process was added Western education. There were thus three steps to attaining social, political, and economic benefits for individuals within incorporated regions: (1) accepting Amhara culture and language, (2) becoming Ethiopian Orthodox Christian, and (3) being Western educated. These steps meant that those wishing access to social benefits from the Ethiopian state had to adapt or acculturate their belief systems to those of the dominant culture and be Western educated.

These processes of internal and external acculturation continue from the 1890s to the present. In traditionally non-Amhara regions of Ethiopia, the indigenous belief systems are undergoing profound changes that are more recent and are rooted in what Donald Donham (1999) has termed "Marxist modern" policies of the post-1974 state of Mengistu Haile Mariam.[57] However, many of the socialist state policies were mere elaborations of previously initiated policies of the Haile Selassie I government. Between 1950 and 1991, non-Christian indigenous religious practices were discouraged, especially as Western education and foreign missionary activity were expanded throughout the provinces. Present internal processes of enculturation are not at the core of this analysis but are helpful for understanding the complexity of ideological dynamics at work within eco-spiritual systems in Ethiopia.

GENDER AND DEVELOPMENT STUDIES IN ETHIOPIA

"Dubartiin Keessummaa hinqabdu." (A woman is never treated as a guest.)

—Oromo saying[58]

Gender and development studies in Ethiopia have tended to draw heavily on Eurocentric and male-focused principles and paradigms. These external social science principles and paradigms have been used to design, collect, process, organize, and interpret much of the social and scientific data about various areas of Ethiopia. Today, many of Ethiopia's gender studies are predicated on development and social issues because they are defined by the Convention on the Elimination of All Forms of Discrimination against Women. Ethiopia ratified the Convention in 1981 and created the

Revolutionary Ethiopian Women's Association (REWA) while Mengistu Haile Mariam was head of state. The association was established to reorient women's associations to focus on women's class issues first and then gender issues as a secondary concern—a totally foreign concept for the average Ethiopian woman. The present government is addressing Ethiopian women's equity issues by coordinating federal legislation on regional, *woreda* (administrative district), and *kebele* (urban dwellers' associations) levels with such various stakeholders as the Women's Affairs Department, nongovernment organizations, civil society organizations, funding agencies, and the Center for Research Training and Information on Women in Development, established in 1991 and centered on the campus of Addis Ababa University.

As Ethiopian women and other women scholars engage in "transnational feminisms," they are reconstructing these older social science paradigms to include perspectives and methodologies drawn from the life experiences of indigenous women. They are transforming the gender and development idiom of the West into one that focuses on the internal patriarchal environment that restricts and constrains women's livelihoods. They are also critiquing the external dynamics that impinge on their societies as a whole. These scholars are defining the race, class, power, and cultural relations from within the context of their specific political economies.

Helen Pankhurst's work *Gender, Development and Identity: An Ethiopian Study* (1991) deals extensively with the political and economic position of women in relation to men and the state in 1988–1989, just before the Mengistu regime came to an abrupt end, in an area located in rural north-central Ethiopia, Menz. Pankhurst's research in Menz illustrates that gender relations are also subsumed in class relations and that the social consequences of this fact can have devastating social effects for women, children, and peasants in general.

Pankhurst describes the richness of "ritual" and "spiritual" aspects that color the lives of the women of Gragn, Menz. The data that she collected and her analyses are sensitive to the local culture. For our purposes, what is most important about this work is that it lends a short lens to the wider concerns of this chapter. Even though Pankhurst acknowledges the importance of female-centered spirituality in the lives of Ethiopian women in Menz, she does not see it as transformative. According to Pankhurst, female-centered spiritual institutions do not directly confront male authority or "mainstream ideology and culture."[59] On this point Pankhurst is correct, for female spiritual institutions in Africa have generally not been a threat to male domination. Nonetheless, they have been a powerful organizing tool within the female socioeconomic and political spheres.

Female institutions may very well be fundamental to Ethiopian women's organizing and activism. Although Ethiopian women's activism may not directly challenge male authority, it lays bare the real lack of male attention to the crucial life concerns of women and their children. Female-centered spiritual institutions offer women a platform for their too-often muted voices. Ethiopian women constitute a real underclass, as a group, and operate according to their view of women's lowly position in their society. How much this position is ideologically determined by older indigenous cosmological concerns is an important question that we should examine. Indigenous spirituality is part of an entire knowledge system that shapes the behavior and choices of women in Ethiopia, as will be described later in this chapter. Yet, scarcely anything has been studied or understood about the content and manifestations of female principles in Ethiopian women's spirituality and activism.

Ethiopian women, then, can and do act in ways that do not disturb the delicate gender balance, in large part, because of their need to uphold the very cultural values embodied in their cosmology. These are values that we in the West often perceive to be the basis of their oppression or political reservation. The eco-spiritual and gender environments in which Ethiopian women operate demand cooperation with males if women and their families are simply to survive. Ethiopian women interpret and affect the world through specific feminine spiritual knowledge that is directed inward, is non-confrontational, but also acts as a catalyst for change. This feminine spiritual knowledge contrasts with that of Ethiopian men, whose spiritual knowledge is directed outward and is institutional.

ETHIOPIAN FEMALE ECO-SPIRITUALITY

It is important to understand that there are several cultural groups and physical environments that make up Ethiopian women's eco-spiritual context. As a historian, I focus on past belief systems in order to understand present belief systems. While the precise antiquity of these beliefs has not been determined, they seem to be shared across gender, religious, socio-economic, and even political borders within Ethiopia. Culture is dynamic and historically determined. For this reason, what may at different historical periods have been elaborate spiritual practices among women from different cultural groups, residing in rural and pastoral areas, may not necessarily carry over into present urban settings. That having been said, many of the spiritual practices of Ethiopian women described here are practiced in the contemporary urban setting among women of differing ages and regional, educational, economic, and cultural backgrounds. Much of the spiritual world of most women in Ethiopia revolves specifically around the feminine body and its reproductive functions, although it is not restricted to the feminine body and its functions.

The aspects of feminine spirituality concerned with pregnancy and birth seem to predate Christianity. Other aspects of spirituality are grounded in Orthodox Christianity, which in itself draws on older indigenous belief systems. Women's spirituality is manifested in existential, everyday life concerns around work, socioeconomic condition, menstruation, birth, and death. Women interpret these concerns as either negative or positive aspects of nature, but they invariably veil these interpretations in spiritual terms. Similar underlying principles are shared by the indigenous eco-spiritual systems of the many cultural and linguistic groups that make up Ethiopia today.[60]

First, there is a strong belief in a supreme deity that resides in the sky. This ancient Cushitic element forms the foundation for such monotheistic religions as Judaism, Christianity (330 CE), and Islam (615 CE) among Ethiopians who practice one or another of these major religions. J. Spencer Trimingham (1965) explains that syncretism abounds in the ritual lives of most of Ethiopia's Christians, Beta Israel (Falasha Jews), and Muslims.[61] Second, there is the universal belief that the soul survives the body after death. Third, such elements of indigenous spiritual belief are practiced with very distinct underlying principles that may be associated with both positive and negative forces and rituals based on natural localities. It is thought, for instance, that spirits reside in particular trees such as the sycamore, or in water.[62] Ometi, for example, believe that the spirit Telehi lives in the Omo River. Certain hills, like Mount Ayalu, are considered sacred for men and women alike among the Afar. These distinct metaphysical entities are known by several names depending on the cultural and linguistic background of individuals.

Some of the more commonly known spirit beliefs are *buda* ("evil-eyes"), explained to me as the ability of a negative or evil person to harm you by looking at you. Adbar is a positive spirit; and many individuals are told, when beginning a journey or leaving a place, "Let the good spirit [Adbar] go with you."[63] Wuk'abi, once a sky-god among the Gurage,[64] is today believed to be a group of malevolent spirits. Because the Wuk'abi ceremonies are considered to be akin to Vudu,[65] Christians are discouraged from participating in them. On the shores of Lake Hoora, a crater lake located in Dabra Zayt, Oromo pilgrims annually celebrate the traditional Oromo deity Waaqa.

Yet, ancient ceremonies associated with these spirits are more clearly manifested in the rituals practiced by urban and rural women today. These spiritual practices are most often identified by Ethiopian women as instrumental in removing obstacles from their daily lives and household activities. As Alemmaya Mulugeta explains, "These traditional rituals [have] given women opportunities to gather and share experiences."[66]

Spiritual strength is derived from a collective practice of female spirituality among women in Ethiopia. For example, the reverence of Maryam,[67] widespread in Ethiopia, is among some Muslim women of Sidama associated with the ancient Cushitic fertility goddess Atete. Among Ethiopian Orthodox Christian women and even men, Maryam is highly revered and even propitiated during many important life events, including death, birth, sickness, and general life crises. Yet, Maryam's special appeal to Ethiopian women is particularly apparent around conception, pregnancy, and childbirth and should be viewed as emanating from the deeper indigenous belief in and concern for the sanctity of life and its protection by the ancient female goddess Atete, embodied in Maryam. It is during these particular female experiences that Ethiopian women pray to Maryam in hopes of conceiving a child or ensuring a child's health and safe entrance into this world. More recently, in Ethiopian society Maryam is an important healing icon for those individuals, both men and women, who are afflicted with HIV/AIDS. It is common to see several portraits of Maryam surrounding a woman, man, or child living with HIV/AIDS.

Jinn, or Jinni, is viewed as Satan or the devil.[68] These types of evil spirits possess individuals and cause either physical or mental illness. Some zar ceremonies are performed in order to extricate or heal these malevolent types of spirits from the possessed, usually women, but not exclusively. Other zar ceremonies are specifically designed to placate particular zar spirits. Though zar is a part of modern Ethiopian spirit belief, it is derived from an ancient Cushitic Agew sky-god. This concept of an ancient Cushitic sky-god (zar) has survived among different linguistic and cultural groups that are related—among the Bilin as Jar, the Gonja as Daro, and the Kaffitcho as Yero. Yet, it is interesting that among the Amhara, who are predominantly Ethiopian Coptic Christians, and among Muslim Somali zar has devolved into a corpus of malevolent spirits.[69]

I. M. Lewis (1969, 1991) has done substantial work on zar in northern Somalia and has propagated the "deprivation theory" as an explanation for the prevalence of zar among Somali women of both non-Muslim and Muslim backgrounds.[70] Lewis's early thesis of zar as a form of female protest against male domination falls short as an explanation for the prevalence and spread of Ethiopian zar and does not adequately address women's spirituality as a salient feature of women's activism. Spirituality is not something that Ethiopian women experience disconnected from their physical reality. Their collective acts of spirituality provide a terra firma upon which they effect substantive change in their lives.

Manak^wsit, or nuns, are Ethiopian Orthodox Christian women who are not married, have married but are past childbearing age, or have been widowed and now dedicate their lives to serving God, the church, and their communities. These *Manak^wsit* sometimes live in monasteries, in their own homes, or in mausoleums. They attend church services and pray several times daily. Their other duties include organizing *mahabers* or *mahaberoch* (money collections to help the church and the parish community) and preparing food for priests.[71]

The ontological and spiritual ecosystems of Ethiopian women provide the platform and the impetus for action in the world. Recognition of the interplay between concrete needs and spiritual sustenance is at the core of Ethiopian women's activism. In order to understand Ethiopian women and how they organize for social change, one must also understand the "invisible world" that is a part of their physical reality.

GENDER, CLASS, EDUCATION, AND ETHNICITY IN ETHIOPIA

Ethiopia is an area of Africa where social class and gender determine one's access to economic, social, and political power and resources. Consequently, class and gender also acutely affect ideology and culture. Valentine Moghadam (1995) explains that "class location shapes cultural practices, patterns of consumption, lifestyle, reproduction, and even 'world-view.' Class divisions find expression in terms of power, income, wealth, responsibility, 'life chances,' style and quality of life, and everything else that makes up the texture of existence."[72]

Although Moghadam is describing the Arab world, this view holds relevance for dominant northern and central highland plow cultures in Ethiopian society. The spread of plow cultures and crops has influenced the agricultural economies of the southwestern areas of Ethiopia since the 19th century. More recently, plow agriculture has begun to dominate other hoe and pastoral cultures of southern Ethiopia, where sorghum, enset, and livestock economies tended to be more widely practiced.[73] In conjunction with the spread of this particular technology and culture has been a system of social stratification akin to that found in highland and central Ethiopia.

Another form of structural domination transferred to other regions of Ethiopia is the patriarchal and patrilineal kinship system. The patrilineal lineage system is presently becoming a prominent feature of many of the cultural groups that were incorporated into the Ethiopian empire in the 19th century. We see this among the Kunama of Eritrea (prior to 1993, Eritrea was part of northern Ethiopia). Once matrilineal, the Kunama are adopting patrilineal kinship as they are drawn into the dominant society. Highland Ethiopian patrilineal kinship and social stratification systems

safeguard and promote mechanisms for senior male control and dominance over junior males, women, and children.[74] These northern systems
of social organization and cultivation technology may have served to erode
the position of women in these areas. Prior to the 19th-century expansion
of the Ethiopian empire into these areas, women's position may not have
been so rigid, especially in pastoral Somali and Oromo areas.[75] Although
the southern region is not our subject here, these are the types of sociopolitical and economic forces that influence hierarchies in Ethiopia and it is
helpful, therefore, to keep the aforementioned processes in mind as we
discuss Ethiopian women and class. While Ethiopian women's lives and
organizations operate in a hierarchical physical world, their spiritual world
in many ways is also stratified.

Adding to this intricacy, Ethiopian women also live in and construct
organizations within highly stratified and hierarchical communities. Educated middle- and upper-class Ethiopian women, like many urban educated women of the nonindustrial world, have access to more choices in
society than do rural and urban poor women who may have little or no
education and are burdened by daily workloads. Yet, these educated
middle- or upper-class women cannot speak for, but certainly do advocate
for, poor urban and peasant women who have only recently (post-1991)
migrated to such large urban areas as Ethiopia's capital, Addis Ababa, from
more remote small towns and rural areas. Educated middle- and upper-
class Ethiopian women do advocate for poor and underserved women precisely because of their class location or their closer proximity to what Valentine Moghadam has termed the "distribution nexus."[76] In Ethiopia,
where there is an ever-widening gulf between those who have what one
Ethiopian woman activist termed "obscene wealth" and those who exist in
desperate poverty, social location and links through kinship and patronage
are crucial to one's own and one's family's survival. Social status in Ethiopia is also determined by an individual's gender, rural or urban location,
ownership of land and other property, level of education, and kinship ties.
To be landless, disconnected from kin, and female is to be placed in
extreme jeopardy in Ethiopian communities. In such conditions, well-to-do
Western-educated Ethiopian women may act as social interpreters for
women in poverty, explicating their predicaments and paving the way for
poor women by bridging the economic or class divide between wealthy
business owners, state bureaucrats, and a large female underclass.

In contemporary Ethiopian society, the majority of Ethiopian women,
especially poor rural and urban women, are not funneled into the "modern" educational system mainly because of a lack of access, the culture, or
gender role expectations. There is no policy of exclusion of women in official government documents. Yet, according to the United Nations' 2002

Human Development Report, only 33.8 percent of the entire adult female population is literate, out of a national adult literacy rate of 41 percent (combined female and male population estimated at 69,127,000). Out of a total of 172,111 university-level students, women represented about 10 percent, mainly as a result of affirmative action programs targeting women and girls (2003–2004, Ministry of Education Statistics).

Despite their scarcity within the higher educational system, Ethiopian women academics have in the past few years been engaged in stimulating scholarship concerned with gender relations in their society. Ethiopian women associated with the Center for Research Training and Information on Women in Development (CERTWID), first launched in 1991 and reinstituted as the Institute of Gender Studies in 2006, have used their skills as academics to expose and provide solutions to the abysmal plight of numerous women and girls in Ethiopian society. They have acted as gender specialists, training and assisting the government in designing policies, dispersing information, and developing gender-sensitive publications. The importance of women academics and their scholarship is further underscored by Ethiopia's unique situation in the global political economy and its past history in relation to gender and globalization and its effects in Africa.[77]

In particular, Ethiopia has suffered from the negative effects of such IMF and World Bank globalization policies as structural adjustment, and much of Ethiopian women's scholarship deals with issues of gender and access to economic and social resources. Gender analysis and feminist economics provide the frameworks for much of this scholarship on Ethiopian women's economic and social conditions. These issues are related to women's survival and are of primary concern to the majority of women living in Ethiopia today. Zeneba N. Bashaw's work "Trajectories of Women, Environmental Degradation and Scarcity: Examining Access to and Control over Resources in Ethiopia" (2004) fits into this category. Bashaw examines the effects of patriarchy on rural Ethiopian women in Tigray and Wollo and the degree to which patriarchy determines rural women's access and control over such a vital natural resource as land. Violence against women and its relationship to economic conditions, culture, and religion is another significant area of gender research in Ethiopia. As Ethiopian women are thrust into what Bashaw calls "acute poverty,"[78] they also become targets of extreme misogynist behavior. The positions that such religions as Christianity and Islam take in sanctioning or condemning violence and oppression of Ethiopian women, in general, is a deep societal concern.[79]

More recently, the Institute of Gender Studies based in Addis Ababa University has been less engaged in gender and development work sponsored by the Ethiopian state, the Economic Commission in Africa (ECA), and other agencies both domestic and foreign. There are also clear indications of the "privatization of aid" as civil society organizations in conjunction with the Ethiopian Women's Development Fund and ECA funding agencies are providing the bulk of monetary assistance to Ethiopia's female underclasses. It is difficult to assess what this privatization means in terms of the state's responsibility to provide equal access to health, education, and economic resources to the masses of its citizens and, more critically, to its weakest and most vulnerable citizens, women and children in the nine regional states that comprise the present Ethiopian polity. That "gender development" programs must be generated from the *kebele* or local level, where women make up at least 30 percent of the councils, is progress, but these local programs are aligned with the broad development expectations set down by the very same funding agencies as the ones that brought in the structural adjustment policies that have served to benefit foreign investment and do little to alleviate the impoverished conditions of Ethiopia's poor.

Therefore, as one delves deeper into the study of Ethiopian women's lives, difficult questions such as the following surface: To what extent, if at all, do the women's organizations in Ethiopia reflect a continuation of previously existing social structures based on class and gender? To what extent, if at all, do Ethiopian women's organizational structures represent class dichotomies that are creating new social hierarchies? And what role does hierarchy play in the spiritual world that acts as a platform on which much of their activism is predicated? Data presented at the end of this section are relevant to exploring these questions.

ECO-SPIRITUALISM, ACTIVISM, AND ETHIOPIAN WOMEN'S ORGANIZATIONS

Lenefsachi (For the benefit of our souls)

—Amharic saying

It is winter, July 2006. Addis Ababa is wet and the clouds are dark gray, pregnant with the promise of strong rains and chilling cold. It is my first time back to the country after a 16-year hiatus. My youngest daughter was two years old the last time we were here. I find myself calculating the time in relation to her present age. The family (*zemad*) will be surprised when they see her. We arrive at the airport. It is late. Degu and Aster come to transport us to a part of the city known as Shola. We arrive at Hanna's house, where we will be staying. We all kiss, laugh, and over a late dinner talk into the night. It seems as though the years apart have been only a brief gap in a continuing conversation.

Hanna is discussing the situation of the poor in Shola and how she and other women are working to alleviate some of their problems. She explains that most of the poor they serve are women and children. She and other Ethiopian women are working closely with a U.S.-based Ethiopian organization called Tesfa Ba Los Angeles. Hanna asked if we wanted to go to the local office in the morning. She had stimulated my curiosity as she discussed how many of the local poor were falling between the cracks in the social system primarily because there were so many poor and so little resources and social services. I was interested in documenting some of these urban women's issues. I was particularly interested in understanding how Ethiopian women use indigenous knowledge systems to organize for social transformation.

As we drove up to the office the next morning, the sign on the building read *Tesfa Ba Los Angeles* (Hope in Los Angeles). I did not really understand the meaning until after I entered the building and met the program participants. I observed several women actively involved ("working the system") in creating economic and social opportunities ("avenues for economic endeavors") for poor and "marginalized" Ethiopian women.[80] These women use the teachings of their faiths (Ethiopian Orthodox Christianity, Catholicism, Islam, and other faiths), female spirituality, and education (often obtained in foreign lands), combined with indigenous cultural forms of organizing. They provide training in small business, resource management, and cottage industries that constitute the basic life-sustaining skills for poor women and their families. Much of the time, family for these women includes children and husbands as well as other kin and even extended family members who are not biological kin but are, certainly, related community. As rural Ethiopian women migrate into cities in hopes of finding a means to feed, clothe, and house their families, it becomes crucial for them to obtain new skills. The women activists of Tesfa are providing a vital link to much-needed social services and skills training on which many of these women will depend.

The work that Tesfa women do in their communities is not easy: they must continually surmount innumerable structures of male dominance and state bureaucracy. Within these systems of control and dominance, many Ethiopian women have discovered and forged ways to use such well-established cultural institutions as *Mahaber* (association) and *Ik'ub* and *Iddir* (mutual aid societies) to create a bridge between those living at the poverty level and those more economically fortunate.[81] Through such cultural institutions and organizations, women network with other women who help to provide them with opportunities for circumventing the restrictiveness of gender expectations that sometimes confine them to "home." But what seems more important is that these cultural institutions and organizations are recognized by Ethiopian women as "insurance."[82] Ethiopian women provide impoverished women with a means for accessing such basic resources as clean water, food, housing, health care, medicine (including HIV/AIDS medicines), and education. Educated women are, as in the past, mobilizing one another and taking up the slack where their government and nongovernment agencies have left gaps in state-sponsored social services and development programs. Many educated women involved in activist activities say they do so because "their education has exposed them to know more about the problems of women [and] to stand for the causes of women."[83]

Although the Ethiopian government has, since at least the mid-1990s, developed a Women's Affairs Office situated in the Prime Minister's Office and initiated a Women's Development Initiative Project and the Ethiopian Women's Development Fund in accordance with their stated aim to "address Ethiopian women's economic poverty, vulnerability and dependency,"[84] government-sponsored programs have been unable to ameliorate the plight of Ethiopian women and girls. This situation is particularly true for uneducated or semiliterate poor women heads of household raising children, destitute and impoverished young girls, or women and girls who are living in abusive situations. Those Ethiopian women and girls who somehow escape their unfavorable living conditions and are able to find work in Addis Ababa are often exploited and sometimes sexually abused by their employers. Many of these women and girls find that they are not getting payment equivalent to that of male workers performing the same jobs. Most recently, for instance, many poor and uneducated urban Ethiopian women and girls work as *yekan sera*, or day laborers, for less pay than awarded men for the same type of work. This disparity is illegal because in Ethiopia women are afforded equal protection under constitutional law. Yet, the government has not been able to protect women and girls from such abuses.[85] As women, girls, and entire families are drawn toward migration into large cities like Addis Ababa, the Ethiopian government is being challenged to find expedient means to address these circumstances.

Aware of the country's lack of capital, trained staff, and natural resources, the Federal Democratic Republic of Ethiopia has adopted an integrated Plan of Action (2004) in order to address environmental stresses, illiteracy, and poverty and the ramifications of these stresses on its citizens. One of the strategies is "household asset building" as a means for eliminating hunger and easing environmental pressures within diverse communities.[86] Under the Plan of Action, the government seeks to enlist donor agencies and Ethiopian women's civil organizations in an effort to coordinate this process and further its commitment to several international conventions on the environment, gender development, and biodiversity. The Ethiopian government and international agencies are recognizing that Ethiopian women and girls are capable of supporting themselves if they are given the proper education and access to economic, social, and political resources.

Thus, such Ethiopian women as Hanna and Tigist, who work at the grassroots level, are mandated to carry out strategies to advance gender equality, economic security, education, and environmental conservation, once primarily the domain of the modern Ethiopian state. Ethiopian women in civil society are now challenged to devise new ways to link gender issues with government agencies, donor communities, and those directly affected by poverty.

The remainder of this chapter weaves together data collected from several Ethiopian women participants in the Tesfa Ba Los Angeles community rehabilitation project. Here, I elucidate the ways in which gender, scholarship, faith, and activism collide, intersect, and even meld as women's survival issues are tackled at the local level in Shola, a section of the capital city, Addis Ababa, Ethiopia. Before continuing, just a little background on Ethiopia's capital city, Addis Ababa.

ADDIS ABABA IN CONTEXT

It is extremely difficult to obtain reliable figures on the demographics of Shola, but it is instructive to view this section of the city within the context of the capital, Addis Ababa. Addis Ababa is one of Ethiopia's largest urban centers and is the economic and political hub of the society. The city's population has been estimated at 2,973,000 inhabitants.[87] Ethiopia, according to the Human Development Index (HDI), is one of the poorest nations in the world. It ranks 171 on a list of 182 countries that were ranked in 2009 on data from 2007. The United Nations' *Human Development Report* (2005) measures development by "three basic dimensions": (1) prospects for a long and healthy life, measured by life expectancy at birth; (2) knowledge, measured by adult literacy rate (two-thirds weight) and combined overall enrollment in primary, secondary, and tertiary education levels (one-third weight); and (3) standard of living, measured by GDP per head, or PPPUS$.[88] The index value assigned to a country lies between zero and one. A value above 0.8 HDI indicates *high human development*, between 0.5 and 0.8 HDI *medium human development*, and below 0.5 HDI *low human development*.[89] Countries with insufficient or no data were excluded from the HDI.[90] Ethiopia's HDI value was 0.367 in 2003 and increased only slightly to 0.414 in 2007. In terms of health and welfare statistics, 22 percent of a total population of 73,908,000 Ethiopians—official estimate for mid-2005—has access to water.[91] Even though 22 percent of the Ethiopian population has access to water, only 6 percent has access to sanitation. It is not necessarily the case that this availability is to "adequate or safe" water and sanitation facilities.[92]

In addition to the foregoing statistics concerning the general standard of life and material conditions for the majority of Ethiopians, there are also statistics relating to the tremendous brain-drain that affects many areas of the social, economic, and political life of the nation. For instance, according to 2007 Ethiopian Central Statistical Agency calculations, there are 187 doctors serving an urban population of 2,973,000 in Addis Ababa.[93] For every 1,000 individuals in the entire country, there are an estimated 0.03 physicians.[94] Considering that just over half of Addis Ababa's population consists of women (some 1,545,000 individuals), out of 57,988 women who received prenatal care, just 23,678 delivered in the hospital, as reported by five government hospitals.[95] Official government statistics report no maternal or infant deaths occurred in Addis Ababa hospitals in 2006–2007. According to UNICEF (2006) statistics, 166 reported infant deaths occur out of every 1,000 live births in the country as a whole.[96] On the average, every woman in Ethiopia, according to the government Central Statistical Agency, gives birth to at least five children in her lifetime.[97] Many of these children will not live past the age of five. By 2015, an Ethiopian woman's life expectancy is projected to be 48.3 years, according to UN statistics.[98] An Ethiopian male can expect to live to 47.5 years.[99]

Against this backdrop, Shola residents are drawn from several cultures, and many are the city's most impoverished. The people in Shola adhere to one of the several religious groups in the area: Ethiopian Orthodox Christians, Muslims, Catholics, and Beta Israel (commonly known as Falasha, 27,000 of whom expatriated to Israel from Gondar, northwestern Ethiopia, under the auspices of Operation Moses between 1984 and 1991; an additional 10,000 emigrated by 2007). Many Shola inhabitants are also Oromo who migrated from the countryside of southern Shewa Province or have resided in the area since the late 19th and early 20th centuries. Others are from rural areas and small towns throughout the country where war, "chronic food insecurity,"[100] and poverty have forced them into the capital city in more recent times. The conditions they find in the urban areas are not that much different from those in the rural areas from which they come: there is a lack of affordable housing, scarcity of clean water, inadequate sanitation, a fuel crisis, and particularly for women, limited job opportunities. This lack of access to social amenities and economic opportunities provides a basis for identification among poorer members of this community as compared to members of more prosperous communities in other parts of Addis Ababa.

In this last section of the discussion, several narratives emerge in the telling of Ethiopian women's activism through Tesfa Ba Los Angeles. The following narratives include my voice; the voices of the women organizers of the U.S.-based Tesfa; those of the women administering the Addis Ababa-based Tesfa programs; and those of the women, men, and children who benefit from the programs of this one organization.

SHOLA REHABILITATION PROJECT: THE TESFA BA LOS ANGELES PROGRAM IN ADDIS ABABA

In 2006, Woizero Hanna, who volunteers her time, took on the task of helping to establish a chapter of Tesfa Ba Los Angeles (based in the United States) in Addis Ababa. Tesfa Ba Los Angeles in Addis Ababa is a state-recognized nonprofit organization that functions as a "family rehabilitation project" in Ethiopia. At the time of this study (July 2006), the Tesfa Ba Los Angeles office had been in operation for four months. Within this short time, Tesfa Ba Los Angeles had organized to directly or indirectly provide assistance to at least 50 families within Shola Kebele.

Hanna, a Tesfa Ba Los Angeles Advisory Board member, and Tigist, who was then the program manager, provided the following details about the programs. The rehabilitation project is dedicated to working with low-income and impoverished women and their families in Shola (some of whom are living with HIV/AIDS) by providing individual households with the technology, training, and skills that will eventually "help them become independent and self-sufficient economically."[101] The women organizers also understood that helping educate the children of these women meant that "the children [would be] able to sustain themselves and support their parents."[102] They also saw the larger picture; that is, by educating children, the society as a whole "avoided social crimes that might be caused by uneducated children."[103] This viewpoint is echoed in the stated purpose of Tesfa Ba Los Angeles's mother organization based in Los Angeles, namely, "to help bring about holistic and sustainable changes" in the lives of poor families in Ethiopia.[104]

While involvement of staff members in these "transformational" projects is aimed at ameliorating material poverty at the household level, there exists a strong undercurrent of spirituality that motivates these and other Ethiopian women activists. As Tigist explains, "It is not only to preach the gospel, but to do what the gospel tells us in our works."[105] We are continually made aware of the fluidity of the spiritual and material as these women describe their involvement in providing resources to "poor families" in Ethiopia. For instance, while presenting an annual progress report on Tesfa's accomplishments in Ethiopia during the fiscal year 2006–2007, the Tesfa Ba Los Angeles Board of Directors repeatedly gave spiritual undertones to Tesfa's work by saying, for instance, "What could be more sacred, more divine than . . . helping others?"

Tesfa women activists are not alone in linking spiritual notions to their social activism. While discussing Tesfa's social activism and programs designed to assist vulnerable women and children in Ethiopia, Tarik Abraha stated, "It is only *morally* the right thing to financially assist all children with shelter, [and] books." He continued, "Although our backgrounds are diverse, we all know that Ethiopian women are the most deprived of education, economic security, and health care. I believe I have a responsibility to speak out on behalf of those who are not as privileged as I am and contribute to their success in life."[106]

Tesfa Ba Los Angeles began in the United States, in 1993, with just three Ethiopian families. It has since grown considerably and has funded several small projects and programs for at least 2,000 households throughout Ethiopia. The organization is funded through donations from Ethiopians living in the United States, especially in Los Angeles, in the Bay Area, as well as through funds from other individual donors. The funds raised are sent to Ethiopia on an annual basis. Presently, these funds finance some of the following educational programs and services: Home Economics Program, Embroidery Skills Program, Orphans and Vulnerable Children's Program, HIV/AIDS Program, and Injera Vendors Program. All these programs are geared toward helping people "to provide for their families" through their own efforts.[107]

According to Wassy Tesfa, the most successful of these programs is the Home Economics Program. Some of the women recruited into this program were "street workers"; others were women heads of household with children; and still others were girls who, like the other women, had few or no prospects for generating an income. Once enrolled in the Home Economics Program, the women received training in both Ethiopian and Western cooking. They were also taught such courses as hygiene, etiquette, English, and "self-esteem." These courses lasted about nine months in total: six months of training and three months as interns. The women are interns in hotels and local restaurants that have developed a partnership with Tesfa. After their training and internships, the women are placed in permanent jobs and receive a steady income.

Tigist discussed some of the problems she and the other organizers have encountered with other programs they offer to women and their families. She explained that many of the individual women Tesfa assists are *gulat* (petty merchants) who sell vegetables on the roadside. Although these women "work very hard," they cannot sustain themselves because they have no designated place to sell their goods legally. In Ethiopia, petty merchants must have a small shop or covered area licensed by the government before they can operate. If they do not have a licensed shop or covered area from which to sell their goods, they are subject to police action, which varies from being asked to move or being beaten off the road. Tesfa is in a position to help with the license, but the *kebele* needs to provide a place where the women can sell their vegetables. In August 2006, the *kebele* in Shola was not in a position to provide a place where the vegetable vendors could sell their produce.

Another concern was the predicament of the vendors of Shola Mountain who sold *injera*, traditional Ethiopian round, flat bread that resembles a large tortilla. Tigist explained that the *injera* sellers sold their *injera* on the mountain, but they were not making much of a profit. Predictably, their problems were connected to scarcity of affordable fuels and accessible clean water, both of which the *injera* vendors needed to produce *injera*. Tesfa was in the process of finding viable solutions to these problems.

SETOCH, SERA, AND BET (WOMEN, WORK, AND HOME): THE CASE OF INJERA SELLERS

Today, the domains of household cottage industries and food preparation are slowly becoming less a part of the general domestic arena. As elsewhere in Africa, in Ethiopia these domains are becoming public services that cater to large urban populations such as found in Addis Ababa. As such, *injera* makers and sellers, vegetable sellers, hairdressers, and food service providers all serve the needs of upper- and middle-class women, in addition to service-oriented businesses, such as the hotels and restaurants in Addis Ababa. In fact, *injera* is quickly becoming the staple form of bread throughout the country. Yet, the women who perform these services are at the same time providers and consumers of these services. According to the program manager of *Tesfa* in Addis, the women who sell *injera* are most at risk for slipping even deeper into poverty. As I step into the world of *injera* sellers, I cannot help but wonder if it is conceivable that *injera* makers and sellers could someday be empowered to take control of their economic lives in ways that would ensure their family's continuous well-being. It is the precarious nature of these women's lives that leaves such a deep impression on me.

The foregoing comments are just a few thoughts that I reflect upon as I enter into Shola's small community of *injera* sellers who have taken advantage of the family rehabilitation programs offered by Tesfa Ba Los Angeles in Addis Ababa.

SHOLA: 7:00 A.M.

Mamush takes me to meet some of the women who are recipients of Tesfa Ba Los Angeles's Family Rehabilitation Project in Addis Ababa. As we walk, I explain to Mamush that I want to let the women know who I am and why I am talking with them about their *injera* businesses. I want to make it clear to the women that they are not obligated to answer any of my questions. Mamush says that in Ethiopian culture, it would be rude for the women to refuse to speak with me. We make our way up the mountain. The road is muddy, steep, and slippery. It is the rainy season and there are puddles of water, making it difficult to walk. I must break the stride of our walk up the mountain because I am feeling the effects of the high altitude. We stop at a small clearing where two or three little houses stand nestled between the eucalyptus trees that are a characteristic feature of Addis Ababa. The houses are constructed of *chiqa* (mud). The highland areas of Addis Ababa are cold, and one feels the chill deep in the bones. Many of the working poor do not have warm clothing or shoes and are especially vulnerable to the elements at this time of the year. The whole city seems to have *gunfan* (cold with a bad cough), especially the children. I feel sympathetic as I remember how I had suffered with the same malady when living in Addis some years ago.

Mamush calls at the door of one of the small houses. A woman steps out to greet us. Mamush introduces me to her, and we exchange greetings and our names. A child continually coughs in the background as we begin a brief introduction. We ask if it's okay to ask questions and take some pictures. We then ask a few questions of Shibera about her and her family's involvement in Tesfa Ba Los Angeles. Tesfa has supplied her with a new *mat'at* (small circular stove with a top) used for making *injera*, a type of round flat bread made from *tef*. The covered *mat'at* is an improvement over the older style, uncovered *mat'at*. The covered *mat'at* is fuel efficient; it prevents the heat from escaping too quickly and thus lessens the women's need to use large amounts of fuel. The covered *mat'at* is also a safer technology. It prevents harmful fumes from escaping into the environment and endangering the health and lives of the women and their families.

Shibera has also been given a few months' supply of fuel (the outer cover and the leaves of the coffee bean). She tells me that "even though the fuel for the fire and the *tef* are expensive, the change is we get more fuel for the fire to make the *injera*."

This fuel has been donated to Tesfa Ba Los Angeles's project by coffee exporters. Responding to the fuel crisis that the *injera* women experience and also to ecological concerns, the women activists offer the outer cover and the leaves of the coffee bean as a replacement for wood fuel obtained by cutting down the trees on Shola Mountain. Prior to these donations of alternative fuels, the *injera* women purchased wood and charcoal or foraged for fuel when money was low. This often meant cutting down the trees near their homes. Also, the women explained to me that the prices for fuel rose or fell according to the season. In the rainy season, the fuel costs were extravagant; during the dry season, the cost for fuel was manageable. These fluctuations in prices affected the profitability of their *injera* businesses. In turn, the household income fluctuations make life difficult. As Shibera says, "So we are putting the money back into fuel and *tef*, now it's gone up and the money is going in circles now." I asked Shibera why she didn't raise her prices to compensate for the expenditures on fuel and *tef* used to make the *injera*. She replied, "*Injera* used to be 90 centime [E$.90] but now it is 1 birr [E$1]. I cannot raise it more, to 1.10 birr [E$1.10], because I want people to buy from me." Shibera is supporting herself and two daughters on the profits she makes from her *injera* business. She says that sometimes she makes enough to pay for food and school supplies for the children.

I spoke with other women who sell *injera* on the mountain. I asked Zenabech if she was making enough profit to take care of herself and her children. She said, "Even though it is enough, it is difficult and I am trying hard to make it." She continues, "And the price for *tef* has gone up. We are selling it for 1 birr [E$1]; when *tef* goes up, we have to raise our prices. Here [Shola], it is not as expensive as other areas. If it were in the middle of the town [such areas as the Piazza, Arat, or Sedist Kilo] or something, we would have sold it for a better price." Zenabech, like the other *injera* sellers, sold her *injera* to other women in her neighborhood. When I asked Zenabech how her life was before being associated with Tesfa, she explained: "I used to work at people's houses making *injera*, washing their clothes. But, now I have this one job making *injera* from my home. I can be with my children. Yes, it is good, thanks be to God."

Ejagayehew explained that without fuel, they could not make their *injera* to sell and the fuel costs were making it difficult for them to make profits. "We used to buy fuel for five or six birr, but now it is twelve birr. The one I just bought is $15 birr [E$15]. During the summer it will go down to 7 or 6 birr [E$7 or E$6], so profits will be better." Ejagayehew has six children to care for and works hard to support them on little income. I asked Ejagayehew, "Does your family eat better now that you are involved with Tesfa?" Her reply was straightforward: "Yes, it's better, thanks be to God. Our living conditions have changed."

Ejagayehew is making *injera* as we speak with her. She pours the *tef* batter onto the *mat'at* in a spiral, beginning in the center and circling outward. She is skillful, as are all the women. "Is there anything that would make your life better for you?" I ask her. As she lays the *injera* on a platter to cool, she replies, "I have no idea. After the winter I will make a decision. During the winter the prices for fuel are always expensive, because it is always wet, but it will go down in the summer. Then I will know. I think business will be up, I will sell more then."

As well as helping to improve the *injera* women's commercial activities, Tesfa provides some of the more destitute women with adequate housing. One woman and her children had been living in a makeshift house before Tesfa stepped in to offer her assistance. In addition to providing technology and resources to the women, Tesfa makes available such educational services as hygiene training and self-esteem lessons. What is impressive is that Tesfa goes to the women where they live on the mountain to offer these services and training. Doing this makes it much easier for the women to receive training, counseling, and other services without having to figure out how to pay for transportation to Tesfa's office. Tesfa also encourages the women to deposit any money saved into a bank account. In this way, the Tesfa women activists hope to create a financial safety net for the *injera* vendors and their families.

Before Mamush and I started our journey down the mountain, I asked Ejagayehew, "How has Tesfa changed your life?" She replied, "Thank God for all of you [Tesfa]. I may not always make a profit, but my children never go hungry, that is the change."

As we leave, Ejagayehew reminds Mamush that she is running out of fuel for the *mat'at*. He assures her that he will bring her more later in the week.

CONCLUSION

The general intention of this chapter is to place Ethiopian women's organizing and activism firmly within the context of the organizing and activism of indigenous African women throughout the African continent. It also focuses on the central role of spiritualism in Ethiopian women's social activism. Drawing on their knowledge of indigenous cultural systems and eco-spiritual systems, Ethiopian women scholars and civil society activists develop strategies to readdress and redirect foreign and domestic funding agencies in ways that will bring about "sustainable changes" in the lives of women, children, and men in Ethiopia. In the process of identifying the ways in which Ethiopian women organize for social change, many new questions emerge about the role of gender in activism, environmental conservation, and culture.

What can scholars and students of Africa learn from Ethiopian women and their style of activism and organization? Ethiopian women, as well as other women on the African continent, face social, economic, and political hardships that are sometimes rooted in external and internal power structures that privilege males over females. As other African women are able to do, Ethiopian women are able to unite across gender, class, religion, and ethnicity in order to cultivate fertile conditions for sustainable changes within their society. On close observation and analysis of Ethiopian women's activism, it is apparent that Ethiopian women draw on multilayered and multifaceted knowledge of their indigenous cultural institutions and eco-spiritual systems. The ways that Ethiopian women use these cultural institutions and eco-spiritual systems in order to navigate and transform their particular environments is life affirming. Ethiopian women's gender activism is not confrontational; it is wholly organic and essentially eco-spiritual.

As the field moves forward, it is critical for researchers on gender issues in Africa to pay closer attention to critical studies written by indigenous African women scholars. The idea is that indigenous women scholars and women activists have legitimate knowledge and issues that should not only inform scholarly research and writing but also act as springboards for directing scholarly exploration on issues that are pertinent to African societies. Researchers must take seriously indigenous African voices, scholarly research, and life experiences. To do so yields methodology, data collection, and analyses of critical gender issues in Africa that provide a fuller and richer picture of women's activism and lives.

NOTES

1. "Eco-spiritual systems and gender approach" is a term I have developed. This approach combines gender analysis from an ecosystems approach. The eco-spiritual systems and gender approach takes into account not only the complexity of relationships involved in physical systems, among them the environmental, socioeconomic, and cultural interactions of human communities, but also recognize their connectedness to spiritual systems. The eco-spiritual systems and gender approach is not an indictment of a Marxist feminist approach to gender studies. It is an acknowledgment of the symbiotic relationship between ecology, gender, and spiritualism.

2. For instance, African women's studies has, in large part, been influenced by writing outside the Africanist field of study and has drawn heavily from various theories, including the early feminist writings of Marxist feminism, feminist anthropology, underdevelopment, and more recent eco-feminism, to name a few. Various other gender studies and women's studies frameworks have also been used.

3. Arvind Sharma and Katherine K. Young, eds., *Feminism and World Religions* (Albany: State University New York, 1999), 16.

4. Sondra Hale, "Colonial Discourse and Ethnographic Residuals: The 'Female Circumcision' Debate and the Politics of Knowledge," in *Female Circumcision and the Politics of Knowledge: African Women in Imperialist Discourses*, ed. Obioma Nnaemeka (Westport, CT: Praeger Publishers, 2005), 209–18.

5. See articles on Gender and Women's Studies for Africa's Transformation (GWS) Project at the University of Cape Town, South Africa, www.gwsafrica.org.

6. Gwendolyn Mikell, ed., *African Feminism: The Politics of Survival in Sub-Saharan Africa* (Philadelphia: University of Pennsylvania Press, 1997), see Acknowledgments, xiii.

7. Obioma Nnaemeka, ed., *Female Circumcision and the Politics of Knowledge: African Women in Imperialist Discourses* (Westport, CT: Praeger Publishers, 2005), 4.

8. See the works of Denise Paulme, ed., *Women of Tropical Africa* (1971); Karen Sacks, *Sisters and Wives* (1979); and Christine Obbo, *African Women: Their Struggle for Economic Independence* (1980). These are some of the early works devoted exclusively to serious studies of African women.

9. Nwando Achebe, *Farmers, Traders, Warrior, and Kings: Female Power and Authority in Northern Igboland, 1900–1960* (Portsmouth, Hants, UK: Heinemann, 2005), 10.

10. Ifi Amadiume, *Male Daughters, Female Husbands: Gender and Sex in an African Society* (London: Zed Books, 1987), 4.

11. See Chimalum Nwankwo, "Parallax Sightlines: Alice Walker's Sisterhood and the Key to Dreams," in *Female Circumcision and the Politics of Knowledge*, ed. Obioma Nnaemeka (Westport, CT: Praeger Publishers, 2005), 219.

12. For a discussion of how African women view Western scholarship that attempts to interpret African cultures, see Caroline B. Brett, ed., *When They Read What We Write: The Politics of Ethnography* (Westport, CT: Bergin and Garvey, 1993).

13. It seems that where traditional hoe cultures dominated (West Africa), women controlled the agricultural knowledge and female rituals were elaborate; where plow cultures dominated (Ethiopia), women had less control over productive resources and female rituals tended not to be as elaborate.

14. See Katsuyoshi Fukui, ed., *Comparative Studies on Indigenous Knowledge Systems in South Ethiopian Societies* (Kyoto: Nakanishi Printing Co., 2003), for a discussion of indigenous knowledge systems.

15. Ifi Amadiume, *Male Daughters, Female Husbands*, 29.

16. See Cheryl Walker, "Women and Gender in Southern Africa to 1945: An Overview," in *Women and Gender in Southern Africa to 1945*, ed. Cheryl Walker (London: James Currey, 1990), 1–32. Also pay close attention to

Walker's discussion in a subheading entitled "Imperialist Research?" Walker critiques a paper written by Dabi Nkululeko, "a black South African woman," who in "The Right to Self-Determination in Research: Azanian Women" (1987) questions the very tools used by "outsiders" to produce knowledge about African women. Nkululeko connects much of the academic work of outsiders to larger issues of oppression and exploitation implicit within the tools of inquiry, a theme that reverberates throughout Edward Said's *Culture and Imperialism* (New York: Knopf, 1993), 239–61.

17. Mikell, "Akan Women and Family Courts," in *African Feminism*, 115. See also Original Wolde Giorgis, "Democratisation Process and Gender," in *Ethiopia: The Challenge of Democracy from Below*, ed. Bahru Zewde and Siegfried Pausewang (Uppsala: Nordiska Afrikainstitutet, 2002), 169–85.

18. Didier N. Kaphagawani and Jeanette G. Malherbe explain that "features of culture like language and religious ceremonies" are keys that unlock a people's "philosophical" including "its epistemology" systems. In P. H. Coeatzee and A. P. J. Roux, eds., *The African Philosophy Reader: A Text with Readings*, 2nd ed. (New York: Routledge, 2003), 219.

19. See Robin D. G. Kelley, *Freedom Dreams* (Boston: Beacon Press, 2002), 5; see also Cedric J. Robinson, *Black Marxism* (Chapel Hill: University of North Carolina Press, 1983; Foreword and Preface, 2000).

20. See Lynda Marion Hill, *Social Rituals and the Verbal Art of Zora Neale Hurston* (Washington, DC: Howard University Press, 1996), 126. Hill discusses Zora Neale Hurston's concept of hieroglyphics as a cultural code that evidences ritual action as cultural knowledge.

21. British ethnographer Geoffrey Parrinder concluded that the "spiritual universe" of most Africans consisted of a "widespread African belief in psychic power." Such other writers as Edwin G. Smith sometimes referred to it as "dynamism"; still others, as "soul-force" or "vital-force," as these beliefs are termed in Geoffrey Parrinder, *African Traditional Religion* (London: Hutchinson House, 1954), 21. See my unpublished master's thesis, "Jamaican Kumina: The Yoruba Contribution," University of Santa Barbara, CA, 1979.

22. Ifi Amadiume, *Male Daughters and Female Husbands*, 134.

23. Kamene Okonjo, "The Dual-Sex Political System in Operation: Igbo Women and Community Politics in Midwestern Nigeria," in *Women in Africa: Studies in Social and Economic Change*, ed. Nancy J. Hafkin and Edna G. Bay (Stanford, CA: Stanford University Press, 1976), 45–58.

24. Omofolabo Ajayi-Soyinka, "Transcending the Boundaries of Power and Imperialism: Writing Gender, Constructing Knowledge," in *Female Circumcision and the Politics of Knowledge: African Women in Imperialist Discourses*, ed. Obioma Nnaemeka (Westport, CT: Praeger Publishers, 2005), 47.

25. See, for instance, Salem Mekuria, "Female Genital Mutilation in Africa: Some African Views," *ACAS Bulletin* 44–45 (1995): 2–6. A recent

article coming out of the Catholic Information Service for Africa (2007) entitled "Diocese Promotes Women's Role in Church and Society" discussed the challenges to women's welfare as being "polygamy and female genital mutilation" and praised African governments for recognizing the need to stop such practices. *News*, October 2, 2007, 1–2.

26. See Obioma Nnaemeka, ed., *Sisterhood, Feminisms and Power: From Africa to the Diaspora* (Trenton, NJ: Africa World Press, 1998).

27. The present government's emphasis on ethnic and regional rights to self-determination has politicized ethnicity in present-day Ethiopian society. Many tensions have arisen in the society as the suppressed ethnicities demand a voice in their own political, economic, and social development within the Ethiopian state structure. But for purposes of this chapter, Ethiopian women are generalized to mean those women regardless of ethnicity who reside within the political boundaries of the Ethiopian state and identify themselves as Ethiopian.

28. Gwendolyn Mikell, *African Feminism*, 5.

29. This is clearly observed in the reigns of such female kings as Hatshepsut in Egypt. Hatshepsut usurped the throne while regent for Thutmose III; she then created for herself a throne name and title of king and ruled Egypt for at least 20 years during the 18th dynasty, roughly between 1473 BCE and 1458 BCE. Hatshepsut was commonly referred to by the designation "His Majesty."

30. Zar is believed to have spread throughout northeastern Africa and the Horn from central Ethiopia in the 18th and 19th centuries by enslaved women of Ethiopia. Although *zar* beliefs and practices have been explained as a modern urban phenomenon, *zar*'s spiritual roots are ancient. It may be that the elaboration and spread of *zar* was a response by enslaved Ethiopian women to their captive status in foreign lands, or it was mainly a result of their loss of kin affiliations and protections. It became a necessary mechanism or act of cohesion that eventually developed into a spiritual support system.

31. Lebisa J. Teffo and Abraham P. J. Roux, "Metaphysical Thinking in Africa," in *The African Philosophy Reader: A Text with Readings*, 2nd ed., ed. P. H. Coeatzee and A. P. J. Roux (New York: Routledge, 2003), 161.

32. Nwando Achebe, *Farmers, Traders, Warriors, and Kings*, 23–28.

33. Ibid., 26.

34. Ibid., 26–27.

35. Diedre L. Badejo, "Authority and Discourse in the Orin Odún Osun," in *Osun across the Waters: A Yoruba Goddess in Africa and the Americas*, ed. Josephe Murphy and Mei Mei Sanford (Bloomington: Indiana University Press, 2001), 128–40. The unedited version of this chapter was provided by the author, and citations are extracted from this version.

36. Judith Van Allen, "'Aba Riots' or Igbo 'Women's War'? Ideology, Stratification, and the Invisibility of Women," in *Women in Africa: Studies in Social and Economic Change*, ed. Nancy J. Hafkin and Edna G. Bay (Stanford, CA: Stanford University Press, 1976), 59–85.

37. Ifi Amadiume, *Male Daughters, Female Husbands*, chap. 12.

38. Janet M. Bujra, "'Urging Women to Redouble Their Efforts . . .' Class, Gender, and Capitalist Transformation in Africa," in *Women and Class in Africa*, ed. Claire Robertson and Iris Berger (New York: Africana Publishing, 1986), 136.

39. *Pray the Devil Back to Hell*. Directed by Gini Reticker. 72 minutes. Pan African Film Festival, 2008.

40. Nakanyike B. Musisi, "The Politics of Perception or Perception as Politics? Colonial and Missionary Representations of Baganda Women, 1900–1945," in *Women in Colonial Histories*, ed. Jean Allman, Susan Geiger, and Nakanyike Musisi (Bloomington: Indiana University Press, 2002).

41. See Ifi Amadiume, *Male Daughters, Female Husbands*, for a discussion of linguistics and gender correlations, 17–21.

42. For an interesting discussion of gender, age, and descent, see Pierre L. van den Berghe, *Age and Sex in Human Societies: A Biosocial Perspective* (Belmont, CA: Wadsworth Publishing Co., 1973), chap. 4.

43. Donald Crummey, "Women, Property, and Litigation among the Bagemder Amhara, 1750s to 1850s," in *African Women and the Law: Historical Perspectives*, ed. Margaret Jean Hay and Marcia Wright (Boston: Boston University, 1982), 19.

44. Chris Prouty, *Empress Taytu and Menilek II: Ethiopia, 1883–1910* (Trenton, NJ: Red Sea Press, 1986).

45. Tsehai Berhane-Selassie, "Ethiopian Rural Women and the State," in *African Feminism: The Politics of Survival*, ed. Gwendolyn Mikell (Philadelphia: University of Pennsylvania Press, 1997), 184.

46. For a discussion of "corporate kin," see Karen Sacks, *Sisters and Wives: The Past and Future of Sexual Equality* (Urbana: University of Illinois, 1982), chap. 3, 115–23.

47. See Tsehai Berhane-Selassie, "Ethiopian Rural Women and the State," in *African Feminism*, ed. Gwendolyn Mikell, 182–82; see also Zenebe N. Bashaw, "Trajectories of Women, Environmental Degradation and Scarcity: Examining Access to and Control over Resources in Ethiopia," in *Gender, Economies and Entitlements in Africa*, vol. 2 (December 2004), http://www.codesria.org/Links/conferences/gender/Zenebe.pdf.

48. Katherine K. Young, Introduction to *Feminism and World Religions*, ed. Arvind Sharma and Katherine K. Young (Albany: State University New York, 1999), 2.

49. One exception is Tsehai Berhane-Selassie's work on female potters in Walayta.

50. For reading on Ethiopian women's issues, see Tsehai Berhane-Selassie, "In Search of Ethiopian Women," *Change 11* (1982); Tsehai Berhane-Selassie, "Ethiopian Women and the State," in *African Feminism: The Politics of Survival*, ed. Gwendolyn Mikell (Philadelphia: University of Pennsylvania Press, 1997), 182–205; and Helen Pankhurst, *Gender, Development and Identity: An Ethiopian Study* (London: Zed Books, 1992). These are just a few selections of the rapidly growing body of works on gender issues in Ethiopia.

51. Donald Johanson and Maitland Edey, *Lucy: The Beginnings of Humankind* (New York: Simon and Schuster, 1981).

52. Taddesse Tamrat, *Church and State in Ethiopia* (Oxford: Oxford University Press, 1972), 38.

53. Bahru Zewde, *A History of Modern Ethiopia, 1855–1991* (Addis Ababa: University Press, 1991), 173. Between 1935 and 1941, women in Addis Ababa and other urban centers in Ethiopia acted as spies for the Tekur Anbassa (Black Lion Patriots) during the war with Italy.

54. Ennis Ford became a citizen of Ethiopia in the 1930s.

55. "Monopolies, [financial] oligarchy, the striving for domination instead of the striving for liberty, [and] the exploitation of an increasing number of small or weak nations by an extremely small group of the richest . . . nations . . . have given birth to those distinctive characteristics of imperialism which compel us to define it as parasitic or decaying capitalism." V. I. Lenin, *Imperialism* (Peking [Beijing]: Foreign Languages Press, 1975), 128.

56. In Ethiopia post-1941, this influence has come primarily from Britain and the United States.

57. Donald L. Donham, *Marxist Modern: An Ethnographic History of the Ethiopian Revolution* (Berkeley: University of California Press, 1999).

58. Fr. George Cotter, *Salt and Stew* (Addis Ababa: United Printers, 1990), 1.

59. Helen Pankhurst, *Gender, Development and Identity*, 165.

60. In Ethiopia today there are more than 75 languages and countless dialects listed under such linguistic and cultural categories as Cushitic, Omotic, Nilo-Saharan, and Semitic. See Grover Hudson, "75 Ethiopian Languages," rev. December 29, 2006, http://www.msu.edu/%7Ehudson/Ethlgslist.htm.

61. J. Spencer Trimingham, *Islam in Ethiopia* (London: Frank Cass & Co., 1965), 257–75.

62. I have personally seen rituals where water is used in acts of spiritual cleansings, healings, and blessings. The hot springs in Soddare near the Awash River are considered a place where body and soul can be healed in this manner.

63. Interview, Helen Shiferaw-Wims, Los Angeles, March 26, 2008.

64. Trimingham, *Islam in Ethiopia*, 257; see also Christopher Ehret, *The Civilizations of Africa* (Charlottesville: University Press of Virginia, 2002), 79.

Ehret's work dates the concept of *Waak'a* or *waq* (sky-god) among Cushitic speakers as early as the seventh millennium BCE.

65. I was told that in the *wuk'abi* ceremony, grass is spread on the ground, special dances are performed, and a chicken is circled three times around the head of a possessed person. The spirit is given special foods like *tela* and *gunfo*. Shiferaw-Wims compared these practices to similar practices in Haitian Vudu.

66. Alemmaya Mulugeta, "Gender and Islam: How Can Violence be Embedded in Religion," in *Reflections, Documentation of the Forum on Gender* ed. Yonas Admassu, No. 7 (June/2002) Ed. Yonas Admassu, (Addis Ababa: Panos Ethiopia, 2002), 53.

67. Maryam (Virgin Mary) may have been syncretized with the ancient Cushitic goddess of fertility, Atete. The survival of this goddess among Oromo Christian and Muslim women has been documented in W. Thesiger, "The Awash River and the Aussa Sultanate," *Geographical Journal* 85 (1935): 8, cited in Trimingham, *Islam in Ethiopia*, 259.

68. Conversation, Ato Assefa Abye, Addis Ababa, Ethiopia, December 1990.

69. In Ethiopia, as in other areas of Africa, once indigenous people accepted Christianity or Islam, the previous gods, deities, and other spirits were not abandoned but sometimes devolved into lesser or negative forces. Many educated Ethiopians consider these older indigenous practices as evil and view them as the practices of low-status, uneducated people. Social status and spiritual beliefs and practices are areas where much research in Ethiopia is yet to be done.

70. I. M. Lewis, "Spirit Possession in Northern Somalia," in *Spirit Mediumship and Society in Africa*, ed. John Beattie and John Middleton (London: Routledge and Kegan Paul, 1969), 188–219. A revised thesis can be found in the introduction to *Women's Medicine: The Zar-Bori Cult in Africa and Beyond*, ed. I. M. Lewis, Ahmed Al-Safi, and Sayyid Hurreiz (Edinburgh: Edinburgh University Press, 1991).

71. Interview, Helen Shiferaw-Wims, Los Angeles, March 26, 2008.

72. Valentine M. Moghadam, "The Political Economy of Female Employment in the Arab Region," in *Gender and Development in the Arab World*, ed. Nabil F. Khoury and Valentine M. Moghadam (London: Zed Books, 1995), 11. For an understanding of production and rural class formation in Ethiopia, see Dessalegn Rahmato, *Agrarian Reform in Ethiopia* (Trenton, NJ: Red Sea Press, 1985), chap. 2.

73. For a discussion of the adoption of *tef* cultivation (plow farming) among southern Ethiopian communities, see Takeshi Fujimoto, "Cereal Agriculture among the Malo of Southwestern Ethiopia: With Special Reference to Their Teff (*Eragrostis tef* [Zucc.] Trotter) Cultivation," in *Proceedings of the*

XIVth International Conference of Ethiopian Studies, vol. 2, ed. Baye Yimam et al. (Addis Ababa: Addis Ababa University Press, 2000), 767–84.

74. For a discussion of some of the issues around production and social stratification I raised here, see Jack Goody, *Production and Reproduction: A Comparative Study of the Domestic Domain* (Cambridge: Cambridge University Press, 1976).

75. See Donald N. Levine, *Greater Ethiopia: The Evolution of a Multiethnic Society* (Chicago: University of Chicago Press, 1974); I. M. Lewis, *A Modern History of Somalia* (London: Longman, 1965, 1980); both these writers describe these societies as being egalitarian.

76. Valentine M. Moghadam, "The Political Economy of Female Employment in the Arab Region," 11.

77. It is ironic that CERTWID was established with funds provided by the government of Ethiopia and the United Nations Population Fund (UNPF). For a short history of the Institute of Gender Studies, see Emebet Mulugeta, "Trajectory of the Institute of Gender Studies at Addis Ababa University, Ethiopia," *Feminist Aftrica* 9 (2007): 85–92, available at http//www.feministafrica.org/uploads/File/Issue_9/profiles_Feminist%20Africa%209_final_27Feb-3.pdf.

78. Zeneba N. Bashaw, "Trajectories . . .," unnumbered pages, http://www.codesria.org/links/conferences/gender/ZENEBA.pdf.

79. See series of papers presented in Ethiopia for the Forum on Gender (2002). See, for example, Hirut Terefe, "Violence against Women from a Gender and Cultural Perspective," in *Reflections: Documentation of the Forum on Gender*, no. 7, June 2002, ed. Yonas Admassu (Addis Ababa: Panos Ethiopia), 6–16. Also see Alemmaya Mulugeta, "Gender and Islam: How Can Violence Be Embedded in Religion?" in the same issue of *Reflections*, no. 7 (June 2002): 33–38.

80. To use the organizers' own language to describe the community of women that they are trying to reach, these women are often "ostracized by kin and community because of the stigma of HIV/AIDS."

81. *Mahaber* can be defined roughly as an association, a society, or a monthly gathering in honor of a saint. *Ik'ub* and *Iddir* are similarly associations or societies established for mutual aid in particular communities. *Iddir* is specifically organized for mutual aid connected to death and burial. In the last two decades or so, women have used these institutions to organize themselves in order to advocate for their specific needs and issues.

82. Electronic communication with Tesfa Ba Los Angeles, Addis Ababa members, September 21, 2007.

83. Ibid.

84. Press Release WOM/1431, UN Committee on Elimination of Discrimination against Women, "Ethiopia Commended for Political Commitment

to Women's Anti Discrimination Convention, Despite Facing Poverty, Natural Disasters, Military Conflict," January 26, 2004, http://www.un.org/News/Press/doc/2004/wom1431.doc.htm (accessed June 30, 2006), 3.

85. Original Wolde Giorgis, "Democratisation Process and Gender," 169–85.

86. Federal Democratic Republic of Ethiopia, Environmental Protection Authority, *The Third National Report on the Implementation of the UNCCD/NAP in Ethiopia*, February 2004 (Addis Ababa, Ethiopia), 16.

87. http://www.csa.gov.et/text_files/national%202007/Health.pdf.

88. Whereas PPP represents "purchasing power parity," PPPUS$-per-head refers to an estimate of a particular country's local currency purchasing power to that of the U.S. dollar.

89. *Europa Regional Surveys of the World: Africa South of the Sahara*, 2007, iv. Such indicators of high or low human development are problematic. Terms such as "low" or "high" human development are highly charged with Eurocentric economic and cultural bias. Are we to view "poor societies" with "low human development" as less human than richer countries or societies of the world that are ranked as "high" in human development?

90. Ibid., vi.

91. These statistics are found in ibid., *Ethiopia*, 467.

92. Ibid., *Health and Welfare Statistics: Sources and Definitions*, vi.

93. http://www.csa.gov.et/text_files/national%202007/Health.pdf, 6.

94. *Regional Surveys of the World: Africa South of the Sahara*, 468.

95. http://www.csa.gov.et/text_files/national%202007/Health.pdf, 25–26.

96. *Regional Surveys of the World: Africa South of the Sahara*, 468. It is likely that these numbers are much higher because often infant mortality and maternal death are a dominant subject of discussion among women in urban and rural Ethiopia; it is likely that infant deaths of rural and urban women and girls who do not give birth in hospitals or clinics are not included in these numbers.

97. Ibid., 468.

98. http://globalis.gvu.unu.kedu/indicator_detail.cfm?IndicatorID=117&Country=ET, 2000.

99. Ibid.

100. "Chronic food insecurity" is an official euphemism for famine or starvation.

101. Interview, Hanna Assefa, Addis Ababa, July 17, 2006.

102. Electronic communication with Tesfa Ba Los Angeles, Addis Ababa members, September 21, 2007.

103. Ibid.

104. Speech, Wassy Tesfa, Tesfa Ba Los Angeles fundraiser, Los Angeles, December 2, 2007.

105. Interview, Tigist Tamirat, Addis Ababa, July 18, 2006.

106. Interview, Tarik Abraha, Los Angeles, September 5, 2007. Tarik Abraha is not a member of Tesfa but is aware of Tesfa's work in Ethiopia.

107. Speech, Wassy Tesfa, Tesfa Ba Los Angeles fundraiser, December 2, 2007.

PART IV

*Sexuality, Power,
and Vulnerability*

CHAPTER 9

Staging Politics: New Currents in North African Women's Dramatic Literature

Laura Chakravarty Box

The body of dramatic literature and performances produced by North African women of the Maghreb is a relatively new area of study, particularly in English-language scholarship. An obscure but rewarding field of inquiry, it poses significant challenges of language, access, and taxonomy to the scholar writing in English. At the same time, this micro-canon offers a unique laboratory in which to consider questions as diverse as the nature of identity and gender formation, the cyclical character of domestic, national, and global violence, and the ways in which the West defines its performance forms in relation to those that its peoples regard as "Other." An extension of a larger study that began in 1997 and ended in 2000,[1] this chapter brings into the present decade some of the observations of the earlier work and its global, and local, sociopolitical contexts.

My work with this body of performance and literary texts, heretofore, has been predicated on the hypothesis that the texts, for the most part, provide a bridge between the sphere of the personal or domestic and that of the national or international. Often, the dramatic conflicts of a troubled household or the struggles of an individual are displayed against a backdrop of national or global violence. Recently, I have sensed the beginnings of a shift in the writing of women from the Maghreb. As the global war on terrorism promulgated by the Bush administration enmeshes more and more of the Middle East and North Africa, the sociological foreground of these plays is receding, the individual and the domestic are becoming less important, and the political backdrop is gaining prominence.

It is very difficult to identify a literary movement as it is happening. Usually, the academy is able to read such currents of thought decisively only when they are in the past. Nevertheless, some recent offerings by two prominent writers of the Maghreb raise this question: have the sociopolitical changes of the last decade been reflected in the recent dramatic literature of women from Maghrebian North Africa? The evidence is thin, and interpreting it is a difficult enterprise, since plays by women in any language are rarely published in North Africa. One of the reasons that Fatima Gallaire, one of the authors considered here, is better known than most of her counterparts from Morocco, Algeria, and Tunisia is that as a diasporic writer who writes in the language of the former colonizer, she has a French publisher. Indeed, the publication of any dramatic literature is a minor enterprise at best for North African publishing houses, and this has to do with the ephemeral nature of theatre as an art form, as well as its difficulties with reputability in the region. Choice of language confounds this issue; an author in the Maghreb, depending on her target audience, may write in Modern Standard Arabic, dialectal Arabic, various Amazigh languages, French, Spanish, Italian, or English. As an investigator in this milieu, I am also challenged by my limited knowledge of Arabic, as well as the type of Arabic (Modern Standard) that I have chosen to study. In large part because of my ability to engage in cultural translation and gloss nonlinguistic elements, I am capable of watching some Arabic-language performances with a fair level of comprehension, but I cannot perform a close reading of a written Arabic text. Thus, while the texts examined in this chapter may be analyzed and parsed as an indication of shifting attitudes among women writers from the region, they cannot be said to constitute a scientific sample; nor do they represent the many voices that space, access, and language do not allow us to consider here.

These very specific limitations, which are inherent to almost all studies of Maghrebian literature, are a useful reminder of the partiality of all knowledge. It is no accident that two major proponents of deconstructionist theory, Jacques Derrida and his disciple Hélène Cixous (herself a playwright), were born in Algeria of European—or in the case of Cixous, multiple—heritage. Derrida's famous "ear of the Other" came into being near Algiers.[2] Like the Indian subcontinent, another crucible for postcolonial and subaltern studies, the Maghreb is a formerly colonized place of tremendous cultural diversity. Scholars and writers born in the region, who may have better access to texts and greater linguistic facility than do

Western scholars, experience linguistic opacity and difficulties obtaining access to materials just as their European and American counterparts do. The field thus demands a level of cooperation between scholars that defies the competitive models currently favored by the academy. This can be seen, for example, in the recent collaboration between Khaled Amine, a Moroccan expert on indigenous Maghrebian performance forms, and the renowned Western theatre historian, Marvin Carlson.[3] The present study, too, owes a debt to Carlson, who shared with me the original French text of Jalila Baccar's *Araberlin*,[4] as well as the new English translation,[5] and alerted me to the new ending of Fatima Gallaire's *Princesses*.[6]

This new ending of Gallaire's best-known and most translated play[7] provided the first clue to a potential shift from the social to the political in North African women's authorial perspective. In the summer of 1997, well before the events of September 11, 2001 sent the U.S. government careening into cycles of aggression in Iraq and Afghanistan, I sat in a café in Paris with the Algerian playwright and novelist, discussing the adaptation and censorship of her plays for foreign markets.[8] At the time, she was in exile because the one-party government of her native country was engaged in a hot civil war with its fundamentalist detractors. Algeria was unsafe for politically committed women artists; and since she now holds French citizenship, she could not at the time obtain a visa to return to Algeria, even to visit her family.

During the interview, the only one she and I have ever had face-to-face, she told me that if she could write her best-known play, *Princesses*, over again, she would change the ending. Gallaire is known for writing plays that pose enormous technical challenges for the director. She likes, for example, to use children, twins, and animals onstage and often asks for settings that are rich in naturalistic detail. She also has a taste for magical realism that can be confounding. The original text for *Princesses* features an ending that is particularly difficult to stage—the protagonist is beaten to death onstage by a group of elder women. At the time of our conversation, the play had rarely been performed as written.[9] Productions and adaptations had either cut the text, as was the case in the UBU Repertory Theatre production that resulted in the only published version of the play in English,[10] or they had changed the staging of the ending, as with the original French production, wherein the protagonist's head was crushed between a door and a wall.[11] In the adaptation of the play that was done in Uzbekistan, the protagonist was beaten to death, not by women, but by men.[12]

Much changed in the intervening decade. Algeria's civil strife cooled down, and Gallaire was able to go home. She even attended an academic conference at the Mentouri University in Constantine in 2006.[13] United

States foreign policy, meanwhile, became controversial even among its own citizens, as it put pressure on the entire region of the Middle East and North Africa. In this new global climate, Gallaire returned to her play and wrote a new ending for it,[14] one of which the English-speaking world is largely unaware, since it has no published English translation. The effect of this re-visioning has been to turn the play's protagonist, Princesse, from an utterly sympathetic, tragic victim into a freedom-fighting icon whose own hands are stained with the blood of her aggressors. As someone who has lived with Princesse since the mid-1990s, I found the change a bit difficult to absorb. I had expected that Princesse would escape death in the new version, but I had not realized that she would also kill.

The premise of the original play is striking, and it captured the imaginations of foreign producers at a time when, even more than now, the Western discourse about women and Islam was focused on rather facile notions of oppression. The published English translation of the piece,[15] for example, eliminated political details that shape the original piece with specificity and nuance, giving that version an Orientalist flavor. Gallaire has always insisted that the oppression depicted in the piece is not symbolic but rather realistic and quasi-autobiographical. The scenario it draws upon is one she claims to have experienced in Algeria, if not firsthand, then through observation of the lives of her close female friends.[16] Gallaire, like her fictional protagonist, was schooled in France, to which she ultimately immigrated and where she married a non-Muslim partner. Unlike Princesse, however, Gallaire's family supported her choices, and she remained close to both her parents, who appear as characters in other plays she has written.

Princesse, like Gallaire and other writers of her generation, is a product of the moment when Algeria gained its independence. In the late 1950s and into the 1960s, many young North Africans were sent abroad to French universities, only to return and, having partaken of cultural hybridity, find themselves out of step with their parents' customs and expectations. The case portrayed in Gallaire's play is an extreme one: Princesse, completely estranged from her powerful and wealthy father following her marriage to a Frenchman, returns to her village to pay respects to her father's grave after his death. Unbeknown to her, he has bequeathed his estate to the control of the village elders, allowing them to build a mosque. In exchange for his generosity, they agree to put Princesse on trial for the crime of having married outside her faith.

The play is structured in two acts. In the first, Princesse returns to her village and is greeted by a group of liminal characters who, while they possess no social standing, remain loyal to her: a beggar, a crippled man, a drunken watchman, a madwoman, and her ancient nurse, Nounou. The fact that she is surrounded by these outcasts punctuates her own ambiguous and transitional state as a female child of the village's social power-base who has fallen from grace through a perceived sexual transgression. Her childhood friends enter, and they celebrate her return with a feast and dancing. During the course of the first act, we hear a number of stories from the young women about the hardship of their lives and the gender inequity that exists in the village; the cries of Mahboula, the madwoman, foreshadow disturbingly the trouble that is to come. The overall tone of the act, however, is one of joy, hospitality, and abundance.

The play darkens in the second act as the young women are replaced by a group of elder women, joined once again by Mahboula, who as a liminal character may pass between the generational groupings. Argumentative and judgmental, the senior women castigate Princesse and Nounou for their lack of breeding and for the lifestyle choices Princesse has made. They accuse her of betraying the laws of Islam through her marriage. In orthodox Islam, Muslim men may take wives or concubines who practice any of the religions of the Book; indeed, the Prophet Mohammed had a Coptic Christian concubine named Maryam. Muslim women, on the other hand, are constrained from marrying outside their faith. In a passage laden with irony, we learn that the most fanatical of Princesse's accusers, Cherifa, is a European convert to Islam. Born Odette, she declares, "Il y a cinquante ans qu'Odette est morte, la chrétienne, l'infidèle! [Odette, the Christian, the infidel, has been dead for fifty years!]"[17] Gradually, we discover that she and the other senior women have been set to the task of putting Princesse on trial by her late father. When she refuses to promise to convert her husband to Islam, the women rise up and, with preternatural strength, execute all the liminal characters who are trying to protect her. Then they beat Princesse to death onstage with the cudgels they have concealed beneath the veils that envelope their bodies. In the final moment of Gallaire's original play, a group of village men enter the scene of carnage, order the women to stop their violent frenzy, and express satisfaction at the deaths of Princesse and her followers. The play ends with a tableau of Princesse's body laid out for burial and the sound of the Muslim call to prayer.[18]

Gallaire's 2004 revision begins in the moment when the elders rise up to attack Princesse. Her followers are killed. She repels her attackers, pushing them into a circle on the ground around her. In a desperate move, she calls the young women to her:

PRINCESSE (*levant farouchement les bras*): À moi la jeunesse! À moi la résistance! (. . . *Princesse arrache sa robe et s'en servant comme un drapeau, enjambe la corolle et fait et se fait Pasionaria.*) À moi j'ai dit! La jeunesse! L'avenir! La résistance! Le passé est là qui va nous étouffer.. . . À moi, vite! Sans honte et sans vergogne!

[PRINCESSE (*lifting her arms fiercely*): To me, young people! To me, re-sistance! (. . . *Princesse tears her dress, using it as a flag. She steps over the corolla of old women and becomes a Pasionaria.*) To me, I say! Youth! The future! Resistance! The past will smother us! . . . To me, quickly! With-out shame!]¹⁹[19]

The young women, astonished that Princesse has survived the onslaught, come to her aid. As they fight, they realize that this is their route to free-dom, and they become infected by the violence of the aggressors. They massacre their elders. As in the previous version, a man enters and calls a halt to the carnage. He explains that the trial Princesse's father has engi-neered was designed to test her resolve and her fortitude in the face of Algeria's willingness to turn a blind eye to religiously inspired terrorism. Calling her "Light of the Orient and the Occident,"[20] he asserts that he will restore her to her father's house after it has been cleansed of blood and bodies. She, in turn, asks him to come with her to the threshold of the house, "que je puisse sous ton ombre tutélaire, m'en aller de nouveau vers la lumière [so that I may, in your protective shadow, make a new jour-ney into the light]."[21] While this last sentence of the play does not quite fall into Alexandrine meter, it is worth noting that it is a rhyming couplet in the classical mode.

What is most startling about this change is its economy. A close com-parison of the play with its earlier versions reveals that it remains exactly the same until roughly two pages from the end. The new version is slightly longer than the older one; the eliminated passages from the older version take up less than a page of text.[22] Nevertheless, the shift in the author's vision is profound. If we hold Gallaire to what she said about the original play and continue to interpret Princesse as a realistic character, then Gallaire has reclaimed Princesse's relationship with her father at the cost of making her a proponent of the same kind of violence her oppressors have used. If Princesse is a metaphor, on the other hand, then we are free to see the killing of the elder women as a symbol of the abolishment of the old order, replete with corruption, intolerance, and ignorance. In either case, the play's revision expresses a deep pessimism, one that is new to Gallaire's work, regarding the ability of the generations to work together for social change in Algeria.

The change also redefines the play's structure. One ambiguity in the original is whether or not the chorus of young women and the group of elders should be doubled. As Jan Berkowitz Gross pointed out to me years ago, the suggestion regarding doubling that appears in the UBU Repertory translation of the original text is an insertion of the translator and does not appear in Gallaire's script.[23] Gallaire has made her wishes more explicit in the revision, wherein the two groups of characters are of necessity discrete. Since they appear onstage at the same time and the young women are the instrument by which Princesse destroys the elders, doubling is not possible. This makes the social narrative of the play linear and progressive; it removes any suggestion that Gallaire believes the situation of these women is cyclical and that, given time, the young women will become like the elders who oppress them.

This structural rejection of the cycle of violence and oppression is particularly interesting when read next to Gallaire's play from the previous year, *La beauté de l'icône* [*The Beauty of the Icon*].[24] One of Gallaire's darkest works, it concerns the citizens of Algeria who were "disappeared" by governmental security forces during the civil strife of the 1990s and includes the reprisals that were carried out well into the present decade against the families of the missing who dared to protest. Unlike the revision of *Princesses*, the structure of *Icon* is decidedly cyclical; the play ends more or less where it begins, in the home of a family celebrating a marriage. In the first scene, Gallaire specifies that the wedding is taking place in a family of dwarves. Gallaire has a respectful fascination with people of small stature, and they are often featured in her plays, where they, like her other liminal characters, exercise the "powers of the weak,"[25] held by people on the margins of society. Into this joyous milieu staggers a woman, apparently a beggar. Dora, the mother of the groom, offers hospitality to the beleaguered woman, taking her into an inner room, away from the other guests, where the woman reveals that her children and grandchildren are among the disappeared and that she has been searching for them for a decade.

This scene shifts into the series of brief, nonrealistic tableaux that make up the heart of the play. A masked group of mothers, along with one male figure, emerge from the substage. They constitute a kind of Greek tragic chorus, recounting and enacting stories of disappearances while Dora stands apart as an onstage witness. On high, the sinister figure of a military official mocks them with a "greasy" laugh.[26] Into this mise-en-scène, Gallaire injects two more iconic figures of liminality. Charib, a water-seller and self-professed *griot*, or storyteller-cum-oral-historian in the mode of West African traditional performance, distributes water to the grieving chorus while recounting an itinerary of Algeria's worst prisons as if reading from a tourism brochure. He offers succor and solidarity to the mothers but slips away before the official can do him harm. The other newcomer, Nina, who is a dwarf like Dora, is not so fortunate. A student who denounces the official, she is physically disappeared before the eyes of the audience and serves as an embodiment of the horrific stories the chorus is recounting. After this strange and terrifying interlude, the final scene of *Icon* returns to the realistic setting of the play's first moments. The government official is replaced by a different one, who looks down on the proceedings from the "gilded Olympus" where the first one had appeared.[27] We are at another wedding, and although Gallaire does not specify that this family should be composed of little people, she does say that the host, "par sa beauté rayonnante [by her shining beauty],"[28] resembles Dora. As in the first scene, a female figure staggers in. It is Dora herself, and the play closes with the suggestion that the members of Dora's own family have been disappeared and that she is searching for them.

It is clear that some time between 2003, when *Icon* was published and performed, and 2004, when she published the new ending for *Princesses*, Gallaire's textual strategies for addressing violence and oppression underwent a radical change. *Icon*, like most of her earlier work, including the original text of *Princesses*, implicitly acknowledges a sociological view of history that is circular and contains characters who rise above the malignancy of oppression through the sacrifice of their lives and happiness. The world view expressed in the revolutionary revision of *Princesses*, on the other hand, demands a rejection of the old order, by any means necessary, however violent. It is as if the playwright, weary of seeing her characters and her country succumb to tragedy, has finally snapped, saying, "Enough! No more!" In turning to violence, this new Princesse loses some of her humanity. She is a glorious revolutionary icon, a true Pasionaria, but she is more difficult for us to empathize with than the dignified victim of her first incarnation.

Perhaps this is Gallaire's intention. Never much of a Brechtian, she employs a strategy for moving audiences to action that, until now, has been to present characters of fine granularity caught up in small moments of living. The march of historical and current events has been present consistently in her oeuvre, but it has never overwhelmed the particularity of the domestic foreground until now. The original Princesse was not designed to be a Courage or a Grusha. Dora and the new Princesse are much more akin to these icons; and because the epic Princesse now sits inside of a structure that was not designed to hold her, she bends the text in which she resides out of shape, producing a *verfremdungseffekt* through sheer incongruity.

Jalila Baccar is a writer who is clearly more comfortable with epic structure than Gallaire. Well-known as an actor and theatrical producer in Tunisia since the mid-1970s, she emerged as a writer of international stature when she began publishing dual versions of her plays in French and Arabic in the late 1990s, winning prizes for both *Araberlin* and *Junun* from the French Société des Auteurs et Compositeurs Dramatiques (SACD) in 2003. It is significant that *Araberlin*, the piece considered here, exists only in French, and Baccar's company, Familia, has not attempted to produce the piece in Tunisia.[29] As Carlson notes in his introduction to *Four Plays From North Africa*,[30] censorship poses a significant problem for Tunisian writers, but Baccar has had only one play, *Khamsoun* [*Corps Otages/Hostage Bodies*], actually banned in her native country. Recently, the one-party government of Ben Ali relented: *Khamsoun* opened at the Masrah Medinat Tunis [Theatre of the City of Tunis] on February 2, 2007,[31] and played the Carthage Festival on August 10, 2008.[32] Although it shares with *Khamsoun* a focus on the problems of Arabs in Europe in the wake of the American war on terrorism, *Araberlin* remains a product for the foreign market. It has been produced in Germany at the Berlin Festspiele in 2002, where Baccar's artistic partner, Fadhel Jaïbi, worked in translation with a German cast.[33] The original text has had productions in France[34] and Belgium,[35] and the English translation has had a staged reading in the United States.[36]

It is fitting that a play that owes such a debt to Bertolt Brecht's legacy and style should be set in his principle city. *Araberlin* is a miniepic for the post-9/11 era, with a large character list played by a tiny cast of five actors. It uses all the tricks of the *V-effekt*: ironic songs, intertexts, a metatheatrical frame to the story, third-person narration of the characters' stories by the actors playing the characters, slapstick comedy that depicts the worst in human behavior, and an ending that is unsettling and unresolved. Just as the word "Arab" dissolves into the name of the German city in the play's title, the ethnic identity of the Arab characters in *Araberlin* is diluted, forcibly or by the characters' own volition, through exile, immigration, intermarriage, and cultural hybridity. Not one of the characters is Tunisian. Baccar, who most resembles her Algerian French counterpart, Hélène Cixous, both in this regard and in her use of the epic form, clearly feels comfortable reaching outside her own country, culture, and personal experience for dramatic subject matter.

Despite its epic and episodic qualities, there is a strong narrative line in *Araberlin*. Mokhtar, a Palestinian student of architecture, loves Katarina, a German florist. His sister, Aïda, a naturalized German citizen and former actor, is married to Ulrich, a native German businessman who has former ties to the Red Army Faction and is unfaithful to his wife. Their son Kaïs, a high school student, is very close to his uncle.[37] Mokhtar, whom we only see for a brief moment at the beginning of the play, bids farewell to Katarina and disappears. His sudden absence causes him to be suspected of Islamist terrorist activities. Aïda and Katarina are questioned, Aïda and Ulrich's house is searched, and the resulting publicity invades all their lives, causing friends, neighbors, and schoolmates to shun them. These tensions destroy Aïda and Ulrich's already troubled marriage, and she leaves him to return to the Levant. The question of Mokhtar's alleged terrorist involvement is never resolved.

The central irony of the play is embedded in its back-story. The evolution of Ulrich from disaffected student-turned-terrorist to rehabilitated businessman highlights the hypocrisy of the hunt for Mokhtar, who may or may not be what he is accused of being. Ulrich's stuffy objections to the disruption of his comfortable life that the accusations occasion are actually expressions of a deep need to conceal his own past. This is a powerful critique of post-revolutionary corruption, and it is a textbook example of critical displacement, one of the most common techniques playwrights use for evading censorship and political oppression. One may read Ulrich as a stand-in for Zine el Abidine Ben Ali, the president of Tunisia, who was himself a member of the resistance to France during Tunisia's struggle for independence and who is now using security as an excuse to crush even moderates who oppose him, a cycle of violence if ever there was one.

Another technique Baccar has used to great effect is slapstick. The scene in which Katrina is questioned at the police station is a classic clown routine, but the subject of the scenario is, of course, torture. In a parallel scene, as the police search the house of Aïda and Ulrich, she must continually excuse herself from the stage because the fear has given her a case of diarrhea. In these moments, the cognitive dissonance between the humorous style of presentation and the gravity of the thematic content pulls one out of the story. To complete the alienation, the scenes are also framed by third-person narrations and discussions of their accuracy, presented by the actors speaking as actors rather than characters. Baccar does not spare anyone in this play. Although, in general, the women fare better than the men, none of her characters are completely sympathetic. True to the epic style, she has left spaces in their ethical framework into which the reader or spectator may choose to step. While jarring, these devices, like the unsettling new ending of *Princesses*, provide small shocks in the interest of provoking critical thought.

It is a great pity that this play has not had a run in Tunisia with Familia's actors. In 2000 I had the privilege of seeing Familia's production of Baccar and Jaïbi's *Sahra Khāssa* [*Soirée particulière/A Certain Night*][38] and was deeply impressed. The company's members constitute a who's-who of Tunisian theatre, including the indefatigable film star Fatma Ben Saïdane, and its production values are among the highest I have witnessed in North Africa. To see Familia play *Araberlin* on its home turf in either Arabic or French would be a powerful thing indeed. It is unlikely, however, that we will see a North African production of any of the three plays under discussion in the near future, and this brings us back to one of the central questions we must face when analyzing the work of playwrights like Baccar and Gallaire: for whom do they write?

It is unquestionable that Gallaire has always written for an international audience, rather than an Algerian one, even though most of her plays bear the mark of her Algerian experiences and identity in some way. According to her Web site, none of her work has been done in Algeria,[39] which is not surprising given the political climate of that country. On the other hand, productions in Bangladesh, Uzbekistan, and Burkina Faso speak to an appeal that reaches beyond her European and U.S. spectatorship. With Baccar, the case is even less clear. For decades, she has written and played for Tunisians; but as she has explored themes that resonate increasingly with current political events, she has had to seek a foreign audience in order for her work to be heard at home. Like so many politically committed playwrights before her, she has sought the relative safety of international recognition so that it is more difficult for her government to ignore or stifle her message. Because of her popularity as a performer in Tunisia, she can exploit this strategy in a way that Gallaire cannot. This is one reason why *Khamsoun* is a major sensation this year at the Carthage Festival, whereas *La beauté de l'icône* remains a closet drama, and *Princesses* plays everywhere but in the Arab world. Another is the language of presentation. Until Gallaire's plays are translated into Arabic, they will not gain popularity in a region that is rapidly moving away from the francophone identity of its past.

It is quite possible that what we are seeing in these three plays is the beginning of a movement away from the styles and strategies that have marked women's dramatic literature since the Maghreb emerged from the independence movements of the 1950s and early 1960s. Like the earliest play in my original study, *Rouge l'aube* [*Red Dawn*],[40] which was written by Assia Djebar and her first husband, Walid Carn, during the Algerian War for Independence, the recent plays of Baccar and Gallaire show a willingness to confront world politics directly, with less reference to the domestic sphere. The individual has become less important, and the political context in which the individual is operating more prominent. North African women of the theatre are notable for their courage, but this marks a new kind of daring that is likely to move their entire oeuvre closer to the international recognition it so richly deserves.

NOTES

1. See Laura Chakravarty Box, *Strategies of Resistance in the Dramatic Texts of North African Women: A Body of Words* (New York: Routledge, 2005).

2. See Jacques Derrida, *The Ear of the Other: Otobiography, Transference, Translation,* ed. Christie McDonald, trans. Peggy Kamuf (Lincoln: University of Nebraska Press, 1985).

3. See Marvin Carlson, Editor's Introduction to *Four Plays from North Africa*, ed. Marvin Carlson (New York: Martin E. Segal Theatre Center Publications, 2008), 1–16.

4. Jalila Baccar, *Araberlin* (Paris: Éditions Théâtrales, 2002).

5. Jalila Baccar, *Araberlin*, trans. David Looseley, in *Four Plays from North Africa*, ed. Marvin Carlson, 86–207.

6. Fatima Gallaire, *Princesses*, in *Theatre 1* (Paris: Éditions des quatre-vents, 2004), 14–78. Although it was originally titled *Ah! vous êtes venues . . . là où il y a quelques tombes,* I will refer to the play by its shorter title, *Princesses,* which was adopted for the play's first French production, directed by Jean-Pierre Vincent at the Théâtre Nanterre-Amandiers in 1991. In English, the play is usually referred to as *You Have Come Back*, the title used by the Ubu Repertory Company's production and subsequent English-language publication. See Fatima Gallaire, *You Have Come Back*, trans. Jill MacDougall, in *Plays by Women: An International Anthology*, vol. 2, ed. Catherine Temerson and Françoise Kourilsky (New York: UBU Repertory Theater Productions, 1988), 166–221. The 2004 published revision is titled *Princesses*.

7. Fatima Gallaire, *Ah! vous êtes venues . . . là où il y a quelques tombes* [*Princesses*] (Paris: Éditions des quatre-vents, 1988); *You Have Come Back* (New York: UBU Repertory Theater Productions, 1988); *Princesses*, in *Theatre 1* (Paris: Éditions des quatre-vents, 2004), 14–78.

8. Fatima Gallaire, interview by Laura Chakaravarty Box, tape recording, Paris, France, August 1997.

9. Ibid.

10. Gallaire, *You Have Come Back* (1988).

11. Jean-Pierre Vincent, interview by Laura Chakaravarty Box, tape recording, Nanterre, France, November 27, 1997.

12. Gallaire, interview by Laura Chakaravarty Box.

13. Fatima Gallaire, *Site official de Fatima Gallaire*, http://www.gallaire .com/fatima (2007).

14. Gallaire, *Princesses* (2004).

15. Gallaire, *You Have Come Back* (1988).

16. Gallaire, interview by Laura Chakaravarty Box.

17. Gallaire, *Princesses* (2004), 67.

18. Gallaire, *Ah! vous êtes venues* (1988), 86.

19. Gallaire, *Princesses* (2004), 77.

20. Ibid., 78.

21. Ibid.

22. Gallaire, *Ah! vous êtes venues* (1988), 86; Gallaire, *Princesses* (2004), 76–78.

23. Gallaire, *Ah! vous êtes venues* (1988), 9; Gallaire, *You Have Come Back* (1988), 167; Jan Berkowitz Gross, e-mails to and telephone conversations with Laura Chakaravarty Box, February 26–March 27, 1998.

24. Fatima Gallaire, *La beauté de l'icône* (Paris: Éditions Art et Comédie, 2003).

25. Elizabeth Janeway, *Powers of the Weak* (New York: William Morrow & Co., 1981).

26. Gallaire, *La beauté de l'icône* (2003), 16–17.

27. Ibid., 42, 46.

28. Ibid., 45.

29. Familia Productions, Compagnie, http://www.familiaprod.com/compagnie.htm.

30. Carlson, "Editor's Introduction," 12–14.

31. Samia Ghachem, *Une catharsis*, in *Réalités*, February 8–14, 2007, http://www.familiaprod.com/presse_realites-fr.htm.

32. Familia Productions, http://www.familiaprod.com/presse.htm.

33. Ibid.

34. Africultures 2008, *Araberlin* par le Collectif Mona, http://www.africultures.com/index.asp?menu=affiche_evenement&no_evenement=15575.

35. Suzane Vanina, *Araberlin* (Bruxelles) Ruedutheatre, May 8, 2007, http://www.ruedutheatre.info/article-6579023.html.

36. Horizon Theatre Rep., 2008, http://www.htronline.org/shows_reading.php.

37. The play is filled with telling names. Mokhtar means "chosen." Aïda means "one who returns." Kaïs is named for the male character in *Majnoun Leïla*, the famous Arabic folk story that resembles *Romeo and Juliet*. In the tale, Kaïs is forbidden by his family from being with his beloved Leïla. He becomes possessed (*majnoun*) and goes mad. Ulrich means "prosperity and power." Katarina means "pure." The most obvious bigot in the play carries the surname "Gross." Hannah Schlicht, the well-meaning member of a humanitarian organization, bears a surname that means both "straightforward" and "defective."

38. Both *"khāss"* in Arabic and *"particulièr"* in French carry the connotation of peculiarity as well as particularity.

39. Gallaire, http://www.gallaire.com/fatima.

40. Assia Djebar and Walid Carn, *Rouge l'aube* (Algiers: SNED, 1969).

CHAPTER 10

Indonesian Women: Activist and Islamist Spiritual Callings

Nelly van Doorn-Harder

SPIRITUALITY AS A TRANSFORMATIVE FORCE

How to define Muslim spirituality within the local context is the topic of many heated discussions all over Indonesia, where especially during the past two decades Muslims are on a major quest to revive, strengthen, and nurture their faith and spirit. Following the fall of the dictator Suharto (1966–1998), which came in the wake of a crippling economic crisis, interest in developing one's personal inner life is booming. Its expressions are manifold and vacillate between intensified practice of the prescribed rituals, studying the Qur'an in small groups, meditation, and Sufi chanting.[1] Islamic healers vie with indigenous practitioners and paranormals; charismatic preachers and inspirational TV and radio programs draw mega audiences while in bookstores works on religious self-education and inspiration fly off the shelves. Artists weave religious themes into their music, songs, and paintings, infusing sound and sight with spiritual meaning. The spectrum ranges from radicals who yearn to relive the pristine times of the Prophet Muhammad to Sufis who communicate with heavenly entities. Whether seeking strict dogmas, discipline, or freedom of the spirit, all are engaged in a reflexive, modern subjective process that helps translate religious faith into the personal life, infusing day-to-day activities with meaning.

Women join this reflexive project, following and creating spiritual expressions that honor their responsibilities and restrictions as mothers, daughters, and spouses. Their beliefs and convictions move them to spend time in prayer, perform religious rituals, and direct the choices they make concerning behavior, work, and service to the community.[2] In Indonesia, many women feel a calling to translate their religious convictions into a career. The goal of their work as Qur'an teachers, preachers, or professors is to promote interpretations of Islam that they consider to be correct and sensitive to women's needs. Indonesian women artists join this process through their art. Understanding the enormity of the concept, for an exhibition on women and spirituality in Jakarta, sixteen women artists interpreted spirituality as "something of a noble aspiration, not easily achieved."[3]

Spirituality is a lived experience that comes in many forms; whether secular or religious, it has dynamic and transformative qualities. In her book *The Search for Spirituality: Our Global Quest for a Spiritual Life*, Ursula King sees it as related to "mind and thought, to consciousness, discerning reflection, and self-aware experience."[4] She suggests we not ask what it *is* but rather what it *does*.[5] Among others, Alister McGrath expresses similar ideas, stressing the transformative potential of what he considers to be of central importance: the process of correlation where spirituality "arises from a creative and dynamic synthesis of faith and life."[6] Consequently, people moved by inner spirituality can transform society. Spiritual teachings in Medieval Europe prepared the believers for the Reformation that shook the foundations of society. Women and men leading religious communities preached their message in town squares, bound by a fever for renewal, a sense that sleeping souls should arise and save humanity from itself. Their aspirations and claims were radical and often misunderstood. At the beginning of this chapter is an impromptu definition of spirituality that coincides with these views and considers the word "transformative" as key to the spiritual life of the women discussed and to what their beliefs move them to do.[7]

This chapter focuses on women whose faith moves them to become advocates for women and transform society according to their specific vision of Islam. Since the fault lines run between *shari'a*-minded and non-*shari'a*-minded activists, I have chosen examples of women who represent each side of the debate: both liberal and Islamist.[8] Although their advocacy has manifold expressions, for all it is Qur'an-based as they consider the Holy Book to hold the blueprint for true spiritual guidance and/or liberation of women. In order to illustrate how the activist agenda connects directly to the women's spiritual life, I will mostly focus on the activities associated with the debates about enforcing *shari'a* law. In particular, the debates and reflections related to the practice of polygamy (more precisely polygyny) provide a rich canvas on which to paint this picture, since they reflect the ongoing struggle for the soul of Muslim women in Indonesia.

The women described in this chapter each play their own specific role in the quest for religious knowledge. Some of them work locally while others reach out on a national level. Following their own call and work, they all preach, teach, and pray. What binds them is that their spiritual lives are the vehicles to bring about change for what they consider to be the societal good for women. Many of them are rooted in traditional backgrounds where they learned the Qur'an in Islamic boarding schools (*pesantren*) or went through religious courses offered by Muslim organizations. Most of the activists who are against the national enforcement of *shari'a* laws are connected to one of Indonesia's two largest Muslim organizations, Muhammadiyah and Nahdlatul Ulama (NU), while the platform of many of the Islamist or *shari'a*-minded activists is the Islamist political party of the Partai Keadilan Sejahtera (Prosperous Justice Party) or PKS. Divisions in opinion concerning the role of *shari'a* run through and at times virtually split families. For example, PKS activist Aan Rohana lobbies for a society-based acceptance of polygamy, whereas her sister Ida Roshida uses her position as a lecturer at the Islamic State University in Jakarta to publish articles against the practice.

A SPIRITUAL CANVAS OF MANY COLORS

In Indonesia, spirituality and social activism have a long history of being wedded together. This union was especially strengthened during the profound social, cultural, and religious changes, as well as natural disasters, of the past decade. When the repressive Suharto regime was forced to step down in 1998, the so-called era of reformation began. Reformation stood for democracy, freedom of speech, and great hopes for social mobility and personal expression. A flood of extremist voices hailed in this new era, as did a host of such natural disasters as the tsunami that on December 26, 2004, killed approximately 130,000 Acehnese. Events such as these represented the pinnacle of the never-ending struggle with natural and manmade disasters ranging from earthquakes and floods to multiple airline crashes in 2006–2007. Indonesia's Muslims felt that along with the disintegration of existing systems and common norms, moral boundaries were also dissolving. Some Muslims reacted with a wish for stricter rules in search of what young Islamic leader Ulil Abshar-Abdalla has called "overmoralization," whereas others found solace in intensified religious practices, groups for Qur'an study, meditation, or Sufi chanting.[9] As Muslim radicalism grew, so did liberal activism for women's rights.

During this period of upheaval, many of the more liberal activists, for example, those whose work shifted to Aceh, perceived an ever-tighter synthesis and correlation between faith, activism, and daily experiences.

Whereas before 1998 most of their activities had been text based, expressed in preaching, teaching, and writing, now many were involved in relief work through which they expressed their spiritual life. "My spiritual life nowadays is to be with all those who suffer," said Rahmawati Husein, who is a university professor and Muhammadiyah leader. "Just to be with them takes up all my energy. I seldom have time for a book anymore" (interview conducted May 22, 2007). Because of the chaos that took up so much mental space, the *hajj* (pilgrimage to Mecca) she made during this period was the only time she had to find mental rest and draw closer to God. "This time was between me and God, during the forty days of the Hajj I read the Qur'an six times."

Masrucha, the national chair of the Koalisi Perempuan, an inter-religious national umbrella organization advocating women's causes, expressed similar sentiments. While dealing with issues ranging from poverty to leprosy, as well as *shari'a*-inspired bylaws that harm women, she nurtured her spirit by performing the rituals and prayers learned as a child in the traditionalist environment of Nahdlatul Ulama Muslims. Fasting on extra days outside the holy month of Ramadan used to give her spiritual strength. When her busy schedule forced her to drop this lifelong practice, the familiar rituals helped her to maintain a spiritual balance. At the same time, the religious practices underscore Masrucha's vision regarding her work. She considers all the issues she encounters, whether concerned with religious pluralism or basic human rights, in direct connection with her spiritual life. With regular reports of scandals of corruption and immoral behavior by male leaders, she considers her most important spiritual assets to be honesty, transparency, sisterhood, and dedication (interview, May 19, 2007).

The bylaws Masrucha is resisting resulted from intense lobbying by Islamist groups that called for the nationwide application of *shari'a* law. Although in 2003 Indonesia's Parliament rejected the law as foundation of the nation, districts (*daerah*) were allowed to introduce *shari'a*-inspired bylaws, while the province of Aceh declared it state law (January 2002). These developments pose intense challenges to liberal activists advocating women's rights as radical Islamic groups try to Arabize Indonesian religious culture by restricting women's participation in public life and limiting their freedom in choice of occupation and moving around without male supervision. Islamist women activists see it as their duty to work toward "socializing" these ideas into society, whereas advocates for women's rights fight against rules that curtail women's religious and civil rights. Many of the bylaws have enforced dress codes for women, engendering, as consequence, much discussion and introspection about the benefits and blessings of wearing the veil. A drive to promote polygamous marriages has triggered discussions and introspection about a woman's role as spouse, her particular call to practice the virtue of *ikhlas*, and about the parameters of psychological, physical, and spiritual domestic violence.

Even before the current national search for meaning, their faith was the activists' main asset. Many of them get up in the middle of the night to do the *tahajjud*, the midnight prayer, and fast on Monday and Thursday. Some even follow the example of the Old Testament king and prophet David and fast every other day, for three or four days a week. Those who are Sufi-minded spend long hours chanting prayers and praises; the women who are more modernist, in contrast, spend much of their energy on developing their theological reasoning: preaching, listening to sermons, and studying the holy texts. Yet, among the entire spectrum of women, we can witness shifts and fusions in tandem with the larger trends going on within society. Where a decade ago many would have been faithful to the rules and directions of their organizations, school, and spouse, now they are choosing and creating their own spiritual practices. Concurrently, while more opportunities for individual choice are becoming available, there is an intense drive going on that aims at keeping women's spirituality within a literalist frame of Qur'anic interpretation. The battle for the spiritual direction of women is thus closely connected with social processes of a society that changes from community oriented to individualistic.

POLYGAMY: DEFINING THE CORE OF A WOMAN'S SPIRITUALITY

Currently, the issue of polygamy has emerged as one of the lynchpins in these battlegrounds where Islamist and non-Islamist activists vie for the public's attention in promoting or condemning the practice. According to the current marriage law (1974), the basis of marriage is monogamy, with polygamy restricted to specific circumstances only. This restriction was challenged in 2007 by an individual in Jakarta whose application to marry a second wife failed.[10] The Constitutional Court's answer to this case, which reconfirmed the monogamous nature of marriage, did not deter the pro-polygamy lobby. Those propagating the practice assume that change in the marriage law is bound to occur naturally in tandem with the eventual application of the *shari'a* law. However, their main arguments are not legal but hinge on a combination of psychological, cultural, theological, and spiritual arguments. While the main pro-polygamy argument remains the Qur'anic text, in order to bring about a change of heart among the Indonesian Muslim public and create a commitment to the practice, spiritual arguments do not suffice. As a result, its promoters rely heavily on a variety of arguments to convince women (and men) to concur with their vision.

SHARI'A-MINDED ACTIVISTS AND THE VIRTUE OF IKHLAS

For nearly a century, Muslim women preachers and activists have toiled to
spread a message of dignity and self-esteem for women across the archipelago. This message led not only to the opening of the first mosque for
women in 1922 but also to the practice of women studying and chanting
the Qur'an, pondering their duties as wives and mothers, and partaking in
the *taraweh* prayers together during Ramadan. More recently, it also led to
such activities as women opening maternity clinics, defending the right to
abortion, and fighting human trafficking.[11] While conveying these messages, Muslim women preachers had to negotiate and overcome deeply
rooted views concerning woman's spiritual capacities and convictions
about her duties and role. Since the Islamic Javanese notion of *ikhlas*
could easily lead to docile subservience, activists had to infuse it with sentiments of ownership and empowerment in order to instill in women a
sense of agency while obeying God's laws.

Ikhlas is a core Islamic virtue explained by Sachiko Murata and
William Chittick as "the human embodiment of *tawhid* (making God one),
by purifying one's religion for God alone."[12] Furthermore, its connotation
of selfless and sincere devotion, to work purely for God without aspiring to
outward appreciation or benefit, matches women's work ethic. In Java,
however, it is also wedded to the virtue of inward resignation, "a readiness
to leave behind one's own individuality and to arrange one's life in accordance with the harmony of the world, as it is destined."[13] Resignation
includes the willingness to live simply and to adopt a lower position in society than others.[14] Its gendered Javanese interpretation is that a woman
remains silent, in the back, serving her husband, family, and environment.
Traditionally, for a woman this dedication meant not only doing the
domestic chores but oftentimes also earning the family's income.

Contemporary interpretations of *ikhlas* consider it to be a transformative force that moves women to become actively involved in finding solutions to problems and situations while remaining faithful to Qur'anic
injunctions. Thus, over the course of a century, women activists and teachers managed to translate the secondary position and passive attitude into
one of self-confidence and spiritual excellence, which were of prime importance in advancing women's rights.[15] However, especially since the fall
of Suharto in 1998, radical-minded Muslim forces are at work to reverse
this reinterpretation of a woman's *ikhlas* into silent compliance with male
desires and acceptance of literalist views of the Qur'anic injunctions concerning women. In this discourse, the stress is on women as obedient
spouses who are perfectly *soleh*: virtuous and pious. Islamist-minded
groups especially push this narrow interpretation of a woman's role onto

society through a spate of youth literature aimed at girls and young adults. Teen novels and magazines are just one part of this pop culture that also finds expressions in blogs, movies, and music.

Thus, the issue of polygamy has become a battleground not only for the application of Islamic law but also for a woman's expression of her spiritual life. Fusing the Islamic and the Javanese concepts of *ikhlas*, radical-minded Muslims consider it the lynchpin to promote and "socialize" the practice of polygamy. Currently, the Indonesian marriage law allows polygamy, but with so many restrictions that most often second and subsequent marriages are entered into through secret contracts. As is the case everywhere, this battle over polygamy does not just concern gender roles but has far-reaching political and legal implications with as prime symbol the role and appearance of women.

A NATION DIVIDED

Acknowledging that polygamy is one of the Qur'anic injunctions, many Indonesians are of a divided mind concerning marrying more than one wife. By the end of 2006, one particular event catapulted the discussion into the limelight.[16] The mega star–preacher Abdullah Gymnastiar, or Aa Gym, was found to have a second wife by secret marriage. Expressing the delight of many Islamists, an Islamic court in West Sumatra promptly awarded him the "polygamy award" for taking this step.[17]

To the Indonesian public, this revelation was a sobering moment. Women, the majority of his audience, were especially devastated by the news. Taking his cue from Sufi doctrines concerning the purification of one's heart as a prerequisite to draw nearer to God, Aa Gym had built a media and business empire by preaching management of the heart (*Manajemen Qolbu*) as the prime Islamic virtue. Through his autobiography or *Qolbugrafi*, he cast himself as the embodiment of this virtue that in public was expressed by serenading his wife Ninih with love songs.[18]

The news about the second marriage was devastating to Ninih, and the task fell to her to save the image of the perfect family with the seven children that her husband used to praise in public. When speaking to the crowds of perplexed journalists about her husband's second marriage, she referred to the virtue of *ikhlas*: "This is the most difficult decision in my life; I am forced to practice *ikhlas*. God does not want that his servant has any other love besides Him. But I consider it as a difficult test and hope that God will bless me."[19]

During other occasions, she mentioned the concept of the pious and virtuous wife: "I want to be a virtuous and pious wife [*soleha*]. During times of anxiety I seek truth via the Qur'an and the Hadith. I found that

Islam does not forbid polygamy so I have to accept it because by being a virtuous wife I can go to Heaven."[20] When meeting her in her home six months later, I asked her what *ikhlas* meant to her, she reiterated this point of view: "To raise good kids and support my husband, always to be optimistic and not to give up easily; the goal is God. It involves submission [*pasrah*]; this is not a passive but an active trait that makes you act without anger or emotion, but with wisdom."[21] Ninih forced herself to take on a passive role. Turning away from her active former self, leaving behind her individual aspirations for her marriage for the greater good of the new community of three spouses, she clung to the virtue of *ikhlas*, which became the transformative force in this process.

Apart from her husband's teaching, Ninih derived religious inspiration and guidance from female leaders from the Islamist-oriented political party PKS (Prosperous Justice Party), which highly stressed the virtue of sacrifice. The PKS Islamists especially helped her navigate the intense media attention. Although it is not being advertised in its political program, according to PKS member of Parliament Aan Rohana, one of the party's goals is to "familiarize or socialize the practice of polygamy among Indonesian Muslims."[22] Rohana sees polygamy as a tool to protect women and to pave a woman's road to heaven. "Every spouse has to sacrifice herself and God will award her. If it is the will of God [*taqdir*] a wife cannot reject it. If she manages to create a harmonious family, she has created a source of blessing." A male supporter of the practice concurs that it allows spiritual and marital benefits for the wives: "For those who can honor their husband deeply with perfect devotion [*ikhlas*], God will soften their husband's heart so that he will love them wholeheartedly [*penuh keikhlasan*]."[23]

Following PKS reasoning, Rohana considers polygamy to be the best medicine against such vices coming in from the West as single parenthood and broken families. It protects women, guarantees large families, and prevents the husband from falling into adultery. It even allows women to focus on their spiritual life, since sharing domestic chores allows them to devote more time to Islam; they could even become a preacher. Rohana realized, however, that the practice can also destroy a family's harmony and advises that the husband prepare not only his wife but also the children and his in-laws to accept the new spouse.

During a televised debate, the other female PKS member of Parliament, Yoyoh Yusroh, defended having more than one wife as "a social choice and solution." She considered the practice of great help to widows, since "women need a husband and companion"; "they need to be guided and educated." In her view, polygamy opens up immense spiritual benefits to the husband since he can make his wives happy, help them, and bear responsibility.[24] During the same debate, one of Indonesia's most prominent male promoters and practitioners of polygamy, Puspo Wardoyo, equally allotted more spiritual power to men, since in his view a woman's *taqwa* or piety depends on her husband.

Aa Gym's popularity plummeted after it became known that he had married a second wife. He lost over 80 percent of his audience, and his female fans started an instant message campaign against him. Some writers considered the public outcry a blessing because of the spiritual struggle it unleashed for Aa Gym. Moreover, they reasoned, it saved him from becoming a cult figure.[25] His high profile, of course, remains an asset to the PKS agenda, which preaches a "soft Islamist" message. It does not officially advocate *shari'a* law but instead works toward its application by recruiting young Muslims and "socializing" especially young women into accepting the practice of polygamy.[26]

Meek acceptance implies narrowing down a woman's spiritual devotions and agency. In their quest to promote polygamy, both Yoyoh and Puspo presented reductionist views on women's spiritual agency. They privileged the fact that the practice provided men with extra opportunities to excel in their spiritual struggles, and they assumed a man's spiritual struggle and burden to be heavier than a woman's. Such views are curious at best in the Indonesian context, which has a long and strong history of Muslim women religious leaders whose sermons and teachings have influenced the devotional and spiritual practices of millions of women and children. Indonesia knows numerous scholars such as Siti Musda Mulia, who participated in the debate and is one of Indonesia's prominent scholars of Islam and a leader in anti-polygamy advocacy. Remarkably, she provided ample quotes from such authoritative sources as the Qur'an, the *hadith* (accounts of the sayings and doings of the prophet Muhammad), and *tafsir* (exegetical works on the Qur'an) in building her argument against the practice. Although representing the Islamist point of view, neither Yoyoh's nor Puspo's main arguments relied heavily on the holy texts.

GUIDING GIRLS TOWARD POLYGAMY

Convincing women to practice a non-active form of *ikhlas* and to transform this quality into one of the main spiritual assets of blind obedience has become a powerful tool to realize Islamist political and social agendas. The burgeoning industry of youth literature, which started to flood the market around 1990, testifies to this development. It processes these themes into teachings palatable to teenagers and young adults. In the words of scholar and journalist Latifah, it aims at showing the "face of friendly Islam," with its ultimate goal being to create acceptance of *shari'a* rules among girls.[27] Appealing to the religious sentiments of this age group is a complex process. On the one hand, it means addressing individualized young adults who feel part of shaping Indonesian Islam. As Nancy Smith-Hefner observed, this future "depends on individuals shaping themselves through self-cultivation and self-fashioning."[28] On the other hand, they teach girls an anti-individualist message. Thus, there is much at stake with Islamist and non-Islamist groups lobbying for the teen soul. Following Sidney Jones's observation, "Radical ideology is alive and well in Indonesia, and JI [Jemaah Islamiyah] publishers are helping disseminate it."[29]

Briskly selling, these writings guide girls on such issues as wearing the veil and on their views on dating and marriage. Finding a pious husband without dating is shown as the ultimate virtuousness. When couples can meet only briefly prior to marriage, there is much at stake for a young woman. In such cases, the virtue of *ikhlas* proves vital because it moves her to accept whomever God sends her way. Similar views infuse the discussions about marrying into a polygamous relationship. One novel describes how the heroine reflects on the fact that the married man she loves could still be available. The fact that he is married need not be an obstruction; when she becomes his second wife, neither she nor the first wife need worry about his divided love. After all, "one of the reasons that a woman is not allowed to marry more than one person is that a man can have multiple loves on an equal level. Psychologically a woman is not capable of loving more than one person."[30]

The theme of Islamic courtship and a woman's appropriate spiritual response is overwhelmingly present in Indonesian religious popular culture and has reached an all-time high in the novel *Ayat Ayat Cinta* (Verses of Love) by Islamic teacher Habiburrahman El Shirazy. The most bestselling novel ever in Indonesian history, it was reprinted 20 times within the first two years of its appearance. While studying at the prestigious Islamic Al-Azhar University in Cairo, its main protagonist, the pious Indonesian Fahri, falls in love with four women. The ensuing battle against his inner vices has gained the novel the label "soul builder." The novel and the blockbuster movie based on it are meant to be antidotes against messages with empty romance and teen love. They portray Islam as being cool and a man's virtuous behavior as lowering the gaze and being courteous.[31]

Although not so in the book, in the movie Fahri marries two of the four women he adores. In the ultimate gesture embodying *ikhlas*, it is not he but his first German-Turkish bride who urges him to take the second wife. The heroines of the movie follow Fahri, cry a lot, and look demure; he is the hero, and his spiritual struggle far outshines theirs.

A female blogger calling herself "warrior princess in training" describes how the novel has made her realize that she should train her obedience to God. Applying this virtue to the choice of a future husband, she contemplates, "If He [God] says, 'muna needs a convert from Italy to be her husband to be closer to Me,' then that is what i need. if He says, 'muna needs a husband who is unable to see to be closer to me,' then that is what i need. i am leaving everything to Allah, the All-Knowing, the Most Wise."[32]

HIGH STAKES

Theoretical works on fundamentalisms mention that part of the attraction of these movements resides in their emphasis on community, order, moral discipline, and demarcation of boundaries. While critiquing the surrounding culture and dominant religious elites, they articulate their agendas within their social environments, locating themselves in particular social spaces.[33] Exploring a theory of cultural articulation, Robert Wuthnow and Matthew Lawson analyze their ordering of social relationships based on analytical dimensions of beliefs, values, and symbols that believers should follow. Yet the boundaries thus created are not fluid but "determined by the questions being asked by the observer."[34] This fluidity of boundaries implies competition. In Indonesia as well as in other places, the agendas of Islamists vary: not all aspire to the restoration of the caliphate that will unite all Muslims, there are different interpretations of the meaning of *jihad*, and movements vary in the degrees to which they accept accommodation to the surrounding society. At the same time, Islamists have to compete with other devout Muslims, among whom are the liberal-minded groups. While competing for new followers, they use the same strategies and similar ideological constructs as their opponents.[35]

One point of reference, whether speaking of soft- or hard-core Islamists, is the highly symbolic meaning of the status and dress of women. Since the majority of Indonesian women are practicing devout Muslims dressed in some degree of appropriate Islamic clothing, including the veil, the issue that can truly be the harbinger of change in mindset is polygamy. Currently restricted by the marriage law and considered not very desirable by the majority of Indonesians, its full acceptance would indicate a change toward a more *shari'a*-minded law and a large pro-polygamy movement and thus a change toward a more Islamist interpretation of Islam. Of course, such a development would not only bring enormous political power but also suffocate such alternative religious interpretations as those by liberals. The lynchpin for this change is a woman's interpretation of her spiritual life as expressed by how the virtue of *ikhlas* moves her to accept the practice, including its potential negative consequences. Convincing women before they marry is crucial, and so much is at stake when addressing teenagers and young adults. Women who promote the benefits of such a

union need not be in one themselves. While singing the praises of a polygamous marriage, both Yoyoh and an Rohana are happily married women
who have no experience with co-wives.

ANTI-POLYGAMY ACTIVISTS

The voices and methods of those advocating against polygamy are just as
numerous and diverse as those lobbying for its acceptance. They range
from those preaching against it through song and poetry, to Sufi women
who have visions, and then on to scholars and preachers who study the
holy texts and their interpretations carefully in order to create sophisticated arguments against the practice.

What differentiates them from the Islamists is that they consider polygamy to be a form of domestic violence or, more precisely, psychological
abuse. Moreover, they interpret it to be against the Qur'anic messages that
at a minimum teach spiritual equality for the sexes. Most activists do not
have access to massive youth journals but present their ideas by means of
Qur'an study groups, journals, and radio and TV discussions. Many of the
activists received their religious training in the educational institutions of
the two large Muslim organizations in Indonesia, the Nahdlatul Ulama
(NU) and Muhammadiyah and still consider these organizations their spiritual and intellectual home.

Several of these activists, men and women, are driven by personal experience or by situations they witnessed in their own circles. For example,
Ruqayya, who teaches the Qur'an in an Islamic boarding school (*pesantren*), was a victim of domestic abuse herself and decided to speak up when
her husband took a second wife. Her case was taken up by Rahima, the
Centre for Education and Information on Islam and Women's Rights
Issues in Jakarta. Hers and similar cases became the inspiration for the
foundation of Puan Amal Hayati, a women's crisis center that works from
within the *pesantren* and provides Islamic counseling for victims of domestic violence. Ruqayya has become a high-profile voice against domestic violence and polygamy, encouraging women with songs she has created from
the Qur'an, from verses that stress equality between men and women.

Much of this struggle centers on Qur'anic injunctions on, and the
interpretation of, marriage. While Islamists read in such texts as Surat An-
Nisa' 4:3 that allowing men to marry more than one wife is a God-given
right, activists point at the texts that remind men that they should practice
justice toward all wives. These interpretations have inspired such activist
scholars as Siti Ruhaini Dzuhayatin and Siti Musdah Mulia to probe the
nature of marriage. Siti Musdah Mulia is one of the main architects of an
alternative draft of the Indonesian marriage law, which starts with the

statement that "the foundation of marriage is monogamy." This statement is followed by the assertion that "marriage is practiced from the principles of voluntary choice, equality, justice, well-being, pluralism and democracy."[36] The current marriage law still allows polygamy, although it requires certain conditions to be met and clearly considers the wife to be more of a helper to the husband, rather than an equal. Siti Ruhaini Dzuhayatin suggests marriage not be considered a legal contract with the potential of being interpreted as a master-servant relation but be seen as a form of worship (*ibadah*). To be valid, acts of worship have to be performed voluntarily and equally require full dedication to God (*ikhlas*).[37]

During the TV discussion with Yoyoh and Puspo, Siti Musdah Mulia argued, inspired by the classical legal scholar Abu Hanifah, that polygamy was in fact "*haram*" (illicit), since the practice led to excesses that made it comparable to "praying in clothes obtained through corruption."[38] The excesses in this case were findings from a research project about the practice, which indicated four prevalent negative consequences from having more than one wife: domestic violence, child neglect, internal conflicts, and a higher risk of contracting venereal diseases.[39]

In her writings, Siti Musdah Mulia has suggested that the core message of the Qur'an is God's *tawhīd*, His Oneness. In her view, "Tawhīd is the basis for human devotion to God, and guides humankind on how to establish harmonious relationships among themselves."[40] *Tawhīd* liberated human beings from other powers and put them on the path of continuous liberation that evolves through gradual changes. Thus, at a time when men were permitted unlimited numbers of women, the Qur'an limited the number of wives to four. At the same time, the Qur'an stresses the principle of justice and indicates that it is almost impossible to practice justice when married to more than one spouse. As proof, Siti Musdah Mulia and other activists point at Qur'an 4:129: "Ye are never able to be fair and just between women, even if it is your ardent desire." Connecting the idea of *tawhīd* with that of justice as presented in the Qur'an brings Mulia to the conclusion that "the limitation to four wives was a first step toward the eventual goal of monogamous marriage as the best guarantee of justice."[41] This analysis brings her to the interpretation that "the Qur'an favors monogamy over polygamy."[42] *Tawhīd* eradicates all forms of discrimination and subordination, which is also shown in the respect the Qur'an shows for a woman's role as mother, while it "is a reflection of God's justice that he takes a woman's physical and mental condition into consideration."[43] Only after presenting these religious arguments does Siti Musdah Mulia consider the social and psychological consequences of a polygamous marriage, many of which she finds to be psychological violence that destroys a woman's self-respect.[44]

CONCLUSION

This chapter can provide only a glimpse of the immense struggle that is going on in contemporary Indonesia with women's religion at the center. For both Islamist and liberal Muslims, spirituality is a transformative power. However, the goals of what this transformation can bring about differ greatly and depend on ideologies concerning the role of Islam in society. Islamist-minded Muslims want a transformation so that women feel renewed enthusiasm to fulfill their roles as wives and mothers in a more secondary, submissive, and perhaps traditional way. Liberal-minded Muslims see the transformative power of spirituality as the engine that liberates women from domestic abuse and subservient roles. In the middle is a large demographic group of devout women who subscribe to neither one nor the other viewpoint but form the undecided mass of potential supporters.

Nothing in this struggle can be taken for granted, since it plays out in a social context of growing individualism and reflexivity. Indonesian Muslims tend to be deeply religious and dedicated to their faith. However, in contemporary society they can choose from a wide array of modes to practice their beliefs. Through literature, radio, TV, and other media, in private, large, or small meetings they can join Sufi groups, practice New Age rituals, don a *burqa* as a sign of belonging to an Islamist sect, or attend the still widely popular gatherings of indigenous Muslim (for example, Javanese Muslim) healer-preachers. Ultimately, the choice of how to practice Islam is left to the people, although Islamist groups would like to direct how these believers should live.

The struggle is so fierce because it confronts a century-old Islamic women's movement that set out to liberate and empower women with verses from the Qur'an that acknowledged their agency and capacity as human beings. Lives filled with prayers, devotions, and Qur'anic recitations became motors of transformation and created vigorous social, cultural, and religious forms of activism. This development gave birth to a range of interpretations of Islam, yielding both liberal and *shari'a*-minded activists.

While the Suharto regime was still firmly in power, the latter type of activism remained invisible, since its goal of applying *shari'a* law in the nation was incompatible with the government's aspirations. The democratizing process that started after the suppressive regime fell in 1998 opened up space for Islamist groups, who carried appealing messages of straightforward belief and honesty in times of chaos and corruption.

The discussions focusing on women can be seen as tools in a fierce battle for political power to rule this vast nation of over 200 million Muslims. Following the Indonesian tradition of discussing issues in public at great length, such cases as those of Aa Gym also have produced much knowledge and new awareness about women's issues. In what seems to be an ironic cycle, they have added new options of individual choice on the vast spectrum that encompasses Islam in Indonesia. On another paradoxical note, Aa Gym, the preacher who once attracted audiences of 100,000, now has withdrawn from the public eye to deepen his study of the Qur'an while Ninik, his first wife, has become a popular guest on religious TV shows.

NOTES

1. Ulil Abshar-Abdalla, quoted in Greg Fealy and Virginia Hooker, *Voices of Islam in Southeast Asia: A Contemporary Sourcebook* (Singapore: ISEAS Publications, 2006), 132.

2. For examples of women's role as teachers and preachers, see my *Women Shaping Islam: Indonesian Muslim Women Reading the Qur'an* (Champaign-Urbana: University of Illinois Press, 2006).

3. Toety Herati, "Introduction," National Gallery, exhibit titled *Women in the Realm of Spirituality* (Jakarta, 1998), 11.

4. Ursula King, *The Search for Spirituality: Our Global Quest for a Spiritual Life* (New York: BlueBridge, 2008), 5.

5. Ibid., 3.

6. Alister E. McGrath, *Christian Spirituality: An Introduction* (Malden, MA: Blackwell Publishers: 1999), 9.

7. Although written for the Christian context, Alister E. McGrath's elaboration on the term is helpful: "To talk about 'the spirit' is to discuss what gives life and animation to someone. 'Spirituality' is thus about the life of faith—what drives and motivates it, and what people find helpful in sustaining and developing it. . . . Spirituality is the outworking in real life of a person's religious faith—what a person *does* with what they believe." *Christian Spirituality*, 2.

8. I use the word "liberal" here following Charles Kurzman's *Liberal Islam: A Sourcebook* (Oxford: Oxford University Press, 1998), 13–26, which uses the term to describe certain modes of interpreting the Islamic sources. In the Indonesian context, activists strive to apply the injunctions of the Holy Qu'ran in non-dogmatic and non-traditional ways, as, for example, interpreting these sources informed by philosophies of basic human rights teachings. They are against an Islamic theocracy, are pro-democracy and uphold free speech, especially in seeking to combine the Qur'anic teachings on women and minorities with human rights discourses.

9. Ulil Abshar-Abdalla, quoted in Greg Fealy and Virginia Hooker, *Voices of Islam in Southeast Asia* (Singapore: ISEAS Publications, 2006), 132.

10. Sally White and Maria Ulfah Anshor, "Islam and Gender in Contemporary Indonesia: Public Discourses on Duties, Rights and Morality," in *Expressing Islam: Religious Life and Politics in Indonesia*, ed. Greg Fealy and Sally White (Singapore: ISEAS Publications, 2008), 147, 148.

11. See Nelly van Doorn-Harder, "Controlling the Body: Muslim Feminists Debating Women's Rights in Indonesia," *Religion Compass* (Oxford: Blackwell Publishing, 2008), n.p.

12. Sachiko Murata and William C. Chittick, *The Vision of Islam* (New York: Paragon House, 1994), 279, 282.

13. Franz Magnis-Suseno, *Javanese Ethics and World-View: The Javanese Idea of the Good Life* (Jakarta: Penerbit PT Gramedia Pustaka Utama, 1997), 141.

14. Ibid., 142.

15. Van Doorn-Harder, *Women Shaping Islam,* 109–113.

16. For example, a poll held by the Women's Study Center of the Islamic University Sunan Kalijaga in Yogyakarta found that the majority view on polygamy was "polygamy: yes, being one of many wives: no." Interview, Inayah Rohmaniyah, on July 26, 2007.

17. http://www.indonesiamatters.com/1014/poligami-award/.

18. For an excellent analysis of the phenomenon of Aa Gym, see James B. Hoesterey, "Marketing Morality: The Rise, Fall and Rebranding of Aa Gym," in *Expressing Islam: Religious Life and Politics in Indonesia*, ed. Greg Fealy and Sally White, 90–107.

19. http://www.indonesia.faithfreedom.org/forum/viewtopic.php?t=8205&sid=2754ecb3b5734b5e94fbe580ae82c0f6.

20. Interview with journalists in Jakarta, December 2, 2006, http://www.kapanlagi.com/h/0000146511.html.

21. Interview, June 23, 2007.

22. Interview, Aan Rohana, member of Parliament PKS, June 26, 2007.

23. Rachmat Ramadhana Al-Banjary and Anas al-Djohan Yahya, *Indahnya Poligami: Menangkap Hikmah di Balik Tabir Poligam: Mengapa Aa Gym Menikah Lagi?* [The Beauty of Polygamy: Capturing the Wisdom behind the Screen (Veiling) Polygamy. Why Did Aa Gym Marry Again?] (Yogyakarta: Pustaka Al-Furqan, 2007), 111.

24. The program "Poligami: Siapa Takut? Perdebatan Seputar Poligami" [Polygamy: Who Is Afraid? A Debate Concerning Polygamy]. Aired on SCTV, December 5, 2006. The program is available on DVD and summarized in a booklet with the same title edited by Eka Kurnia (Jakarta: QultumMedia, 2007). The participants in the debate were Yoyoh Yusroh, member of Parliament on behalf of the PKS; Puspo Wardoyo, married to four wives and the president of Poligami Indonesia, an organization that promotes the practice; Siti Musdah Mulia, a women's rights activist and professor of Islamic studies;

and M. M. Billah, a human rights activist and member of the Indonesian Commission for Human Rights, KOMNAS HAM.

25. This argument is used, for example, by Al-Banjary and Yahya in *Indahnya Poligami* [The Beauty of Polygamy], 2007.

26. For recruitment techniques, see, for example, Ulla Fionna, "PKS Gets Serious about Recruitment in Malang," *Inside Indonesia* 92, April–June 2008, available online at http://insideindonesia.org/.

27. Latifah, "Writing the Self, Ascribing Islam. Islamic Teen Fiction: Reforming the Moslem Identity" (unpublished manuscript, 2007).

28. Nancy J. Smith-Hefner, "Youth Language, *Gaul* Sociability, and the New Indonesian Middle Class," *Journal of Linguistic Anthropology* 17, no. 2 (2007): 190.

29. Sidney Jones, "Indonesia: Jemaah Islamiyah's Publishing Industry," ICS Asia Report 147, February 28, 2008, available at http://www.crisisgroup.org/home/index.cfm?id=5324&l=1.

30. Latifah, "Islamic Teen Fiction," 13, quoting from the novel *Tak Bisa ke Lain Hati* by Azimah Rahyu (Jakarta: Khairul Bayaan, 2003).

31. http://www.hafihz.com/islam/ayat-ayat-cinta-in-english-signs-of-love/.

32. http://munirfa.wordpress.com/2007/03/23/ayat-ayat-cinta-made-me-stronger-inside/.

33. Robert Wuthnow and Matthew P. Lawson, "Sources of Christian Fundamentalism in the United States," in *Accounting for Fundamentalisms: The Dynamic Character of Movements*, Martin Marty and Scott Appleby (Chicago: University of Chicago Press, 1994), 22. Wuthnow applies the so-called theory of cultural articulation to the phenomenon of fundamentalist movements.

34. Ibid., 23 and 24.

35. This point has been stressed by Vincent Cornell, who refers to the works of French philosophers Henri Lefebvre, Rene Girard, and Gilles Deleuze on pseudo-repetitions, mimetic rivalry, and the artistic use of repetition to underpin his argument how extremist movements use these tactics to create and delineate their agendas. In *"Mimesis* and the Logic of Repetition in Islamic Extremism: The Cosmic Shari'a in the Works of Sayyid Qutb and the Brethren of Purity" (unpublished manuscript, 2009).

36. TIM Pengurusutamaan Gender, *Pembaharuan Hukum Islam: Counter Legal Draft Kompilasi Hukum Islam* [Renewal of Islamic Law] (Jakarta: Ministry of Religious Affairs RI, 2004), 36.

37. Siti Ruhaini Dzuhayatin, "Marital Rape, Suatu Keniscayaan?" [Marital Rape, a Certainty?], in *Islam dan Konstruksi Seksualitas*, ed. Edy S. Santoso (Yogyakarta: PSW IAIN, 2002), 128.

38. Eka Kurnia, *Poligami. Siapa Takut?* 33.

39. Ibid., 34.

40. Siti Musdah Mulia, "Tauhid: A Source of Inspiration for Gender Justice," in *Dawrah Fiqh Concerning Women: Manual for a Course on Islam and*

Gender, ed. K. H. Husein Muhammad, Faqihuddin Abdol Kodir, Lies Marcoes Natsir, and Marzuki Wahid (Cirebon, Indonesia: Fahmina Institute, 2006), 39.

41. Ibid., 49.

42. Siti Musdah Mulia, *Islam Menggugat Poligami* [Islam Criticizes Polygamy] (Jakarta: Gramedia, 2007), 100.

43. Musdah Mulia, "Tauhid," 56 and 55.

44. Musdah Mulia, *Islam Menggugat Poligami*, chap. 3.

CHAPTER 11

The Dialogics of a New Orientalist Discourse: Telling Tales of Iranian Womanhood

Khani Begum

"So what's with all the Iranian Memoirs?" asks Gina Barkhodar Nahai, responding to the proliferation of published literary memoirs by Iranian women in recent years. During the early 1990s, Nahai was one of two Iranian women authors publishing in the West. In 1991, when Crown published her first book, *Cry of the Peacock*, a story about Iranian Jews, and eight years later, when her second novel, *Moonlight on the Avenue of Faith*, found its way on to the *Los Angeles Times* bestseller list, there still was no appreciable mass reading audience in the West for stories about Iranian women, regardless of whether they were Muslims, Jews, or Christians. In 2007, Nahai is surprised that an Amazon search for "Iran, Memoirs, and Novels" reveals over 600 entries.[1] During promotional readings for her fourth novel, *Caspian Rain*, Nahai faces the following questions from her audience:

·Why are so many Iranian women writing books? Why so many memoirs? Is each one of these lives interesting enough to merit a book? Is there a market for all these books? Are Iranian women getting paid by the Bush administration to write bad things about Iran to convince the American people that a military attack against the country is a noble idea?[2]

While such questions speak to the susceptibility of the publishing industry to trends much like any other industry, they also elide underlying sociopolitical and psychological reasons for *this* particular trend at *this* particular time in the West. In addition, they implicate U.S. political and economic interests with the phenomenon of literary and filmic output by Iranian women in the last two decades by drawing attention to the relevance of these personal memoirs for U.S. and Western policies regarding the West's relations with Islamic societies in general and Iran in particular. Rather than expressing a genuine desire to understand the experiences of Islamic women and their culture on their own terms, these questions reflect the perceptions and attitudes similar to those Edward Said cataloged in his analysis of U.S. and Western media's coverage of the Iran hostage crisis of January 1981 in *Covering Islam*. Said, in this work and in *Orientalism* (1978), makes a key point that historically, knowledge, representation, and the construction of knowledge or how knowledge is acquired are all imbricated with issues of power, class, and materiality.

The notion that knowledge and power are intertwined has been raised by a number of theorists in the West and the East. Sankaran Krishna brings up the work of Michel Foucault to discuss how genealogies and knowledge about the postcolonial are constructed:

> [Foucault] argues that we can never truly and finally know something; all we can do is conduct an archeology that plumbs the series of meanings that humans have attached to that something over the ages. Whether it is our concepts of madness, illness, crime, "normal" sexual behavior, the individual, or political agency, for Foucault, the meanings that humans attach to these aspects of reality, in other words, interpretations, are indissociable from issues of power.[3]

"In the spirit of Foucault," Krishna finds that the genealogy of the postcolonial is imbricated with issues of power and political action. Said's argument in *Orientalism* and in *Covering Islam* follows Foucault in reiterating this connection between knowledge, its construction, and its investment in power with regard to the ways in which the West has constructed its views about the Orient. In his introduction to *Covering Islam*, bringing attention to the ways in which all discourse on Islam is vested in some authority or power, Said says:

> Let us say that discourse on Islam is, if not absolutely vitiated, then certainly colored by the political, economic, and intellectual situation in which it arises: this is as true of East as it is of West. For many evident reasons, it is not too much of an exaggeration to say that *all* discourse on Islam has an interest in some authority or power. On the other hand, I do not mean to say that all scholarship or writing about Islam is

therefore useless. Quite the contrary; I think it is more useful than not, and very revealing as an index of what interest is being served. I cannot say for sure whether in matters having to do with society there is such a thing as absolute truth or perfectly true knowledge; perhaps such things exist in the abstract—a proposition I do not find hard to accept—but in present reality truth about such matters as "Islam" is relative to who produces it. It will be noted that such a position does not rule out gradations of knowledge (good, bad, indifferent), nor the possibility of saying things accurately. It simply asks that anyone speaking about "Islam" remember what any beginning student of literature knows: that the writing or reading of texts about human reality brings into play many more factors than can be accounted for (or protected) by labels like "objective."[4]

Written two years after the Iran hostage crisis, *Covering Islam*, primarily a critique about Western media's coverage of Islam, rings just as true of the West's attitudes toward Islam and Iran in 2009 as it did in 1981. Said's point regarding the importance of recognizing that the truth about Islam is relative to who produces it is equally, if not more, valid today as it relates to media coverage of Islamic countries and issues, literary works, documentaries, and other types of films. Said argued that Orientalism is a discourse, one that "is not an airy European fantasy about the Orient, but a created body of theory and practice in which, for many generations, there has been considerable material investment."[5] Today, the West's "Orientalist" attitudes surrounding the discourse of Islam and non-Western societies that Said's *Orientalism* and *Covering Islam* brought to the forefront are also reflected in the scholarly and creative work produced by insider subjects. As Said and later postcolonial theorists have noted, one of the effects of colonization is the internalization of the colonizers' perceptions of their own culture. Krishna points out that "the 'truth' about representations hinges more on the power inhering in the locus of enunciation—who is describing whom, who is representing, and who is being represented."[6] Insider narratives that may replicate Orientalist representations of their own culture occupy varying positions of power, especially during critical global political crises. Hence, to understand the relevance of contemporary Iranian women's narratives and memoirs to contemporary global discourses about Islam, Iran, and terrorism, it becomes necessary to critically analyze the "truth tales" presented by insider speaking subjects and their vested interest in whatever authority or power.

East-West discourses of Islam and Iran in 2009 have now been supplemented by the addition of new insider and exiled or diasporic subjects' literary and filmic narrative expressions of the experiences of women during the Iranian Revolution of 1979 and after. Additionally, there has arisen another stream of critical and academic discourse around these insider and diasporic responses that attempts to either validate or call into question their credibility and authenticity. In this chapter, by implicating myself in this last stream, I maintain that certain insider and diasporic narratives and films and the discourses around them together, on the one hand, empower Iranian women and all women readers and audiences and, on the other, through their reification of Western stereotypes of Islamic culture and Islamic women, participate in and at times function as a new type of Orientalist discourse. The popularity in the West of select narratives derives from their insider position, which allows them to function as a form of subaltern speech, thereby providing for the West a lens into the mysterious lives of women in the Orient. In exploring how the discourses around some of these narratives, both literary and filmic, have given birth to a new kind of Orientalist discourse, I examine what characteristics make certain narratives and films more accessible and desired in the West, whereas others are virtually ignored despite the insider status they both inhabit. The media and academic discourse around the celebrated narratives and films too functions as another form of this new Orientalist discourse.

Although literature and the arts have occupied an important position in Iran's history for centuries, Iran's rich literary tradition, like many early literary traditions, privileges male writers; furthermore, writing by women historically has not been as highly respected. These earlier literary traditions also favor the genres of poetry and drama, and, when in the 18th and 19th centuries Iran witnesses the development of the novel, the new genre evolves in the form of the historical novel. The autobiographical memoir, much less prevalent, is discouraged particularly for women writers. Also, Iranian women are either actively dissuaded from writing in general, or their work is often subjected to greater critical scrutiny than that of their male counterparts. This makes the current flood of Iranian women's poetry and memoir (both the most personal of genres) an even more curious phenomenon. By choosing to write in the form of the personal memoir, these writers trespass against traditional literary practices, and the very act of writing constitutes for them a personal rebellion. Additionally, since the memoir documents events, it serves as witness and bears testimony. It takes on connotations of the forbidden through the transgressive act of telling tales outside the family, outside the tribe, and outside the societal unit—tales that the family, the tribe, and the societal unit may not want told to the world at large. Also, because the autobiographical format provides these women with a means to challenge traditional notions of women's self-effacement found in previous third-person narratives, it enables them to write women's stories back into their cultural and national history.

Through this retelling, the subaltern voices of these women discover a newfound subjectivity and agency of their own.

During the Iranian Revolution of 1979 both men and women writers experienced a hiatus of freedom of expression. The initial revolutionary freedom in literary and filmic expression did not last long once the religious fundamentalist elements came to power. Iran witnessed a cultural revolution that prohibited any expression that did not adhere to the religious ideologies set forth by the new Iranian Republic. Despite the censorship and restrictions placed upon them, the generation that went through the revolution, grew up in it, or escaped it still managed to give literary, artistic, and filmic expression to their experiences in unprecedented terms. These women writers began using the autobiographical form to come to terms with the 1979 Iranian Revolution and those who escaped it to adjust to their new lives in the diaspora. The memoirs that detail experiences of women growing up during the revolution constitute a body of writing that is written against the grain and ends up taking on permutations of protest.

Persis Karim, in her introduction to an edited collection of writing by contemporary Iranian women, notes that one of the most interesting byproducts of the revolution was the "explosion of women's writing both in Iran and abroad." This explosion of Iranian women's writing in the diaspora, Karim finds, "has met with remarkable success in part because [the writings] complicate our notions of Iranian women and articulate ways that women respond to 'Iranian-ness'—on more than one continent and in more than one political and social context."[7] Women, confined to private spaces, found new ways to express their desires and feelings, and one could say that ironically the repressive regime made them even more creatively engaged. Iranian cinema too experienced a phenomenal growth of similar proportions, and for the first time more women entered the arena, with many of them winning awards for their films in Iran as well as at international film festivals. Many of these women are making films that at times radically critique Iranian society and explore women's lives from a variety of traditional and nontraditional perspectives. While some of these women work in the Iranian diaspora, almost as many are working in Iran making films within strict censorship codes and government regulations that were instituted by the new regime's desire "to create a national culture devoid of foreign influences, and by extension to create a national culture that would remain detached from both East and West."[8] The regulations have challenged these directors, leading them to devise new and creative cinematic techniques in representing women and male-female relationships on camera. As a result, Iranian films have been celebrated at a variety of international film festivals and have acquired a reputation for creating innovative styles that have broken many traditional rules of European and

Western film technique. Negar Mottahedeh, examining this phenomenon, notes that in 1992 the Toronto International Film Festival called Iranian cinema "one of the pre-eminent national cinemas in the world," and years later a *New York Times* reviewer echoed this sentiment by calling it "one of the world's most vital national cinemas."[9]

Karim, paralleling the experiences of Iranian women during the revolution with those of American women during the same period, says:

> While Americans were experiencing the effects of American feminism, Iran's post-revolutionary Islamic identity was being rigidly defined by perceptions about women and their appropriate social and sexual conduct. While Iran expressed its post-revolutionary ideology in part through its policies toward women, Americans became fixated on the veil as an icon of the essential identity of Iranian women. While women in Iran were limited in their opportunities and in their ability to vocalize dissent, Americans too participated in their silencing by assuming that they had little or no agency and were uninvolved in dissent.[10]

The significant point here is that despite limitations placed upon them within a fundamentalist regime, Iranian women assert themselves and vocalize dissent in their own way. That this is not always recognized by Western media coverage, along with critical discourses of the veil, testifies to another form of silencing of Iranian women and an undermining of their subjectivity. Discourses of the veil and its literal and symbolic silencing of woman have been a constant preoccupation in both the Occident and the Orient. Reza Shah Pahlavi's modernization measures prohibited veiling in public, one of the prohibitions that contributed to the growing frustration with his regime among more traditional Iranians. In the 19th century, European scholars and travelers in their quest to understand the Orient were fascinated with issues relating to veiling and the harem. The actual and symbolic connotations of the veil aside, this fixation on the veil also typifies the West's historical fascination with the Oriental Other. Perceiving veiling only in terms of its limitations, however, only furthers an Orientalist perspective of Islamic culture, ignoring other, more nuanced and diverse readings of not only veiling but also other traditional Islamic cultural practices.[11]

In the wake of the Iranian Revolution and the Iranian hostage crisis, this fixation on the veil along with the West's renewed interest in the Islamic Orient contributes to the increased desire to know, to unveil, the women living under the fundamentalist regime of the new Republic of Iran. Flexing their artistic muscle, Iranian women too want to unveil themselves for both Iranian and non-Iranian reading and viewing publics as well as for themselves in their quest for subjectivity and the desire to create their own autonomous identities. In pursuit of this desire, they have produced a wide array of literary and filmic representations of Iranian womanhood. The dynamic between the tales told by Iranian and Iranian diasporic women and the reception of these tales in the West embodies elements of the specularization found in earlier Orientalist discourses noted and discussed in Edward Said's body of work as well as in the work of many postcolonial scholars. It is necessary to examine this dynamic through a postcolonial theoretical perspective to reveal the underlying implications and motivations of both the creators of these narratives and their audiences in the West, thereby enabling readers to decode the real truth of these tales. The West's curiosity in the "lives of others"—Others, whose experiences are expressed in personal narratives and autobiographies by women of color and by women from non-Western cultures in general—has spawned a new popular audience outside the academy and out of the purview of feminist, multicultural, and postcolonial scholars. The reasons for the popularity in the West (especially among this new popular readership, a readership typified by Nahai's audiences) of personal narratives of women's struggle set against the backdrop of calamitous political, cultural, and social upheavals are threefold: First, the complexities of personal and political identity construction within these different geographical and cultural spaces are inherently engaging and good fodder for literature and film. Second, they mirror the continued fascination of the West with the exotic Other. And, third, they connect with female experiences around the globe, thereby participating in the larger dissemination of the human values of transnational feminism. Ironically, despite the popularity of the values of feminism, the reach of globalization, and the ease of acquiring knowledge in the digital information age, the exotic Other continues to resist analysis and comprehension for the mass media and the academy in the West. As a result, this resistance on the part of the Other has fueled the desire of the West to unmask and know the unknowable and to make it manageable. This is not dissimilar to precolonial and colonial interests of European scholars and travelers to conquer the Orient through knowing and seeing the "real" Orient. This desire notwithstanding, these scholars and travelers invariably interpret what they see and learn in terms of their own culture; and what they cannot explain in terms of their own experience, they categorize as exotic and mysterious. As Said maintained, the knowledge the West sought and gathered of the Orient enabled it to constitute the Oriental Other in specific ways and also constituted the West's own sense of self in specific ways. Orientalism was as much about the West as it was about the Orient. In other words, the discourse of Orientalism was not so much about the verifiable truth of Eastern or Oriental societies, their religions, economy, politics, languages, grammars, and texts, but rather a rhetoric of Western self-fashioning and enabling of its dominance and control over the rest of the world.[12]

The average European visitor to the Orient, when faced with its mystery, often overreacts, as does E. M. Forster's female protagonist in his novel *A Passage to India*. Adela, a young British woman, travels to colonial India in the 1920s desiring to see the "real" India. When confronted with India's mysterious unknowability, she becomes unnerved and, losing her grip on reality, accuses Aziz, the Indian who befriends her, of rape. Forster's novel critiques the British colonial presence in India for its callous disregard for, and its inability and lack of desire to understand, the Other culture as well as the naïvete of the average Britisher who expects readily to acquire knowledge of the Other and his/her culture with the help of a *Baedekar Travel Guide* and a day trek to an Indian historic site.

Although scholarship on Islam and Islamic cultures today has increased from the lamentable lack of it noted by Said in *Covering Islam*, the understanding of Islam and Islamic societies that emerges in some of this scholarship still resembles the flawed perceptions of existing scholarship criticized by Said in 1981. What has changed since then is the urgency and haste with which new scholarship is willing to interpret literary and filmic outpourings from insider sources as "real" truth tales. As noted earlier, in 1981, memoirs and novels from Iran had begun appearing in the global literary marketplace; and except for the work of a handful of internationally acclaimed film directors, most filmic work by Iranian women and men had been virtually unknown in the West. Over the past two or more decades, however, Iranian films have found a receptive global audience. Despite this increased literary and filmic output by Iranian men and women that has become accessible to Western audiences, only certain select works have been singled out for praise and have received greater than usual critical and scholarly attention. These selections are often works that traverse a fine line between representing an exotic Other (but not so exotic as to be alienating) while they also resonate with a universalism that increases their accessibility to Western readers and audiences. The more authentic and/or nuanced evaluations of life under the Iranian Republic are often subordinated in lieu of those works that celebrate literary and humanistic values—values that closely resemble those of European humanism. In 19th-century colonial discourse, the Orient figures as a desired place of fantasy and the exotic Other as desired Object. In the 21st century's "war against terrorism discourse," the Orient (particularly the

Islamic Orient) has become the place of chaos and the exotic Other; and rather than being the desired Object, it has become the Object to be feared. The psychological shift from desired exotic to feared terrorist complicates the relationship of the reader/viewer and the producer of the literary or filmic representation of the Iranian experience. For the Western reader/viewer today, the fear overrides the desire; hence, works that express a position or worldview that challenges the reader's/viewer's worldview are less likely to find an audience. Also, in light of the new threat of a nuclear Iran and the even more recent threat of cyber spies and Internet hackers from Iran,[13] the anxiety and need felt by the West to bring Iranian culture under control and to understand the threat it may pose to Western societies has increased.

The increase in the scholarly and journalistic coverage on Islam and Islamic cultures has also resulted in a greater number of studies on the role of women in non-Western cultures and histories. Despite this, the female subject from non-Western cultures remains an enigma, not only to the West, but often also to herself. The need to decipher, to know, and to understand this Other and the culture that formed her, reminiscent of the 19th-century colonial desire that specularized the female Other,[14] is mirrored in the 21st century by the subaltern narrator's own subjective desire to bear testimony and to come to terms with her own sense of self in the midst of a conflicting and conflicted new postcolonial reality. For the woman narrator, this twofold struggle to give voice to her story as woman and her story as racial/postcolonial/female subject, because of the inevitable compromises between the two, becomes a process invariably defined by loss, especially when placed in relation to Western feminist, cultural, and aesthetic ideals. All of Nahai's novels (like many Iranian women's memoirs) are about exile and the loss that results from it. In an interview included as an appendix to her novel *Moonlight on the Avenue of Faith*, speaking of exile and loss, she concludes that "exile can be as freeing as it is devastating." Many women who have given voice to their experiences in personal memoirs and films, however, have resisted seeing themselves as victims of circumstance or of oppressive political and sociocultural structures. In some cases, the loss, or the experience of loss in terms of their physical freedom to live their lives as they choose, has been transmuted and used to redefine themselves and to find a new kind of subjectivity.

The key question, "why private and personal tales of true experiences of growing up Muslim and female in locations outside Western skies have preoccupied public and global discourse in unprecedented ways in recent years," still remains. The first reason is that these tales of women's survival and their overcoming of insurmountable odds resonate for all women battling against patriarchal structures around the globe. Despite the experiences of loss they express, they also carry a life-affirming message. The desire to read this "life-affirming literature" or view the "life-affirming film"—both the literature and films either directly or indirectly also affirm Western humanistic values, particularly the values of Western feminism—has increased exponentially with the escalation of the war on terror after 9/11. Another reason for this desire to know the Other, especially the Iranian female Other, results from the Other's rejection of the West. Iran, in the aftermath of the 1979 Islamist Revolution, becomes a geographical and cultural space that escapes comprehension and provides no reasonable (at least to the Western scholar) explanation for its rejection of Western modernity. Iranian feminist scholar Parvin Paidar discusses how different feminist movements in Iran had been active since before the Shah's regime and had functioned as secular organizations prior to the 1970s: "Iranian Feminism was essentially secular until the rise of Shi'i modernism in the 1970s. It was only then, that the new trend of Islamist feminism (gender activism within an Islamic framework), joined other feminisms in Iran."[15] Feminist movements in Iran during the reign of the two shahs (Reza Shah Pahlavi and his son), as well as after the Revolution, were closely linked to nationalism. During the two Pahlavi reigns, they gained ground primarily in the secular realm; and while the forced modernization of the Pahlavi regimes provided educational and career opportunities for women in the public sector, it did little to change the status of women's rights within the family. Also, during the early years of the 20th century, the feminist movements in Iran were brought under greater state control than ever before. Following the Revolution, the link to nationalism remained crucial; however, nationalism as a

mobilizing force was transformed and redefined. The state attempted this by constructing nationalism as synonymous with anti-imperialism on the one hand, and replacing nationalism with Islam as the mass mobilization force on the other.[16]

The rejection of Western culture and values following the 1979 Iranian Revolution became part of the rallying force for the establishment of a theocratic Islamist regime. This puzzling turn of events suddenly made Iran less accessible to the West, both physically and imaginatively. So, when President George W. Bush declared Iran to be one of the "Axis of Evil" powers post-9/11, it furthered the sense of incomprehension in the West of this culture and community, leaving the West wondering, "Why do they hate us?" Seeking an answer to this question, many in the West have turned to Iranian narratives and films from Iran and the Iranian diaspora as well as to works from other countries previously invisible to the West. Hence, in the last few years we have seen a rise in the number of literary works and films published in the West that are not only from Iran but also from countries like Afghanistan, Bosnia, Turkey, and North Korea, among others.[17]

The writers and directors from these countries have begun to draw attention internationally at this juncture in history partly because their voices have occupied subaltern positions and we are now in an era when subaltern voices are not only being listened to but are being urged to speak out. The early work of the Subaltern Studies Group and in particular Gayatri Spivak's account of the subaltern and his/her speech during the colonial period in India and postindependence suggests that most topics were foreclosed from being speaking subjects.[18] Maki Kimura, writing on the Korean comfort woman debates, perceives of narrative as a site of subject construction. Many women who had survived the Korean-Japanese war as comfort women and who gave their testimonies soon after went unheard, or their tales were of little interest to the public at the time. It was only after a call to tell their stories in the 1990s that their voices were heard, giving them subjectivity and agency. Kimura, citing Judith Butler's argument, itself based on Louis Althusser's theory of interpellation, concludes that in order to become subjects and to be recognized, individuals have to be "hailed" by and submitted to the dominant ideology. Since this "hailing" into speech also confers subjectivity, it can be deduced that the subject is constituted by and within discourse—a discourse comprised of "a prior and authoritative set of practices" that precedes and conditions the moment of this action of speech. In this view of the subject's constitution in and through speech, Kimura sees the possibilities for an international and global collaboration that can help enhance the awareness of women's human rights within international institutions.[19] Along a similar vein, post-9/11 anxieties have led to a public and academic discourse that has recognized subaltern voices from Iran and other Islamic countries and in essence "hailed" them into speech. Iranian women are being called upon by the global public to voice their experiences. And, as Nahai says, "Iranian women are writing, I imagine, because they can,"[20] implying that they can write now that they have something to say that is of interest to the rest of the world and that they can do so because the opportunities to have their say have suddenly opened up.

This opening up of opportunities to speak, to represent in narrative and film her cultural and political experience, also places the subaltern woman in the role of "native informant" and authenticates her experience as the "real" truth tale and not another colonialist Orientalist representation of the Other culture and regime. What is still problematic is that, while the subaltern in this case has spoken, the subaltern's voice, in so far as it is heard in the West, has been "hailed" into speech more in response to publishing trends in the West driven primarily by current events that have generated the fear and paranoia evidenced in the rhetoric of the war on terrorism. So, while many of these narratives express individual responses to a national and secular situation, their manipulation in literary, media, and governmental interpretations points either to their compliance with or their co-option for official global and political critiques of not just the current Iranian government but also Iranian culture, and by extension all Muslim culture in general, thus proving that this discourse, in Said's terms, is vested in "some authority or power." It is the native informant aspect of these memoirs that makes them so desirable and marketable. While this nativist position attests to the veracity of these Iranian women's narratives, at the same time it makes them vulnerable to manipulation.

The age and rhetoric of colonialist and Orientalist discourses and narratives may be over, but a new kind of Orientalist discourse surrounding the publication and translation process, media coverage, reviews, and debates over these "telling tales" of the native informant, tales that can be manipulated and used to do the work of the earlier Orientalist narratives, has come into being. When the native informant's narrative speaks out against the fundamentalist antihumanistic ideals of the native culture, just as the old colonialist and Orientalist narratives did, the native informant's narrative, like the old colonialist narratives, valorizes values of Western humanism. The us/them dialectic is reinstated with even greater vigor and force because this time it is now the insider voice of the female subaltern of the native culture that decries the native regime and makes the case for the superiority of Western values and culture. Gayatri Spivak, along with Homi Bhabha, argues that the project of imperialism has been to transform the radically Other into the domesticated Other in a way that consolidates the Western self.[21] The new Orientalist discourse, by being hailed into speech and being celebrated (often indiscriminately and uncritically) through the lens of universal feminism, transforms what otherwise is the speech of the radically Other into a managed domesticated product produced by what can be termed the protégé and prodigy of Western feminism.

Hamid Dabashi sees a connection between narratives by "native informers" and President George W. Bush's empire-building initiatives through the rhetoric of the war on terrorism. Citing a number of political historians from Eric Hobsbawn, V. G. Kiernan, Michael Hardt and Antonio Negri, Chalmers Johnson, Michael Mann, and Robert D. Kaplan, Dabashi holds that the United States, especially post -9/11, was undergoing a form of *collective amnesia* and needed to fabricate instantaneous enemies and moving targets, one on the trail of the other, [which] thus became the principal *modus operandi* of the virtual empire. An empire lacking, in fact requiring an absence of, long term memory, and banking heavily on the intensity of short term memories that last only for about one to two years—one to two wars per one presidential election.[22]

Arguing that this act of collective amnesia is accompanied by selective amnesia, he finds evidence of this selective amnesia in the increasing body of memoirs by people from Islamic backgrounds that ever since the commencement of the United States' war on terrorism has flooded the U.S. market.[23] This body of literature, perhaps best represented by Azar Nafisi's *Reading Lolita in Tehran* (2003), ordinarily points to legitimate concerns about the plight of Muslim women in the Islamic world and yet "puts the predicament squarely at the service of the US ideological psy-op, militarily stipulated in the US global warmongering."[24] Dabashi recognizes how Nafisi's memoir plays a key role in this global scenario as a form of an insider narrative. Claiming that *Reading Lolita* coincides with the most belligerent period in recent U.S. history, he finds that

> the text has assumed a proverbial significance in the manner in which native informers turned comprador intellectuals serve a crucial function in facilitating public consent to imperial hubris. With one strike, Azar Nafisi has achieved three simultaneous objectives: (1) systematically and unfailingly denigrating an entire culture of resistance to a history of savage colonialism; (2) doing so by blatantly advancing the presumed cultural foregrounding of a predatory empire; and (3) while at the very same time catering to the most retrograde and reactionary forces within the United States, waging an all out war against a pride of place by various immigrant communities and racialised minorities seeking curricular recognition on university campuses and in the American society at large.[25]

Dabashi's criticism here further emphasizes that any discourse about Islamic cultures and the literary, media, and filmic documents addressing Islam and Islamic societies is invested in some sort of power and authority. The discourse surrounding Nafisi's memoir and its reception in the West reflected in the reviews and interviews, as well as its rapid inclusion in university courses across the United States, speaks to how the memoir *and* the discourse surrounding it has functioned as a new kind of Orientalist discourse. The "native informant" position the memoir appears to occupy has been questioned by critics, even as the work is accepted widely as a "truth tale" of the reality of women's lives under the fundamentalist regime in Iran; and Nafisi's role as teacher and mentor to her young Iranian women students itself is seen as giving her an insider position of sorts. What is more problematic about the content of the work, however, is that the liberatory power of literature the book addresses rests primarily in examples of Western and American modernist novels, the majority of them having been written by "dead white males." Iran's rich literary tradition is completely overlooked, probably because the focus for Nafisi's women students and the memoir is on learning English and on accessing the West. The students, through this foreign language and literature, find a way to express their own desires and find a kind of subjectivity they are denied in their contemporary world. They are able to empathize with characters from alien cultures because of the universality of the human condition. In the process of valorizing the values of universal humanism, the memoir elides a more nuanced evaluation of individual cultural differences and ignores the rich literary and cultural history of Iran.

It is this factor of empathy that also makes the Western reader connect with works like *Reading Lolita*, for the book readily provokes empathy in its readers for the women presented in the text. Empathy for the plight of others is critical for furthering and improving global political and cultural connections, and a readership and audience that embraces literary and filmic works from cultures other than its own is more likely to promote global understanding and peace. Theresa Kulbaga, citing Nafisi's radio address on NPR, *This I Believe*, where Nafisi speaks about how "mysterious connections can be formed between people despite vast differences," points out that for Nafisi these "mysterious connections are forged through stories, specifically humanist narratives of individual triumph over tyranny" and though "Nafisi refers to actual people from Afghanistan, Iraq, Algeria, Rwanda, and North Korea," she uses the example of Huckleberry Finn to explain how it is empathy that allows Huck to see Jim as a human being instead of as a slave.[26] Nafisi's memoir, *Reading Lolita*, fulfills both the voyeuristic appetite for knowledge of the exotic Other in the West and the need for an Iranian woman to voice the experience of Iranian womanhood. The text, in its critique of the conditions under the fundamentalist regime in Iran, problematizes other autobiographical revelations by women from those countries and cultures that have acquired enigmatic and demonist symbolism in the wake of a rising fear around Islamic fundamentalism. The Western readers of Nafisi's memoir are able to empathize more readily with the women she represents because this readership, along with the women who take her classes in the 1980s and 1990s, sees in the works of Henry James, Jane Austen, and Vladimir Nabakov (all great books of the Western literary canon) the ideals of humanism. The cross-cultural empathy, first experienced by the Iranian women reading Western literature, is reciprocated by the empathy of the Western readers for the plight of these women. The question arises whether this empathy would be as readily possible were it not for the common shared experience of the Western literary greats. Nafisi's memoir's reign on the *New York Times* bestseller list beginning in September 2004 lasted for over 36 weeks. Also, as Kulbaga notes, the success of *Reading Lolita*, regardless of any debate over its veracity, suggests "the cultural triumph and powerful transnational appeal of feminism and women's human rights."[27]

The novel, however, has been critiqued by Iranian scholars (Bahramitash, Dabashi, Keshavarz, and Mottahedeh) for the accuracy of its "insider" position and its "mobilization of stereotypes about Islam in general."[28] For Kulbaga, the rhetoric surrounding Nafisi's memoir, however, is significantly more pertinent than these critiques because it "appeals to U.S. audiences by mobilizing fundamentally *nationalist* discourses and affective responses that position the United States as the geopolitical center of freedom, choice, feminist empowerment and human rights."[29] Kulbaga goes on to connect the call to empathy voiced by Nafisi, both in her radio address and through her memoir, with the tone of Oprah Winfrey's book club discussions, which like other contemporary book clubs offer members "pleasurable pedagogies of power and privilege."[30] In this context, the Iranian woman's narrative, like other narratives of triumph from different and difficult cultural landscapes, becomes a commodity to be devoured by the enlightened liberal Western reader who seeks to understand and empathize with the story of the distressed, disadvantaged female Other who overcomes her circumstances through self-determination and grit, much like the pioneer men and women of the Wild West. It is precisely because these narratives can be loosely mapped over the American West's most enduring tales of empowerment and colonization that they draw empathetic reactions, particularly from American readers. The patriarchal regime from which the narratives' heroines make their escape or to which they succumb functions as the elemental hurdle the heroines must overcome. The new Orientalist narrative reestablishes the power of the Occident with even greater emphasis because it is voiced now by the native informant herself, and the Occident is never directly implicated. Instead, it stands by offering moral support and a pat on the back to the subaltern for having validated the Occident's own long-held assumptions about the subaltern's culture and for having brought them out for view by the global public. In so doing, the Occident along with the subaltern narrative elides any real historical assessment of East-West relations. As Dabashi notes:

Nafisi's book is the *locus classicus* of the ideological foregrounding of the U.S. imperial domination at home and abroad in three simultaneous moves: (1) it banks on the collective amnesia of historical facts surrounding successive U.S. imperial moves for global domination—for paramount in *Reading Lolita in Tehran* is a conspicuous absence of the historical and a blatant white washing of the literary; (2) it exemplifies the systematic abuse of legitimate causes (in this case the unconscionable oppression of women living under Muslim laws) for illegitimate purposes; and (3) through the instrumentality of English literature, regarded and articulated by an "Oriental" woman who deliberately casts herself as a contemporary Sheherezade, it seeks to provoke the darkest corners of the Euro-American Oriental fantasies and thus neutralizes competing sites of cultural resistance to U.S. imperial designs both at home and abroad.[31]

The predominantly Western perspective in Nafisi's work, to some extent, accounts for the unmediated and unprecedented embrace of this memoir by not just Western audiences in general but also the U.S. government. Negar Mottahedeh and Hamid Dabashi have separately pointed to Nafisi's connections with U.S. leaders. Dabashi, particularly critical of Nafisi's memoir, finds it to be

> the most cogent contemporary case of yet another attempt at positing English literature yet again as a *modus operandi* of manufacturing transregional cultural consent to Euro-American global domination. The factual evidence of Azar Nafisi to the US leaders of the neo conservative movement and her systematic depreciation of Iranian culture, and by extension local and regional cultures of actual potential resistance to the US empire, glorifying instead a canonized inner sanctum for an iconic celebration of "Western Literature," are additional factors in placing her squarely at the service of the predatory US empire—the service delivered via the most cliché-ridden invocation of the most retrograde Oriental fantasies of her readers in the United States and Europe.[32]

Ironically, while Nafisi's memoir invokes "the most retrograde Oriental fantasies of her readers," the Western classics that her students avidly devour invoke the Occidental fantasies of Nafisi's students. So, on the one hand *Reading Lolita* stimulates a new Orientalist discourse in the West that allows its readers, both popular and academic, to indulge their latent fantasies of the Other as immanent and desiring and needing liberation. This liberation becomes possible only abstractly through the powerful spell of the Western literary canon. On the other hand, *Reading Lolita* also participates in the new Orientalist discourse in its valorization of Western culture and literature that becomes doubly convincing in the obvious absence of positive examples of Iranian literature and culture, as Dabashi has so emphatically decried.

Not only have Iranian women been telling their personal and national stories, they have also taken them to the screen and been directing films that have fearlessly portrayed the realities of life under cultural and political oppression. The Islamist regime's destruction of over 180 theaters during the Revolution was incurred because the theaters were perceived as morally corrupting Iranian society with Western propaganda. This same sentiment accounts for the film industry in general coming under greater scrutiny with the regime's attempt at establishing an Islamic nationalist cinema. New censorship codes and regulations about pre- and postproduction script approval, review of films prior to release, screening permits, and so on, were instituted. Iranian women directors have managed to make films under these more difficult circumstances, and they carry out an active role in positions of social, political, and economic importance within the arts and continue to achieve international acclaim. Some of the more significant women directors who have emerged during this period have made films that are radically feminist and also culturally authentic in expressing an Iranian feminism rather than an imported brand of universal humanism. Sheri Whatley, addressing the fearless role taken by Iranian women directors, draws attention to the work of several women directors, among them Tahmineh Milani, Manijeh Hekma, Samira Makhmalbaf, Maryam Shariar, Rakshan Bani-Etemad, and Puran Derakhshandeh.[33] Many of the films made by these women have brought attention to a variety of social issues and have actually resulted in improving some of the conditions for women. Many of these portrayals highlight the active roles women have taken in contemporary Iranian life while still wearing the *hijab* and conducting themselves within the laws of the current fundamentalist regime. One portrayal, among many, is a film by Tahmineh Milani, *The Hidden Half*, in which a *hijab*-wearing wife and mother recalls her radical participation along with other militant university students, both men and women, in the Iranian Revolution (participation undertaken while she was also wearing a *hijab*). The film's unflinching portrayal of this troublesome period in Iranian history aside, the traditional and the modern ways of life are presented in the film as coexisting naturally. Tahmineh Milani was arrested for making *The Hidden Half*, a politically radical film; although released, she still faces charges that could result in a death penalty if convicted. *The Circle* and *Offside*, two films by male directors, also present women's experience in multifaceted terms. *Offside* addresses a young female teen's interest in soccer, a sport from whose public matches women were barred, and follows her attempts along with the help of some male teens to sneak into the stadium to watch one of the most significant soccer wins for Iran. Although many of these films by Iranian women and men are readily available in the West, through Iranianmovies. com and other distributors, they are not as widely seen or celebrated as a more recent film nominated for an Oscar in the Foreign Film category in 2008, *Persepolis*, by Marjane Satrapi made with her French co-director Vincent Parronaud.

Since the release of Satrapi's animated film version of her graphic novel series named for its collected republication in 2004, *The Complete Persepolis*,[34] Satrapi's work with both the graphic novel and the animated film has drawn much critical acclaim and attention and can be viewed as one of the "hailed" subaltern voices. Part of the appeal of Satrapi's work, as Naghibi and O'Malley point out, has to do with the fact that "there is currently in the West a greater interest in hearing from a member of the axis of evil, especially in an autobiographical form that promises to disclose the intimate secrets of an exotic other."[35] Naghibi and O'Malley place Satrapi's novel, *Persepolis,* within the new wave of autobiographical writing by Iranian women writers post the 1979 Iranian Revolution.[36]

First-time readers and audiences of Satrapi's work are struck by how easily the reader enters the world she creates because it seems so familiar. Iranian Americans, male and female, respond to her expatriate experiences and find in her works a realization of their own. Most critics too, citing the universality of her characters and their feelings, marvel at how she has made Iranian culture so readily accessible to Western audiences. They praise her feminism and how her books and film speak to women's issues and female subjectivity globally. The rave reviews of *Persepolis*, a story that ostensibly is the experience of the "radical Other," all stress its *accessibility* and *universality*. I find in this attempt to domesticate by homogenizing and making the radical other "Western," not just a paternalistic impulse on the part of Western media, but something integral to Satrapi's own vision of her experience as a European cosmopolitan in much the same way that Nafisi's impulse operates to find a liberating experience for her Iranian women students only in the Western literary canon. Even the production history of Satrapi's film, with its culturally European and American cast, its use of the French language, its graphic style reminiscent of such earlier French graphics as the Madeleine series, all make this a European domesticated product or at best a transnational global product, rather than a product created by one who is "radically Other."[37] All the diversity and multiculturality (or lack thereof) the film incorporates makes the film accessible and entertaining globally, but it must not be perceived, as it has been in several reviews, as representational of *the* Iranian woman's experience, for it happens to be a very particular experience and *an* Iranian woman's experience—the Iranian woman in question being a cosmopolitan upper-class Western-educated and relatively well-off woman from an aristocratic Iranian family. Just as all memoirs document particular experiences, Satrapi's is no exception; Satrapi herself should not be expected to provide the quintessential Iranian woman's tale, nor is that her intent. It is important, however, to acknowledge how the discourse around her books and the film, especially in Western academic circles and the media, has embraced these works as *true* (and for some, *only*) representations of life in Iran during the country's turbulent times and to be aware that other perspectives may tell somewhat different tales and present quite different perspectives.

What is troubling about the discourse around Nafisi's and Satrapi's work is that alternative or different perspectives from theirs, abundant in written memoirs and films produced by other Iranian women, are rarely brought into dialogue with them. The work of some of the women writers and directors who present varying perspectives on Iranian women's experiences has received some recognition through awards and exhibitions but has not gained the same level of popular media and academic attention as the work of Nafisi and Satrapi. Shirin Neshat's art gallery installations and accompanying films, most produced in New York and outside Iran, have garnered a following in the art world globally. Her work is unique for the ways in which she shifts between mediums from photography to video and also in the way her works reflect the trauma of her own personal displacement. In her installations and videos, "she detects and evokes the powers of suppressed passions; dignity amidst submission, liberation amidst restriction, and transgression amidst taboo."[38] Neshat's photographs and videos critically characterize the veiling practices of women in the urban space that at the same time express a sense of power inherent in her subjects and a respect in the way she presents them. Even though veiled, her women express spirituality, power, and strength belied by the very practice of veiling. Dabashi characterizes Neshat as "a revolution, a war," and finds that "defining the visual 'virility' of Shirin Neshat's femininity is a fragmented subjectivity now beyond her or anybody's else's control."[39] Neshat's work pits the colonial and the patriarchal against each other and deploys the masculine colonial gaze against the feminine veiled Oriental's gaze. Neshat's work portrays Iranian women's experiences through a lens that incorporates a feminism that shares a vision with global feminism while also representing traditional Iranian and Islamic cultural practices that embody a dignity and power not as readily visible in the work of Nafisi and Satrapi. Neshat's vision and critique shares more with the vision found in the films of Milani and Makmalbaf and in the work of other, lesser-known women directors and memoirists in presenting Iranian women's lives under the fundamentalist regime that, while critiquing the political condition, recognizes the dualistic nature of traditional and religious customs. In these works, the influence of Western feminism and ideology is used and applied in a way that does not deny or negate the cultural authenticity of Islamic culture of the women being portrayed. As a result, these works do not participate in the new Orientalist discourse and may be perceived as more authentic and possibly closer to being the "truth tales" of Iranian womanhood. They preserve a cultural and particular authenticity of individual women whether from the city, the village, or the university, presenting the vulnerable and the strong, the militant and the obediently passive, thereby giving voice to the diversity and individuality of the experiences of women's lives on their own terms without reference to Western notions of women's experiences and a continued invocation of universalism.

While several of these women are being recognized in academic writing, their work has not appeared quite as readily on booklists of college courses and public library reading groups, nor have their films become even half as popular as Satrapi's *Persepolis*. Neshat's work is better known partly because of the many genres it crosses over—from art and photography installations to literature and video and even a type of performance. Film as a medium allows for easier accessibility, but so far only diasporic Iranians and eclectic foreign film enthusiasts have an interest in these films, with the exception of a few Iranian film courses at select universities. The fact that many extremely well-made and powerful films and several incisive memoirs have missed the radar of Western readers and the work of the same celebrated few is repeatedly invoked as representative of Iranian women's experiences reflects the myopic and self-involved character of current concerns about the West's relationship with Iran and Islamic cultures and also speaks to the continuation of Orientalist attitudes in the West. The power of the press, the audiences at Nahai's book readings, university course selections, library reading groups, all contribute to the production of the new Orientalist discourse by celebrating only those "truth tales" that reflect a universalist world view privileged in the West.

APPENDIX

List of selected Iranian women's memoirs and novels, poetry, drama, graphic novels, and anthologies published in the West in recent years.

MEMOIRS AND NOVELS

Asayesh, Gelareh. *Saffron Sky: A Life between Iran and America*. Boston: Beacon Press, 1999.

Bahrampour, Tara. *To See and See Again: A Life in Iran and America*. New York: Farrar, Straus, and Giroux, 1999.

Dumas, Firoozeh. *Funny in Farsi: A Memoir of Growing Up Iranian in America*. New York: Villard, 2003.

Dumas, Firoozeh. *Laughing without an Accent: Adventures of an Iranian American at Home and Abroad.* New York: Villard, 2008.

Hakakian, Roya. *Journey from the Land of No: A Girlhood Caught in Revolutionary Iran.* New York: New Rivers Press, 2004.

Keshavarz, Fatemeh. *Jasmine and Stars: Reading More than Lolita in Tehran.* Chapel Hill: University of North Carolina Press, 2007.

Latifi, Afschineh. *Even after All This Time: A Story of Love, Revolution, and Leaving Iran.* New York: HarperCollins, 2005.

Moaveni, Azedeh. *Lipstick Jihad: A Memoir of Growing Up Iranian in America and American in Iran.* New York: Public Affairs, 2005.

Moaveni, Azedeh., and Shirin Ebadi. *Iran Awakening: A Memoir of Revolution and Hope.* New York: Random House, 2006.

Moshiri, Farnoosh. *Against Gravity.* New York: Penguin, 2006.

Moshiri, Farnoosh. *At the Wall of the Almighty.* New York: Interlink Publishing, 1999.

Moshiri, Farnoosh. *The Bathhouse.* Boston: Beacon Press, 2003.

Moshiri, Farnoosh. *The Crazy Dervish and the Pomegranate Tree: A Mystic Tale.* Seattle: Black Heron, 2004.

Nafisi, Azar. *Honeymoon in Tehran.* New York: Random House, 2009.

Nafisi, Azar. *Reading Lolita in Tehran: A Memoir in Books.* New York: Random House, 2003.

Nahai, Gina. *Caspian Sea.* New York: MacAdam Cage, 2007.

Nahai, Gina. *Cry of the Peacock.* New York: Crown, 1991.

Nahai, Gina. *Moonlight on the Avenue of Faith.* New York: Crown, 1999.

POETRY

Atefat-Peckam, Susan. *That Kind of Sleep.* New York: Coffee House Press, 2001.

Atefat-Peckam, Susan. *The Soul Lives There, in the Silent Breath.* New York: Coffee House Press, 2006.

Hakakian, Roya. *For the Sake of Water.* (in Persian) Los Angeles: Intisharat Tasvir, 1993.

Kalaam, Niloofar. *In Relation.* Toronto: Lyrical Myrical Press, 2005.

Khalvati, Mimi. *Entries on Light.* Manchester, UK: Carcanet Press, 1997.

Khalvati, Mimi. *In White Ink.* Manchester, UK: Carcanet Press, 1991.

Khalvati, Mimi. *Mirrorwork.* Manchester, UK: Carcanet Press, 1995.

Khalvati, Mimi. *Selected Poems.* Manchester, UK: Carcanet Press, 2000.

Khalvati, Mimi. *The Chine.* Manchester, UK: Carcanet Press, 2002.

Wolpe, Sholeh. *The Scar Saloon.* Granada Hills, CA: Red Hen Press, 2004.

Zandvakili, Katayoon. *Deer Table Legs.* Athens, GA: University of Georgia Press, 1998.

DRAMA

Dowlatshahi, Layla. *Joys of Lipstick*. Reading at the Lark Play Development Center.

Dowlatshahi, Layla. *Waiting Room*. Staged at the Annenberg Studio Theater of the University of Pennsylvania.

GRAPHIC NOVELS

Satrapi, Marjane. *Chicken with Plums*. London: Jonathan Cape, 2006.

Satrapi, Marjane. *The Complete Persepolis*. New York: Pantheon Books, 2007.

Satrapi, Marjane. *Embroideries*. New York: Pantheon Books, 2005.

ANTHOLOGIES

Karim, Persis M. *Let Me Tell You Where I've Been: New Writing by Women of the Iranian Diaspora*. Fayetteville: University of Arkansas Press, 2006.

Mozaffari, Nahid, and Ahmad Karimi Hakkak. *Strange Times, My Dear: The PEN Anthology of Iranian Literature*. New York: Arcade Publishing, 2005.

NOTES

1. Gina Barkhodar Nahai, "So What's with All the Iranian Memoirs? An Original Tries to Explain," *Publishers Weekly*, November 26, 2007, 58.

2. Ibid.

3. Sankaran Krishna, *Globalization and Postcolonialism: Hegemony and Resistance in the Twenty-first Century* (New York: Rowan and Littlefield, 2009), 63.

4. Edward Said, *Covering Islam: How the Media and the Experts Determine How We See the Rest of the World* (New York: Pantheon Books, 1981), xvii–xviii.

5. Edward Said, *Orientalism* (New York: Pantheon Books, 1978), 6.

6. Krishna, *Globalization and Postcolonialism,* 75.

7. Persis M. Karim, ed., *Let Me Tell You Where I've Been: New Writing by Women in the Iranian Diaspora* (Fayetteville: University of Arkansas Press, 2006), xxiv. The title of Karim's collection is telling in its implication of secrets and private stories it promises to reveal. The title suggests a personal one-on-one relationship between the memoirist and the reader, so the telling of where the memoirist has been becomes a secret shared, a conversation between two women. The world at large is not invoked except in the telling of experiences occurring in diasporic spaces traveled by the memoirist.

8. Negar Mottahedeh, "New Iranian Cinema: 1982–Present," in *Traditions in World Cinema*, ed. Linda Badley, R. Barton Palmer, and Steven Jay Schneider (New Brunswick, NJ: Rutgers University Press, 2006), 177.

9. Ibid., 176.

10. Karim, *Let Me Tell You Where I've Been*, xix.

11. Frantz Fanon's "Algeria Unveiled," in Frantz Fanon, *A Dying Colonialism*, trans. Haakon Chevalier (New York: Grove Press, 1967), addresses the power dynamics inherent in the act of veiling in his analysis of the Front de Libération Nationale's (FLN) tactics during their resistance to French rule in Algeria. This is another instance of how knowledge and power intertwine, for the resistance fighters played upon the Europeans' knowledge or lack thereof of Islamic practices in regard to women and were able to exploit it to their own advantage.

12. Krishna, *Globalization and Postcolonialism*, 74.

13. "The Internet remains a welcome mat for enemies seeking to take advantage," reported Paul Hearst on a news story regarding the dangers of cyber spies and Internet hackers on a CNN broadcast, April 9, 2009. The gist of this broadcast piece was that the Internet was another avenue through which such terrorist groups as Al Qaeda could damage economic, political, and societal structures in the West.

14. Malek Alloula's examination of the visual specularization of Algerian women in postcards during the 19th century in *The Colonial Harem* (Minneapolis: University of Minnesota Press, 1986) aptly points to issues of colonial desire for the exotic Other and the covert and overt power relationships embedded in the visual texts. Alloula's work is the most obvious example and analysis of the specularization of the Muslim female Other in the project of colonialism.

15. Parvin Paidar, "Feminism and Islam in Iran," in *Gendering the Middle East*, ed. Deniz Kandiyoti (Syracuse, NY: Syracuse University Press, 1996), 57.

16. Ibid., 58.

17. From Afghanistan, Khaled Hosseini's *The Kite Runner* (2005) and *A Thousand Splendid Suns* (2007), the former having touched the American imagination in its harking back to 19th-century immigrant experiences of the American dream. Hosseini's text naturalizes his story within the context of American literary history, thereby making an otherwise inaccessible culture accessible. Also, U.S. interest in Afghanistan as the habitat of Al Qaeda and the Taliban added to the West's desire to voyeuristically consume this experience. The plotline of child abuse and possible homosexuality adds to this voyeurism and feeds the specularistic desire to "know" the cultural Other and its "transgressive" and hence exotic behaviors. *The Kite Runner* resonated so much with Western audiences that it became required reading for first-year college students at Bowling Green State University in Ohio in Freshmen Bowling Green Experience courses and as well as made it on the reading lists of several middle-American small-town public library reading groups. In the fall of 2006, a regional public library invited me to present a talk and lead book discussions on

Hosseini's second novel (they had already devoured the first). I was invited again in spring and fall of 2008 to talk and lead discussions on two more works written by Muslim writers—*The Reluctant Fundamentalist* by Mohsin Ahmed (2007) and *The Complete Persepolis* (2007) by Marjane Satrapi. Clearly, the appetite for works by and about the Islamic world is growing; however, why and how this material is consumed and interpreted deserves further analysis.

18. Gayatri Spivak and Ranajit Guha, eds., *Selected Subaltern Studies* (Essays from 5 vols.) (New York: Oxford University Press, 1988); Gayatri Spivak, *A Critique of Postcolonial Reason* (Boston: Harvard University Press, 1999).

19. Maki Kimura, "Narrative as a Site of Subject Construction: The 'Comfort Woman' Debate," *Feminist Theory* 9, no. 1 (2008): 13.

20. Nahai, "So What's with All the Iranian Memoirs?" 58.

21. Gayatri Spivak, "Three Women's Texts and a Critique of Imperialism," *Critical Inquiry* 112 (1985): 253.

22. Hamid Dabashi, "Native Informers and the Making of the American Empire," *Al Ahram Weekly Online*, June 15, 2007, 2, http://weekly.ahram.org.eg/2006/797/special.htm.

23. For a selected list of Iranian women's writing, including memoirs and poetry, see the appendix to this chapter.

24. Dabashi, "Native Informers," 2.

25. Ibid., 3.

26. Theresa A. Kulbaga, "Pleasurable Pedagogies: Reading Lolita in Tehran and the Rhetoric of Empathy," *College English* 70, no. 5 (May 2008): 506.

27. Ibid., 507.

28. Ibid., 506.

29. Ibid., 508.

30. Ibid., 510. The experience of leading book discussions on *The Reluctant Fundamentalist* and *Persepolis* at a regional public library gave me the opportunity to experience in person this phenomenon of "pleasurable pedagogies of power and privilege." The responses from some of the group members completely elided the significant cultural and historical elements of the works and focused instead on how both Ahmed and Satrapi were lucky to have had the experience of living in the West outside their oppressive homelands. One group member, seriously offended by Ahmed's work for its critique of American consumerism, commented that Ahmed was ungrateful, given that he was lucky enough to have received an education in the United States. In courses on contemporary fiction, where I have taught both works to different types of student audiences, the responses have been slightly more open to different perspectives; however, there are a handful of students who express a similar sense of power and privilege. The sum of the attitudes to both works has been

that the cultures of both writers are oppressive and cruel and life in Iran and Pakistan is unimaginable and to be feared.

31. Dabashi, "Native Informers," 4.

32. Ibid., 5.

33. Sheri Whatley, "Iranian Women Film Directors: A Clever Activism," *International*, March-April 2003, 31–32. Tahmineh Milani's films include *The Hidden Half, Two Women, The Legend of a Sigh, The Children of Divorce*, and *Cease Fire*; Manijeh Hekma's *The Day I Became a Woman*; Samira Makhmalbaf's *The Apple, Blackboards*, and *At Five in the Afternoon*; Maryam Shariar's *Daughters of the Sun*; Rakshan Bani-Etemad's *Under the Skin of the City, Narges, The May Lady, The Blue Veined*, and *Our Times*; and Puran Derakhshandeh's *Candle in the Wind, Love across Frontiers, Lost Time*, and *The Small Bird of Happiness*.

34. The Persepolis series, originally published in French in France as four separate volumes in 2000 and 2001, and the English-language publication in two volumes in 2003 and 2004 are the most well known, but her shorter and less political work, *Embroideries*, also speaks to women of all cultures. The graphic novel form has historically been conducive to autobiographical and semiautobiographical writing and graphic art, with some successful examples being Art Spiegelman's *Maus I* and *Maus II* and Joe Sacco's journals of his travels in Bosnia and Palestine.

35. Nima Naghibi and Andrew O'Malley, "Estranging the Familiar: 'East' and 'West' in Satrapi's *Persepolis*," in *English Studies in Canada* 31, no. 2–3 (2005): 225.

36. Nima Naghibi and Andrew O'Malley list some of the autobiographies by Iranian women: Tara Bahrampour (*To See and See Again: A Life in Iran and America*, 2000), Gelareh Assayesh (*Saffron Sky: A Life between Iran and America*, 2002), Firoozeh Dumas (*Funny in Farsi: A Memoir of Growing Up Iranian in America*, 2003), Azar Nafisi (*Reading Lolita in Tehran: A Memoir in Books*, 2003), Roya Hakakian (*Journey from the Land of No: A Girlhood Caught in Revolutionary Iran*, 2004), and Azadeh Moaveni (*Lipstick Jihad: A Memoir of Growing Up Iranian in America and American in Iran*, 2005). Also, a second memoir by Azar Nafisi, *Honeymoon in Tehran*, was published in 2009.

37. The diasporic nature of this film is further universalized or diasporized, or diversified, or domesticated within a European-Western context despite the fact that the story is about a radical Iranian experience. It is written and produced in France by a graphic and film production team made up of French, English, and American artists and technicians; the language is French; the music, American, Austrian, French, and English; the actors, French, Spanish, and English. The English-dubbed version, which includes Sean Penn and Iggy Pop, further homogenizes the film for Western and American audiences. In

fact, there is very little attributable to Iranian influences other than that the story is Iranian and one of its directors, who is the author and inspiration behind the entire production, is also Iranian. It is a global international film as much as or as little as it is an Iranian film.

38. Sherri Geldin, in Shirin Neshat, Bill Horrigan, and Sherri Geldin, *Shirin Neshat: Two Installations* (Columbus, OH: Wexner Center for the Arts, 2000), 4.

39. Shirin Neshat, Francisco Bonami, Hamid Dabashi, and Octavia Zaya, *Women of Allah* (Torino, Italy: Marco Noire, Editore, 1997), 7.

PART V

Women, Worldview, and Religious Practice

CHAPTER 12

Religious Practice and Worldview of Muslim Women in Western Europe

Kari Vogt

The presence of Islam in Western Europe has been strongly determined by immigration flows from the Muslim world that started around the 1950s. Thus, religious practices, commitments, and worldviews of Muslim women should be seen in the broader political and social context of decolonization and specific economic and political choices made by European countries during times of economic growth or decline.[1]

Islam is now the second-largest religion in Western Europe. Reliable statistics are still lacking, however, and the exact size and composition of its Muslim population is still unknown, but believed to be between 15 million and 20 million.[2] Large numbers of Muslims in such countries as France and Britain have become full citizens while their families have lived there for two or three generations. The experiences and views of these citizens are often quite distinct from those of the newcomers who arrived in Europe as refugees in times of political crisis and upheaval in their countries of origin. This is one of the reasons why a mosaïc of different trends and attitudes to social, moral, and religious questions is the main characteristic of Europe's Muslim communities.

The feminization of migration began relatively late. When European countries started to restrict their immigration policies because of the global economic crisis of the early 1970s, large groups of male immigrants who were already in Europe decided to settle for good and bring their families over. This increase and diversification of the Muslim population put a strain on the welfare systems of European societies with rising demands concerning state schooling, social housing, and health care.

The population of Muslim women living in Western Europe naturally reflects the variety of the broader Muslim population. Belonging to manifold traditions within Islam, they have quite distinct backgrounds in terms of ethnicity, culture, language, nationality, and personal history. When describing women's religious practice, their understanding of Islam, intellectual interpretation, and emotional commitment to Islamic precepts, we should keep this diversity in mind.

Since the mid-1980s, different categories of women's groups, networks, and associations have become increasingly visible, not only among Muslims themselves but also in society at large. Public debates on a variety of issues, among them forced marriages, Islamic divorce practices, and polygamy, actually have prompted a number of Muslim women to engage in the public sphere and to establish groups and associations to support and represent their community.

One of the more contentious issues remains the Islamic dress code; especially the headscarf. Since the mid-1990s, exclusion of women and girls from schools—mainly in France—or from jobs has led to multiple support groups. How the hijab question was handled will remain a long-term issue for debates and initiatives. Especially after France passed the law forbidding the wearing of the hijab in 2003, the issue has grown in symbolic importance both within and outside Muslim communities.

Religious practice is, of course, a wide category, and the private home has traditionally been defined as a women's domain for prayer and religious celebrations. In this respect, today a noticeable development is taking place in Europe, where also the local mosque has become an important arena for women's activities.[3]

MOSQUE ACTIVITIES: SUNNI AND SHI'A

In many instances, the mosque has taken on new importance in the Western context as the place where women can meet regularly with others who share the same faith, language, and culture. Increasingly, mosque activities seem to reflect a recent, slowly growing trend toward solidifying a collective Muslim identity in the public domain, as the mosque has become the main center for community functions and religious instruction for all: men, women, and children. Teaching activities in the local mosques usually include girls' Qur'an classes, which are quite often, at least at the basic level, organized and carried out by women. Some mosques, for example, certain South Asian Deobandi and most Tablighi-oriented mosques, remain closed to women. However, women belonging to these circles have found other venues for their religious and social lives.

Informal women's groups in many mosques are linked by a gender-segregated participation in the annual religious festivals and rituals. Meeting regularly throughout the year in the women's section of the mosque, they provide *iftar* [food for breaking the fast] for women during Ramadan, arrange *mawlid* celebrations on the Prophet's birthday, and sometimes even organize *hajj* or pilgrimage groups for women. At times they also perform particular rituals during Ramadan or on occasion of a death, for example, the *Qur'an-khwani*, the recitation of the whole Qur'an, or the *aqiqa* (hair-shaving) ritual for a newborn child. These rituals are especially performed in South Asian Brelwi mosques. *Mawlids* are held during the entire Muslim calendrical month of Rabi al-Awwal and also on such auspicious occasions as when moving into a new house or at family events. These celebrations, very popular among Muslims with a South Asian background, are predominantly a women's tradition. Originally, these rituals took place in the homes; but with increasing mosque activities, they are now taking place at the mosque as well as in the home. This development also concerns *dhikrs* (repetitive chants) performed by members of Sufi groups or by communities that recommend *dhikr* as an optional part of their devotional practice.[4]

In the Shi'a communities, women's groups meet on a regular basis in private homes during the month of Muharram for *majlis-e aza*, mourning assemblies. Muharram activities in the women's section of the *hosainiyeh*, or mosque, are often extensive and include recitation of religious poetry and preaching by the women themselves. When organizing traditional ritual activities, these groups had to take into account their new environment and long-distance traveling. Overcoming obstacles women faced in fulfilling their wish to participate and perform forced them to develop new social networks and organizing skills. First-generation immigrants seem to be the most dedicated participants in these informal groups. While second- and third-generation women often credit their mosque experience with learning the basics of Islam, some of them leave their parents' experience of Islam in search of more "authentic" and "pure" forms of belief and practice. In search of alternative teachings, they may look for another mosque community or find a personal mentor. Several Sufi shaykhs based in the Middle East, in Turkey, and in South Asia have male and female murids in Western Europe and provide spiritual and other forms of guidance by e-mail or on the phone.

Local mosques also provide room for women's groups to initiate new social and cultural activities, at time even allowing new rituals. Especially younger women rally around such mosques. For example, the largest Arab mosque in Oslo, Norway (1,688 members in 2006), had four women's groups that each organized courses for women and girls: one on *tajwid*, Qur'anic recitation; one on *tafsir*, explanation of the Qur'an; and an art class. The fourth group organized lectures on religious and cultural topics, which were open to mixed audiences of men and women, Muslims and non-Muslims.

Such activities, when well organized, also attract women from mosques of different ideological and ethnic affiliations and may thereby help build bridges between different communities. These groups also occasionally initiate and encourage innovative participation in traditional rituals. For example, since 1990, in the same Arab mosque in Oslo, women follow the men's Id prayer in a separate room. This particular ceremony is attractive to Turkish and Pakistani women and draws women from some African mosques as well.

Converts to Islam often play a central role in women's mosque-related activities; probably a majority of European converts to Islam are women, and some of them bring organizational skills into the community and encourage those born as Muslims to engage in new activities.[5] These local activities can easily be combined with membership in women's associations outside a particular mosque, and active women often become members of autonomous Muslim women's associations. Well known are the activities of An-Nisa Society, founded in 1985, headquartered in London and with related groups in Bradford and Birmingham. An-Nisa Society provides a range of services not provided by the larger society or by male-dominated Muslim associations or mosque groups. Their activities include social work (counseling, providing information concerning the rights of women, etc.); at the same time, they also promote cultural activities like art exhibitions, encouraging women's creative and artistic abilities.

A number of mosques are affiliated with specific Islamic movements and international organizations that have a more traditional approach to women's questions. Women belonging to these movements, among them the Jamaat-i Tabligh, organize devotional practices at their homes. Others such as those affiliated with the Pakistani Minhaj ul-Qur'an or the Turkish Milli Görüs will use the women's quarters in their respective mosques, or they reserve the use of a mosque, as is the case among the Turkish Sulaymancis.[6]

The Jamaat-i Tabligh, founded in British India in the late 1920s, recruits mainly from the South Asian and Arab communities, particularly Moroccan, and has established preaching networks and mosques throughout the world. Although women are expected to conform to strict rules of modesty and seclusion, those married to active Tabligh members are often encouraged to engage in *da'wa* (calling to the faith) activities as long as they do not mix with unrelated men. In Norway, women's *jama'ats* (congregations) gather in small preaching groups of two to four women, addressing Muslim women in their neighborhood. As the Tabligh movement mainly focuses on devotional practice, "an arena where women and men are, fundamentally, on the same ground,"[7] the Tablighis remain open to a certain degree to women's ritual activities. Wives of active members of the Tabligh can travel with their husbands and organize parallel gatherings for women.

Several associations are linked to one particular ethnic or linguistic community. The Pakistani Idara Minhaj ul-Qur'an, founded in the 1980s in Lahore, Pakistan, has established branches in several European countries. Idara has succeeded in recruiting a number of followers from Pakistani communities. In particular in Denmark and Norway, mosque-related activities of Idara's women's groups are centered on *dhikr* as well as on regular gatherings during which social, legal, and medical instructions are given by educated women members who are working as medical doctors or teachers.

The Turkish Milli Görüs, as well as the Sulaymancis, have women's branches that organize both religious education and devotional activities; they also, at least to some extent, provide social aid to Turkish women and to families in need. The Sulaymancis offer an interesting example of a traditional, hierarchical, and Sufi-oriented organization with an active female branch that is led by a hierarchy of women who organize devotional and teaching activities. At their headquarters in Cologne, Germany, the women's house is spacious and well kept, receiving girls for religious instruction from the Turkish community for the weekend. The girls also participate in devotional activities, mainly *dhikr*-meetings, twice a day, and receive spiritual guidance from their female teachers. The ideal, both for men and women, is to realize the *imitatio muhammadi* (emulation of Muhammad). A recent study of the female branch of the Sulaymancis also indicates that "these women constantly make *suhbat* [(spiritual) conversation] among themselves, which is something the men are not doing habitually. This means that whenever they have a moment of time together, while waiting in line for classes to begin, these women choose a verse from the Qur'an and apply its content to their own situation."[8]

The Sulaymanci women's centers are now established in numerous cities and smaller towns in Western Europe, where the female teachers can also function as preachers.[9] These communities include different Sufi networks where women organize *dhikr*-gatherings or participate in the men's *dhikr*. Especially Sufi orders have recruited a number of European converts, and the gender relations among members of Sufi orders vary greatly.[10] The Persian Ni'matu'llahi *tariqa*—particularly popular in Western

Europe in the 1990s—observes strict gender segregation in the Muslim world (also before the revolution in Iran), while in Europe men and women freely say their prayers together and meditate side-by-side. Such associations as the Turkish Diyanet or the Pakistani Idara, firmly anchored in the Muslim world—even though they differ greatly among themselves—are all based on a strict ideology of segregation, with women having little or nothing to say in the leadership. This pattern is repeated by most of the new and influential European-based, male-dominated networks and associations. In reaction to this reality, women have organized increasing numbers of autonomous associations. This trend can be traced back to the mid-1980s and became clearly visible during the 1990s.

Although many Muslims—in particular, Turkish, Moroccan, and Pakistani Muslims—interact almost exclusively with Muslims of the same ethnic origin, a growing number of women's networks and associations are crossing or superseding ethnic, national, and linguistic barriers. Such groups, often launched by an individual or a small circle of people, are popular among the younger generations. They communicate in European languages and commit themselves to women's concerns in their various localities and often cooperate with non-Muslim authorities while interacting with European society at large. These groups offer counseling services and address social, moral, and religious problems within the Muslim community. For example, they provide remedial classes for young girls, organize space for sporting activities, sell and sometimes even publish Islamic books, and open telephone hotlines for women. All these activities are, of course, based upon an explicit commitment to their Islamic faith.

PREACHING AND TEACHING

Throughout history, Islamic scholars have unanimously agreed that a woman cannot deliver the Jum'ah *khutba*, Friday sermon, and that women are excluded as prayer leaders in mixed assemblies. In the past, women were also excluded from the Islamic institutions in the Muslim world, where the formal training of teachers and preachers took place. However, traditional communities often allowed women to practice legitimate, nonofficial religious activities such as nonritual preaching. Thus, while the *katib*, preacher of *khutba*, is a man, a woman can serve as a *da'iyah*, missionary preacher, or as a *wa'ezah*, preacher. Thus, several categories of female religious specialists developed separately from their male counterparts. Albeit, the variety of expressions of ritual activities has been constricted, and it remains so by certain interpretations of orthodoxy or by local customs. Nevertheless, nowadays there are female *mullahs, shaykhas,* and *nakibas*, while in Sufi circles—also in the European diaspora—the *muqadamat*, female religious leaders, officiate at gender-segregated ceremonies.[11] In premodern times,

Sufi circles in particular seem to have encouraged women preachers, and their competency and popularity are frequently underlined in hagiographies. Traditional practices are thus being transferred to new surroundings; for example, Muslim communities from Eastern European developed the role of the *bola*, a female religious leader who leads the women's *dhikr* during *mawlids*, preaches and teaches, and prepares funerals. The *bola*, now also called *muallima*, is often the spouse of the *imam* (*hocca*). The Islamist movement does not seem to have any influence in diminishing these activities in Western Europe.

Since the 1970s, women have been admitted to several traditional Islamic institutions of learning, including al-Azhar University in Cairo. As a result, more women study to be *'ulama*, Islamic scholars, and since the 1990s they have started to participate in nonritual preaching in several Muslim countries. A similar development seems to be taking place in Western Europe. Currently, two types of women preachers are active in Europe: those who belong to a network of Islamic organizations that remain firmly rooted in their country of origin, and individuals who have the required skills to preach, teach, and perform traditional rituals in local mosques. At the same time, a new category is emerging of women born and raised in the West. They tend to claim active roles for women in non-segregated Islamic teaching and preaching activities.

Again, the Turkish Sulaymancis offer an interesting example. Their teaching programs, based in Turkey, include advanced religious studies for those who aspire to the title *hocca hanum*, "madam *imam*" (a parallel to *hocca effendi*), becoming female teachers who function as preachers, of whom the most talented are sent on preaching tours during Ramadan. For example, in 1998, a 24-year-old woman who was the preacher in two Sulaymanci mosques (that is, mosques permanently reserved for women) in Norway made a preaching tour to Sydney and Melbourne. The question of traveling alone without a *mahram*, a related male, was solved by designating women's groups to accompany the preacher to and from the airport.

Another example is the Jamaat Tabligh organization that recruits mainly among South Asian and Moroccan immigrants. Although women are not allowed in Tablighi-dominated mosques, the organization encourages the wives, daughters, and sisters of its active members to engage in *da'wa* activities provided they do not mix with unrelated men. As a result, Norwegian women's *jama'ats*, or congregations, gather in small preaching groups of two to four women that meet with Muslim women in their neighborhood. Usually, one of the women gives a short sermon, followed by a commentary of Qur'anic verses that concern such familiar practices and tenets of faith as prayer or the *shahada*, the profession of faith. Thus, to a certain degree, the Tablighis accommodate organized women's *da'wa* activities that are customarily centered on exhortations to uphold traditional lifestyles and morals.

The *majlis-e aza*, mourning assemblies, during the month of Muharram and commemorations of the *imams* for women in Shi'a communities take place in private homes. Muharram activities in the women's section of the *hosainiyeh* or the mosque are often extensive and include reciting, singing, and preaching. As already pointed out, Iraqi women *mullahs* are trained by other *mullahs* and start studying at the time of puberty.[12] For example, in Oslo, Iraqi women in their thirties and forties preach in the women's part of the main Shi'a center, using as sources of reference works compiled in their home country.

Most preaching activities mentioned so far are performed in the languages of the country of origin. However, women's networks that arose in Western Europe are changing this pattern. In formal and informal ways, they encourage women to take up religious studies so they can propagate and revitalize the Islamic message in European languages. These women frequently provide *dars*, or religious lectures and sermons, at times to a mixed audience. In spite of these developments, women preachers are still controversial among the majority of European Muslims. At the same time, however, a small number of Muslim women are not only preaching to mixed audiences but also challenging the idea that only men can serve as *katib*.

Although Muslim women are still far behind Muslim men in organizational activities, the number of small-scale activities carried out by mostly anonymous Muslim women's groups is growing. These groups are still based on the values of segregation and tradition; most of them emphasize ritual and moral obligations. However, considering the fact that traditional mosques in the countries of origin often had no place for women, their present inclusion in most European mosque communities, even in low numbers, can be interpreted as an accomodation to changing circumstances.

DEVOTIONAL PRACTICE AND ISLAMIC LAW

The extent to which Muslim women in Europe engage in traditional devotional practice is unknown. Few reliable statistics exist, but according to M. Tribalat's study of immigrant communities in France, women are practicing more intensely than men.[13] When it comes to *hajj*, an interesting development seems to have taken place: reports from Saudi authorities show that in 2006, as many as 45 percent of the *hajj* pilgrims were women, compared to less than 10 percent before 1995.[14] These female pilgrims were not only from Europe, of course. However, several Muslim associations, including the Turkish Diyanet, are catering to numerous women *hajj* groups from European countries. Women enthusiastically participate, with some of them saving money to go every year.

Another development in women's religious practice concerns the application of precepts from Islamic law. This law is not limited to rules for the *ibadat* (worship), for to be a good Muslim has traditionally been linked to the observance of legal precepts, in particular those concerning family law and inheritance. In this area, gender differences in attitudes are particulairly salient, since Muslim women are generally more supportive of European secular legal systems than are their male counterparts.[15] In Sara Silvestri's study, none of the female informants appeared to long for living in one of the Muslim countries that apply Islamic law. The possibility to enjoy a range of freedoms and to be respectful of the majority's rule of law was constantly regarded as the most valuable feature of European society and a reason why people preferred to live in Europe. Many Muslims in Europe, both men and women, consider the legal aspects of Islamic tradition as "changeable" aspects of faith, subject to new interpretations, and consider only the five pillars "unchangeable."[16] In many circles, especially among young Muslims, individual experience of faith, *islam du coeur*, is highly appreciated, perhaps much more than social and legal Islam.[17] It also seems that a growing number of women are interested in promoting the empowerment of women by reinterpreting the Islamic sources.

Among the younger generation of European Muslim women, a process of identity formation is taking place as personal religious growth. Many women have taken up the study of Islam, attend lectures, and join Islamic associations. Recent studies show that young Muslim women long to find their own way in experiencing and understanding Islam intellectually and spiritually. Drawing closer to their faith does not seem to impinge upon their appreciation of their Western environment. These young women take Europe for granted as a natural platform of professional and individual engagement. This attitude also implies belief in the values of fundamental rights and the expectation to be respected as individuals by European society.[18] Pious and educated Muslim young women thus wish to gain respect and recognition from the majority society as being both pious and modern. This struggle for recognition is regularily framed in terms of claiming the right to live as practicing Muslims in European societies.

A Sense of Belonging

A life in diaspora may at first cause a crisis of meaning and require a restructuring of emotions and beliefs. This, in turn, may produce a strengthening of religious points of reference and, potentially, further segregation. There is plenty of evidence, however, that religious communities function as bridges of integration into the new society. If we understand the term "worldview" as a sense of belonging to a global faith community as well as to a local and highly complex social setting, we can easily observe how religious practice is the focus of interest and activity and how devotional practice is naturally linked to social action.

Higher levels of education, as well as economic independence, have given increasing numbers of women expanding degrees of autonomy, greater courage to affirm their rights, and the ability to assume new responsibilities, including female religious leadership. Consequently, women are gradually becoming more active in creating new networks, often based on gender cooperation. They actively participate in debates concerning the visible roles they can play in the devotional and organizational life of their community. Until now, the most vital and original contributions to women's religious life have been the steadily increasing number of autonomous female associations and European-Muslim associations based on cooperation between men and women. Together with new networks and informal groups, they provide new training fields for women. They attract members and followers from different ethnic and linguistic backgrounds, thus counteracting the present fragmentation and lack of cooperation in local Muslim communities. This development can be interpreted as a sign of how political, social, and cultural priorities of the Muslim community—and probably also of their European interlocutors—are beginning to produce new types of women's commitments. While formulating their own agendas, the founding members of women's groups are not blind to the shortcomings of male-biased mosque leadership or of male-dominated associations. Until now, the women's groups had to articulate their criticisms mostly in guarded terms. Clearly, many Muslim women are fighting patterns of prejudice on two fronts, prejudices that exist both within and outside their communities.[19] The current process of reappropriation of the Islamic faith through a search for knowledge, renewed religious commitment, and the rallying around networks initiated by a young Muslim generation could and should enable women, in the long run, to withstand the pressures of social conventions within their communities.

NOTES

1. A comprehensive picture is given in Sara Silvestri's research report *Europe's Muslim Women: Potential, Aspirations and Challenges* (London: City University and Cambridge University, 2008).

2. Only one European country, the United Kingdom, has officially begun to collect, for the first time with the census of 2001, information about its residents' religious affiliation. The number of Muslims given currently also includes those who either are nonpracticing or have explicitly rejected their faith.

3. Kari Vogt, "Women, Gender and Religious Associations: Western Europe," in *Encyclopedia of Women and Islamic Cultures*, vol. 2: *Family, Law and Politics*, ed. Suad Joseph (Leiden: E. J. Brill, 2005), 715–19.

4. This is typical for Turkish Muslim organizations, like the state-based Diyanet, as well as for Brelwi-oriented South Asian mosque communities. The term *"dhikr"* (or *zikr*) is used for rituals where the constant repetition of certain pious formulas is intended to create a spiritual-emotional experience of nearness to God.

5. See Haifaa Jawad, "Female Conversions to Islam: The Sufi Paradigm," in *Women Embracing Islam: Gender and Conversion in the West*, ed. Karin van Nieuwkerk (Austin: University of Texas Press, 2006), 154.

6. That is, members of the Avrupa Islam Kültür Merkezleri Birligi.

7. Barbara Daly Metcalf, "Tablighi Jama'at and Women," in *Travellers in Faith: Studies of the Tablighi Jama'at as a Transnational Islamic Movement for Faith Renewal*, ed. Muhammad Khalid Masud (Leiden: E. J. Brill, 2000), 56.

8. Gerdien Jonker, "The Evolution of the Naqshbandi-Mujaddidi Sulaymancis in Germany," in *Sufism in the West*, ed. Jamal Malik and John Hinnells (New York: Routledge, 2006), 82.

9. The ICC has 350 centers all over Western Europe, as well as some branches in the United States and Australia. The majority of the centers (299) are concentrated in Germany, with aproximately 60,000 to 80,000 active members. See Jonker, in *Sufism in the West*, 76.

10. Leonard Lewison, "Persian Sufism in the Contemporary West: Reflections on the Ni'matu'llahi Diaspora," in *Sufism in the West*, ed. Maik and Hinnells, 54.

11. R. Fernea and E. Fernea, "Variations in Religious Observance among Islamic Women," in *Scholars, Saints, and Sufis: Muslim Religious Institutions since 1500*, ed. Lois Beck and Nikkie R. Keddi (Berkeley, CA: Berkeley University Press, 1972), 399.

12. Ibid.

13. Michèle Tribalat, *Une enqête sur les immigrés et leurs enfants: La Découverte* (Paris: Faire France, 1995), 95–96; Jytte Klausen, *The Islamic Challenge: Politics and Religion in Western Europe* (Oxford: Oxford University Press, 2005), 140–41.

14. *Le Monde*, December 28, 2006, based on information from the Saudi Hajj Department, 2006.

15. Klausen, *The Islamic Challenge*, 194–95.

16. See Abdolkarim Soroush, "The Changeable and the Unchangeable," in *New Directions in Islamic Thought: Exploring Reform and Muslim Tradition*, ed. Kari Vogt et al. (London: I. B. Tauris, 2008), 9–15.

17. Leïla Babès, *Islam Intérieure, Passion et Désenchantemant* (Paris: Editions Al Bourak, 2000) 189.

18. See Silvestri, *Europe's Muslim Women*, 31.

19. See also Silvestri's conclusion, *Europe's Muslim Women*, 63–67.

CHAPTER 13

From Ritual to Redemption: Worldview of Shi'a Muslim Women in Southern California

Bridget Blomfield

Shi'a Muslim women base their worldview on the redemptive suffering of the Prophet Muhammad's martyred family and the justice that God will bring forth in the future. This chapter focuses on the efforts of Shi'a Muslim women to abide by their religious tenets and to construct meaningful rituals that support their beliefs. Dress code, the construction of sacred space, ritual symbols, and the functions of specific rituals are examined. Also addressed are the relationships these women maintain with their spiritual role models and how they commemorate these role models and elicit their support for intercession. Finally, given the ethnographic research methods, Shi'a Muslim women in southern California express, through personal interviews, how their beliefs and rituals create meaning, identity formation, and personal agency.

Much of the meaning in Shi'a redemptive theology is based on suffering, intercession, and redemption. Shi'a believe that because of their privation and persecution, their sufferings are rewarded. This belief compensates for the chronic persecution and oppression of the Shi'a historically and in modernity. Their worldview is partially developed through narrative and ritual. Participating in the ritual defines the participant, forming identity and establishing meaning.

The roles of female religious models are integral to a Shi'a woman's sense of self. These role models instruct piety, bravery and femininity, establishing clear-cut gender roles for the female participants. They call on these exemplary women during their rituals seeking intercession and guidance. The point of their religious rituals is the honoring, recognition, and repetition of sorrow of universal suffering and the universality of the struggle against human tragedy and oppression. Revisiting this space annually commemorates not only the holy family but also honors the history of human suffering at the hands of oppressors. For this reason, Shi'a Muslims reenact and commemorate the suffering of the Prophet Muhammad's family and their friends who were martyred fighting for what they believed to be the true Islam.

THE BATTLE OF KARBALA

Following the death of the Prophet in 632 CE, his close companion, Abu Bakr, became the first caliph. Shi'a believe that Ali, first cousin of the Prophet Muhammad, should have been the immediate successor. Ali was finally placed as the fourth caliph, but his leadership was short lived. His son Husayn tried to carry on the message to Muslims to return to the rightly guided path but was murdered at the battle of Karbala along with a party of 72 family members and followers. Husayn is depicted as the martyred son of a martyr in Shi'a hagiography and foreshadows the coalescence of Shi'ism as a political identity based on allegiance to Ali and his bloodline. From this bloodline stems the Shi'a Imamate, a succession of spiritual authorities or Imams (to be distinguished from the Sunni imam, who leads the prayer) commencing with Ali. Depending on the genealogies followed, there are several Shi'a groups such as the Zaydis, the Ithna Ashari, the Ismaili, and others. The majority of the Shi'a, the Ithna Ashari, hold that the 12th Imam went into occultation. Hence, this group of Shi'a have come to be known as the Ithna Ashari, or Twelver Shi'a. Husayn as "martyred son of martyr" thereby established martyrdom as the theme for Alid Shi'ism.[1] This chapter deals exclusively with women of the Ithna Ashari Shi'a. To this day, Husayn, the grandson of the Prophet Muhammad, is revered by the Shi'a, for he gave his life willingly in the name of Islam. The Battle of Karbala, where he died, is the focal point of justice and injustice to which Shi'a women adhere, giving them purpose spiritually and communally. Their ritual enactments during Muharram tie them to the past and give them direction for the future.

As one of the few surviving family members at Karbala, Husayn's sister Zaynab became the carrier of the message to stand against oppression and injustice. She held the first lamentation ceremony that in honor of her brother is still enacted today. She stood in the face of her oppressors and demanded justice, leading her to be forever revered by the Shi'a. This message is a focal point to Shi'a all over the world. Today Shi'a women still reenact the ritual initiated by Zaynab.

From the perspective of Shi'a women, justice is one of the most important tenets of their worldview. Their belief in divine justice gives them the strength to continue in the face of oppression. Faith in Allah's divine judgment on *yawm al-din*, considered the Day of Reckoning, and their honoring of those who suffered before them create piety in the lives of the Shi'a and also take care of the things over which they have no control. Belief that the holy family and their descendants are the rightful heirs to Muhammad's spiritual authority establishes believers as propagators of the faith, encouraging piety and activism in their daily lives. Their proof lies not only in the Qur'an but also in the *hadiths* of Imam Ali and Imam Husayn. These figures, as well as Fatima and Zaynab and other members of the family, are the focal point of devotion and inspiration that lead to intercession and redemption for Shi'a women.

ROLE MODELS

Although Shi'a women adore Imam Ali and Imam Husayn, they often focus on Fatima, the daughter of the Prophet Muhammad and the wife of his first cousin Ali. For the Shi'a, Fatima's daughter Zaynab is also a historical figure and spiritual guide. Loved and admired for their courageous resistance against oppression and for an unwavering promise of the final attainment of justice, Fatima and Zaynab serve as models for familial and community devotion. They play an important role in the construction of women's spiritual and social identity.

Depicting images of piety and resistance, Fatima and Zaynab serve as important role models for Shi'a women, guiding them to fight for human rights and justice. As revealed in early Shi'a history, Fatima and Zaynab were, and continue to be, integral parts of the community spiritually and politically. Shi'a women continue to emulate both of these women as exemplary role models. Fatima, known for her purity and piety as a daughter, wife, and mother of the Imamate, works as an intercessor for both male and female Shi'a. Standing at the gates of paradise, she holds a 70-yard scroll wherein the merits and transgressions of the believers are written. She is a mediator between this world and the next. If one has loved her and joined in her suffering, shedding tears for her family's martyrdom, one will be stamped lover and will gain instant admission into paradise. Fatima teaches love, compassion, and patience. She offers hope to the suffering and the possibility of redemption to those who emulate her. As a virtuous wife and mother, she exemplifies piety. Tears cried on her behalf, and on behalf of her family, for the injustices done to humanity will be recorded and taken into cosmic account, balancing transgressions that may be judged sinful. Anyone who is a relative of Fatima, a *sayyed* or *sayyeda,* and creates an uprising against any injustice and defends the truth can become an Imam, which is a most exalted role even today.[2]

A *hadith* attributed to the Prophet Muhammad says, "Paradise lies at the feet of the mothers," suggesting that motherhood is the highest honor for a woman. From a spiritual perspective, Fatima is also the mother of *al-rahmah,* mercy and compassion. She appears as a Sophia, a bearer of the purest feminine wisdom; in Shi'ite theology, "her luminous aspect of the feminine is indicated by the power with which it is invested and the masculine attributes which are bestowed upon it, thereby compensating for the situation in which it is maintained by a patriarchal world on the social plane."[3] Derived from these two qualities, she emits them to those who pray on her behalf. Her *rahm* (womb) is the growing place for every action that comes to life and initiates *rahmah* (compassion) through the tradition of spiritual virtue. Fatima-*Batul*, the Virgin Fatima, is the physical and spiritual mother. She is the divine creative power and represents spirit embodied.[4] These narratives uphold the feminine side of the religion that places value on women and their deeds. Fatima is more than a metaphor: she is alive in every woman who turns to her for patience, courage, compassion, and love. A woman who has been filled with the spirit of Fatima will have these qualities emanate from her very essence—the divine feminine that the Prophet sired.

Her daughter Zaynab is revered for her brave speech at the palace of Yazid. It is believed that Zaynab offered the first mourning ritual after the murder of her brother Imam Husayn and other members of her family. Her strong and powerful roles were as angered sister and outraged mother. As the daughter of Fatima and Ali, Zaynab assumed a majestic defiance of the limitations assigned to her by her culture and religion, enabling her to "betray [their] political, social, and religious agenda" and to "transcend gender expectations and regulations."[5] Zaynab has become a symbol of courage for Shi'a women, especially the younger generation. It is through her that the message of Islam is carried. She is considered a patron saint to mothers, orphans, and the oppressed. Regarded as the embodiment of purity, justice, kindness, and generosity, Fatima instills faith and hope. Her role as protector of orphaned children and widowed women makes her the only female saint referred to by the title *"al-Sayyida"* (descendant of the Prophet), without use of a first name.[6] She is "the mother to those who cannot look after themselves: the poor, the old and incapacitated, in short, Mother of the Incapable."[7]

Shi'a women believe that they must strive to embody the qualities of Fatima and Zaynab. Numerous stories depicting the behavior of these women are told year round at gatherings and particularly during Muharram, thereby keeping Fatima and Zaynab alive in the consciousness of the community. Considered the source of wisdom for all women, Zaynab is called *zinat*, the Jewel of Paradise, the light of God, because "she is a representative of Zahra's [Fatima] side for women's welfare."[8] She is a constant reminder that the human spirit will fight against and triumph over oppression. Although Zaynab suffered tremendously during her lifetime, Shi'a Muslim women see her as a heroine, not as a victim. Her combined qualities make her a perfected human being.

FINDING FATIMA AND ZAYNAB IN THE CONTEMPORARY WORLD

The modern Shi'a woman can be religious and pious as a means to combat the Western notions of modernity. The gender-coded models of Fatima and Zaynab promote a preservationist model of womanhood and thus pass on the true nature of Shi'ism. In his book *The Martyrs of Karbala*, Kamran Scot Aghaie says that the image of woman has changed among the Shi'a. Today, women are seen "as [a] symbol of morality and resistance to foreign moral corruption."[9] Karbala symbolism expresses the "new woman" in the modern Shi'a world. In countries like Iran, this "new woman" is a woman that is removed from the "modernized woman" of the past administration, where women's bodies were politicized to express modernity by Western standards of dress and behavior, something to which many Shi'a women object. He adds that today, female characters have taken on empowered narratives and roles in opposition to Western oppression. One might also say that this "new woman" is also a politicization of women's bodies by Islamist regimes. Aghaie writes:

> A woman who has attained the level of belief chooses her own life, her way of thinking, her very being and even her own form of adornment. She actualizes herself. She does not give herself over to television and passive consumption. She does not do whatever consumerism tells her to do. She is not afraid to choose the color of her dress because it may not be in style this year! She has returned and returned vigorously! To what? To the modern dress of Islam. As what? As a believer and committed human being.[10]

As a revolt against Westernization by the Shah, Iranian women took up the veil as a form of protest and defiance against imposed Western standards. They used Zaynab as a role model to construct piety and as an example of a strong woman who stood against oppression in the face of her oppressors. In other words, she was a political activist, standing for a cause. Farah Azari, a member of the Iranian Women's Solidarity Group stated:

> For a time it was Zeinab [Zaynab] who came to the forefront to symbol-ize the ideal of the modern revolutionary woman in Iran. Those enig-matic young women clad in a black chador . . . bearing machine guns, aspire to follow Zeinab. It is not inappropriate that they have been some-times referred to as "commandos of her holiness Zeinab."[11]

Zaynab is the model of revolutionary woman, whereas Fatima is the model that restores faith and justice. These qualities combine to make a modern, pious woman who is politically and religiously involved.

Shi'a women have reinterpreted the role of Fatima and Zaynab, espe-cially elevating Zaynab because "it is Zaynab who carries the history of Ashura forward to future generations of Shi'i Muslims."[12] The role of Zay-nab is emphasized in the modern elegies recited during ritual observances and has moved from traditional narratives of a weeping, wailing victim to an empowered protester who stood against incredible suffering and was strong, courageous, and resilient. In other words, she never gave up. In Lebanon today women emulate Zaynab as they participate in "authenti-cated public piety," which is women's involvement in social activism in the public arena. For these women, Zaynab carries a critical message against oppression and is outspoken about it. She also exemplifies strength of mind, compassion, dedication to others, and the courage to speak. Moth-ers who have lost their children during the current tensions in the Middle East especially express these qualities. They can compare their losses to the grief that Zaynab suffered when her family was martyred. She did not collapse but continued to bravely speak out against the oppressor. Like Zaynab, these women establish a strong sense of self in response to the suffering they experience when their sons, daughters, or husbands are mar-tyred.[13] Today, public piety displays the emergence of Zaynab as a role model through public activism that ultimately leads to a global awareness of the Shi'a struggle. The image of Zaynab provides a normative moral system of behavior that is based on Shi'a values of piety through self-expectations that include appropriate Islamic dress styles and codes of behavior, thereby making public expressions of piety a form of women's *jihad*. Scholar Lara Deeb suggests that the Shi'a woman emulates Zaynab for the good of the community but also for herself because doing so develops her faith. She writes:

> The ultimate goal of gender *jihad* was to facilitate women's abilities to be good, moral, pious Muslims, unhindered by patriarchal social norms that limited their public participation, norms that they viewed as standing in the path of their piety. While they were confronting patriarchal norms, their major motive for doing so was not the emancipation of individualized selves but for equity in the possibilities for practicing a pious and moral lifestyle.[14]

Shi'a women's relationship with Zaynab makes their lives meaningful and gives them a sense of the importance of struggle. Fatima gives them the courage to remain pious and patient, using love and compassion as rewards in the afterlife.

Shi'a women insist that Islam expressly ensures the rights of women. They argue that it is their religious right and the critical element of choice that gives them freedom. For example, Shi'a women in Lebanon see themselves as modern and pious. These women create a space for their faith and the practice of Islam within the modern world and make the case that the notions of Islam and modernity are not contradictory but complementary. They practice "authenticated" Islam, an Islam that has a modern interpretation based on knowledge and understanding in contrast to a traditional, unquestioned Islam that is blindly followed by older generations. This "enchanted modern" form of piety emphasizes the importance of both material and spiritual progress, and it encompasses a "new kind of religiosity, one that involves conscious and conscientious commitment."[15] Pious women's identity is created through the visibility of their faith, where faith is seen in activism. For them, progress and modernity are not about materialism but about social welfare, where women are active agents in ending oppression and injustice through their centers that offer education and support. These women see feminism as activism; it is the commitment to make the world a better place through their actions.

Modern and pious, they continue to participate in the ancient women's rituals during Muharram. During the ritual observances, the women tell stories about the martyrs of Karbala, stressing the importance of observance of Ashura to the younger women and girls. These narratives passed down from generation to generation and from culture to culture preserve the importance of spiritual qualities and ethical behavior in the practicing women. Girls and women learn about the roles of Fatima and Zaynab through stories, sermons, elegies, and prayers. Besides engaging in the rituals during the month of Muharram, Shi'a women celebrate the birthdays of the saints, and Fatima's birthday is often celebrated as Mother's Day, but the most celebrated are those remembered during Muharram.

MUHARRAM RITUALS

Participating in the Muharram rituals defines the participants, forming identity and establishing meaning. Much of the meaning in Shi'a redemptive theology is based on suffering, intercession, and redemption, a personal and social suffering that creates meaning for the society. The promise of salvation and divine mercy offered in these religious ritual gatherings that commemorate the death of the holy family serves to cleanse and redeem everyone who participates in them. These rituals are an act of piety and a form of protest, making visible the suffering of the Prophet's family and the present suffering of the Shi'a in modernity. Every year, Shi'a are still martyred in various parts of the world where they are oppressed and marginalized, giving the practitioners proof of their never-ending struggle and establishing the need to continue ritual enactment and protest against tyrannical groups.

For the Shi'a, the rituals have a religious and political meaning. The tragedy at Karbala holds universal significance because it continues to be commemorated by the Shi'a in the modern world. The rightful heirs of Islam, the Prophet's family, were rejected, persecuted, and killed. The Shi'a rituals honor the holy family while voicing and recognizing a universal suffering and the universality of the struggle against human tragedy and oppression. Participation for Shi'a women is crucial because it works as a cultural response to a given situation, helping participants to interact and define who they are.

FUNCTION OF THE RITUAL

Ritual enactments create an environment for the spirit of the holy family and for the women, Fatima and Zaynab. They establish the women's worldview and order their lives in a system of redemption. The rituals communicate a political and religious statement and express piety and resistance to oppression by providing symbolic vocabulary and using symbols that create meaning. Such symbols as altars, banners, special clothing, and foods represent specific elements developing the psychological and spiritual needs of the women. By reenacting the stories, Shi'a women gain a sense of identity. The women's difficulties are resolved through the motifs of the fight against oppression made by women. Through the direct ritual context, there are oral paradigms, the efficacy of mourning, and most importantly the remembrance of God. The recitation of these poignant tales of the Prophet's family are performed by women for women, and it is considered inappropriate for men to recite them because they are the property of women's worlds.[16] Women participate in Muharram rituals of mourning to ask for intercession and redemption through the use of imagery, ritual objects, and elegiac poetry so that they might cross the threshold of everyday life to enter into sacred space.

The Ashura rituals practiced during Muharram and specifically the *azadari* (sorrow) ritual create order and bind community members together, making the rituals personal and collective. These rituals are religious, psychological, and cultural and are rites of passage that develop meaning. For the Shi'a, their rituals are a response to a historical event but also a means to deal with current world events. Surprisingly, women, not men, are at the center of these rituals. They prepare and decorate the sacred ritual space whether in their homes or at a Shi'a center. They have specific clothing that they wear for the rituals and specific foods that they prepare to represent the needs of the historical community. An example of this ritual food is the making of *sorbet*, a drink that quenches the thirst of an infant that has lost its mother and can no longer be nursed. Shi'a rituals create a social system that attempts to foster and maintain in the community's members a commitment to what they believe and is a larger and more important cause—the meaning of the suffering experienced by the holy family. These rituals are agreed upon by the community and cultivate an inner experience as well as a group experience. Participating in the ritual defines the participant, forming identity and establishing meaning.

Shi'a women's rituals have grown out of a personal and collective need to give voice to their lived experiences and connect these voiced experiences to larger structures of meaning.[17] Ritual communication, having its own language, expresses something that cannot be expressed in any other way. It temporarily structures a time-space environment through a series of physical movements, thereby molding the actors into new persons. As the Shi'a participants become intimately involved in the suffering of the members of the Prophet's family, they know and enter into the spiritual world. This ritual mastery is the ability to make and remake schemes from the shared culture that can transform or privilege the ritual experience. The relationship of power is being negotiated directly and also indirectly, and that power is claimed to be redemptive. Passed from generation to generation, the rituals are organized by experts creating a 1,300-year continuity with the past. By using collective images from the past and melding them into current affairs, the women become involved and identified. The ritual, therefore, creates and maintains an identity that establishes a worldview. Reproducing and valorizing tradition keeps it alive and active, allowing it to dominate the present and honor the past. The Shi'a rituals integrate the group and codify them through specific prayers and physical movements. Their religious reality is structured and restructured through the rituals that are redemptive and spiritually healing. The experience within a ritual releases through each individual's body. Suffering and grief are embodied; therefore, it is through ritual that they become expressed and transformed. Through ritual enactment, the experience is transformative; it becomes "nothing more nor less than the meaningfulness of meaning."[18] The ritual tells the story, and it narrates the meaning of suffering, giving it value. Through ritual expression, women give voice to their sacred aspirations. The rituals are framed historically and practiced currently, making them a timeless extension of the past, where the meaning and efficacy never change, thus making the rituals a source of religious truth where collective grieving transpires.

Shi'a women take on leadership roles through the rituals, creating sacred space, cooking, hostessing, writing and reciting elegies, and organizing the community. They have regulated specific aspects of such gatherings that included recitation of elegies, expressions of sorrow and grief, and ritual closures through breaking for a meal. The gatherings are also occasions to educate the participants on the events at Karbala and their religious significance. The function of the gatherings is to create a soteriological dimension to the awareness of the audience; the gatherings also elicit deep feeling and foster critical thinking about the meaning of faith on the part of the listeners. As well, the gatherings contain a historical component while also providing the opportunity for salvation. Most gatherings that I observed among Shi'a women in southern California began with a call for blessings upon the Prophet Muhammad and his family. Next, there was a reading from the Qur'an, followed by an elegy, a poetic tale about one of the issues the family was facing. This elegy, in poetic form, was lyrical and later became highly emotional as the recitation progressed. It also was accompanied by a discourse on a religious topic that reminded people to learn from history, taught ethics, and was a tool for "the dissemination of traditional wisdom."[19] It restored the importance of piety and reminded believers to stand against oppression and injustice. It told the tales of the suffering of those people who had died for love—the love of Islam. As the participating members became more aroused, they beat their breasts and wept. When they were finished, they usually shared a meal.

Among the Southern California Shi'ite communities that I observed, there are specific leaders who give scholarly lectures, preach, and are administrators who are also trained to recite elegies; yet anyone who is so moved may host a gathering or lead an elegy. There are professional reciters who can be hired to recite dirges at a gathering. These dirges are specific to the appropriate night during Muharram and are relegated to a specific person or persons. The dirges are known to have often been extremely explicit, bloody, and violent in the past. Ritual elegies are also recited in groups, some large and some small. Participants spend months in training to recite and sing elegies as a group in a sort of competition. Sisters and cousins will practice and perform at a special gathering held by a relative. The ritual elegies they perform can be extremely heartfelt and moving, especially when they are written and chanted by children or teenage girls. Participants memorize elegies that have been written hundreds of years ago and also create contemporary ones. Recitations typically move the audience to tears, and there is group participation in self-mortification to varying degrees. Most important, ritual leaders orchestrate the rituals from beginning to end, preserving the lessons of Karbala.

The mourning ritual illustrates through gestures and elegies a dramatic presentation that laments the martyrs of Karbala and is always performed publicly; it is never a solitary practice. As part of the ritual process, there exists a culturally defined lamentation. As the ritual draws to an end, people start to weep. They cry as they stand, beating their chests, or sit down and wail. Pakistani women beat their chests, whereas Iraqi women slap their faces as they stand in a circle chanting and releasing their sorrows. Women of the various ethnic groups shed tears on behalf of Husayn and his family, tears that are critical for salvation. Lady Fatima is a witness to the tears, and those believers who weep on her behalf are rewarded in paradise. The practitioners' tears and pious actions will rescue them from hellfire, releasing those "in whose heart is the weight of an atom of love for *ahl al-bayt* [holy family]."[20]

SACRED SPACE

Commemorations for Husayn and his party are held privately and publicly, in homes or prayer halls. Depending on the culture, there are specially built centers and rooms displaying ritual objects like standards, miniature coffins, and tombs that are decorated. Walls are draped in black fabric, and salutations are painted in glitter. Each group stresses specific décor particular to its culture, but the meaning and goal of the activity remains the same. The services are almost always segregated by gender either in separate rooms or with a curtain between the men and women or with women sitting behind the men. In some countries there is segregation, but participants move freely between groups. Children are always welcome and wander and play between both men and women. The rituals are always done in a group, and included on the most important day of Muharram is Ashura, a procession that usually involves the carrying of coffins and standards. A procession can be enacted in the prayer hall or on the streets the night of Ashura. For people who live in countries where they have no shrines and cannot perform this ritual, it may be done symbolically. Where Shi'a are repressed, in places like Afghanistan and Saudi Arabia, participants are quiet and hidden in people's homes; but in India and the United States, where more expression is allowed, Shi'a practice in the streets (in India) and hold gatherings late into the night (in both India and the United States).

RITUAL SYMBOLS

There always exists a cultural component to the Muharram gatherings. In the Pakistani and Indian community, the most common ritual symbols are kept in *imambargahs* (special centers). There is often a formalized alcove or altar at one end of the building where the replicas are kept. Sometimes floor-length curtains conceal them; in other facilities, they are enclosed in glass. On the platform or in the alcoves *alams* (standards) are placed. Standards are usually the hand of Fatima that represents the five family members or *ahl al-bayt*—the Prophet Muhammad, Ali, Fatima, Hasan, and Husayn. Pounded from metals that range from pewter to sterling silver, the standards extend on poles that are draped in beautiful fanciful cloth. Miniature coffins, baby cradles, replicas of the tombs, and banners accompany the standards. They are often draped with garlands of flowers. There are incense burners ready to be filled and lit and often vases of fresh flowers. Sometimes, for large processions, there is a life-sized coffin that is covered with cloth, sometimes black, green, or white. Usually the white cloth is spattered with red paint to replicate the blood of the martyrs. Homes that have altars display a smaller version of the draped coffin. When Muharram is over, the replicas are packed carefully and stored until the next year.

Unlike the Pakistanis, Iranian and Iraqi communities do not have *imambargahs* (altars) in their homes or centers. Iran and Iraq boast numerous holy sites, tombs, and shrines of the holy family and the Imams, so immigrants from these countries say that they don't need such replicas. Those Shi'a lucky enough to live in Iran or Iraq can make *ziyarat* (pilgrimages) whenever they wish. For the Pakistanis, however, their *ziyarat* must be done symbolically through the *imambargahs*.

Gatherings held in the homes of Iranian and Iraqi women are similar to those held by Pakistanis in Southern California. Although they do not have *imambargahs*, they create sacred space through intention. They do not have small rooms converted into sacred space, as have the Pakistanis; instead, they make their living rooms into sacred space, for it is there that their presence and prayers create holy space. Some homes have a room that is completely cleared of furniture, a room where the carpets are covered with white sheets and everyone sits on the floor; but others leave their furniture in place, sometimes adding more chairs to receive the maximum number of guests. Chairs are placed against the walls of the room, creating an empty circle so that women can see the elegist while she chants the elegies. Depending on the home, gatherings may have a more formal setting.

In the Iraqi and Iranian centers, large portions of the walls are covered with black fabric that is painted with Arabic prayers, poetry, and *suras* from the Qur'an. Sometimes the black cloths are painted with glitter or embroidered, creating something somber yet beautiful. The carpets remain the same on the floor, and the room itself differs only in that numerous boxes of tissues are placed at hand to dry the tears of the mourners. In the front of the room is a chair draped in black cloth, and it is there the elegist sits. Most often, however, when in women-only congregations, the female leader sits on the floor with everyone else as she leads the prayers or recitations for that day.

Clothing too becomes a symbol. Everyone wears black. Pakistanis and Indians wear simple *shalwar kameez*, and Iranians sometimes wear expensive black dresses with black stockings and high heels. There are special black robes made of lace that are especially beautiful and are given as gifts to family members. Iraqi women wear black *abayas* and headscarves. It is a time of sadness, so people do not go out to dinner or to movies. Even teenagers stay in during Muharram because it is considered a time of mourning.

THE FEMALE BODY AS SACRED SITE

Like the sacred space that the women create in their homes and centers by assembling the ritual sites, the participating women's bodies also become the sites of the ritual, embodying the suffering and piety of Fatima and Zaynab. By internalizing the message of Muharram, women create agency and authority that is grounded in piety. They protest against oppression and injustice, and the tears they weep are considered to be spiritually and psychologically cleansing. Women's lives are made meaningful through participating in the religious rituals that hold spiritual and emotional cleansing properties as each woman gives voice to her religious convictions. The rituals allow women a different perspective of human suffering by putting their personal sufferings in the context of the larger issues that the Prophet's family faced. Many of the women state that their sorrows are diminished in comparison to the suffering of the Prophet's family at the hands of their oppressors. The rituals connect them to the holy family and keep their faith alive and fluid.

THE IDEOLOGICAL BASIS OF THE RITUALS

Not only do the Muharram rituals commemorate the death of members of the early Shi'a community, but they are also grounded in ideological beliefs that form Shi'ism a bit differently than Sunni Islam. Woven throughout the rituals are the tenets of Shi'ism. *Tawhid,* the divine unity and the oneness of God, is acknowledged in every Shi'a event. The importance of *nubuwwa* (prophethood) is vocalized in the elegies and prayers expressing the role of Muhammad in the salvation and redemption of the Shi'a. Their belief that the Imamate will be present on their behalf for *ma'ad* (the resurrection) after the Day of Judgment soothes their fears regarding salvation. By honoring the Imamate, Shi'a believe they will be spared divine persecution and that *adl* (divine justice) will prevail, with God's subsequent judgment rewarding or punishing individuals for their actions. Shi'a stress that God will read their intentions and commitment to Islam through their rituals of devotion, prayer, and visitation of holy shrines.

Shi'a use of *ijtihad* to arrive at points of religious law through reasoning uncovers knowledge that would be transmitted by the Imams were they still alive. Consensus comes through numerous *marj'as* (those whose authority is considered worthy of being followed) offering differing opinions and then finally agreeing between themselves on modern issues that are not covered in the Qur'an or *hadiths.* Above all, Shi'a stress *niyyat* (intention) and the importance of *du'as* (devotional prayer) and *ziyarat* (visitation of shrines). By visiting the sacred sites, Shi'a maintain an intimacy with Fatima, Zaynab, and the Imamate.

Shi'a belief in the return of the last Imam, the Mahdi, helps them to cope with the injustices that they see in the modern world. The final Imam, who is in occultation, will return to restore piety and justice throughout the world. Martyrdom or selfless service to the Prophet and his family keeps the past alive in the hearts of the women and their community. Their rituals address the immediate situation—for example, the war in Iraq or the suffering of Shi'a in Pakistan—and also reserve a place for them in the afterlife. They maintain a direct relationship with the holy family that transcends the temporal world, for they believe that the holy family is present at all rituals in their honor. The rituals do not create closure but establish a never-ending relationship with the Prophet, his family, and the subsequent Imams. By enacting their rituals, they experience a sense of their own spiritual and political agency.

Shi'a rituals hold tremendous significance for the participating women. Tears are shed on behalf of the sorrowful story of the past and also express today's troubles, whether the loss of a sister, the death of a husband, or the war in Iraq. Most of the women in Southern California have practiced the Muharram rituals since childhood. They preserve these memories of the past and create new ones for themselves and the younger generation of women that will take their place in the ritual, maintaining it for future generations every time a gathering is held. The women carefully teach their children the chants, the stories, and the ritual movements to ensure the safekeeping of their traditions. Their lifelong participation in the rituals leads them to the individuation process through which personal and communal identity is built.

Through participation in the rituals, practitioners are able to create a sense of self within their cultural context. For these women, agency and authority are attached not necessarily to Western notions of agency but to religious authority that is validated through their religious and ritual enactments and experiences. The women define themselves through their religion and culture, where their religious belief forms agency. Rather than resist, they collaborate as a community of women to maintain their rituals and religious identity. Most notably, all the women believed that the importance of Muharram was the meaning behind it whether it was spiritual, psychological, or political. During interviews, women divulged the following information.

B: Why do you cry during Muharram?

H: Well, you want to cry you know, you get emotional about the Prophet's family and then other things too. I cry for my own children's well-being and especially my family who is still in Iraq. They are suffering just like others did hundreds of years ago. I guess I feel better when I cry. I feel closer to Allah and to the Prophet's family. I guess it helps me cope with things I have no control over . . . like the war [in Iraq]. I know that life holds suffering but it is important that some people die for a reason that has a greater meaning.

The foregoing woman examines the importance of weeping on behalf of the Prophet's family and reminds us of the importance of personal sacrifice. The significance of the doctrine of martyrdom for Shi'a women's agency is important to investigate. This form of martyrdom is located in the personal and communal realm. From the Shi'a perspective, the martyrdom of Husayn for the greater good of the community models a deeply spiritual connection to perfection through individual selfless martyrdom. Considered to be the noblest way to die, it is "sanctified when it is motivated by a desire and willingness to negate oneself for the sake of a greater whole."[21] The concept of martyrdom stems from a deeply spiritual concept of life, which does not see death as "a tragic form of leaving the world, but a means of attaining eternal life."[22] By internalizing these beliefs, the women can make some sense of human suffering. There is meaning in the message of Imam Husayn.

H: I think it's the message behind it. It is the whole message of Imam
Husayn and why he sacrificed his life. What was the purpose of that?
How he and his group stood up to his enemies. Still, today people
remember them, while the enemies, nobody remembers. The role that
Zaynab, (sallallaha alayhi wa sallam—may peace be upon her), and
Fatima and all these people played in the religion. So, they make me
reflect on my own life, our own life as people, what are we doing for
religion, how much are we doing for the religion? What bad things
are we doing, what good things are we doing? What things do we
need to improve on, what do we need to harbor more of? So it's really
a month of reflection and of self-cleansing and feeling sorry about
some acts that some people who call themselves Muslims did, and
the same thing we see happens nowadays. So it is that kind of cycle
of thinking and reflection.

She suggests that reenacting the rituals is a reminder of the importance of
keeping the religion alive and also a time to reflect on what really matters
to her. She stresses the importance that Muharram is a reminder to keep
things sacred. It is a time to think about one's choices and what is important in life. I asked another woman if Muharram can be seen as a political
statement, and she responded:

S: Yeah, I mean to an extent yes, because when you see people being tyr-
annized, you see things that are not supposed to be done and yet be
quiet and do nothing about it. So Muharram and Karbala teach you not
to be quiet about issues that take place around you. You should be aware
of everything that is happening and play your role the way you should
and not only be concerned about your life, but be concerned about the
people around you. So Karbala has to do with politics too. But then it
was not achieving the status, I mean being the ruler. I mean Imam
Husayn didn't want to be the ruler, he wanted to implement justice.

Another woman interviewed stresses the message of Imam Husayn to "be
yourself." This shows the importance of standing up for one's identity and
one's belief. It encourages a strong statement about Shi'a identity.

B: Do you see Muharram as a political statement?
T: I see Muharram as psychological, physical, love, and also political, yes.
As far as passion and love, when you practice you have the opportunity
to sit in the majalis or read more about Imam Husayn, it just touches
you. It teaches you how to deal with your family, with your neighbors,
and how to act. As far as politics, it teaches you that Husayn teaches

everyone, I always say this, even to non-Muslims, "Be yourself, don't let someone give you an idea or show you their way, try to be as close to yourself, be in touch with your insides." That is why Imam Husayn was offered to be a ruler: they offered good money, everything. He said, "Do I live for this short lifetime or do I live for eternity?" This is the message that Imam Husayn gives to everyone every year: be yourself. In the last message on Ashura, he said to the enemy, "Even if you are not Muslim and you do not believe in the Day of Judgment, just be free men. Don't follow your ruler just because he tells you so." Think about it.

"Being yourself" is the formation of an important identity construction that Shi'a women find through the teachings and practices of their religion and their religious rituals. Developing a strong sense of self creates agency and authority.

One interviewee embraces the importance of tradition and how that is kept alive through ritual participation. She feels that as a Shi'a, she finds much of her identity created by the Muharram rituals. She expresses the importance of humility and patience and examines the notion that allowing oneself to be a victim is un-Islamic. The 20th-century Shi'a philosopher Ali Shariati, who is often quoted by the women in the Shi'a community, echoes this belief. He says, "One is the oppressor and the other is the one who accepts the oppression. It is the co-operation of these two which brings about oppression."[23] This is a very important value for women because it keeps them from being victimized by others. This interviewee refuses to be a victim anywhere in her life, whether at home or at work.

B: Can Muharram be seen as a political statement?
S: Yeah, I mean to an extent yes, because when you see people being tyr-annized, you see things that are not supposed to be done and yet be quiet and do nothing about it. So Muharram and Karbala teach you not to be quiet about issues that take place around you. You should be aware of everything that is happening and play your role the way you should and not only be concerned about your life, but be concerned about the people around you, especially those being oppressed for any reason. So Karbala has to do with politics too. It is really about justice, and women can really relate to that.

The Shi'a women in Southern California also put tremendous importance on the messages left by Fatima and Zaynab. Fatima, the daughter of the Prophet Muhammad, the wife of Imam Ali, and the mother of Imam Husayn holds a tremendously important role in the construction of these women's sense of self. Her daughter Zaynab is especially beloved and admired by young Shi'a women. When in a difficult situation, women examine their actions and ask themselves and each other, "What would Zaynab have done?"[24] For the Shi'a, Zaynab is a primary example of a woman who was publicly pious. She is central to the gendered dimension of women and Islam, for "having observed the historical conditions, can any person claim that in those forceful and trying moments, Zaynab's tongue had any knots, her heart any intimidation, or that she herself had any fear or dread? . . . She is the voice of truth in the face of tyrannical government and an oppressive sultanate."[25] Shi'a Muslim women can turn toward Zaynab as a role model and to Fatima as an intercessor, but ultimately each woman is responsible for her own salvation, redemption, and life choices. Given these role models, women assume many roles; but the ultimate role is to become oneself through spiritual commitment and action. Every woman in the Shi'a community has the opportunity to be like Fatima, to be her sacred self, to find personal agency and religious authority by emulating the piety and bravery that she and Zaynab represent.

Most important, these Shi'a women stress knowing oneself and standing up for oneself. They do not need to define themselves by external means, as urged in the popular image of woman that is created by media images. A Shi'a woman is not a "slave" to what others think; she makes her own choices based on her religious convictions and the role modeling of Fatima and Zaynab. Young women respect the piety of Fatima and the activism of Zaynab, who is seen as a radical feminist who is brave and fearless in the face of adversity. Modernize her, and she fights for what she believes in just as she did hundreds of years ago. Today's Zaynab is an attorney, a doctor, a social activist, and an educator.

Because Fatima and Zaynab embody piety, righteousness, bravery, and courage, modern Shi'a women can do the same. They see Fatima and Zaynab as women who stand up for themselves and others and speak the truth. One interviewee says:

> Z: I always admire them when I hear stories about Fatima Zahra. She's always so outspoken, and what I love about it, that whenever a woman can get up and speak her mind, because she would always say things in front of her father, the Prophet, and he would never tell her to be quiet or to sit down or anything like that. If there was something she thought was wrong, even after when her father passed away and it was the companions and everybody discussing things, she would speak to them and say, "No this isn't correct or whatever," you know, and just state her opinion. And she would get up and speak after his passing, [she] got up in front of everyone and said those words and, you know, I just love how they were so outspoken. You don't hear about that with many other women at that

time. A lot of Muslims nowadays, I think this has to do with the culture affecting the religion, like that's embarrassing or they'll tell you not to do it. It's not really *haram*, but they're always telling you, they don't want you to be outspoken. They're, like, "That's not nice for a girl to speak her mind or anything." They discourage that, and I think that's what I'm talking about, that, her mind or anything. They discourage that, and I think that's what I'm talking about that has to do with culture. But if you look at Fatima or Zaynab, you see the opposite of that.

The foregoing interviewee uses historical narratives of Fatima and Zaynab to frame her perspective of what a pious woman is. As a young college graduate, she works to procure voting rights for Iraqis who have been displaced in the United States. She belongs to a generation of young women who are religious, educated, and politically savvy, demanding equality for all people everywhere. She sees the importance of the qualities that both Fatima and Zaynab exude when she says:

Z: I love Zaynab (my namesake!). She stood up against tyranny and oppression, something very few women have the courage to do. Now that I am in law school, I think about how I will be like her someday fighting for justice for people that have been mistreated. She was so courageous.

Shi'a women do not have to dismiss history to be modern. On the contrary, they take from the past and meld their beliefs and religious rituals into actions that they can exemplify in their daily lives as mothers, career women, and social activists. They have their feet planted firmly in the soil of modernity yet can reach for the heavens knowing they will be rewarded for their courageous and pious efforts while still here on Earth. They believe that their religion allows women to be and do anything. They have the freedom to choose. Once again, the theme that women are empowered and have personal agency is articulated.

When All Is Said and Done

The rituals that Shi'a Muslim women perform keep their religion alive and meaningful in their everyday lives as mothers, wives, career women, and community activists. They rest in the belief that the last Imam, the Mahdi, will appear at the end of time as the final avenger who will bring justice to those who have suffered for their beliefs. His return will be preceded by a long period of chaos and degeneration, yet he will restore "peace, prosperity and the final triumph of truth over falsehood when justice and equity will reign forever."[26] His return is the concrete symbol for the rewards of the holy family and the vindication of their suffering; it is the antithesis of the house of sorrows. The Mahdi, as mediator between humans and God, will return as Christ to the followers of the world at the end of his concealment. All sorrow will be forgotten, and for the Shi'a the final days will be blessed.

Commemoration of the deaths of those martyred at Karbala creates cohesion in the Shi'a community and serves as a timeless, symbolic act of solidarity. The scholar Mahmoud Ayoub stresses the importance of this commemorative ritual when he writes:

> Through ritual, religious men and women can relive an event in their spiritual history and renew their relationship with it. Through the enactment of an important event of the past, the "now" of a religious community may be extended back into the past and forward into the future. Thus, history is no longer the mere flow of happenings in time without purpose or direction. Rather, through the present moment, that is, the ritualistic moment, time and space become unified and events move toward a definite goal. In the ritualistic moment, serial time becomes the bridge connecting primordial time and its special history with the timeless eternity of the future. This eternal fulfillment of time becomes the goal of human time and history.[27]

The past becomes the now whenever there is a remembrance of suffering at the hands of oppressors, whether that might be historical or in modernity. Participating in the ritual defines the participant, forming identity and establishing meaning.

CONCLUSION

Shi'a Muslim women regard themselves as women who have consciously chosen the paths of Fatima and Zaynab. They make a commitment to a larger, more fundamental goodness that is based on the preservation of femininity, gender roles, and religious authority. They would adamantly argue that they are not oppressed by their religion but that they enjoy God-given rights as Muslim women. Proofs of the freedoms designated to women are the important and elevated roles given to Fatima and Zaynab. These Shi'a women implement such concepts of feminism as independent thinking, standing up to injustice, showing compassion, patience, and bravery, earning a living, and still maintaining allegiance to their religion while creating change through the system, rather than completely alienating themselves from spiritual and cultural values. Shi'a women can respond in the same way that Fatima and Zaynab did to oppression; they can resist the evils of globalization and forced modernization by Western influences that are just as much a battleground for women today as they were historically.

The worldview of practicing Shi'a women is based on intercession, salvation, redemption, and justice by Allah on Judgment Day. Through their religious beliefs, practices, and rituals, they believe that they must be activists against oppression and constructers of piety by reenacting their religious rituals. The female role models Fatima and Zaynab and the Muharram rituals are important ingredients in the construction of the women's spiritual identity. Meaning is established by observance of specific days that depict, love, death, loss of children or husbands, and other sufferings that women of all times have had to bear. The women's ritual offerings reveal the importance of piety, ethics, moral lessons, and community interaction through the practice of ritual purity, devotion, and prayer. Their rituals commemorate the holy family and other members of the Prophet's family, honoring them and asking for intercession in return. Their redemption rests in their devotion and sincerity. They argue that they are not oppressed but fully visible and conscious actors in their own lives and the lives of others. Pious Shi'a women are empowered through their religious expression as they pass their worldview from one generation to the next.

NOTES

1. Maria Massi Dakake, *The Charismatic Community: Shi'ite Identity in Early Islam* (Albany: State University of New York Press, 2007), 81–86, based on the earliest historical sources, including Abu Mikhnaf, *Maqtal al-Husayn*, ed. Hasan al-Ghaffari (Qum: Ilmiyya, 1985), 91. The phrase "martyr son of martyr" is found in Tabari, cited on 73, 269.

2. 'Allamah Sayyid Muhammad Husayn Tabataba'i, *Shi'ite Islam*, trans. Seyyed Hossein Nasr (New York: State University of New York Press, 1977), 77.

3. Henry Corbin, *Cyclical Time and Ismaili Gnosis* (London: Kegan Paul International, 1983), 182.

4. Mahmoud Ayoub, *Redemptive Suffering in Islam* (The Hague: Mouton Publishers, 1978), 213.

5. Mary F. Thurkill, "Chosen among Women: Mary and Fatima in Early Medieval Christianity and Shi'ism" (unpublished thesis, Indiana University, 2001), 2.

6. Ibid., 99.

7. Nadia Abu-Zahra, *The Pure and Powerful: Studies in Contemporary Muslim Society* (Reading, Berks, UK: Ithaca Press, 1997), 120.

8. Ibid., 110.

9. Kamran Scot Aghaie, *The Martyrs of Karbala* (Seattle: University of Washington Press, 2004), 115–16.

10. Ibid., 47.

11. Farah Azari, "Islam's Appeal to Women in Iran: Illusions and Reality," in *Women of Iran: The Conflict with Fundamentalist Islam*, ed. Farah Azari (London: Ithaca Press, 1983), 70.

12. Lara Deeb, *An Enchanted Modern: Gender and Public Piety in Shi'i Lebanon* (Princeton, NJ: Princeton University Press, 2006), 149.

13. Ibid., 163.

14. Ibid., 218.

15. Ibid., 5.

16. Ibid., 53.

17. Catherine Bell, *Ritual Theory, Ritual Practice* (Oxford: Oxford University Press, 1992), 109.

18. Thomas J. Csordas, *Body/Meaning/Healing* (New York: Palgrave Macmillan, 2002), 11, 53.

19. Vernon Schubel, *Religious Performance in Contemporary Islam* (Columbia: University of South Carolina Press, 1993), 90.

20. Ayoub, *Redemptive Suffering in Islam*, 201.

21. Nader Ahmadi and Fereshteh Ahmadi, *Iranian Islam* (New York: St. Martin's Press, 1998), 168.

22. Ibid., 169.

23. Ali Shariati, *Shariati on Shariati and the Muslim Women*, trans. Laleh Bakhtiar (Chicago: ABC Group International, 1996), 136.

24. Ibid., 204–5.

25. Syed Akbar Hyder, *Reliving Karbala: Martyrdom in South Asian Memory* (New York: Oxford University Press, 2006), 169.

26. Ayoub, *Redemptive Suffering in Islam*, 217.

27. Ibid., 148.

CHAPTER 14

Religion as a Spring for Activism: Muslim Women Youth in Canada[*]

Katherine Bullock

C lad in a *hijab* (headscarf) and holding a placard containing an antiwar slogan is a young Canadian Muslim woman attending a rally partly organized by a student group of which she is the chair; another young *hijabi*[1] speaks on behalf of her university's interfaith council at a memorial to honor 14 women shot in a shooting tragedy on another Canadian university; and yet another young *hijabi* sits at an information booth to explain to a passer-by her positive view of Islam's teachings about women and how these teachings differ from negative cultural teachings that adversely affect Muslim women.

Nadira, Mona, and Samana are three young Canadian Muslim women who have written autobiographical stories about their lives as activists.[2] Though there are obviously differences among their lives' trajectories, since each human life has its own unique life history, there are striking parallels among their stories: their sense that their activism stems from their faith and that their activism is also in part related to a defense of that

[*]Adapted from *Muslim Women Activists in North America: Speaking for Ourselves*, edited by Katherine Bullock. Portions taken from Chapter 11: "In Pursuit of Truth and Justice" by Nadira Mustapha; Chapter 13: "Activism: A Part of Life" by Mona Rahman; and Chapter 16: "Taking the Bus to the World of Islamic Activism" by Samana Siddiqui. Copyright © 2005. Reprinted with permission of University of Texas Press.

faith from the negative stereotypes of Islam and Muslim women that abound in Canadian and, indeed, Western society as a whole.

This chapter is an attempt to draw out of these three autobiographical narratives some reflections about the relationship between religion and women's activism in a Canadian context. I have always found autobiography to be a useful way to investigate broader trends in society. Thus, while I would never claim that three narratives speak to the experiences of all Muslim women the world over, I do suggest that Nadira's, Mona's, and Samana's stories are reflective of a subsection of contemporary young Muslim women. These are young women who have grown up Muslim in Western society and who self-consciously choose to identify themselves as Muslims by wearing a headscarf and long wrist- and ankle-length clothes out of a conviction that this is a religiously mandated dress. They become activists through interactions with Muslim student associations, many of which adhere to an activist interpretation of Islam founded in the reformist and anticolonial movements of the Middle East and South Asia. Thus, an activist lifestyle is combined with particular interpretations of Muslim women's role. These perspectives differ from other traditionalist and modernist perspectives on Muslim women and also are not always considered liberatory from a Western liberal feminist point of view. One of the arguments advanced in this chapter is that adopting this activist-inflected interpretation of Islam indicates that religion can contribute to women's empowerment, rather than necessarily being a source of oppression, as is more commonly understood, particularly when it comes to Islam.

Moreover, these three narratives reveal the salience of religion as a positive source of identity in an otherwise chaotic and instable world. Growing up in Canada, these young women could have embraced many different lifestyles, and yet, all three chose to adopt a reformist-conservative religious lifestyle.[3] Theirs is a decision naturally reflective of their upbringing and environment, but contrary to any simplistic notion that equates young Muslim girls' behaviors with Muslim community brainwashing and/or intimidation, their decisions are made by young, thoughtful, self-reflective women, demonstrating their agency as actors in their society. The overarching negative images of Muslims that permeate Canadian culture are ever present in the lives of Muslims in Canada—as, indeed, they are in the lives of all Canadians—so a decision, say, to start wearing a *hijab* and keep wearing it (that is, not take it off when out of the sight of parents) is a decision of an agent acting as an individual, making decisions, and sustaining them through a complex cognitive process that interacts with all aspects of society.

This chapter proceeds in three parts. Part One introduces the women and their arenas as activists. Part Two delves more deeply into the relationship between their faith and activism. Part Three looks at their understanding of religion, women, and activism in the contemporary era.

PART ONE: INTRODUCING NADIRA, MONA, AND SAMANA

Nadira was born in Winnipeg, a city in western Canada, in the early 1970s. Her ethnic heritage is Caribbean, and her religious upbringing began from an early age, since her parents and siblings were activists in the local community. Nadira remembers being taken to Islamic study circles by an older brother to learn about Islamic law when she was ten.[4] When she was 12, her youth group, the Muslim Youth Council of Winnipeg, gave her her first project, and ever since then she has moved from project to project, even into her PhD years, where at the time of (her) writing, she was studying Islamic law at McGill University in Montréal, on the eastern side of Canada. Nadira's university activism comes as no surprise, given this probably intense upbringing in an activist environment. Whereas other high school students might have congregated after school at the mall to "hang out" and shop, Nadira was busy organizing study circles, being a summer camp counselor for Muslim youth, fundraising for children orphaned in Afghanistan as a result of the Soviet-Afghan War, and so on.[5] As a university student, she has turned her activism to the political sphere, including learning how lobbying and advocacy works in the United States, engaging in antiwar lobbying, and being an advocate for justice for Palestinians.

Mona was born in Kingston, a small university town in eastern Canada, in the early 1970s. Her parents had come from Bangladesh in the late 1960s. Her father was a graduate student and later professor at Queen's University; and, like Nadira's parents, Mona's parents were activists in the then very tiny Muslim community in Kingston. Mona remembers that because the community was so small, all the adults of her parents' generation were "aunt" and "uncle," no matter their background.[6] Her father served as the president of the Islamic society for about 18 years, most of her formative years. "Thus, I recall," writes Mona, "many evenings when my sister and I were recruited to stuff envelopes for the community newsletter."[7] At age 12, Mona was the treasurer-secretary of the Kingston Muslim Youth Club, although she thinks the president really did most of the work. From being active in the youth club, it was a natural move for Mona to become active in her high school, where she and others produced a standard presentation about Islam that could be given by the members of the youth groups at their respective high schools. At the university (still in Kingston), Mona was an active member of the Queen's University Muslim Student Association (QUMSA), organizing religious study circles, alternative FROSH (first-year students) events, and a precursor to the continent-wide "Islam Awareness Week," "Islam Days." As a graduate student at the same university, Queen's, Mona served as a president of QUMSA. One of her responsibilities was to sit on the Campus Interfaith Council. The chair of that council, the Rev. Brian Yealland, asked Mona to give the memorial speech for the "Montréal massacre," a shooting at the Ecole Polytechnique in Montréal that resulted in the deaths of 14 young women.

Samana's autobiographical narrative is less detailed than Nadira's or Mona's. From her story we learn that she was born in the mid-1970s in Montréal, a big city in the eastern French province of Québec in Canada, to parents who had emigrated from Pakistan. Samana's activism was sparked when she was 16 by hostile looks she received during the 1991 Gulf War, when she determined to be a journalist. She began by becoming active in her high school Muslim students' association and writing a column about Islam for the high school newspaper, *Phoenix*. At Concordia University she continued this activism, writing for the university's student newspaper and being active in the Muslim Student Association (MSA), as well as pursuing her studies. After an internship at the *Montréal Gazette*, she took time off to study Arabic at McGill, until she landed her "dream" job of writing a practical advice column about how to live Islam, especially in North America, for the Sound Vision Web site. Sound Vision is a Muslim-owned company that aims to produce multimedia materials for Muslims. Samana prepares articles, including sample letters to get time off for Eid, instructions about how parents can interact with the school, sample in-class presentations about Ramadan, and the like.[8]

PART TWO: RELIGION AND ACTIVISM

One of the striking themes of the autobiographical narratives of these three young Canadian Muslim women is how they privilege the role of religion in their activism. While we might be familiar with social justice activism stemming from Catholic liberation theology, social justice activism stemming from Islamic discourses is less known. Nadira opens her chapter with two paragraphs on the relationship of activism to dreams of achieving "peace and justice." Indeed, her opening sentence declares, "The quest to achieve peace and justice remains the heartbeat of every activist."[9] She proceeds from such generalized statements about activism to an eight-paragraph discussion about Hasan al-Banna and how his religious teachings inspired activism in her. Hasan al-Banna is the founder of the Egyptian Muslim Brotherhood (Ikhwan al-Muslimun, 1928). Al-Banna's

Muslim Brotherhood grew rapidly in Egypt, claiming about a million followers by 1949. Because of the organization's Islamic and popular nature, the Egyptian state has alternated between allowing the Muslim Brotherhood to function and banning and suppressing it.

In the West, the Muslim Brotherhood is seen as a controversial Islamist movement whose commitment to democracy, human rights, and the rule of law is rendered suspect by its support for *shari'a*, Islamic law. Certainly, its traditional prescriptions for male and female roles in society run contrary to mainstream Western feminist notions of women's liberation and equality. And yet, al-Banna's teachings and the movement for reform under the auspices of Islam he initiated have garnered admiration, respect, and devotion from millions of Muslims in the world. Nadira is one of these. She believes that the "Ikhwan al-Muslimoon works to establish worldwide peace by first establishing peace within the individual. Thereafter, this internal peace, sincerity, love, and compassion should follow to the development of the family, the community, the 'state,' and eventually throughout the world."[10]

Nadira credits Hasan al-Banna with sparking her commitment to activism:

> Hasan al-Banna and aspects of his inspiring, prestigious, and sincere movement prompted my religious activism from an early age. . . . [His] spiritual philosophy is one of the major factors that led me to a spiritual awakening. This philosophy remains the backbone of my religious-related activism, and is one of the key elements that channelled me to select my first career as a teacher at the secondary level in order to work for the next generation.[11]

A clearer statement relating activism to religion is hardly needed.

After the lengthy discussion of Hasan al-Banna and his relationship to her activism, Nadira relates the influence of her family and her environment on her activism. Once again, she privileges the religious aspect as opposed to possible nonreligious aspects of these. Regarding her family, Nadira writes:

> Born in Canada and of Caribbean descent, and thus raised in a Western environment, I grew up within a family embracing strong Islamic morals that engraved in me the true meaning of the oneness of God, the logic of religion, the dynamics of spirituality, the meaning of this temporary life, the importance of humility, the significance of ethical and physical purity, the value of organizational and leadership skills, and the permissibility of enjoying this temporary life within God's guidelines.[12]

And regarding her environment, she notes:

> The exposure to Hasan al-Banna's spiritual teachings, my family, and the environment cultivated by my youth group all contributed to my religious activism. The dream to establish an Islamic niche for the Muslims in our community was instilled in the youth's [sic] minds from an early age. The youth organisation, the Muslim Youth Council (MYC) of Winnipeg, Manitoba, encompassed various elements of an independent, self-governed as well as coexisting Islamic niche within the larger environment. Thus the projects that were implemented tended to be in the following spheres: spiritual, educational (secular and religious), political, economical, and recreational.[13]

So, when Nadira talks about her upbringing, she places religious influences at the top of the list. Religion for her has played a positive formative role in her identity as a Canadian Muslim.

Nadira closes her chapter with a paragraph returning to the theme of activism, peace, and justice:

> The quest to achieve peace and justice at a worldwide level both politically and religiously is not a simple endeavour. It commences with one's own personal and pure understanding of his/her religion and the implementation of amalgamating politics and religion within one's own life. When we have true and sincere leaders of this disposition and spirit, we will be in a better position to make substantial and permanent changes throughout the world, by the will of God.[14]

The final phrase, "by the will of God," recalls a traditional Islamic saying, insha'allah, whereby a Muslim recognizes that while individuals plan and work and mean to achieve things in the world, none of this happens except by the permission of God. Thus Nadira ends her chapter with a very strong nod to a religious perspective.

These three somewhat lengthy quotations reveal the very strong linkage for Nadira between her activism and her religion. We are able to get a sense through these quotations that while her upbringing was obviously very infused with religious perspectives, she wholeheartedly approves and celebrates that upbringing. Nowhere does she imply youthful rebellion against her parents for their religious upbringing of her, nor does she suggest any sense of doubt or discomfort at being raised so strongly Muslim in such a Western environment as Canada. Indeed, through her narrative, the reader feels the approval Nadira gives to her parents and youth leaders for their "instilling" Islam so strongly, yet as a continuation of her activism.

The very act of writing the narrative is obviously meant to say something positive about being a religious Muslim woman activist in Canada. It is a subtext to be understood against the overarching negative Western stereotype about Islam as violent and oppressive to women. It can be contrasted with such narratives as those of Irshad Manji or Raheel Reza, who talk depressingly of the awful *madrassas* (weekend Islamic schools) they attended as young girls and tell how they have been propelled into a radically different understanding of Islam from that of Nadira.[15]

Like Nadira, Mona also opens her chapter with a short discussion on the relationship between religion and activism. However, Mona has a different understanding of the two, even though hers is also an understanding that privileges religion as a motivator for activism. The first paragraph discusses how Mona does not see herself as an "activist" because to her mind, activists are people who "go beyond the call of duty to work for changes in society," whereas she sees her work to bettering society as part of her "duty as a Muslim."[16] She proceeds to talk about how she sees the link between religious faith and doing "righteous deeds," and she quotes one of her favorite verses in the Qur'an (Surah al-'Asr, 103) in support. For Mona, "activism," which she sees as a multilevel arena—from educating oneself about one's religion to assisting one's family and community, educating others about Islam, contributing to the broader Canadian society, and helping alleviate the suffering of others throughout the world[17]—is part of "righteous deeds." Moreover, she argues, Islam is about "balance—between the spiritual world and the *dunya* (material world)."[18] So a Muslim must have more than simply faith; a Muslim must translate that faith into action—and not just any kind of action, but good actions done for the sake of God's pleasure (i.e., activism, or in her terminology, "righteous deeds"). She writes, "The linkage of faith with doing righteous deeds is a recurring theme within the Qur'an; in fact, to my understanding, references to 'those who believe' in the Qur'an are often (if not always) followed by the phrase 'and do righteous deeds.'"[19]

While her understanding of the meaning of the word "activist" is evidently different from Nadira's, the parallels between their understandings of their faith are also clear. It is mostly a semantic difference, with Nadira using the phrase "religious activist," and Mona collapsing that term into the very meaning of "being Muslim." Note also the parallels between their understandings of the overlaying levels of activism, from the individual, to the family, to the society. The end result is very similar, with both being active in MSAs on campus, organizing youth camps, participating in study circles, and the like. Nadira has taken a more overtly political advocacy route out of her conviction that Islamic activism must address itself to the political realm in order to be complete,[20] whereas Mona has mostly focused on community-building projects, especially as the administrator of an e-mail list for Muslim women called Sisters Net.

Mona ends her chapter, as did Nadira, with a traditional Islamic invocation. Hers is a prayer asking God for forgiveness if she "erred or misled anyone in any way [in her essay]. Anything good in this essay is from Allah (swt [*subhanahu wa ta'ala*—glory be to God]); all mistakes are due to my own weaknesses,"[21] she finishes.

Samana starts her chapter differently from that of Nadira or Mona. True to her journalistic sense, she starts by narrating a story, with dramatic phrases that signal the import of the story she narrates for her subsequent life as a Muslim activist. She gets on the bus for school, "weary" and looking for a seat. "The next move I made changed me forever," she foreshadows. It was during the 1991 Gulf War, and without a second thought she had put on a black headscarf that day: "It wasn't a political statement . . . maybe I just threw it on because it was the first thing I could find. Or maybe it was because black was one of my favourite colors. Whatever the reason, I probably looked very, very 'Muslim.'" And during the Gulf War, it was not a good thing in many Western cities to look "very, very 'Muslim.'"[22]

Samana continues her story by recounting the hostile glances she received from the adults as she walked down the aisle looking for a seat. The looks "caught me off guard," she says. "Instead of the usual mild curiosity or obliviousness when they saw me, I could feel hostility in the air, like electricity during a lightning storm. One particular woman's expression remains imprinted on my brain to this day: narrowed, angry eyes looking straight into mine. She frowned at me, offering me a hard, grim expression."[23]

So, unlike Nadira and Mona, who were raised in activist environments, Samana experienced an outside catalyst for her activism, in this case anti-Muslim sentiment during a time of tension between the West and the Muslim world. Samana writes that while compared with other Muslims, she thinks her family "got off lightly" during the Gulf War (CSIS [Canadian Security Intelligence Service] didn't visit, no one crank-called the house), but the incident on the bus "unnerved" her. She wondered, "Why did people look at me so hatefully? I was normal, wasn't I, a teenager catching the (late) bus to school? Did those who stared think I was going to blow up the bus or kill somebody? Did they think I was related to Saddam Hussein?"[24]

Samana writes that she had learned from her political science professors that perception is reality, and the bus incident showed her that as a result of the negative coverage Islam was getting in the media, people had negative perceptions of Islam. She resolved to defend her faith through journalism, to try to give rise to a different media perspective that she hoped would translate into different reactions from those around her.

> The bus incident propelled me into what is called "Islamic activism." It was the desire to stand up for my beliefs and make it clear that Islam is not what the prevailing "wisdom" in the West says it is. No, I'm not a terrorist. No, Islam is not a murderous, violent religion bent on destroying and suppressing life, beauty and the good. The vision behind my activism was simple: to clear up misunderstandings and refute lies against Islam.[25]

Samana's "sudden but seamless"[26] entrée into activism sets her story apart from those of Nadira and Mona. The latter two conceive of their activism as an outgrowth of their spiritual development, Samana to an external catalyzing event. Had the bus incident never happened, would she have become a Muslim activist? The differences between these stories indicate that while it is evident that religion plays a powerful and positive motivating factor in Muslim women's activism, even in that connection, nuances and differences exist. Nadira, Mona, and Samana mobilize religion in their activism in different ways. So, while they may all look quite similar—brown-skinned young Canadian women in headscarves—it is important to recall that they are also individuals with unique stories. Their life experiences also dispel the effacing and negative stereotype of the "veiled" silent and submissive Muslim woman, an archetype deeply ensconced in Western popular culture.[27]

The rest of Samana's story shows that even though she pegs down her activism to the bus incident, there were other "seeds" of activism planted long before that, and she goes on to talk about her family and her decision in grade nine to wear *hijab*. In these aspects of her biographical narrative, we can discern more similarities among her and Nadira and Mona. Samana talks about how her parents, especially her mother, "made it a point to teach me that I am a Muslim, I'm different, and that this is not something to I should be ashamed of." Samana attributes to this teaching a seed of activism, as if to say that merely holding to one's own identity is in and of itself an act of activism, of social justice. Of course, in a racist environment, holding to one's identity is exactly a form of activism because the opposite, ceding one's identity and being required to "blend in" is an act of social injustice. This is indeed what has happened throughout the whole history of European colonization of the Middle East, Asia, and Canada, where the indigenous peoples were taught to despise their own identities, forbidden to talk their own languages, and required to be educated in the "civilizing" language of the colonizer. Here, we can recall Edward

Said's observation that "for almost every Muslim, the mere assertion of an Islamic identity becomes an act of nearly cosmic defiance and a necessity for survival."[28]

And in Samana's case, as with other people of color, blending in is not truly allowed anyway. Samana recalls:

> Growing up in Canada in the 1980s, and attending a public school where my brother and I were among barely a handful of Muslims, this message [not being ashamed of being different] needed to be reinforced regularly. Our worthiness, our "different-ness" was not something to be embarrassed about. Being a minority because of my beliefs and skin color also made me acutely aware of how futile "fitting in" eventually was. You could dress and talk like everyone else, but when push came to shove, you were never like everyone else. You would still be called a "Paki," a "terrorist," or be excluded at some level. With this realization, standing up for my beliefs became easier. So did being who I really was, instead of kowtowing to the majority.[29]

With this memory, Samana also talks about how her decision to wear *hijab* in grade nine was "a turning point," and also another activist seed being planted. She interprets the wearing of a *hijab* as "the point of no return. I could no longer try to hide myself and deny who I was. *Hijab* set me apart. It was a marker that indicated I was no longer embarrassed by my 'different-ness.'"[30] And thus, while Samana can see the activism inherent in these prior experiences, as a young woman of color, growing up in a mostly white neighborhood, feeling the sting of racism and exclusion, she still interprets her life story as becoming an activist after the incident on the bus:

> My parents fully supported me in my new role as "activist." Whether it was driving me places, letting me call during odd hours of the night to prepare MSA work, or letting me stay late when I needed to attend meetings or gatherings, their support was always there. It was a significant turnaround from high school, when coming home late would never have been tolerated. But for Islam, their hearts and their resources were always there for me.[31]

And yet the prior seeds must be considered important, for other young Muslim women have experienced being turned away from their faith because of the negative media portrayals of Muslims during the 1991 Gulf War.[32]

Samana ends her chapter with an appreciation of activism that brings her story much closer to that of Nadira and Mona:

I've come to realise that activism is not something we can simply do on the side, apart from our other daily activities. The early Muslims did not compartmentalize their lives into the "mundane" and the "activist-oriented activities." This was reflected by their drive to serve Islam in any way, with whatever their capacities, because they loved Allah and wanted to establish the truth. They were all activists.

And maybe one, day, *insha'allah*, I'll be one too.[33]

Here, Samana echoes Mona's perspective that to be an activist is part of "being Muslim," where one does not divide life into activist and nonactivist spheres. And also like Nadira and Mona, Samana ends her chapter with a traditional Islamic invocation, the same one as had Nadira; in this case, in its original Arabic.

These three young Canadian Muslim women's stories remind us of the multifaceted ways in which Muslim women mobilize religion for their activism. Samana's story, emphasizing an external propeller into activism, differentiates her from Nadira and Mona, who "grew up" in activist families. Nadira and Mona themselves express different perspectives on the meaning of the term "activism," and each has focused her activist energies in a different sphere. And yet there are intersections and criss-crosses between these three young women activists: they all do things consciously to "defend" Islam from detractors in the West; they see themselves as serving God through their activism; they may describe their activism differently, yet they all refer to similar concepts about activism and how it relates to being Muslim; and they all end their chapters with a traditional Islamic understanding of the relationship between individual endeavor and God's power.

PART THREE: RELIGION, WOMEN, AND ACTIVISM IN THE CONTEMPORARY ERA

Not surprisingly, given the overloaded negative Western stereotype about Islam's oppression of women, all three young women discuss being Muslim and female in their chapters. Nadira talks about women and Islam in two separate parts of the chapter, once when discussing her youth and finally in her conclusion as she sums up her thoughts on being an activist, a Muslim and a woman. Nadira tells us that as she was being raised in the activist environment of her family and youth group, the boys and the girls were treated equally, and equality was a "strong focus" of the youth group.[34] In fact, she says, "The experience of gender equality was so phenomenal that I personally did not realize, while in junior and senior high school, that in certain pockets of the Muslim world inequalities existed between men and women."[35]

This somewhat astonishing claim is testament both to the laudable vision of the parents, teachers and leaders of her youth group (there are numerous Muslim communities in Canada that only educate the boys in Qur'an and Islam, leaving the girls at home to play or engage in household duties) and to their success in imparting to Nadira an Islamic concept of gender justice that differs from that of mainstream secular Western society. For in the same paragraph, Nadira talks about her decision to wear a *hijab* in grade 10. Now, *hijab*, or wearing the veil, is considered by many feminist scholars and commentators in the West to be a sign of Islam's submission of women—for its way of sexualizing, controlling, and containing the female body; for its stiflingness, especially in summer; and for its inequality in that men do not have to wear it.[36] Needless to say, Nadira's perspective on *hijab* is radically different, so that she can choose to wear the veil and still experience growing up and being a Muslim female as being "equal" with her coreligionist boys and men. She does not discuss this in depth, but given the contemporary discourse on *hijab* from the perspective of those who claim *hijab* is not (necessarily) oppressive, it would not be a misplaced assumption to think that Nadira imbibed and agreed with this perspective as she grew up till now. This positive view of *hijab* often describes the wearing of the veil in feminist terms, as being a dress that frees women from the tyranny of the beauty myth, that treats a woman as a person and not a sex object, that provides a liberatory experience as against the commodification of women in Western capitalist culture, and that it is an expression of devotion to God, a source of peace. It is an acknowledgment that Islam views men and women differently but equally.[37]

Nadira's paragraph describing her decision to wear a *hijab* is worth quoting at some length for the way it connects these points about women's position, spirituality, and dress:

> The right to education was also a matter of absolute equality for both genders. From attending basic or intensive study circles to praying night prayers at the mosque during the month of Ramadan, from attending Friday prayer to attending month-long educational retreats, both males and females experienced equal opportunity. As a result of the religious environment cultivated for both genders, in addition to the religiously oriented work I was involved in, I entered into a period of high spirituality with Muhammad Al-Ghazali (a famous Muslim scholar and mystic, d. 1111 CE) as my mentor and guide commencing at the age of fifteen. Engaging in acts of worship on an increasingly high level, followed by an appreciation for the seriousness of this life and our duty as God's servants within the world, became the cornerstones of my life. When I was in grade ten, I altered my style of dress from wearing baggy pants to

wearing long skirts; in grade eleven, I wholeheartedly wore the *jilbab*, a long-flowing outer garment. Al-Ghazali states that modesty remains the infrastructure of Islam and reflects the internal condition of the heart.[38]

Rather than seeing *hijab* as a symbol of oppression, Nadira has a positive view of *hijab*:

The role of the Muslim woman in Islam is one of grave importance to which we, Muslims, seem to be oblivious at times. The Muslim woman wearing the *hijab* remains a symbol that portrays, for Islam, educational advancement and moral liberation. By her own conduct and her activism, the Muslim woman can demonstrate to the world the reality and dynamics of the gender equity within Islam. This in turn reflects the beauty of Islam at all levels of society: individual, family, and the community.[39]

Nadira goes on to lament the treatment of Muslim women in some cultures in the world and attributes this poor treatment to "culture and/or personal, selfish and wanton desires, not of faith as taught and implemented by the last Prophet of God, Muhammad, may peace and blessings be upon him."[40] Nadira argues that the solution to women's poor treatment by fellow Muslims is to "return back to the pristine teachings of the Qur'an and Sunnah."[41] She attributes unequal treatment of women in Islamic law to the lack of qualified Muslim women in *shari'a*, which results in the implementation of *shari'a* rulings being "imbalanced or misapplied."[42] Muslims, both men and women, must be educated about the proper rights and responsibilities of both men and women in the *shari'a*: hence her decision to change her career from being a teacher to study for a PhD in Islamic law at McGill University.

In her chapter, Mona also addresses the position of women in Islam, in a section titled "Sisters' Activism." Not surprisingly, given her active involvement in the Queen's University MSA (QUMSA), Mona has ideas about women and Islam that are very similar to Nadira's. Her formative years in the youth group also seem to have been with a forward-thinking group of parents. She opens this section with a quote from the Qur'an, verse 9:71, which states that "men and women are protectors one of another." She writes, "'Sisters activism' is not a phrase that I used until after my undergraduate days, mainly because the phrase implies that, in general, there is little or no participation of women."[43] But she found that women have always been involved:

Masha'allah, while I was growing up, my family and my community never differentiated between brothers' and sisters' activism, just as the

ayah [verse] in the Qur'an states. Both men and women are equally accountable for their deeds and for the building of a community, by
enjoining good and forbidding evil and observing the fundamental duties
of Islam; gender is not a factor. Moreover, there was always support and
encouragement to be active. Our "parental generation" strove to ensure
that we were educated in both our duties and our rights in Islam as
Muslims and females in particular, and that our opinions were to be
voiced and considered. . . . Like many executive councils, our community has a "women's representative" to ensure that the perspectives of
the sisters are taken into account. However, the sisters of the community have always been actively involved in community affairs, beyond
participation in the "sisters' group." To this day, there has always been at
least one sister holding an executive position in addition to that of wom-
en's representative.[44]

Both Nadira and Mona were lucky to have grown up in Muslim communities where consideration and attention is paid to girls and where
youth and women's education and involvement are promoted. These environments are reflective of many Muslim communities in North America,
though other communities reflect such less encouraging environments as
mosques that restrict women's attendance and do not encourage women's
involvement at the executive level.[45] These affirmative formative experiences have clearly affected the positive identification Nadira and Mona have
with being Muslim women in a Canadian environment. Mona went on to
become the president of the QUMSA, an association in which frequently
half its office bearers are women. One year there was only one brother executive (not the president, either), Mona says, "whom I suspect felt rather
outnumbered at times!"[46] She recalls her surprise during her term as president at receiving an e-mail from another MSA to "get advice about having
sisters as leaders of an MSA." Since QUMSA had had at least three
women as presidents prior to her, Mona was taken aback by this question.
Indeed, her term as president was the first time she was the only woman
on the executive.[47]

Mona talks about older Muslim women role models that have inspired
and guided her in her activism. These women, she believes, are reflecting
the situation of women's involvement in community life as evidenced
"at the time of the Prophet (pbuh) and the early Muslims."[48] She says that
the women role models showed her the importance of "standing firm to
the principles of Islam as outlined in the Qur'an and Sunnah in our non-
Muslim society," and she appreciates them for having paved the way for
young women like her to follow in their footsteps, young women who are
able to do things they now "take for granted."[49]

This appreciation for older women who broke down barriers leads Mona to lament the situation of Muslim women in today's world. She writes, "Unfortunately, there are many misconceptions regarding women in Islam, their rights, their duties, and indeed even their position, among non-Muslims and even among Muslim women themselves."[50] She notes, "This is why it seems that, throughout the years, no matter what the forum, we always come back to discussing the rights of women in Islam, the myths and misconceptions regarding women in Islam."

Since high school Mona has been giving presentations to non-Muslims as well as Muslims about women and Islam. "I recall, as a youth, during one presentation to a high school class in which we talked about the rights and duties within a family, one girl raised her hand and commented that it seemed that the men were at a disadvantage. Perhaps we went a bit overboard in trying to dispel the myths about Muslim women!"[51]

As an undergraduate student, she was on a subcommittee for organizing "Islam Days" whose responsibility was to arrange a display presentation and be present at the table for "Islam's view on women." The QUMSA was careful to include men and women on this committee, and especially to have women present at the display to answer questions, since "no matter how knowledgeable a brother may be about women's rights in Islam (e.g., the right to an education, that the *hijab* is not a means of oppression, etc.), unfortunately, his view is not as credible as if it were being stated and demonstrated by a woman."[52]

Mona's insight demonstrates a profound understanding of the depth of the negative stereotype about women and Islam in Western culture and also speaks to a clever strategic wisdom behind the planning of "Islam Days." That young women like Mona were actively present at the planning as well as the execution stage of a poster display about women and Islam meant to address skeptical Western passers-by (in this case, fellow undergraduate students) demonstrates Mona's commitment and dedication to her faith. She is not avoiding extracurricular activities on campus out of an embarrassment to be visibly Muslim; neither has she given up the rituals and traditions of the faith into which she was socialized as a child, as is very common at university. Rather, she is an active interlocutor with the negative Western discourse, represented in the bodies of the undergrads who pass by the display and stop to ask questions or challenge the young women, about Muslim women, aiming to demonstrate the latter's errors, as she sees it. Her anecdote about her presentation in high school indicates the effort that has gone into this for her whole life, to the point that in order to compensate for the negative image, perhaps the young women went too far in the other direction of praise. This aspect of her story demonstrates that she is, like Nadira, an individual who daily makes rational and strategic choices related to supporting and confirming her identity as a devout young Muslim woman in Canada.

Indeed, so immersed is Mona in this commitment to demonstrating that Islam does not oppress women, that when she talks about what it is like to wear the headscarf, she considers it a "blessing." She states:

> *Masha'allah* for the most part, I have not encountered any negative attitudes toward me because of my *hijab*. I once had an elderly person approach me to inquire about the significance of the color of my pink scarf, as he had only ever seen women wear white or black. I responded that the color matched my outfit; this could easily lead to a discussion on the reasoning behind the *hijab*. The visibility of the *hijab* is [a] blessing as it serves as a reminder to us, as individuals, of our own behavior. As one of my friends put it, it is like "the weight of the Ummah is on your shoulders," since no matter where we go, people will associate Islam and Muslims with how you behave.[53]

This is a big sense of responsibility for young 20-year-old women to feel as they move about their day. And yet this daily challenge does not seem to daunt them. They make an effort to rise to the challenge and deal with it head on, figuratively and literally.

Mona has managed to maintain an admirable sense of tranquility, since she has grown up as a Muslim woman activist. She talks of the blessings she has experienced, the positive opportunities of being Muslim in a North American context of freedom of religion. And she is convinced that "granted, we must also constantly deal with the ignorance of those within this society about Islam and Muslims, but *insha'allah*, with time and patience this will change."[54]

Samana's story, as mentioned, is shorter and less detailed about her time growing up as a Muslim in Montréal. The experiences that drew her to activism and her decision to wear *hijab* have already been highlighted here. Like Mona, Samana talks of the impact of older Muslim women activists in helping her learn her faith and motivating her to follow in their footsteps as an activist. Samana singles out one woman in particular, Dr. Sheema Khan, the director of the Council on American-Islamic Relations, Canada, who connected Samana to "a number of worthy projects and organizations. But more importantly, she was a role model of a Muslim woman activist for me. I have great respect for her drive and dedication to serve Allah and to use her many talents and skills for Islam, *masha'allah*."[55]

Samana's thoughts on the questions related to women's position in Islam and Western culture, albeit brief, do shine through in her story through a few anecdotes that she narrates about her activism. The way her words appear on the printed page actually convey some aspect of this story, so they are reproduced in full here. She starts by talking about how embarrassed she sometimes feels when she rereads the stories she wrote about Islam for her high school newspaper:

> How immaturely ideas were put forth. How badly sentences were structured. But little did I know that, *alhamdulillah* [thanks be to God], my efforts were having a small but significant impact. A woman named Sonia put it into perspective for me. I actually met her when I was in university and she was conducting an interesting experiment: wearing *hijab* and acting "Muslim" for a class project. After a couple of meetings with her, she said something that surprised me.
>
> "Those articles you used to write in the paper at Vanier really changed the way I saw Islam and Muslims," she told me. "They helped me develop a more open mind."
>
> Really? Wow. *Alhamdulillah.* And here I was thinking no one read them—or at least dismissed them as the ravings of a religious fanatic.
>
> I experienced something similar sitting one day at a booth set up by the Vanier Muslim Students' Association. A tall, burly student came over and started telling me how horribly Muslim women were treated in his native Morocco. He was of Moroccan Jewish background. After explaining the role cultural traditions antithetical to Islam play in how Muslim women are often treated, he said to me, "You know, it takes a lot of guts to do what you guys are doing by explaining your faith. I really admire that. Thanks."
>
> That was another "Really? Wow. *Alhamdulillah*" moment for me.[56]

Her one-line reactions—"Really? Wow. *Alhamdulillah*"—written separately from the rest of the paragraph in a way that emphasizes them more strongly, capture something very deep about these exchanges. We have here a young woman being challenged about her faith and the way it treats women. For her, as a *woman of that faith*, this is an existential challenge. But Samana feels deeply in her heart that the challengers are mistaken, and she spends time writing articles for a newspaper and sitting at a booth during the day. She could be anywhere else, doing anything else, studying, shopping, or watching TV. She is not even sure that all this time she commits to this endeavour is changing anyone's mind about her faith. Then she has two positive encounters that affirm her efforts, though they are very small compared to the number of hours she would have invested. These positive encounters give her the courage, conviction, and strength to continue being an activist, eventually propelling her toward a job that would allow her to "merge [her] love of Islam with [her] love of writing."[57]

We also see in her anecdotes the similarities between Nadira's and Mona's perceptions of women and Islam. Muslim women are suffering in the world, but this is because of local cultural customs that discriminate against women, not the Islamic religion. The predominant discourse in MSAs across North America emphasizes this concept of the difference between "true Islam" and "untrue" Muslim cultures. Thus, there is a conviction that the Qur'an emphasizes women's equality with men and that this can be found in the *shari'a*, Islamic law. Some of the more traditional practices that are embraced by these youth that appear to contradict these statements about equality, such as wearing *hijab* or praying behind men, are interpreted in women-positive ways. For instance, concepts of gender equity in Islam,[58] as articulated by such Islamic scholars as Jamal Badawi, a management professor and preacher based in Halifax, Canada, enable such women to hold their Islamic practices in conjunction with their affirmation of the positive valuation of women in Islam. Gender "equity" is embraced rather than "equality," which is conceived of as "identicality." Gender equity means that men and women are different but equal. There are different rights and duties that exist in harmony and a just balance with each other; they are given to human beings by the Creator, the One who knows human nature best, and hence these varying roles and responsibilities are to be welcomed as a commitment to, and expression of, faith. The *shari'a* is held to be perfect, but some expressions of it in positive law, or applications of it, are considered to be unjust to women. The problem is the implementation, not the *shari'a* itself. Thus, where the historical *shari'a* may contain legal rulings that do not seem to promote gender equity, the response is either to try to interpret the legal opinion in the most women-friendly way or to open the idea of the need for reform to bring it in line with the Qur'an's equal treatment of women, on the premise that different historical conditions require different legal opinions. Hence, Muslims of this persuasion are reformers and traditionalists all at the same time, depending on the issue.

The foregoing is a discourse that is profoundly satisfying to many Muslims in North America because it allows for a way to resolve apparent discrepancies between a love for the faith, a conviction in its rightness and perfection, and the dissonance that can be experienced by a woman treated unjustly. It is akin to a Western secular person being convinced in the perfection of liberal ideology in the abstract, and dismayed at persistent racism in Western culture as a disease that can be educated out of the citizens in a liberal polity. Through this cognitive method, many such traditional practices as *hijab* or praying behind men in the congregation are accepted as part of the "different but equal" metaphor. Not all Muslim women in Western societies resolve these dissonances this way; some decide to reject Islam as irredeemable, and others turn to different expressions of women's equality, including that advanced by the "progressive Muslims" where women can lead mixed-gender congregational prayer. For yet others, *hijab* can be considered oppressive. It is part of my argument in this chapter that these concepts of gender equity advanced through MSAs not be dismissed as "false consciousness" but, rather, be engaged seriously because they offer many Muslim women a profoundly satisfying experience of spiritual life in the modern West. Nadira, Mona, and Samana fit into this category of Muslims; their stories reflect the contours of the discourse as I have outlined it.

CONCLUSION

In an article on Muslim women and political participation in Canada, Yasmeen Abu-Laban makes the point that Western social scientists have obscured a proper understanding of such a relationship because of their reliance on behaviorist categories.[59] She advises studying Muslim women's political behavior based on their own understandings. In the case of Muslim women activists in North America and the relationship between religion and activism, I urge the same point. Since Canadian society is supportive of the individualistic development of a person, Muslims living here have the space to forge their own identities. Young Muslim women are able to meld the strong messages about women's equality stemming from their Western milieu, with deep commitments to their faith. They find in such reformists as Hasan al-Banna strong messages about women's equality and the need for women's commitment to achieving justice in society alongside their male counterparts. What counts for us, the observers, is to notice their own understandings and possible adaptations of Islamic messages, rather than a priori (and generally negative) categories about Islam and the position of women.

Thus, through the autobiographical narratives of three young Muslim women in Canada, I have been able to highlight several things: Some young Muslim women in Canada are activists, working hard to better their societies—and not just their own communities, but the wider, non-Muslim community too. The source for their activism is their religion, their understanding that Islam requires them to better the world, or their sense of injustice at its negative image in the West and their desire to alter that image from a negative into a positive one; that through this commitment to their faith in the face of negativity, we can see rational choice and strategic decision making. These are agents, not victims. And finally, we can observe the positive effect their commitment to their faith and to activism has on their identity. We can see its stability, its high self-esteem, and its remaining strong in the face of negative encounters with the West.

NOTES

1. The epithet *hijabi* is for a Muslim woman who wears *hijab*.

2. Nadira Mustapha, "In Pursuit of Peace and Justice"; Mona Rahman, "Activism: A Part of Life"; and Samana Siddiqui, "Taking the Bus to the World of Islamic Activism," in *Muslim Women Activists in North America: Speaking for Ourselves*, ed. Katherine Bullock (Austin: University of Texas Press, 2005).

3. See the later discussion where I outline how a Muslim can be both a reformer and a conservative.

4. Bullock, ed, *Muslim Women Activists*, 119.

5. Ibid., 120.

6. Ibid., 137.

7. Ibid., 141.

8. Ibid., 181.

9. Ibid., 117.

10. Ibid., 118.

11. Ibid.

12. Ibid.

13. Ibid., 119–20.

14. Ibid., 127.

15. Radio and TV interviews on the CBC, 2005.

16. Bullock, ed., *Muslim Women Activists*, 135.

17. Ibid., 136.

18. Ibid., 135.

19. Ibid.

20. Ibid., 122.

21. Ibid., 149.

22. Zuhair Kashmeri, *The Gulf Within: Canadian Arabs, Racism and the Gulf War* (Toronto: James Lorimer, 1991); Nabeel Abraham, "The Gulf Crisis and Anti-Arab Racism in America," in *Collateral Damage: The New World Order at Home and Abroad*, ed. Cynthia Peters (Boston: South End Press, 1992).

23. Bullock, ed., *Muslim Women Activists*, 177.

24. Ibid., 178.

25. Ibid.

26. Ibid.

27. Jasmin Zine, "Muslim Women and the Politics of Representation," *American Journal of Islamic Social Sciences* 19, no. 4 (2002): 1–22.

28. Edward Said, *Covering Islam: How the Media and the Experts Determine How We See the Rest of the World* (New York: Pantheon Books, 1981), 72.

29. Bullock, ed., *Muslim Women Activists*, 179.

30. Ibid.

31. Ibid.

32. A young Muslim woman recalled being in eighth grade at the time of the Gulf War: "Everything I was reading [about Saddam Hussein] was so negative . . . that in a way you start to question your own people, you just believe whatever you read." Katherine H. Bullock and Gul Joya Jafri, "Media (Mis)-Representations: Muslim Women in the Canadian Nation," *Canadian Woman Studies* 20, no. 2 (2000): 38.

33. Bullock, ed., *Muslim Women Activists*, 181.

34. Ibid., 120.

35. Ibid., 20.

36. Katherine Bullock, *Rethinking Muslim Women and the Veil: Challenging Historical and Modern Stereotypes* (Herndon, VA: International Institute of Islamic Thought, 2002), chap. 4, passim.

37. Ibid., chap. 5, passim.

38. Bullock, ed., *Muslim Women Activists*, 120.

39. Ibid., 126.

40. Ibid.

41. Ibid., 126–27.

42. Ibid., 127.

43. Ibid., 143–44.

44. Ibid., 144.

45. Yvonne Haddad et al. argue that only a minority of traditionalists from the Indian subcontinent and Salafi leaders are not supportive of women's more public role. Yvonne Yazbeck Haddad, Jane I. Smith, and Kathleen M. Moore, *Muslim Women in America: The Challenge of Islamic Identity Today* (New York: Oxford University Press, 2006), 66.

46. Bullock, ed., *Muslim Women Activists*, 146.

47. Ibid., 146. Sadly, Mona recently told me that an influx of male Salafi graduate students has pushed women out of this Queen's University tradition of heavy participation by women in the QUMSA. This reveals how fragile women's position in community life can be.

48. Ibid., 147.

49. Ibid.

50. Ibid.

51. Ibid., 144.

52. Ibid., 145–46.

53. Ibid., 147–48.

54. Ibid., 148–49.

55. Ibid., 180.

56. Ibid., 179–80.

57. Ibid., 181.

58. Jamal Badawi, *Gender Equity in Islam: Basic Principles* (Indianapolis: American Trust Publications, 2003), 13–14.

59. Y. Abu-Laban, "Challenging the Gendered Vertical Mosaic: Immigrants, Ethnic Minorities, Gender and Political Participation," in *Citizen Politics: Research and Theory in Canadian Political Behaviour*, ed. J. Everitt and B. O'Neill (Toronto: Oxford University Press, 2002), 278–79.

Abbreviations

ADFM	Association Démocratique des Femmes du Maroc (Democratic Association of Moroccan Women)
BCE	Before the Common Era
CE	Common Era
CEDAW	Convention on the Elimination of All Forms of Discrimination Against Women
CERTWID	Center for Research Training and Information on Women in Development
DOM	Daerah Operasi Militer
ECA	Economic Commission in Africa
FGM	Female Genital Mutilation, also known as FGC, Female Genital Cutting
FLN	Front de Libération Nationale (National Liberation Front), Algeria
FOSIS	Federation of Student Islamic Societies
FROSH	Freshman-related activities
GAM	Gerakan Aceh Merdeka (Aceh Freedom Movement)
GDI	Gender Development Index
GWS	Gender and Women's Studies
HDI	Human Development Index
HIV/AIDS	Human Immunodeficiency Virus/Acquired Immune Deficiency Syndrome
IDP	Internally Displaced Person(s)
IFL	Islamic Family Law
IMF	International Monetary Fund
ISA	Internal Security Act
JAKIM	Jabatan Kemajuan Islam Malaysia (Department of Islamic Development)

JAWI	Jabatan Agama Islam Wilayah Persekutuan (Federal Territory Islamic Affairs Department)
JI	Jamaat-e Islami, Islamic political party founded in 1941 in Lahore (now Pakistan) by Abu al-Ala Mawdudi; also Jemaah Islamiyah in Indonesia
LBH APIK	Lembaga Bantuan Hukum Asosiasi Perempuan Indonesia Untuk Keadlilan, nongovernmental organization providing legal support for women
MA	Master of Arts
MAAP	Malaysians Against Moral Policing
MCB	Muslim Council of Britain
MENA	Middle East and North Africa
MP	Member of Parliament
MSA	Muslim Students Association
MYC	Muslim Youth Council
NGO	Nongovernmental Organization
NKRI	Negara Kesatuan Republic Indonesia (Unitary State of the Republic of Indonesia)
NU	Nahdlatul Ulama, Muslim organization in Indonesia
PAS	Parti Islam Se-Malaysia (All-Malaysia Islamic Party)
pbuh	"Peace be upon him," uttered at mention of revered persons, especially the Prophet Muhammad
PEKKA	Pemberdayaan Perempuan Kepala Keluarga (Female-Headed Household Empowerment Program in Aceh)
PJD	Party of Justice and Development
PKK	Pembinaan Kesejahtraan Keluarga (Family Welfare Movement)
PKS	Partai Keadilan Sejahtera (Prosperous Justice Party)
PPP	Purchasing Power Parity relative to the U.S. dollar
QUMSA	Queen's University Muslim Student Association
RELA	Ikatan Relawan Rakyat Malaysia (People's Volunteer Reserve Corps), a paramilitary force
REWA	Revolutionary Ethiopian Women's Association
RPuK	Relawan Perempuan untuk Kemanusiaan (Women's Volunteers for Humanity)
SAP	Structural Adjustment Program
SARA	*suku* (ethnicity), *agama* (religion), *ras* (race), *antar golongan* (intergroup), collectively known as SARA as the sources of conflicts
SeIA	Serikat ureung Inong Aceh (Aceh Mother Association or Women's Union)
SIS	Sisters in Islam
swt	*subhana wa ta'ala* (Glory Be to God, the Most High), inserted after every mention of God (Allah)

UK	United Kingdom
UN	United Nations
UNDP	United Nations Development Program
UNICEF	United Nations Children's Fund; originally United Nations International Children's Emergency Fund
UNPF	United Nations Population Fund
USA	United States of America
WAO	Women's Aid Organisation

Glossary

abaya   long, flowing, cloaklike garment worn over clothes

adat   concepts, rules, and codes of behavior

adbar   good spirit

adl   justice

agama   religion

ahl al-bayt   lit. "people of the house," that is, the Prophet Muhammad's family

alam   standard, flag, or sign

alhamdulillah   "All praise be to God," usually indicating thanks to God

alim/alima   male/female religious scholar

al-rahmah   mercy or compassion

anchi   you, feminine

antar golongan   intergroup

aqiqa   hair-shaving ritual, usually for a newborn child

ayat   verse (of the Qur'an)

azadari   sorrow; rituals commemorating sorrow at the martyrdom of the Prophet's grandson Husayn, predominantly observed by the Shi'a

bangsa melayu   Malay race

batul   virgin

birr   unit of currency in Ethiopia

bola   female religious leader able to conduct rituals

buda   evil eye

burqa   black floor-length garment with a separate headpiece allowing face to be covered in part or fully

351

chiqa   mud

communitas   unstructured community in which people are equal

daerah   districts

da'iyah   female missionary

dakwah   proselytization; missionary work, lit. "the call"; Ar. *dawah*

dalang   puppet master

dapur   kitchen

dars   religious instruction

dars-e-nizami   study curriculum used in *madrassas*

dawah   religious outreach or call to Islam

demokrasi terpimpin   guided democracy

dhikr   chantlike repetition, usually of one of the names of God, or a religious phrase

du'a   supplicatory prayer

dunya   (material) world

dupatta   long rectangular scarf worn by South Asian women draped over the head and shoulders

farz   obligatory

fatwa   legal pronouncement

feqh-e puya   dynamic jurisprudence

feqh, fiqh   jurisprudence

fiqh-ul-ibadat   Islamic jurisprudence on worship

fuqaha'   jurists; sing. *faqih*

griot   storyteller

gunfan   cold, with a cough

hadith   reports of what the Prophet Muhammad said and did during his lifetime; pl. *ahadith*

hahdari   civilizational

hajj   pilgrimage to Mecca

haram   illicit

hejab, hijab   head covering worn by Muslim women

hijabi   one who wears *hijab*

hocca/hojja   one who is learned in religious subjects

hocca effendi   female preacher

hocca hanum female *hocca*; or a *hojja*'s wife

hosainiyeh/husayniya Shi'ite place of worship and commemoration

hudud punishments for severe crimes, including theft, adultery, and slander

ibadah worship

ijtihad critical independent reasoning; lit. intellectual effort or struggle; independent rational investigation of tradition and text

ikhlas lit. "sincerity"; purifying one's religion for God alone

imam lit. "leader." For Sunni Muslims, the imam is the leader of the prayers; for Shi'a Muslims, the Imam is the legitimate spiritual and often temporal authority succeeding the Prophet.

imambargah place where ritual material objects are kept and where people gather to commemorate the martyrdom of Husayn

imitatio muhammadi emulation of (the prophet) Muhammad

injera traditional Ethiopian round, spongy flatbread

inongbale female Freedom Aceh Movement (GAM) member

insha'allah God willing

islah reform

islam du coeur Islam of the heart; individual experience of faith

islamiyat study of Islam

jahiliyya pre-Islamic times, considered age of ignorance

jama'at congregation

jeda kemanusiaan humanitarian ceasefire

kachi basti slum

kasur bed

katib preacher

kebele local-level urban dwellers' association

ketuanan melayu Malay supremacy

khalifah trustee; vicegerent

khalwat close proximity cases between unmarried males and females in a secluded space

khutba sermon, usually delivered before the Friday noon prayer

limina on the boundary

locus classicus passage from a classic or benchmark work that is cited to illustrate a point

ma'ad return, resurrection

madrassa   Islamic religious school

mahaberoch   fundraising events

mahabers   association

mahr   sum endowed by husband to wife upon marriage to be given to her at his death or at divorce

mahram   male relative

majalis   religious gatherings, s. *majlis*

Majles   Iranian Parliament

majlis-e aza   mourning assembly, held by Shi'ite Muslims to commemorate the death of Imam Husayn

managemen qolbu   management of the heart

manak^wsit   unmarried Ethiopian Orthodox Christian women

masha'allah   phrase denoting respect, "God has willed it"

mat'at   small circular stove with a top

maulvi sahib   Qur'an or religious teacher, derived from *mawlavi*, our master/teacher

mawlid   celebration of a holy person's entrance into the divine presence, that is, the date of mortal death

mélange   mixture, mixing

mestiza   mixture, mixing

métissage   mixture, mixing

modus operandi   mode of operation

mu'amalat   ethical accountability between humans

muallima   female teacher

mudawana/moudawana   personal status codes in Morocco

muhibah   goodwill

mullah   religious cleric

muqadamat   female Sufi religious leaders

nafs   soul; self

nakibah   female religious teacher

namaz   prayer

ngandani   advice

ngantepi   certainty

ngayani   basic household needs

ngayemi   security

ngayomi   protection

nikkah marriage

niyyat intention

nubuwwa prophethood

pancasila five principles

pasrah submission

penuh keikhlasan wholehearted love

pesantren Islamic religious (often also a boarding) school

pribumi native Indonesians

purdah veil; separation of men and women; lit. curtain

qur'an khwani recitation of the entire Qur'an

rahm womb

ras race

rumah geudong Geudong House

salafi reformist; lit. those who follow the predecessors, or early generations

santri class and religious identity

sayyed* or *sayyeda male or female person related to (the prophet) Muhammad

shahada profession of faith, through the statement, "I witness there is no god but God" (*lā illāha ila allāh*)

shalwar kameez tunic and trousers worn by South Asian women

shari'a Islamic law, lit. "the way"

shaykhah female authoritative figure, considered advanced on the spiritual path; m. *shaykh*

Shi'a Muslims who believe that (the prophet) Muhammad passed the mantle of spiritual authority to his son-in-law and cousin, Ali.

sokoguru central pillar

soleh virtuous and pious

soleha virtuous and pious woman

Sufi Muslims who, whether they are Shi'a or Sunni, strive to follow a *tariqa* or path that will lead to an experiential understanding of reality, through love of God, often seeking guidance from one who has already attained such spiritual understanding

suku ethnicity

sumur well

sunna customary practice of Muhammad

Sunni Muslims who believe that spiritual authority resides, after (the prophet) Muhammad's death in the Qur'an, and the Prophet's *sunna* (custom) as recorded in the *hadith* (narratives detailing the sayings and actions of Muhammad)

sura   chapter from the Qur'an

tafsir   exegesis; commentary on the Qur'an

tahajjud   midnight prayer

tajdid   revival

tajweed/tajwid   Qur'anic recitation

takaful   insurance

talaq   a type of Islamic legal divorce in which the male verbally divorces his wife three times in front of witnesses by pronouncing the word *talaq*

taqdir   will of God

taqlid   following or imitation, sometimes seen as blind obedience

taqwa   piety

taraweh   prayers during the month of fasting, Ramadan

tariqa   Sufi path/organization

tarjumah   translation

tawhid   doctrine of unity; Oneness of God

tef   cereal grown primarily in Ethiopia from which *injera* is made

tesfa   hope

thealogy   feminist theological reconstruction; also study of the divine feminine

tokoh   spiritually advanced consultant

tudung   headscarf

ujrat al-mithal   fair price

ulama   religiously learned scholars; sing. *alim*

uloom-ul-Hadith   Hadith sciences

uloom-ul-Qur'an   Qur'anic sciences

umma   community, referring to worldwide Muslim community

umrah   pilgrimage to Mecca undertaken at any time of year, entailing non-obligatory but highly recommended rituals separate from the *hajj* rituals, such as performing the circumambulation of the Ka'ba; running between Safa and Marwa; shaving one's head (for men)

usool-ul-fiqh   principles of jurisprudence; also *usul al-fiqh*

V-effekt   *verfremdungseffekt*

verfremdungseffekt   distancing effect; lit. "making [the familiar] strange or alien"

wa'ezah   female preacher

wali   guardian

waq or **Waak'a**   sky-god

woreda administrative district

wuk'abi malevolent spirits

yekan sera day laborers

zar spirit possession and healing

zemad family *zikr*; see *dhikr*

zinat jewel

ziyarat pilgrimages or visitations to shrines

Bibliography

Abaza, Mona. "Images of Gender and Islam: The Middle East and Malaysia, Affinities, Borrowing, and Exchanges." *Orient* 39, no. 2 (1998): 271–84.

Abdullah, Nazri. "Undang-undang Kekeluargaan Islam: Siapa yang Keliru?" [Islamic Family Law: Who Is Confused?]. *Berita Minggu*, August 5, 1990.

Abou El Fadl, Khaled. *The Authoritative and Authoritarian in Islamic Discourses.* Riyadh: Taiba Publishing House, 1997.

Abou El Fadl, Khaled. *Speaking in God's Name: Islamic Law, Authority and Women.* Oxford: OneWorld Publications, 2001.

Abou-Bakr, Omaima. "Islamic Feminism? What's in a Name? Preliminary Reflections." *Middle East Women's Studies Review* 15:4–16:1 (2001), http://www.amews.org/review/reviewarticles/islamicfeminism.htm.

Abraham, Nabeel. "The Gulf Crisis and Anti-Arab Racism in America." In *Collateral Damage: The New World Order at Home and Abroad*, edited by Cynthia Peters, 255–78. Boston: South End Press, 1992.

Abu Mikhnaf. *Maqtal al-Husayn.* Edited by Hasan al-Ghaffari. Qum: Ilmiyya, 1985.

Abu-Laban, Y. "Challenging the Gendered Vertical Mosaic: Immigrants, Ethnic Minorities, Gender and Political Participation." In *Citizen Politics: Research and Theory in Canadian Political Behaviour,* edited by J. Everitt and B. O'Neill, 268–82. Toronto: Oxford University Press, 2002.

Abu-Zahra, Nadia. *The Pure and Powerful: Studies in Contemporary Muslim Society.* Reading, Berks, UK: Ithaca Press, 1997.

Achebe, Nwando. *Farmers, Traders, Warriors, and Kings: Female Power and Authority in Northern Igboland, 1900–1960.* Portsmouth, Hants, UK: Heinemann, 2005.

Afshar, H., R. Aitken, and M. Franks. "Feminisms, Islamophobia and Identities." *Political Studies* 53:2 (2005): 262–83.

Afzal-Khan, Fawzia. "Betwixt and Between? Women, the Nation and Islamization in Pakistan." *Social Identities* 13:1 (2007): 19–29.

Aghaie, Kamran Scot. *The Martyrs of Karbala*. Seattle: University of Washington Press, 2004.

Ahmad, Sadaf. "The Story of Islamic Revivalism amongst Urban Pakistani Women." PhD dissertation, Syracuse University, NY, 2006.

Ahmad, Salbiah. "Zina and Rape under the Syariah Criminal Code (11) Bill 1993 (Kelantan)." In *Hudud in Malaysia: The Issues at Stake*, edited by Rose Ismail, 13–21. Kuala Lumpur: SIS Forum Bhd, 1995.

Ahmadi, Nader, and Fereshteh Ahmadi. *Iranian Islam*. New York: St. Martin's Press, 1998.

Ahmed, Fauzia. "Modern Traditions? British Muslim Women and Academic Achievement." *Gender and Education* 13:2 (2001): 137–52.

Ahmed, Leila. *A Border Passage: From Cairo to America—A Woman's Journey*. New York: Penguin Books, 1999.

Ahmed, Leila. *Women and Gender in Islam: The Historical Roots of a Modern Debate*. New Haven, CT: Yale University Press, 1992.

Ajayi-Soyinka, Omofolabo. "Transcending the Boundaries of Power and Imperialism: Writing Gender, Constructing Knowledge." In *Female Circumcision and the Politics of Knowledge: African Women in Imperialist Discourses*, edited by Obioma Nnaemeka, 47–77. Westport, CT: Praeger Publishers, 2005.

Alexander, C. "Imagining the Asian Gang: Ethnicity, Masculinity and Youth after 'the Riots.'" *Critical Social Policy* 24:4 (2004): 526–49.

Ali, Kecia. "Acting on a Frontier of Religious Ceremony: With Questions and Quiet Resolve, a Woman Officiates at a Muslim Wedding." *Harvard Divinity Bulletin* 32:4 (2004). Available at http://www.hds.harvard.edu/news/bulletin/articles/ali_ceremony.html.

Ali, Kecia. *Sexual Ethics and Islam: Feminist Reflections on Qur'an, Hadith, and Jurisprudence*. Oxford: Oneworld, 2006.

Allen, Judith Van. "'Aba Riots' or Igbo 'Women's War'? Ideology, Stratification, and the Invisibility of Women." In *Women in Africa: Studies in Social and Economic Change*, edited by Nancy J. Hafkin and Edna G. Bay, 59–85. Stanford, CA: Stanford University Press, 1976.

Alloula, Malek. *The Colonial Harem*. Minneapolis: University of Minnesota Press, 1986.

Amadiume, Ifi. *Male Daughters, Female Husbands: Gender and Sex in an African Society*. London: Zed Books, 1987.

Amin, Camron M. *The Making of the Modern Iranian Woman: Gender, State Policy, and Popular Culture, 1865–1946*. Gainesville: University Press of Florida, 2002.

Andaya, Barbara Watson, and Leonard Y. Andaya. *A History of Malaysia*. Basingstoke, Hants, UK: Palgrave, 2001.

An-Naim, Abdullahi. "The Application of Shari'a Islamic Law and Human Rights in the Sudan." In *Islamic Law Reform and Human Rights, Challenges and Rejoinders: Proceedings of the Seminar on Human Rights and the Modern Application of Islamic Law, Oslo, 14–15 February 1992*, edited, with an introduction, by Tore Lindholm and Kari Vogt, 135–48. Copenhagen: Nordic Human Rights Publications, 1993.

An-Naim, Abdullahi. "The Cultural Mediation of Human Rights: The Case of Al-Arqam in Malaysia." In *The East Asian Challenge for Human Rights*, edited by Joanne Bauer and Daniel Bell, 147–68. Cambridge: Cambridge University Press, 1999.

An-Naim, Abdullahi. "The Future of Shari'a and the Debate in Northern Nigeria." In *Comparative Perspectives on Shari'a in Nigeria*, edited by Philip Ostien, Jamila Nasir, and Franz Kogelmann, 327–57. Ibadan, Nigeria: Spectrum Books, 2005.

An-Naim, Abdullahi. "Mahmud Muhammad Taha and the Crisis in Islamic Law Reform: Implications for Religious Relations." In *Muslims in Dialogue: The Evolution of a Dialogue*, edited by Leonard Swidler, 37–54. Lewiston, NY: Edwin Mellon Press, 1992.

Anthias, F., and N. Yuval-Davis. *Racialised Boundaries: Race, Nation, Gender and Class and the Anti-racist Struggle*. London: Routledge, 1992.

Anwar, Etin. *Gender and Self in Islam*. London: Routledge, 2006.

Anwar, Zainah. *Islamic Revivalism in Malaysia: Dakwah among the Students*. Kuala Lumpur: Pelanduk Publications, 1987.

Anwar, Zainah. "Sisters in Islam and the Struggle for Women's Rights." In *On Shifting Ground: Muslim Women in the Global Era*, edited by Fereshteh Nouraie-Simone, 233–47. New York: Feminist Press at the City University of New York, 2005.

Arber, S. "Designing Samples." In *Researching Social Life*, edited by N. Gilbert, 58–82. London: Sage Publications, 2003.

Archer, L. "'Muslim Brothers, Black Lads and Traditional Asians': British Muslim Young Men's Constructions of Race, Religion and Masculinity." *Feminism and Psychology* 11:1 (2001): 79–105.

Arendt, Hannah. *The Human Condition*. Chicago: University of Chicago Press, 1998.

Ariffin, Rohana. "Feminism in Malaysia: A Historical and Present Perspective on Women's Struggles in Malaysia." *Women's Studies International Forum* 224 (1999): 417–23.

Arkoun, Mohammed. *The Unthought in Contemporary Islamic Thought*. London: Saqi in association with the Institute of Ismaili Studies, 2002.

Armstrong, Karen. *Muhammad: A Biography of the Prophet*. San Francisco: Harper San Francisco, 1992.

Ayoub, Mahmoud. *Redemptive Suffering in Islam*. The Hague: Mouton Publishers, 1978.

Azari, Farah. "Islam's Appeal to Women in Iran: Illusions and Reality." In *Women of Iran: The Conflict with Fundamentalist Islam*, edited by Farah Azari, 1–71. London: Ithaca Press, 1983.

Babès, Leïla. *Islam Intérieure, Passion et Désenchantemant*. Paris: Editions Al Bourak, 2000.

Baccar, Jalila. *Araberlin*. Paris: Éditions Théâtrales, 2002.

Baccar, Jalila. *Araberlin*. In *Four Plays from North Africa*, edited by Marvin Carlson and translated by David Looseley, 86–207. New York: Martin E. Segal Theatre Center Publications, 2008.

Badawi, Jamal. *Gender Equity in Islam: Basic Principles*. Indianapolis: American Trust Publications, 2003.

Badejo, Diedre L. "Authority and Discourse in the Orin Odún Osun." In *Osun across the Waters: A Yoruba Goddess in Africa and the Americas*, edited by Josephe Murphy and Mei Mei Sanford, 128–40. Bloomington: Indiana University Press, 2001.

Badlishah, Nik Norani Nik. *Marriage and Divorce under Islamic Law*. Kuala Lumpur: International Law Books Services, 1998.

Badran, Margot. "Between Secular and Islamic Feminism/s: Reflections on the Middle East and Beyond." *Journal of Middle Eastern Women's Studies* 1:1 (2005): 6–28.

Badran, Margot. *Feminism in Islam: Secular and Religious Convergences*. Oxford: Oneworld, 2009.

Badran, Margot. *Feminists, Islam, and Nation: Gender and the Making of Modern Egypt*. Princeton, NJ: Princeton University Press, 1995.

Badran, Margot. "Islamic Feminism Revisited." *Countercurrents.org* 10 (2006).

Badran, Margot. "Islamic Feminism: What's in a Name?" *al-Ahram Weekly*, January 17–23, 2002. http://weekly.ahram.org.eg/2002/569/cu1.htm.

Badran, Margot. "Toward Islamic Feminism: A Look at the Middle East." In *Hermeneutics and Honor*, edited by Asma Afsarudin and Anan Ameri, 159–88. Cambridge: Harvard University Press, 1999.

Bahramitash, Roksana. "The War on Terror, Feminist Orientalism and Orientalist Feminism: Case Studies of Two North American Bestsellers." *Critique: Critical Middle Eastern Studies* 14:2 (2005): 221–35.

Banjary, Rachmat Ramadhana Al-, and Anas al-Djohan Yahya. *Indahnya Poligami: Menangkap Hikmah di Balik Tabir Poligam: Mengapa Aa Gym Menikah Lagi?* [The Beauty of Polygamy: Capturing the Wisdom behind the Screen (Veiling) Polygamy: Why Did Aa Gym Marry Again?] Yogyakarta: Pustaka Al-Furqan, 2007.

Barlas, Asma. *"Believing Women" in Islam: Unreading Patriarchal Interpretations of the Qur'an*. Austin: University of Texas Press, 2002.

Barnard, Timothy. *Contesting Malayness: Malay Identity across Boundaries*. Singapore: Singapore University Press, 2004.

Baron, Beth. *The Women's Awakening in Egypt: Culture, Society, and the Press.* New Haven, CT: Yale University Press, 1994.

Basarudin, Azza. "Interview with Asma Barlas." *Islamic Institute for Human Rights,* 2002.

Bashaw, Zenebe N. "Trajectories of Women, Environmental Degradation and Scarcity: Examining Access to and Control over Resources in Ethiopia." Accessed at http://www.codesira.org/links/conferences/gender/Zeneba.pdf.

Baumann, Martin. "Conceptualizing Diaspora: The Preservation of Religious Identity in Foreign Parts, Exemplified by Hindu Communities outside India." *Temenos* 31 (1995): 19–35.

Baumann, Martin. "A Diachronic View of Diaspora, the Significance of Religion and Hindu Trinidadians." In *Diaspora, Identity and Religion: New Directions in Theory and Research,* edited by Waltraud Kokot, Kachig Tölölyan and Carolin Alfonso, 170–88. New York: Routledge, 2004.

Baumann, Martin. "Diaspora: Genealogies of Semantics and Transcultural Comparison." *Numen* 47 (2000): 313–37.

Belarbi, Aïcha. "Mouvements des Femmes au Maroc." In *La Societe Civile au Maroc,* ed. Noureddine El Ayoufi, 186–96. Rabat: Imprimerie El Maârif Al Jadida, 1992.

Bell, Catherine. *Ritual Theory, Ritual Practice.* Oxford: Oxford University Press, 1992.

Beng, Ooi Kee, Johan Savaranamuttu, and Lee Hock Guan. *March 8: Eclipsing May 13.* Singapore: Institute of Southeast Asian Studies, 2008.

Berghe, Pierre L. van den. *Age and Sex in Human Societies: A Biosocial Perspective.* Belmont, CA: Wadsworth Publishing Co., 1973.

Berhane-Selassie, Tsehai. "Ethiopian Rural Women and the State." In *African Feminism: The Politics of Survival,* edited by Gwendolyn Mikell, 182–205. Philadelphia: University of Pennsylvania Press, 1997.

Berhane-Selassie, Tsehai. *In Search of Ethiopian Women.* London: Change, 1990.

Bernal, Victoria. "Gender, Culture, and Capitalism: Women and the Remaking of Islamic 'Tradition' in a Sudanese Village." *Comparative Studies in Society and History* 36:1 (1994): 36–67.

Berry, John W. "Immigration, Acculturation, and Adaptation." *Applied Psychology: An International Review* 46:1 (1997): 5–35.

Bhabha, Homi. *The Location of Culture.* London: Routledge, 1994.

Bhabha, Homi. "The Third Space: Interview with Homi Bhabha." In *Identity: Community, Culture, Difference,* edited by Jonathan Rutherford, 207–21. London: Lawrence and Wishart, 1990.

Bhopal, K. "How Gender and Ethnicity Intersect: The Significance of Education, Employment and Marital Status." *Sociological Research Online* 3:3 (1998). http://www.socresonline.org.uk/3/3/6.html.

Bouma, Gary D., ed. *Many Religions, All Australians: Religious Settlement, Identity and Cultural Diversity.* Kew, Australia: Christian Research Association, 1996.

Bouma, Gary D. *Mosques and Muslim Settlement in Australia.* Canberra: Australian Government Publishing Service, 1994.

Box, Laura Chakravarty. *Strategies of Resistance in the Dramatic Texts of North African Women: A Body of Words.* New York: Routledge, 2005.

Brah, A. "'Race' and 'Culture' in the Gendering of Labour Markets: South Asian Young Muslim Women and the Labour Market." *New Community* 29 (1993): 441–58.

Brand, Laurie. *Women, the State, and Political Liberalization: Middle Eastern and North African Experiences.* New York: Columbia University Press, 1998.

Brenner, Suzanna A. "Why Women Rule the Roost: Rethinking Javanese Ideologies of Gender and Self Control." In *Gender in Cross-Cultural Perspective,* edited by Caroline B. Brettell and Carolyn F. Sargent, 135–56. Upper Saddle River, NJ: Prentice Hall, 2000.

Brett, Caroline B., ed. *When They Read What We Write: The Politics of Ethnography.* Westport, CT: Bergin and Garvey, 1993.

Brown, Graham, Christopher Wilson, and Suprayoga. *Overcoming Violent Conflict.* Vol. 4, *Peace and Development Analysis in Maluku and North Maluku.* Jakarta: CPRU-UNDP, LIPI and BAPPENAS, 2005.

Brown, K. "Realising Muslim Women's Rights: The Role of Islamic Identity amongst British Muslim Women." *Women's Studies International Forum* 29:4 (2006): 417–30.

Brubaker, R. "Ethnicity without Groups." *European Journal of Sociology* 43:2 (2003): 163–89.

Bujra, Janet M. "'Urging Women to Redouble Their Efforts . . .' Class, Gender, and Capitalist Transformation in Africa." In *Women and Class in Africa,* edited by Claire Robertson and Iris Berger, 117–40. New York: Africana Publishing, 1986.

Bulbeck, Chilla. *Re-orienting Western Feminisms: Women's Diversity in a Postcolonial World.* Cambridge: Cambridge University Press, 1998.

Bullock, Katherine, ed. *Muslim Women Activists in North America: Speaking for Ourselves.* Austin: University of Texas Press, 2005.

Bullock, Katherine, ed. *Rethinking Muslim Women and the Veil: Challenging Historical and Modern Stereotypes.* Herndon, VA: International Institute of Islamic Thought, 2002.

Bullock, Katherine H., and Gul Joya Jafri. "Media (Mis)Representations: Muslim Women in the Canadian Nation." *Canadian Woman Studies* 20:2 (2000): 35–40.

Bunch, Charlotte. "Peace, Human Rights, and Women's Peace Activism: Feminist Readings." In *Peace Work: Women, Armed Conflict and Negotiation,* edited by Radhika Coomaraswamy and Dilrukshi Fonseka, 28–53. New Delhi: Women Unlimited, 2004.

Buskens, Leon. "Recent Debates on Family Law Reform in Morocco: Islamic Law as Politics in an Emerging Public Sphere." *Islamic Law and Society Journal* 10:1 (2003): 70–131.

Carlson, Marvin. Editor's Introduction to *Four Plays from North Africa*, edited by Marvin Carlson, 1–16. New York: Martin E. Segal Theatre Center Publications, 2008.

Centre d'Etudes et de Recherches Démographiques (CERED), ed. *Population et Développement au Maroc*. Rabat, Morocco: CERED, 1997.

Charrad, Mounira. *States and Women's Rights: The Making of Postcolonial Tunisia, Algeria, and Morocco*. Berkeley: University of California Press, 2001.

Clifford, James. "Diasporas." *Cultural Anthropology* 9:3 (1994): 302–38.

Coeatzee, P. H., and A. P. J. Roux, eds. *The African Philosophy Reader: A Text with Readings*. 2nd ed. New York: Routledge, 2003.

cooke, miriam. "Multiple Critique: Islamic Feminist Rhetorical Strategies." *Nepantla: Views from South* 1:1 (2000): 91–110.

cooke, miriam. "Multiple Critiques: Islamic Feminist Rhetorical Strategies." In *Postcolonialism, Feminism and Religious Discourse*, edited by Laura E. Donaldson and Kwok Pui-lan, 142–60. London: Routledge, 2002.

cooke, miriam. *Women Claim Islam: Creating Islamic Feminism through Literature*. New York: Routledge, 2001.

Coomaraswamy, Radhika, and Dilrukshi Fonseka. Introduction to *Peace Work: Women, Armed Conflict and Negotiation*, edited by Radhika Coomaraswamy and Dilrukshi Fonseka, 1–13. New Delhi: Kali for Women, 2004.

Corbin, Henry. *Cyclical Time and Ismaili Gnosis*. London: Kegan Paul International, 1983.

Cotter, Fr. George. *Salt and Stew*. Addis Ababa: United Printers, 1990.

Crouch, Harold. "Malaysia: Neither Authoritarian nor Democratic." In *Southeast Asia in the 1990s: Authoritarianism, Democracy and Capitalism*, edited by Kevin Hewison, Richard Robison, and Gary Rodan, 133–158. Sydney: Allen & Unwin, 1993.

Crummey, Donald. "Women, Property, and Litigation among the Bagemder Amhara, 1750s to 1850s." In *African Women and the Law: Historical Perspectives*, edited by Margaret Jean Hay and Marcia Wright, 19–32. Boston: Boston University, 1982.

Csordas, Thomas J. *Body/Meaning/Healing*. New York: Palgrave Macmillan, 2002.

Dabashi, Hamid. "Native Informers and the Making of the American Empire." *Al Ahram Weekly Online*, June 15, 2007. http://weekly.ahram.org.eg/2006/797/special.htm.

Dakake, Maria Massi. *The Charismatic Community: Shi'ite Identity in Early Islam*. Albany: State University of New York Press, 2007.

Danaher, Geoff, Tony Schirato, and Fen Webb. *Understanding Foucault*. St Leonards, NSW Australia: Allen & Unwin, 2000.

Dawood, Shiamala Matri. "Will the Real Pakistani Woman Please Stand Up?" *Newsline*, March 2005.

Deeb, Lara. *An Enchanted Modern: Gender and Public Piety in Shi'i Lebanon*. Princeton, NJ: Princeton University Press, 2006.

Derrida, Jacques. *The Ear of the Other: Otobiography, Transference, Translation.* Edited by Christie McDonald and translated by Peggy Kamuf. Lincoln: University of Nebraska Press, 1985.

Djebar, Assia, and Walid Carn. *Rouge l'aube.* Algiers: SNED, 1969.

Donham, Donald L. *Marxist Modern: An Ethnographic History of the Ethiopian Revolution.* Berkeley: University of California Press, 1999.

Doorn-Harder, Nelly van. "Controlling the Body: Muslim Feminists Debating Women's Rights in Indonesia." *Religion Compass.* Oxford: Blackwell Publishing, 2008.

Doorn-Harder, Pieternella van. *Women Shaping Islam: Indonesian Muslim Women Reading the Qur'an.* Champaign-Urbana: University of Illinois Press, 2006.

Dywer, C. "Veiled Meanings: British Muslim Women and the Negotiation of Differences." *Gender, Place and Culture* 6 (1999): 5–26.

Dzuhayatin, Siti Ruhaini. "Marital Rape, Suatu Keniscayaan?" [Marital Rape, a Certainty?]. In *Islam dan Konstruksi Seksualitas,* edited by Edy S. Santoso, 118–32. Yogyakarta: PSW IAIN, 2002.

Ehret, Christopher. *The Civilizations of Africa.* Charlottesville: University Press of Virginia, 2002.

Dale F. Eickelman and Jon W. Anderson. "Redefining Muslim Publics." In *New Media in the Muslim World,* edited by Dale F. Eickelman and Jon W. Anderson, 1–18. Bloomington: Indiana University Press, (1999) 2003.

Eklöf, Stefan. *Indonesian Politics in Crisis: The Long Fall of Suharto, 1996–98.* Copenhagen: Nordic Institute of Asian Studies, 1999.

Ennaji, Moha, and Fatima Sadiqi. "The Feminization of Public Space: Women's Activism, the Family Law, and Social Change in Morocco." *Journal of Middle East Women's Studies* 2:2 (2006): 86–107.

Environmental Protection Authority, Federal Democratic Republic of Ethiopia. *The Third National Report on the Implementation of the UNCCD/NAP in Ethiopia.* Addis Ababa: Environmental Protection Authority, February 2004.

Errington, Shelly. "Recasting Sex, Gender, and Power: A Theoretical and Regional Overview." In *Power and Difference: Gender in Island Southeast Asia,* edited by Shelly Errington, 1–58. Stanford, CA: Stanford University Press, 1990.

Europa Regional Surveys of the World: Africa South of the Sahara, 2007.

Fanon, Frantz. "Algeria Unveiled." In Frantz Fanon, *A Dying Colonialism.* Translated by Haakon Chevalier, 35–68. New York: Grove Press, 1967.

Fausto-Sterling, Anne. "Hormone and Aggression: An Explanation of Power." In *Myths of Gender: Biological Theories about Women and Men,* authored by Anne Fausto-Sterling, 123–54. New York: Basic Books, 1985.

Fealy, Greg, and Virginia Hooker. *Voices of Islam in Southeast Asia: A Contemporary Sourcebook.* Singapore: ISEAS Publications, 2006.

Fekete, L. "Anti-Muslim Racism and the European Security State." *Race and Class* 46:1 (2004): 3–29.

Fekete, L. "Enlightenment Fundamentalism? Immigration, Feminism and the Right." *Race and Class* 48:2 (2006): 1–22.

Fernea, Robert, and Elizabeth Fernea. "Variations in Religious Observance among Islamic Women." In *Scholars, Saints, and Sufis: Muslim Religious Institutions since 1500,* edited by Lois Beck and Nikkie R. Kęddi, 385–401. Berkeley, CA: University of California Press, 1972.

Fisher, William F. "Doing Good? The Politics and Antipolitics of NGO Practices." *Annual Review of Anthropology* 26 (1997): 439–64.

Foucault, Michel. *The History of Sexuality: An Introduction.* Vol. 1. Translated by Robert Hurley. New York: Vintage Books, 1990.

Foucault, Michel. *Power/Knowledge: Selected Interviews and Other Writings.* Edited by C. Gordon. New York: Pantheon, 1980.

Fujimoto, Takeshi. "Cereal Agriculture among the Malo of Southwestern Ethiopia: With Special Reference to Their Teff (*Eragrostis tef* [Zucc.] Trotter) Cultivation." In *Proceedings of the XIVth International Conference of Ethiopian Studies,* edited by Baye Yimam et al., 767–84. Addis Ababa: Addis Ababa University Press, 2000.

Fukui, Katsuyoshi, ed. *Comparative Studies on Indigenous Knowledge Systems in South Ethiopian Societies.* Kyoto: Nakanishi Printing Co., 2003.

Gallaire, Fatima. *Ah! vous êtes venues . . . là où il y a quelques tombes.* Paris: Éditions des quatre-vents, 1988.

Gallaire, Fatima. *La beauté de l'icône.* Paris: Éditions Art et Comédie, 2003.

Gallaire, Fatima. *Princesses. Theatre 1,* 14–78. Paris: Éditions des quatre-vents, 2004.

Gallaire, Fatima. *You Have Come Back.* Translated by Jill MacDougall in *Plays by Women: an International Anthology,* vol. 2, edited by Catherine Temerson and Françoise Kourilsky, 166–221. New York: UBU Repertory Theater Productions, 1988.

Gatsiounis, Ioannis. *Beyond the Veneer: Malaysia's Struggle for Dignity and Direction.* Singapore: Monsoon Books, 2008.

Geldin, Sherri, in Shirin Neshat, Bill Horrigan, and Sherri Geldin, *Shirin Neshat: Two Installations.* Columbus, OH: Wexner Center for the Arts, 2000.

Gheytanchi, Elham. Appendix (to Nikkie Keddie) titled "Chronology of Events regarding Women in Iran since the Revolution of 1979." *Social Research Journal* 67:2 (2000).

Giorgis, Original Wolde. "Democratisation Process and Gender." In *Ethiopia: The Challenge of Democracy from Below,* edited by Bahru Zewde and Siegfried Pausewang, 169–85. Uppsala: Nordiska Afrikainstitutet and Forum for Social Studies, 2002.

Göle, Nilüfer. *The Forbidden Modern: Civilization and Veiling.* Ann Arbor: University of Michigan Press, 1996.

Goody, Jack. *Production and Reproduction: A Comparative Study of the Domestic Domain.* Cambridge: Cambridge University Press, 1976.

Grillo, R. "Islam and Transnationalism." *Journal of Ethnic and Migration Studies* 30:5 (2004): 861–78.

Guehenno, Jean. *The End of the Nation State*. Minneapolis: University of Minnesota Press, 1995.

Haddad, Yvonne Yazbeck, Jane I. Smith, and Kathleen M. Moore. *Muslim Women in America: The Challenge of Islamic Identity Today*. New York: Oxford University Press, 2006.

Hale, Sondra. "Colonial Discourse and Ethnographic Residuals: The 'Female Circumcision' Debate and the Politics of Knowledge." In *Female Circumcision and the Politics of Knowledge: African Women in Imperialist Discourses*, edited by Obioma Nnaemeka, 209–18. Westport, CT: Praeger Publishers, 2005.

Hale, Sondra. *Gender Politics in Sudan: Islamism, Socialism, and the State*. Boulder, CO: Westview Press, 1996.

Halper, Louise. "Law and Women's Agency in Post-Revolutionary Iran." *Harvard Journal of Law and Gender* 28 (2005): 85–142.

Halper, Louise. "Law, Authority and Gender in Post-Revolutionary Iran." *Buffalo Law Review* 54 (2007). http://papers.ssrn.com/sol3/papers.cfm?abstract_id=933078.

Harper, Tim. *The End of Empire and the Making of Malaya*. Cambridge: Cambridge University Press, 1999.

Hashim, Rizal Chek. "Justice and Jurisdictions: The Shamala Sathiyaseelan v. Dr Jeyaganesh C Mograrajah (Muhammad Ridzuan) Custody Case." *Aliran Monthly* 7 (2004): 7–10.

Hassan, Riffat. "Brief Comment on Feminist Misunderstandings." *Journal of Women's History* 13:1 (2001): 46–46.

Hassan, Riffat. "Challenging the Stereotypes of Fundamentalism: An Islamic Feminist Perspective." *The Muslim World* 91:1 (2001): 55–69.

Hassan, Riffat. "The Issue of Woman-Man Equality on the Islamic Tradition." In *Eve & Adam: Jewish, Christian, and Muslim Readings on Genesis and Gender*, edited by Dristen E. Kvam, Linda S. Schearing, and Valerie H. Ziegler, 464–76. Bloomington: Indiana University Press, 1999.

Hassan, Riffat. "Islam and Human Rights in Pakistan: A Critical Analysis of the Positions of Three Contemporary Women" (2004). Published on Islamic Research International Foundation (IRFI) http://www.irfi.org/articles/articles_101_150/islam_and_human_rights_in_pakist.htm.

Hassan, Saliha. "Islamic Non-governmental Organizations." In *Social Movements in Malaysia: From Moral Communities to NGOs*, edited by Meredith Weiss and Saliha Hassan, 97–114. New York: RoutledgeCurzon, 2002.

Hefner, Robert, and Patricia Horvatich, ed. *Islam in the Era of Nation States: Politics and Religious Renewal in Muslim Southeast Asia*. Honolulu: University of Hawaii Press, 1997.

Hill, Lynda Marion. *Social Rituals and the Verbal Art of Zora Neale Hurston*. Washington, DC: Howard University Press, 1996.

Hoesterey, James B. "Marketing Morality: The Rise, Fall and Rebranding of Aa Gym." In *Expressing Islam: Religious Life and Politics in Indonesia*, edited by Greg Fealy and Sally White, 90–107. Singapore: ISEAS, 2008.

Hoodfar, Homa. *The Women's Movement in Iran: Women at the Crossroads of Secularization and Islamization*. The Women's Movement Series, no. 1. Grabels Cedex, France: Women Living Under Muslim Laws, 1999.

Hooglund, Mary. "The Village Women of Aliabad and the Iranian Revolution." *Review of Iranian Political Economy and History* 4:2 (1980): 27–46.

Hyder, Syed Akbar. *Reliving Karbala: Martyrdom in South Asian Memory*. New York: Oxford University Press, 2006.

Ibrahim, Ahmed Mohammed. *The Administration of Islamic Law in Malaysia*. Kuala Lumpur: Institute of Islamic Understanding Malaysia (IKIM), 2000.

Ibrahim, Ahmed Mohammed. "The Administration of Muslim Law in Southeast Asia." 13 *MLR* 124, 1971; also *Islamic Culture* 46:3 (1972): 245–63.

Ibrahim, Samina. "Interview with Farhat Hashmi." *Newsline*, May 2001.

Irfani, Suroosh. "Pakistan's Sectarian Violence: Between the 'Arabist Shift' and Indo-Persian Culture." In *Religious Radicalism and Security in South Asia*, edited by Satu P. Limaye, Robert G. Wirsing, and Mohan Malik, 147–70. Honolulu: Asia-Pacific Center for Security Studies, 2004.

Janeway, Elizabeth. *Powers of the Weak*. New York: William Morrow & Co., 1981.

Jawad, Haifaa. "Female Conversions to Islam: The Sufi Paradigm." In *Women Embracing Islam: Gender and Conversion in the West*, edited by Karin van Nieuwkerk, 153–71. Austin: University of Texas Press, 2006.

Johanson, Donald, and Maitland Edey. *Lucy: The Beginnings of Humankind*. New York: Simon and Schuster, 1981.

Johns, A. H. "Perspective of Islamic Spirituality in Southeast Asia: Reflections and Encounters." *Islam and Christian-Muslim Relations* 112 (2001): 5–21.

Johnson, Allan G. "Patriarchy, the System: An It, Not a He, a Them, or an Us." In *Women's Lives: Multicultural Perspectives*, edited by Gwyn Kirk and Margo Okazawa-Rey, 29–30. New York: McGraw Hill, 2000.

Jones, Sidney. "Indonesia: Jemaah Islamiyah's Publishing Industry." ICG Asia Report 147. Karachi, Pakistan: International Crisis Group, 2008.

Jonker, Gerdien. "The Evolution of the Naqshbandi-Mujaddidi Sulaymancis in Germany." In *Sufism in the West*, edited by Jamal Malik and John Hinnells, 71–85. New York: Routledge, 2006.

Joseph, Suad. "Gender and Citizenship in Middle Eastern States." *Middle East Report* 198 (1996): 4–10.

Kamali, Muhammad Hisham. *Islamic Law in Malaysia: Issues and Developments*. Kuala Lumpur: Ilmiah Publishers, 2000.

Kamaruzzaman, Suraiya. "Violence, Internal Displacement, and Its Impact on the Women of Aceh." In *Violent Conflicts in Indonesia: Analysis, Representation, Resolution*, edited by Charles A. Coppel, 258–85. London: Routledge, 2006.

Kamaruzzaman, Suraiya. "Women and the War in Aceh: These Women Want to Silence All the Guns, Whether Indonesian or Acehnese." *Inside Indonesia*, no. 64, October–December 2000.

Kandiyoti, Deniz. "Bargaining with Patriarchy." *Gender and Society* 2:3 (1988): 274–90.

Karim, Persis M., ed. *Let Me Tell You Where I've Been: New Writing by Women in the Iranian Diaspora*. Fayetteville: University of Arkansas Press, 2006.

Karim, Wazir Jahan. *Women and Culture: Between Malay Adat and Islam*. London: Westview Press, 1992.

Karimi-Taleghani, Patricia. "Jamaican Kumina: The Yoruba Contribution." Unpublished MA thesis, University of Santa Barbara, CA, 1979.

Kashmeri, Zuhair. *The Gulf Within: Canadian Arabs, Racism and the Gulf War*. Toronto: James Lorimer, 1991.

Kassam, Tazim. "Balancing Acts: Negotiating the Ethics of Scholarship and Identity." In *Identity and the Politics of Scholarship in the Study of Religion*, edited by José I. Cabezón and Sheila G. Davaney, 133–61. New York: Routledge, 2004.

Kassam, Tazim. "On Being a Scholar of Islam: Risks and Responsibilities." In *Progressive Muslims on Justice, Gender, and Pluralism*, edited by Omid Safi, 128–44. Oxford: Oneworld, 2003.

Kearney, Michael. "The Local and the Global: The Anthropology of Globalization and Transnationalism." *Annual Review of Anthropology* 25 (1995): 547–65.

Kelley, Robin D. G. *Freedom Dreams*. Boston: Beacon Press, 2002.

Khan, Shahnaz. *Muslim Women: Crafting a North American Identity*. Gainesville: University Press of Florida, 2000.

Khomeini, Ruhollah. *The Position of Women from the Viewpoint of Imam Khomeini*. Edited and translated by Juliana Shaw and Behrooz Arezoo. Tehran: Institute for the Compilation and Publication of Imam Khomeini's Works, 2001.

Kian-Thiebaut, Azadeh. "Women and the Making of Civil Society." In *Twenty Years of Islamic Revolution: Political and Social Transition in Iran since 1979*, edited by Eric Hooglund, 56–73. Syracuse, NY: Syracuse University Press, 2002.

Kimura, Maki. "Narrative as a Site of Subject Construction: The 'Comfort Woman' Debate." *Feminist Theory* 9:1 (2008): 5–24.

Klausen, Jytte. *The Islamic Challenge: Politics and Religion in Western Europe*. Oxford: Oxford University Press, 2005.

Klinken, Gerry van. "The Maluku Wars: 'Communal Contenders' in a Failing State." In *Violent Conflicts in Indonesia: Analysis, Representation, Resolution*, edited by Charles A. Coppel, 129–43. London: Routledge, 2006.

Knott, Kim, and Sadja Khokher. "Religious and Ethnic Identity among Young Muslim Women in Bradford." *New Community* 19:4 (1993): 593–610.

Krishna, Sankaran. *Globalization and Postcolonialism: Hegemony and Resistance in the Twenty-first Century.* New York: Rowman and Littlefield, 2009.

Kulbaga, Theresa A. "Pleasurable Pedagogies: Reading Lolita in Tehran and the Rhetoric of Empathy." *College English* 70:5 (2008): 506–21.

Kurzman, Charles, ed. *Liberal Islam: A Sourcebook.* Oxford: Oxford University Press, 1998.

Lan, Thung Ju, Abdul Rahman Patji, et al. *Penyelesaian Konflik di Aceh: Aceh dalam Proses Rekontruksi & Rekonsiliasi.* Jakarta: Lembaga Ilmu Pengetahuan Indonesia, 2005.

Lenin, V. I. *Imperialism.* Peking [Beijing]: Foreign Languages Press, 1975.

Levine, Donald N. *Greater Ethiopia: The Evolution of a Multiethnic Society.* Chicago: University of Chicago Press, 1974.

Lewis, I. M. *A Modern History of Somalia.* London: Longman, 1965, 1980.

Lewis, I. M. "Spirit Possession in Northern Somalia." In *Spirit Mediumship and Society in Africa*, edited by John Beattie and John Middleton, 188–219. London: Routledge and Kegan Paul, 1969.

Lewis, I. M., Ahmed Al-Safi, and Sayyid Hurreiz, eds. *Women's Medicine: The Zar-Bori Cult in Africa and Beyond.* Edinburgh: Edinburgh University Press, 1991.

Lewison, Leonard. "Persian Sufism in the Contemporary West: Reflections on the Ni'matu'llahi Diaspora." In *Sufism in the West*, edited by Jamal Malik and John Hinnells, 49–70. New York: Routledge, 2006.

Macey, M. "Class, Gender and Religious Influences on Changing Patterns of Pakistani Muslim Male Violence in Bradford." *Ethnic and Racial Studies* 22:5 (1999): 845–66.

"Madrassas, Extremism and the Military." ICG Asia Report 36. Karachi: International Crisis Group, July 29, 2002.

Magnis-Suseno, Franz. *Javanese Ethics and World-View: The Javanese Idea of the Good Life.* Jakarta: Penerbit PT Gramedia Pustaka Utama, 1997.

Mahmood, Saba. "Feminist Theory, Embodiment, and the Docile Agent: Some Reflections on the Egyptian Islamic Revival." *Cultural Anthropology* 16:2 (2001): 202–36.

Mahmood, Saba. *Politics of Piety: The Islamic Revival and the Feminist Subject.* Princeton, NJ: Princeton University Press, 2005.

Malik, Jamal, ed. *Madrassas in South Asia: Teaching Terror?* London: Routledge, 2008.

Mandaville, Peter. *Transnational Muslim Politics: Reimagining the Umma.* London: Routledge, 2004.

Marcotte, Roxanne D. "Identity, Power, and the Islamist Discourse on Women: An Exploration of Islamism and Gender Issues in Egypt." In *Islam in World Politics*, edited by Nelly Lahoud, Anthony H. Johns, and Allan Patience, 67–92. London: RoutledgeCurzon, 2005.

Marcotte, Roxanne D. "The Qur'ān in Egypt: Bint al- Shati' on Women's Emancipation." In *Coming to Terms with the Qur'an: A Volume in Honor of Professor Issa Boullata*, edited by Khaleel Mohammed and Andrew Rippin, 179–208. North Haledon, NJ: Islamic Publications International, 2008.

Marcotte, Roxanne D. "What Might an Islamist Gender Discourse Look Like?" *Australian Religion Studies Review* 19:2 (2006): 141–67.

Marcus, George E. "Ethnography in/of the World System: The Emergence of Multi-sited Ethnography." *Annual Review of Anthropology* 24 (1995): 95–117.

Martin, Vanessa. *Creating an Islamic State: Khomeini and the Making of a New Iran*. London: I. B. Tauris, 2000.

Martinez, Patricia, and Saliha Hassan. "Malaysia and Singapore: Early 20th Century to the Present." In *Encyclopedia of Women & Islamic Cultures*. Vol. 1, *Methodologies, Paradigms, and Sources*, edited by Suad Joseph, 222–27. Leiden: E. J. Brill, 2003.

Mauzy, Diane, and R. S. Milne. "The Mahathir Administration in Malaysia: Discipline through Islam." *Pacific Affairs* 56:4 (1983–84): 617–48.

Mazrui, A. A. "The Black Woman and the Problem of Gender." In *Race, Gender, and Culture Conflict: Debating the African Condition: Mazrui and His Critics*, edited by Alamin Mazrui and Willy Mutunga, 211–35. Trenton, NJ: African World Press, 2004.

McGrath, Alister E. *Christian Spirituality: An Introduction*. Malden, MA: Blackwell Publishers, 1999 and 2004.

Megawangi, Ratna. *Membiarkan Berbeda: Sudut Pandang Baru tentang Relasi Gender*. Bandung: Mizan, 1999.

Mekuria, Salem. "Female Genital Mutilation in Africa: Some African Views." *ACAS Bulletin* 44–45 (1995): 2–6.

Melchert, Christopher. "Whether to Keep Women out of the Mosque: A Survey of Medieval Islamic Law." In *Authority, Privacy and Public Order in Islam: Proceedings of the 22nd Congress of l'Union Européenne des Arabisants et Islamisants*, edited by Barbara Michalak-Pikulska and A. Pikulski, 59–69. Leuven, Belgium: Peeters, 2006.

Menon, Ritu. "Doing Peace: Women Resist Daily Battle in South Asia." In *Peace Work, Women, Armed Conflict and Negotiation*, edited by Radhika Coomaraswamy and Dilrukshi Fonseka, 54–72. New Delhi: Kali for Women, 2004.

Mernissi, Fatima. *Beyond the Veil: Male-Female Dynamics in Modern Muslim Society*. Rev. ed. Bloomington: Indiana University Press, 1987.

Mernissi, Fatima. *Doing Daily Battle: Interviews with Moroccan Women*. Edited by Fatima Mernissi and translated by Mary Jo Lakeland [reprint of 1988]. New Brunswick, NJ: Rutgers University Press, 1989.

Mernissi, Fatima. *The Forgotten Queens of Islam*. Translated by Mary Jo Lakeland. Minneapolis: University of Minnesota Press, 1993.

Mernissi, Fatima. *Islam and Democracy: Fear of the Modern World*. Rev. ed. Translated by Mary Jo Lakeland. Cambridge, MA: Perseus, 2002.

Mernissi, Fatima. *The Veil and the Male Elite: A Feminist Interpretation of Women's Rights in Islam*. New York: Perseus, 1991.

Metcalf, Barbara Daly. "Tablighi Jama'at and Women." In *Travellers in Faith: Studies of the Tablighi Jama'at as a Transnational Islamic Movement for Faith Renewal*, edited by Muhammad Khalid Masud, 44–58. Leiden: E. J. Brill, 2000.

Midden, E. "Faith in Feminism: Rethinking the Relationship between Religion, Secularism and Gender Equality." Unpublished paper, 2007.

Mikell, Gwendolyn, ed. *African Feminism: The Politics of Survival in Sub-Saharan Africa*. Philadelphia: University of Pennsylvania Press, 1997.

Min, Sai Siew. "'Eventing' the May 1998 Affair: Problematic Representations of Violence in Contemporary Indonesia." In *Violent Conflicts in Indonesia: Analysis, Representation, Resolution*, edited by Charles A. Coppel, 39–57. London: Routledge, 2006.

Mir-Hosseini, Ziba. "The Construction of Gender in Islamic Legal Thought and Strategies for Reform." *Hawwa* 1:1 (2003): 1–28.

Mir-Hosseini, Ziba. *Islam and Gender: The Religious Debate in Contemporary Islam*. Princeton, NJ: Princeton University Press, 1999.

Mir-Hosseini, Ziba. *Marriage on Trial: A Study of Islamic Family Law*. London: I. B. Tauris, 1993.

Mir-Hosseini, Ziba. "Women and Politics in Post-Khomeini Iran: Divorce, Veiling and Emerging Feminist Voices." In *Women and Politics in the Third World*, edited by Haleh Afshar, 145–73. London: Routledge, 1996.

Mirza, Qudsia. "Islam, Hybridity and the Laws of Marriage." *Australian Feminist Law Journal* 14 (2000): 15–21.

Modood, T. "Muslims and the Politics of Multiculturalism in Britain." In *Critical Views of September 11: Analyses from Around the World*, edited by Eric Hershberg and Kevin W. Moore, 193–207. New York: New Press, 2002.

Modood, Tariq. "Anti-essentialism, Multiculturalism and the 'Recognition' of Religious Groups." *Journal of Political Philosophy* 6:4 (1998): 378–99.

Modood, Tariq. *Multicultural Politics: Racism, Ethnicity, and Muslims in Britain*. Edinburgh: Edinburgh University Press, 2005.

Modood, Tariq. *Multiculturalism: A Civic Idea*. Cambridge: Polity, 2007.

Modood, Tariq, and Fauzia Ahmad. "British Muslim Perspectives on Multiculturalism." *Theory, Culture and Society* 24:2 (2007): 187–213.

Moghadam, Valentine. "Islamic Feminism and Its Discontents: Towards a Resolution of the Debate." *Signs: Journal of Women in Culture and Society* 27:4 (2002): 1135–71. Also in *Gender, Islam, and Politics*, edited by Theresa Saliba, 15–52. Chicago: University of Chicago Press Journals, 2002.

Moghadam, Valentine. "The Political Economy of Female Employment in the Arab Region." In *Gender and Development in the Arab World*, edited by Nabil F. Khoury and Valentine M. Moghadam, 6–34. London: Zed Books, 1995.

Mohamad, Mahathir. *The Malay Dilemma*. Kuala Lumpur: Federal Publications, 1995.

Mohamad, Maznah, ed. *Muslim Women and Access to Justice: Historical, Legal, and Social Experience in Malaysia*. Penang: Women's Crisis Centre, 2000.

Mohammed, Khalid. "Noorkumalasari Appeals to Trader's Wife." *The Star*, August 4, 1990.

Mohammed, Khalid. "Sejauh manakah undang-undang boleh halang poligami?" [How Far Can the Laws Restrict Polygamy?]. *Mingguan Malaysia*, August 5, 1990.

Mohanty, Chandra. *Feminism without Borders: Decolonizing Theory, Practicing Solidarity*. Durham, NC: Duke University Press, 2003.

Mojab, Shahrzad. "Theorizing the Politics of 'Islamic Feminism.'" *Feminist Review* 69 (2001): 124–46.

Mottahedeh, Nigar. "New Iranian Cinema: 1982–Present." In *Traditions in World Cinema*, edited by Linda Badley, R. Barton Palmer, and Steven Jay Schneider, 176–89. New Brunswick, NJ: Rutgers University Press, 2006.

Mulia, Siti Musdah. *Islam Menggugat Poligami* [Islam Criticizes Polygamy]. Jakarta: Gramedia, 2007.

Mulia, Siti Musdah. "Tauhid: A Source of Inspiration for Gender Justice." In *Dawrah Fiqh concerning Women: Manual for a Course on Islam and Gender*, edited by K. H. Husein Muhammad, Faqihuddin Abdol Kodir, Lies Marcoes Natsir, and Marzuki Wahid, 39–59. Cirebon, Indonesia: Fahmina Institute, 2006.

Mulugeta, Alemmaya. "Gender and Islam: How Can Violence Be Embedded in Religion?" In *Reflections: Documentation of the Forum on Gender*, no. 7 (June 2002), ed. Yonas Admassu, 33–38. Addis Ababa: Panos Ethiopia, 2002.

Mulugeta, Emebet. "Trajectory of the Institute of Gender Studies at Addis Ababa University, Ethiopia." *Feminist Africa* 9 (2007): 85–92.

Mumtaz, Khawar. "Identity Politics and Women: 'Fundamentalism' and Women in Pakistan." In *Identity Politics and Women: Cultural Reassertions and Feminisms in International Perspective*, edited by Valentine Moghadam, 228–42. Boulder, CO: Westview Press, 1994.

Murad, Abdal-Hakim. "Boys Will Be Boys," http://www.masud.co.uk/ISLAM/ahm/boys.htm.

Murata, Sachiko, and William C. Chittick. *The Vision of Islam*. New York: Paragon House, 1994.

Murniati, Nunuk P., and Komnas Perempuan. "Women in Aceh and Women's NGOs." *Asia Pacific Forum on Women, Law, and Development, Forum News* 16, Aug.–Sep. 2003.

Musisi, Nakanyike B. "The Politics of Perception or Perception as Politics? Colonial and Missionary Representations of Baganda Women, 1900–1945." In

Women in African Colonial Histories, edited by Jean Allman, Susan Geiger, and Nakanyike Musisi, 95–115. Bloomington: Indiana University Press, 2002.

Mutalib, Hussin. *Islam and Ethnicity in Malay Politics.* New York: Oxford University Press, 1990.

Muzaffar, Chandra. *Islamic Resurgence in Malaysia.* Kuala Lumpur: Fajar Bakti, 1987.

Naciri, Rabéa. *The Women's Movement and Political Discourse in Morocco.* United Nations Research Institute for Social Development, Occasional Paper 8, March 1998.

Nagata, Judith. *The Reflowering of Malaysian Islam: Modern Religious Radicals and Their Roots.* Vancouver: University of British Columbia Press, 1984.

Nagata, Judith. "What Is a Malay? Situational Selection of Ethnic Identity in a Plural Society." *American Ethnologist* 1 (1974): 331–50.

Naghibi, Nima, and Andrew O'Malley. "Estranging the Familiar: 'East' and 'West' in Satrapi's *Persepolis.*" *English Studies in Canada* 31:2–3 (2005): 223–47.

Nahai, Gina Barkhodar. "So What's with All the Iranian Memoirs? An Original Tries to Explain." *Publishers Weekly,* November 26, 2007.

Najib, Ala'i. "Perempuan dan Perdamaian: Catatan tentang peacebuilding." *Tashwir* 22 (2007): 9–25.

Nakamura, M. "Nahdlatul Ulama." In *The Oxford Encyclopedia of the Modern Islamic World,* edited by John L. Esposito, 217–22. New York: Oxford University Press, 1991.

Nasr, Seyyed Vali R. *The Vanguard of Islamic Revolution: The Jama'at-i-Islami of Pakistan.* Berkeley: University of California Press, 1994.

Nelson-Pallmeyer, Jack. *Is Religion Killing Us? Violence in the Bible and the Qur'an.* New York: Continuum International Publishing Group, 2003.

Neshat, Shirin, Francisco Bonami, Hamid Dabashi, and Octavia Zaya. *Women of Allah.* Torino, Italy: Marco Noire, Editore, 1997.

Netto, Anil Noel. "A Battle of Wills in Malaysia's Perak." *Asia Times Online,* February 11, 2009, at http://www.atimes.com/atimes/Southeast_Asia/KB11Ae01.html.

Netto, Anil Noel. "Malaysia-Religion: Crackdown of Shiah Muslims Puzzles Many." *Inter Press Service,* November 11, 2007.

Nnaemeka, Obioma, ed. *Female Circumcision and the Politics of Knowledge: African Women in Imperialist Discourses.* Westport, CT: Praeger Publishers, 2005.

Nnaemeka, Obioma, ed. *Sisterhood, Feminisms and Power: From Africa to the Diaspora.* Trenton, NJ: Africa World Press, 1998.

Nwankwo, Chimalum. "Parallax Sightlines: Alice Walker's Sisterhood and the Key to Dreams." In *Female Circumcision and the Politics of Knowledge: African Women in Imperialist Discourses,* edited by Obioma Nnaemeka, 219–44. Westport, CT: Praeger Publishers, 2005.

O'Connor, June. "Rereading, Reconceiving and Reconstructing Traditions: Feminist Research in Religion." *Women's Studies* 17 (1989): 101–23.

Obbo, Christine. *African Women: Their Struggle for Economic Independence*. London: Zed Books, 1980.

Ohmae, Kenichi. *End of the Nation State: The Rise of Regional Economies*. New York: Touchstone Press, 1996.

Okin, Susan Moller. "Is Multiculturalism Bad for Women?" In *Is Multiculturalism Bad for Women?* edited by J. Cohen, M. Howard, and M. C. Nussbaum, 7–26. Princeton, NJ: Princeton University Press, 1999.

Okonjo, Kamene. "The Dual-Sex Political System in Operation: Igbo Women and Community Politics in Midwestern Nigeria." In *Women in Africa: Studies in Social and Economic Change*, edited by Nancy J. Hafkin and Edna G. Bay, 45–58. Stanford, CA: Stanford University Press, 1976.

Ong, Aihwa. "State versus Islam: Malay Families, Women's Bodies and the Body Politics." In *Bewitching Women, Pious Men: Gender and Body Politics in Southeast Asia*, edited by Aihwa Ong and Michael G. Peletz, 159–94. Berkeley: University of California Press, 1995.

Orr, Deborah. "Why This Picture Offends Me." *The Independent*, July 8, 2006.

Othman, Norani. "Grounding Human Rights Arguments in Non-Western Culture: Shari'a and the Citizenship Rights of Women in a Modern Islamic Nation-State." In *The East Asian Challenge for Human Rights*, edited by Joanne R. Bauer and Daniel A. Bell, 169–92. New York: Cambridge University Press, 1999.

Othman, Norani. "Islamization and Modernization in Malaysia: Competing Cultural Reassertions and Women's Identity in a Changing Society." In *Women, Ethnicity and Nationalism: The Politics of Transition*, edited by Rick Wolford and Robert Miller, 170–92. London: Routledge, 1998.

Othman, Norani, Zainah Anwar, and Zaitun Mohamed Kasim. "Malaysia: Islamization, Muslim Politics and State Authoritarianism." In *Muslim Women and the Challenge of Islamic Extremism*, edited by Norani Othman, 78–108. Selangor, Malaysia: Vinlin Press, Sdn, Bhd, 2005.

Paidar, Parvin. "Feminism and Islam in Iran." In *Gendering the Middle East: Emerging Perspectives*, edited by Deniz Kandiyoti, 51–68. New York: Syracuse University Press, 1996.

Paidar, Parvin. "Gender of Democracy: The Encounter between Feminism and Reformism in Contemporary Iran." United Nations Research Institute for Social Development: Democracy, Governance, and Human Rights, Programme Paper 6, October 2001.

Paidar, Parvin. *Women and the Political Process in Twentieth-century Iran*. Cambridge: Cambridge University Press, 1995.

Pankhurst, Helen. *Gender, Development and Identity: An Ethiopian Study*. London: Zed Books, 1992.

Parrinder, Geoffrey. *African Traditional Religion*. London: Hutchinson House, 1954.

Paulme, Denise, ed. *Women of Tropical Africa*. Translated by H. M. Wright. London: Routledge, 1971.

Peacock, James. *Purifying the Faith: The Muhammadiyah Movement in Indonesian Islam*. Menlo Park, CA: Benyamin/Cumming Publishing, 1978.

Pfeifer, Karen. "How Tunisia, Morocco, Jordan and Even Egypt Became IMF 'Success Stories' in the 1990s." *Middle East Report*, no. 210 (1999): 23–27.

Phillips, A. *Multiculturalism without Culture*. Princeton, NJ: Princeton University Press, 2007.

Plaskow, Judith, and Carol Christ, eds. *Weaving the Visions: New Patterns in Feminist Spirituality*. San Francisco: Harper and Row, 1989.

Poya, Maryam. *Women, Work and Islamism: Ideology and Resistance in Iran*. London: Zed Books, 1999.

Prouty, Chris. *Empress Taytu and Menilek II: Ethiopia, 1883–1910*. Trenton, NJ: Red Sea Press, 1986.

Pui-lan, Kwok. "Unbinding Our Feet: Saving Brown Women and Feminist Religious Discourse." In *Postcolonialism, Feminism and Religious Discourse*, edited by L. E. Donaldson and K. Pui-lan, 62–81. London: Routledge, 2002.

Purdey, Jemma. "The 'Other' May Riots: Anti Chinese Violence in Solo, May 1998." In *Violent Conflicts in Indonesia: Analysis, Representation, Resolution*, edited by Charles A. Coppel, 72–89. London: Routledge, 2006.

Rahmato, Dessalegn. *Agrarian Reform in Ethiopia*. Trenton, NJ: Red Sea Press, 1985.

Rahyu, Azimah. *Tak Bisa ke Lain Hati* [I cannot turn to another heart]. Jakarta: Khairul Bayaan, 2003.

Ramazani, Nesta. "Women in Iran: The Revolutionary Ebb and Flow." *Middle East Journal* 47 (1993): 409–28.

Reid, Anthony. *Southeast Asia in the Age of Commerce, 1450–1680: Expansion and Crisis*. New Haven, CT: Yale University Press, 1993.

Reid, Anthony. "Understanding Melayu (Malay) as a Source of Diverse Modern Identities." *Journal of Southeast Asian Studies* 32 (2001): 295–313.

Roald, Anne Sofie. *Women in Islam: The Western Experience*. London: Routledge, 2001.

Robinson, Cedric J. *Black Marxism*. Chapel Hill: University of North Carolina Press, 1983; Foreword and Preface, 2000.

Rodinson, Maxime. *Muhammad*. London: Penguin Books, 1971.

Roff, William. "Indonesian and Malay Students in Cairo in the 1920s." *Indonesia* 9 (1970): 73–87.

Roff, William. "Patterns of Islamization in Malaysia, 1890s–1990s: Exemplars, Institutions, and Vectors." *Journal of Islamic Studies* 9:2 (1998): 210–28.

Roudi-Fahimi, Farzaneh. *Iran's Family Planning Program: Responding to a Nation's Needs*. Washington, DC: Population Reference Bureau, 2002.

Roussillon, Alain, and Fatima Zahra-Zryouil. *Être femme en Égypte, au Maroc et en Jordanie* [To be Female in Egypt, Morocco, and Jordan]. Paris: Aux lieux d'être; Cairo: Cedej; Rabat: Cjb, coll. documents, 2006.

Sacks, Karen. *Sisters and Wives: The Past and Future of Sexual Equality.* Urbana: University of Illinois, 1982.

Safi, Omid. "*The Times Are A-Changin'*—A Muslim Quest for Justice, Gender Equality and Pluralism." Introduction to *Progressive Muslims on Justice, Gender, and Pluralism*, edited by Omid Safi, 1–29. Oxford: Oneworld, 2003.

Safran, William. "Deconstructing and Comparing Diasporas." In *Diaspora, Identity and Religion: New Directions in Theory and Research*, edited by Waltraud Kokot, Khachig Tölölyan, and Carolin Alfonso, 9–29. London: Routledge, 2004.

Said, Edward. *Covering Islam: How the Media and the Experts Determine How We See the Rest of the World.* New York: Pantheon Books, 1981.

Said, Edward. *Culture and Imperialism.* New York: Knopf, 1993.

Said, Edward. *Orientalism.* London: Penguin, 2003. First published, New York: Pantheon Books, 1978.

Saigol, Rubina. "Ter-Reign of Terror: 11 September and Its Aftermath." In *Peace Work, Women, Armed Conflict and Negotiation*, edited by Radhika Coomaraswamy and Dilrukshi Fonseka, 14–27. New Delhi: Kali for Women, 2004.

Sanghera, G., and S. Thapar-Björkert. "'Because I am Pakistani . . . and I am Muslim . . . I am political'—Gendering Political Radicalism: Young Femininities in Bradford." In *Islamic Political Radicalism: A European Perspective*, edited by T. Abbas, 173–88. Edinburgh: Edinburgh University Press, 2007.

Sarjono, Maria A. "Rekonsiliasi dalam Perspektif Gender: Suatu Refleksi atas Timpang antara laki-laki dan perempuan [Reconciliation from a Gender Perspective: A Reflection on Male and Female Inequality]." In *Rekonsiliasi, Menciptakan Hidup Damai dan Sejahtera: Tinjauan Perspektif Religiusitas*, edited by A. Widyahadi Seputra, Afra Siowarjaya, et al., 94–107. Jakarta: Kerjasama Sekretariat Komisi PSE/APP-KAJ, LDD-KAJ, Komisi PSE-KWI, and LPPS-KWI, 2002.

Sassen, Saskia. "Spatialities and Temporalities of the Global: Elements for a Theorization." *Public Culture* 12:1 (2000): 215–32.

Schubel, Vernon. *Religious Performance in Contemporary Islam.* Columbia: University of South Carolina Press, 1993.

Setiawan, Chandra, ed. *Direktori Penelitian Agama, Konflik dan Perdamaian* [Directory of Religious Studies, Conflict and Peace]. Jakarta: Komisi Nasional Hak Asasi Manusia and Institut Pluralisme Agama, 2005.

Shaaban, Bouthania. "The Muted Voices of Women Interpreters." In *Faith and Freedom: Women's Human Rights in the Muslim World*, edited by Mahnaz Afkhami, 61–77. Syracuse, NY: Syracuse University Press, 1995.

Shadi, Jaleh. "Officials Concerned about Controversy over Women's Employment and Housewifery." *Zanan*, no. 77, July 2001.

Shahidian, Hammed. *Women in Iran*. Westport, CT: Greenwood Press, 2002.

Shamsul, A. B. "A History of an Identity, an Identity of a History: The Idea and Practise of 'Malayness' in Malaysia Reconsidered." *Journal of Southeast Asian Studies* 32 (2001): 355–66.

Shariati, Ali. *Shariati on Shariati and the Muslim Women*. Translated by Laleh Bakhtiar. Chicago: ABC Group International, 1996.

Sharma, Arvind, and Kathrine K. Young, eds. *Feminism and World Religions*. Albany: State University of New York Press, 1999.

Siew, Zedeck. "PAS Muslimat Oppose Unity Govt." *The Nut Graph*, June 18, 2009.

Silvestri, Sara. *Europe's Muslim Women: Potential, Aspirations and Challenges*. Research report. London: City University and Cambridge University Press, 2008.

Smith, Christian, ed. *Disruptive Religion: The Force of Faith in Social-Movement Activism*. New York: Routledge, 1996.

Smith-Hefner, Nancy J. "Youth Language, *Gaul* Sociability, and the New Indonesian Middle Class." *Journal of Linguistic Anthropology* 17:2 (2007): 183–203.

Sökefeld, Martin. "Religion or Culture? Concepts of Identity in the Alevi Diaspora." In *Diaspora, Identity and Religion: New Directions in Theory and Research*, edited by Waltraud Kokot, 133–55. New York: Routledge, 2004.

Soroush, Abdolkarim. "The Changeable and the Unchangeable." In *New Directions in Islamic Thought: Exploring Reform and Muslim Tradition*, edited by Kari Vogt et al., 9–15. London: I. B. Tauris, 2008.

Spivak, Gayatri Chakravorty. "Can the Subaltern Speak?" In *Marxism and the Interpretation of Culture*, edited by C. Nelson and L. Grossberg, 271–316. Basingstoke, Hants, UK: Macmillan Education, 1988.

Spivak, Gayatri. *A Critique of Postcolonial Reason*. Boston: Harvard University Press, 1999.

Spivak, Gayatri. "Three Women's Texts and a Critique of Imperialism." *Critical Inquiry* 112 (1985): 243–61.

Spivak, Gayatri, and Ranajit Guha, eds. *Selected Subaltern Studies*. Essays from 5 vols. New York: Oxford University Press, 1988.

Statham, P. "Political Mobilisation by Minorities in Britain: A Negative Feedback of 'Race Relations'?" *Journal of Ethnic and Migration Studies* 25:4 (1999): 597–626.

Tabataba'i, Allamah Sayyid Muhammad Husayn. *Shi'ite Islam*. Translated by Seyyed Hossein Nasr. New York: State University of New York Press, 1977.

Taha, Mahmoud Mohamed. *The Second Message of Islam*. Translated by Abdullahi An-Na'im. New York: Syracuse University Press, 1987.

Tamrat, Taddesse. *Church and State in Ethiopia*. Oxford: Oxford University Press, 1972.

Teffo, Lebisa J., and Abraham P. J. Roux. "Metaphysical Thinking in Africa." In *The African Philosophy Reader: A Text with Readings*, edited by P. H. Coetzee and A. P. J. Roux, 134–48. 2nd ed. New York: Routledge, 2003.

Teik, Khoo Boo. *Paradoxes of Mahathirism: An Intellectual Biography of Mahathir Mohamad*. Oxford: Oxford University Press, 2003.

Terefe, Hirut. "Violence against Women from a Gender and Cultural Perspective." In *Reflections: Documentation of the Forum on Gender*, no. 7 (June 2002), edited by Yonas Admassu, 6–16. Addis Ababa: Panos Ethiopia, 2002. Thesiger, W. "The Awash River and the Aussa Sultanate." *Geographical Journal* 85 (1935): 1–21.

Thurkill, Mary F. *Chosen among Women: Mary and Fatima in Early Medieval Christianity and Shi'ism*. Notre Dame, IN: University of Notre Dame Press, 2007.

TIM Pengurusutamaan Gender. *Pembaharuan Hukum Islam. Counter Legal Draft Kompilasi Hukum Islam* [Renewal of Islamic Law]. Jakarta: Ministry of Religious Affairs RI, 2004.

Tohidi, Nayereh. "The Global-Local Intersection of Feminism in Muslim Societies: The Cases of Iran and Azerbaijan." *Social Research* 69:3 (2002): 851–88.

Toynbee, Polly. "Only a Fully Secular State Can Protect Women's Rights." *The Independent*, October 17, 2006.

Tribalat, Michèle. *Faire France: Une grande enqête sur les immigrés et leurs enfants* [Making France: A Grand Survey of Immigrants and their Children]. Paris: La Découverte, 1995.

Trimmingham, J. Spencer. *Islam in Ethiopia*. London: Frank Cass & Co., 1965.

Turner, Victor W. *The Ritual Process: Structure and Anti-Structure*. Chicago: Aldine, 1969.

Umar, Nasaruddin. *Argumen Kesetaraan Gender: Perspektif al-Qur'ân*. Jakarta: Paramadina, 1997.

Vertovec, S. "Three Meanings of 'Diaspora,' Exemplified among South Asian Religions." Working paper, Oxford University, 1999.

Vogt, Kari. "Women, Gender and Religious Associations: Western Europe." In *Encyclopedia of Women and Islamic Cultures*. Vol. 2, *Family, Law and Politics*, edited by Suad Joseph, 715–19. Leiden: E. J. Brill, 2005.

Wadud, Amina. *Inside the Gender Jihad: Women's Reform in Islam*. Oxford: Oneworld Press, 2006.

Wadud, Amina. *Qur'an and Woman: Rereading the Sacred Text from a Woman's Perspective*. New York: Oxford University Press, 1999 [1992].

Wadud, Amina. "Towards a Qur'anic Hermeneutics of Social Justice: Race, Class and Gender." *Journal of Law and Religion* 12:1 (1995–96): 37–50.

Walker, Cheryl. "Women and Gender in Southern Africa to 1945: An Overview." In *Women and Gender in Southern Africa to 1945*, edited by Cheryl Walker, 1–32. London: James Currey, 1990.

Watt, W. Montgomery. *Muhammad: Prophet and Statesman*. London: Oxford University Press, 1961.

Webb, Gisela. *Windows of Faith: Muslim Women Scholar-Activists in North America*. Syracuse, NY: Syracuse University Press, 2000.

Welsh, Bridget. "Election Post-Mortem: Top 10 Factors." *Malaysiakini*, March 12, 2008.

Werbner, Pnina. "Essentialising Essentialism, Essentialising Silence: Ambivalence and Multiplicity in the Constructions of Racism and Ethnicity." In *Debating Cultural Hybridity: Multi-cultural Identities and the Politics of Anti-racism*, edited by P. Werbner and T. Modood, 226–54. London: Zed Books, 1997.

Werbner, Pnina. *Imagined Diasporas amongst Manchester Muslims: The Public Performance of Pakistani Transnational Identity Politics*. Oxford: James Currey, 2002.

Werbner, Pnina. "The Making of Muslim Dissent: Hybridized Discourses, Lay Preachers, and Radical Rhetoric among British Pakistanis." *American Ethnologist* 13:1 (1996): 102–22.

Werbner, Pnina. "Public Spaces, Political Voices: Gender, Feminism and Aspects of British Muslim Participation in the Public Sphere." In *Political Participation and Identities of Muslims in Non-Muslim States*, edited by W. A. R. Shahid and P. S. van Koningsveld, 53–70. Kampen, Neth.: Kok Pharos Publishing House, 1996.

Werbner, Pnina. "Theorizing Complex Diasporas: Purity and Hybridity in South Asian Public Sphere in Britain." *Journal of Ethnic and Migration Studies* 30:5 (2004): 895–911.

Whatley, Sheri. "Iranian Women Film Directors: A Clever Activism." International, *Off Our Backs*. 33:3/4 (March/April 2003): 30–33.

White, Sally, and Maria Ulfah Anshor. "Islam and Gender in Contemporary Indonesia: Public Discourses on Duties, Rights and Morality." In *Expressing Islam: Religious Life and Politics in Indonesia*, edited by Greg Fealy and Sally White, 137–58. Singapore: ISEAS, 2008.

Wuthnow, Robert, and Matthew P. Lawson. "Sources of Christian Fundamentalism in the United States." In *Accounting for Fundamentalisms: The Dynamic Character of Movements*, edited by Martin Marty and Scott Appleby, 18–56. Chicago: University of Chicago Press, 1994.

Yeğenoğlu, M. *Colonial Fantasies: Towards a Feminist Reading of Orientalism*. Cambridge: Cambridge University Press, 1998.

Yeğenoğlu, M. "Sartorial Fabrications: Enlightenment and Western Feminism." In *Postcolonialism, Feminism and Religious Discourse*, edited by Laura E. Donaldson and Kwok Pui-lan, 82–99. London: Routledge, 2002.

Young, I. "The Logic of Masculinist Protection: Reflections on the Current Security State." *Signs: Journal of Women in Culture and Society* 29:1 (2003): 1–25.

Young, Katherine K. Introduction to *Feminism and World Religions*, edited by Arvind Sharma and Katherine K. Young, 1–24. Albany: State University of New York Press, 1999.

Yuval-Davis, N. "Ethnicity, Gender Relations and Multiculturalism." In *Debating Cultural Hybridity, Multi-cultural Identities and the Politics of Anti-racism*, edited by P. Werbner and T. Modood, 193–208. London: Zed Books, 1997.

Yuval-Davis, N. "Human Rights and Feminist Transversal Politics." Lecture presented at University of Bristol series on Politics of Belonging, June 2004.

Yuval-Davis, N. "Intersectionality and Feminist Politics." *European Journal of Women's Studies* 13:3 (2006): 193–209.

Yuval-Davis, N. "Is There a Space in Religion for Feminists?" In *Women Against Fundamentalism Journal*, 1996, http://waf.gn.apc.org/.

Zahiid, Syed Jaymal. "Hadi: SIS Know Nothing about Islam." *The Malaysian Insider*, June 12, 2009.

Zaman, Muhammad Qasim. *The Ulama in Contemporary Islam: Custodians of Change*. Princeton, NJ: Princeton University Press, 2002.

Zewde, Bahru. *A History of Modern Ethiopia, 1855–1991*. Addis Ababa: Addis Ababa University Press, 1991.

Zine, Jasmin. "Muslim Women and the Politics of Representation." *American Journal of Islamic Social Sciences* 19:4 (2002): 1–22.

Web Resources[*]

Al-Ahram Weekly: http://weekly.ahram.org.eg.
    Al-Ahram Weekly is an Egyptian English-language weekly established in 1991 providing news and commentary, owned by Egypt's largest publishing house.
Al-Huda International: http://www.alhudapk.com.
    Al-Huda International is an NGO active in the promotion of Islamic education. Its objectives are to promote purely Islamic values and thinking based on sound knowledge and research and to plan and work for the welfare of the deprived classes of society.
Asian Human Rights Commission: http://ahrchk.net.
    The Asian Human Rights Commission works with local and regional human rights groups to create greater awareness of human rights groups and prevent their violation. It works alongside the Asian Legal Resource Centre (ALRC), which is an NGO founded by jurists and human rights activists committed to legal self-reliance emphasizing the areas of cultural, social, and economic rights and the right of development.
Association for Women's Rights in Development: http://www.awid.org.
    AWID is an international organization committed to achieving gender equality, sustainable development, and women's human rights.
Central Statistic Agency of Ethiopia: http://www.csa.gov.et.
    The CSA is responsible for the countrywide statistical information gathered through surveys and census data for Ethiopia.
Council for the Development of Social Science Research in Africa: http://www.codesria.org.
    CODESRIA was established in 1973 in Dakar, Senegal, as an independent pan-African research organization with a primary focus on the social sciences.

---

[*]Descriptions adapted from relevant Web site

Fatima Gallaire: http://www.gallaire.com/fatima/accueilsite.html.

The official Web site for Franco-Algerian author Fatima Gallaire.

Feminist Africa: http://www.feministafrica.org.

Feminist Africa is a publication of the African Gender Institute and is strengthening gender and women's studies for the Africa's Transformation (GWS Africa) Project.

Inside Indonesia: http://www.insideindonesia.org.

Inside Indonesia is an online journal set up in Melbourne, Australia, by the Indonesian Resources and Information program to provide a deeper image of Indonesia than that painted by the mainstream media.

International Crisis Group: http://crisisgroup.org/home/index.cfm.

ICG is an international NGO recognized as the world's leading independent, nonpartisan source of analysis and advice to governments and intergovernmental bodies on the prevention and resolution of deadly conflict.

Iran Chamber Society: http://www.iranchamber.com.

The Iran Chamber Society aims to educate and create global awareness about Iranian society.

Islamic Research Foundation International: http://www.irfi.org.

IRFI is an organization that has as its goal an Islamic renaissance through the intellectual advancement of the Muslim *ummah*.

Online Women in Politics: http://www.onlinewomeninpolitics.org.

The Asia Pacific Online Network of Women in Politics, Governance and Transformative Leadership is managed by the Center for Asia-Pacific Women in Politics (CAPWIP), a nongovernmental organization promoting equal participation of women in politics and decision-making from the Asia-Pacific region.

PeaceWomen: http://www.peacewomen.org.

The PeaceWomen Project of the Women's International League for Peace and Freedom monitors and works toward rapid and full implementation of United Nations Security Council Resolution 1325 on women, peace, and security.

Pemberdayaan Perempuan Kepala Keluarga: http://pekka.or.id.

PEKKA (Women Headed Household Empowerment) was founded as an NGO originally devoted to empower widows who were victims of the conflict in Aceh, Indonesia, but is now more broadly attuned to the needs of households headed by women.

Sisters in Islam: http://www.sistersinislam.org.my/BM.

SIS is an NGO in Malaysia committed to promoting the rights of women within the framework of Islam, believing that Islam does not endorse the oppression of women and the denial of their basic rights of equality and human dignity.

Transnational Communities Program, University of Oxford: http://www.transcomm
.ox.ac.uk.

    Although this program has ended, the reports and working papers of University of
Oxford's research project on transnational communities are held on this site.

United Nations Educational, Scientific, and Cultural Organization Documents
Database: http://unesdoc.unesco.org.

    UNESCO promotes international cooperation among its member states in the
fields of education, science, culture, and communication.

United Nations Human Development Reports: http://hdr.undp.org/en/reports.

    UNDP is the United Nations' (UN) global development network. The annual
Human Development Reports focus on the global debate on key development
issues.

Women Against Fundamentalism: http://www.womenagainstfundamentalism.org
.uk.

    WAF was formed in 1989 in the United Kingdom to challenge the rise of fun-
damentalism in all religions.

Women Living Under Muslim Laws: http://www.wluml.org.

    Women Living Under Muslim Laws, an international network that provides
information, solidarity, and support for all women whose lives are shaped, conditioned, or governed by laws and customs said to derive from Islam.

World Bank GenderStats: http://www.worldbank.org/genderstats.

    World Bank GenderStats is a compilation of data on key gender topics.

Index

About the Editor and Contributors

EDITOR

Zayn R. Kassam is Professor of Religious Studies at Pomona College, Claremont, California. She has been honored with two Wig Awards for Distinguished Teaching at Pomona College, as well as an American Academy of Religion Excellence in Teaching Award. She is the author of a reference textbook on Islam (Greenwood Press, 2005) and is also at work on a feminist theology in Islam. Her published articles include "Gender Violence in Islam," "The Case of the Animals versus Man: Towards an Ecology of Being," "Islamic Ethics and Gender Issues," and "Reflections on Teaching Islam at a Liberal Arts College."

CONTRIBUTORS

Etin Anwar is Assistant Professor of Religious Studies at Hobart and William Smith Colleges, Geneva, New York. She is the author of *Gender and Self in Islam* (Routledge, 2006) and has published several articles in various journals. She has also been featured in the XXI TV documentary called *Muslim Women in Our Midst: The Path to Understanding*, in conjunction with America at the Crossroads (2006).

Azza Basarudin received her PhD in Women's Studies at the University of California Los Angeles (UCLA) in 2009, after which she was a Postdoctoral Fellow of The Future of Minority Studies Research Project in the Department of Women's and Gender Studies at Syracuse University. Currently a research scholar at the Center for the Study of Women at UCLA, her work explores feminist and religious knowledge production through hermeneutic projects and memory work in Southeast Asia and the Middle East. She is also a recipient of awards from the Wenner-Gren Foundation for Anthropological

Research, the Social Science Research Council (SSRC), and the National Science Foundation (NSF), among others.

Khani Begum, Associate Professor of English at Bowling Green State University, teaches courses in Modern British, Postcolonial, and Middle Eastern Literatures, Transnational and African Cinemas, Postcolonial Theory, and Africana Studies. She has published essays on the work of James Joyce, Lawrence Durrell, E. M. Forster, Tsitsi Dangarembga, and Maxine Hong Kingston.

Bridget Blomfield is Assistant Professor of Religion at the University of Nebraska in Omaha. She teaches courses on Islam, Sufism, American Muslims, and women in Islam. Her key areas of research and publication are American Shi'a and Sufism.

Katherine Bullock received her PhD in Political Science from the University of Toronto in 1999. Her books are *Rethinking Muslim Women and the Veil: Challenging Historical and Contemporary Stereotypes* and *Muslim Women Activists in North America: Speaking for Ourselves*. She is currently president of The Tessellate Institute, a not-for-profit policy research institute based in Toronto, Canada.

Laura Chakravarty Box is a stage actor, director, dramaturge, and independent scholar whose primary research interest is North African women's drama and performance. From 2002 to 2009, she served as Assistant Professor of Theatre and African Studies at Colby College in Waterville, Maine, where she taught directing, acting, African drama, and world theatre history. Her monograph titled *Strategies of Resistance in the Dramatic Texts of North African Women* was published by Routledge in 2005.

Nelly van Doorn-Harder is Professor of Religion at Wake Forest University. Her research straddles issues concerning women and religion and those concerning minorities, minority cultures, and human rights in Muslim countries. She has conducted fieldwork on indigenous Christianity in Egypt and on Muslim organizations in Indonesia and has authored and coauthored books, papers, and book chapters in these areas. Her latest book, titled *Women Shaping Islam: Indonesian Muslim Women Reading the Qur'an* (2006), analyzes the various religious strategies Indonesian Muslim feminists have developed to strengthen the position of women. She has held fellowships from Fulbright, the Ford Foundation, the American University at Cairo, and the Norwegian Institute for Human Rights Studies.

Louise A. Halper (in memoriam) was Professor of Law and Director of the Frances Lewis Law Center at Washington and Lee University, where she taught for 17 years, after a distinguished career in public interest law.

She published and traveled widely and held a Fulbright Fellowship at Marmara University, Istanbul, Turkey, as well as visiting professorships at institutions in Europe, the Middle East, and North America, including one at Harvard University. She is the author of many papers in noteworthy law reviews, including more recently studies on gender in Iran and Turkey. At the time of her unexpected and untimely death in June 2008, following complications from surgery, she was editing a volume of papers from a conference jointly sponsored by the Frances Lewis Law Center and the Islamic Legal Studies Program at Harvard Law School on gender-relevant legislative change in Muslim and non-Muslim countries.

Patricia H. Karimi-Taleghani is a PhD candidate in African History at the University of California, Los Angeles, and specializes in Ethiopian History. She has researched and taught in such areas as African History, Africana/Black Studies, Caribbean Studies, and African Gender and Women's Studies. She is currently working on her dissertation, titled "Education under Haile Selassie I, 1941–1974: The Political Economy of Education in Ethiopia."

Roxanne D. Marcotte is Lecturer in Arabic and Islamic Studies at the University of Queensland in Australia. Her research and publication on gender issues include studies on Muslim women in Canada, Islamist discourse on women in Egypt, gender and sexuality on Australian Muslim online forums, women and reforms in various Muslim societies, Muslim veils and the dynamics and paradoxes of resistance, and the "religionation" of bodies in contemporary (online) *fatwas*.

Narzanin Massoumi is a PhD student at the Centre of the Study of Citizenship and Ethnicity, Department of Sociology, University of Bristol. Her areas of research include feminism and religion; antiracism and multiculturalism; and political and social movements. She has also been active in the antiwar movement in Britain since 2003.

Rachel Newcomb received her PhD in Anthropology from Princeton University in 2004. Her book *Women of Fes: Ambiguities of Urban Life in Morocco* was recently published by University of Pennsylvania Press. Currently she is Associate Professor of Anthropology at Rollins College in Winter Park, Florida.

Khanum Shaikh earned her PhD in Women's Studies from the University of California, Los Angeles, in 2009. Her scholarship lies at the intersection of gender, transnational feminisms, postcolonial, and diaspora studies. She has received numerous awards to complete research for her dissertation, titled "New Expressions of Religiosity: A Transnational Study of Al-Huda International." Currently she is a University of California

Presidential Postdoctoral Fellow for the year 2010–2011 at the University of California, Santa Barbara, after holding a Research Fellowship with the Arab and Muslim Ethnicities and Diasporas (AMED) Initiative in the College of Ethnic Studies, San Francisco State University.

Kari Vogt is Associate Professor at the Institute of Cultural Studies and Oriental Languages at the University of Oslo, Norway. She has written widely on Christian and Islamic issues. She is also editor and coeditor of several books, the most recent of which is titled *New Directions in Islamic Thought and Practice: Exploring Reform and Tradition*, published by I. B. Tauris, London, in 2009.